Ecstatic Subjects, U . . . . ,

SUNY Series in the Philosophy of the Social Sciences

Lenore Langsdorf, Editor

Ecstatic Subjects, Utopia, and Recognition: Kristeva, Heidegger, Irigaray

Patricia J. Huntington

State University of New York Press

Published by
State University of New York Press, Albany

Printed in the United States of America

Cover art entitled *Auca Beastiarium* (1992, etching, 8/60) provided and
granted by Stano Černý. Overall cover design by Amy Stirnkorb.

For information, address State University of New York
Press, State University Plaza, Albany, N.Y. 12246

Production by Diane Ganeles
Marketing by Nancy Farrell

Library of Congress Cataloging-in-Publication Data

Huntington, Patricia J.
    Ecstatic subjects, utopia, and recognition : Kristeva, Heidegger,
Irigaray / Patricia J. Huntington.
        p.   cm. — (SUNY series on philosophy of the social sciences)
    Includes bibliographical references and index.
    ISBN 0-7914-3895-3 (alk. paper). — ISBN 0-7914-3896-1 (pbk. :
alk paper)
    1. Agent (Philosophy) 2. Utopias. 3. Recognition (Philosophy)
4. Postmodernism. 5. Social sciences—Philosophy. 6. Feminist
theory. 7. Heidegger, Martin, 1889–1976. 8. Kristeva, Julia, 1941–
. 9. Irigaray, Luce, I. Title. II. Series.
    BD450.H867   1998
    149'.97—dc21   97-41269
                                                                CIP

10   9   8   7   6   5   4   3   2   1

To Martin
for being my joy

Contents

Acknowledgments

Like all projects, this work reflects the support, encouragement, and feedback of many people. I express my gratitude to
friends, family, teachers, and colleagues for the insights and human encounters that nourished this project to the light of day.
During my studies in New York, numerous people and events set
this project underway. Merold Westphal, James L. Marsh, and John
D. Caputo provided much needed professional guidance and im-
pressive knowledge during the early phases of this work. At Fordham
University, Margaret Walker's and Jean Walton's respective semi-
nars on feminist theory offered discussion formats for the conception of these ideas. I especially thank Drucilla Cornell for her
support, friendship, and the timely conversations we had in the
village. Fordham University supported my study abroad in Frankfurt am Main. There Mathius Jung discussed Heidegger with me;
and I benefited from Seyla Benhabib's guest seminar on feminist
theory and Cornell's guest lecture (1990).

At Purdue University, the Akropolis group—William McBride,
Charlene Seigfried, Lewis Gordon, and Leonard Harris—provided
dialogue that has influenced these pages. I wish to thank Calvin
Schrag for asking me to give a lecture on Kristeva to his graduate
seminar and for his public support of my work. Other stimulating
outlets for discussion included: Leonard Harris's seminar on "Rationality and Relativism," conversations with Dorothy Leland, the
Purdue Cultural Studies Collective, and the Purdue Feminist Theory
Reading Group. Two special colleagues, first met at Purdue, have
given me loyal friendship, professional support, and expertise: Lewis
R. Gordon and Ramsey Eric Ramsey.

My ideas found resonance with the Czech reception of Heidegger
and Kierkegaard. I am grateful to those people and institutes in
Prague that supported my visit during fall 1996: Ivan Havel at the
Center for Theoretical Study for integrating me into Czech intellectual life; Zdeněk Pinc, Chair of the Philosophy Faculty at Charles

University, and Douglas Dix and Věra Trávníčková, both of Internacionální Institut Interkulturních Studií, for having me teach and give a public lecture at the Kafka Society; Petr Brabec for his superb translation of my lecture; my students at Charles; and Hana Havelková for her professional support, personal friendship, and use of the Prague Gender Studies Centrum facilities.

Warm thanks to Lenore Langsdorf for publishing this book in her series and for being a fine role model. Clay Morgan, the former senior editor for SUNY Press, was a wonderfully patient and supportive editor. Andrew Cutrofello made meticulous comments and gave immensely helpful advice on an earlier draft of this manuscript. His generous criticisms helped make this a much improved work. The comments by two anonymous readers were also much appreciated. Kathleen League's copyediting and Jeff Paris's index were excellent. Midwest SWIP, SPEP, and the Philosophy and Social Science Conference sponsored by the Czech Academy of Sciences let me voice certain ideas printed here. I am especially thankful for conversations with Linda Alcoff, Iris Young, and Cynthia Willett. Thanks also to Alison Brown and Tamsin Lorraine for putting together the Kierkegaard panel at SPEP (1993). My department chair at American University, David Rodier, merits special mention for doing everything within his power to clear time and space for me to complete this work. Joanne Molina gave research support and an attentive ear. My students in the Kristeva seminar of fall 1996 stimulated my thought. And Beth Turner of Purdue did a super job editing citations.

I am fortunate to receive much encouragement from very special friends (in addition to those already mentioned): Diane Gruber, Heidi Bostic, Stephen Pluháček, Gail Presbey, Bill Martin, Bill Wilkerson, Jeff Paris, Loretta Kensinger, Natalija Mićunović, Karin Dienst, and Richard Dienst. Rarely do I have occasion to extend public recognition to my family. My grandmother, Cecile Pierce, gave me a sense of adventure. Magdalena Beck's memory inspires my work. My mother always believed in my artistry. My father's practical wisdom suffuses the competencies I have developed and helps me negotiate the world much more than he knows. Bettyanne, my big sister–second mother, provides a haven for me when I need rest. I have five wonderful siblings, all of whom have become tried-and-true friends. My Californian and Czecho-Slovakian families make me happy: Elizabeth Matustik and Pavel Matustik with friendship; Radek Matuštík and Kyra Matuštíková with excursions into the world of Slovakian art. My life would not be the same without my best girlfriend, Dianna Holt-Autrey, and our lengthy phone conversations. Other spirited folk appeared in the creative process: *modrá zebra, Kráska,* Red, Brown, *Smutný, Bhomus, mrzutá,* my little *hněv,* and *Oaxaquena.* Above all, this project owes much to my partner and true friend, Martin J. Beck Matuštík. He also commented on earlier drafts and assumed responsibility for the practical burdens of our intertwined lives in past months.

I wish to acknowledge the following journals and publishers for permission to use material from copyrighted works I authored:

In chapters 1 and 2, from "Heidegger's Reading of Kierkegaard Revisited: From Ontological Abstraction to Ethical Concretion," in *Kierkegaard in Post/Modernity,* ed. Martin J. Matuštík and Merold Westphal (Bloomington: Indiana University Press, 1995): 43–65.

In chapter 3, from "Toward a Dialectical Concept of Autonomy: Revisiting the Feminist Alliance with Poststructualism," *Philosophy and Social Criticism* 21, no. 1 (1995): 37–55.

In chapter 7, "Fragmentation, Race, and Gender: Building Solidarity in the Postmodern Era," in *Existence in Black: An Anthology of Black Existential Philosophy,* ed. Lewis R. Gordon (New York: Routledge, 1997): 185–202.

Introduction

The Anglo-feminist alliance with French philosophy bypasses one important precursor to poststructuralist thought: Martin Heidegger's existential phenomenology. Yet understanding this Heideggerian inheritance, both as a productive and an ambiguous legacy for feminist theorizing, proves of central importance. The indelible influence of Heidegger on Derridean deconstruction and at least two of the "holy Trinity"—Luce Irigaray and Hélène Cixous—cannot be denied. If importing French theory hurries beyond this Heideggerian inheritance, then French-influenced feminist theory may be destined to repeat Heideggerian-type errors as well as overlook fundamental Heideggerian contributions to its endeavors. My book begins to fill that lacuna.[1]

Two recent books offer sustained engagements with Heideggerian thought and a positive contribution to feminist theory. These include Jean Graybeal's *Language and "The Feminine" in Nietzsche and Heidegger* (1990) and Carol Bigwood's *Earth Muse: Feminism, Nature, and Art* (1993). Linking Heidegger's *practice* of thinking in nonmetaphysical ways to Kristeva's semiotic theory, Graybeal demonstrates that Heidegger's work tacitly, though not explicitly, exposes the gender-differential underlying western metaphysics as well as relies upon feminine metaphorics in order to press beyond metaphysics. Whereas Graybeal's study substantiates the extent to which Heidegger is a precursor to Lacanian-influenced feminist theory, Bigwood applies Heidegger's thought in a more reconstructive direction. Against the nominalist claim within feminist poststructuralism—that woman's identity as such cannot be named—she argues that Heidegger's concept of *Dasein* (being-there) proves weighty enough to resist abstracting from the historical continuity of women's various identities (as emphasized in nominalism) without lapsing into essentialism (EaM, chap. 1). In developing her ecofeminist theory, she goes back to later Heidegger's existential phenomenology so as to move beyond the "dangerous" and nihilistic "neo-Nietzschean underpinnings" of French post-structuralism (EaM, 7). Joanna Hodge, Sandra Bartky, Tina Chanter, Ellen Mortensen, Ellen Armour, Nancy Holland, Iris Young, Sandra Adell, and Noëlle McAfee also explore specific elements of Heidegger's thought in connection with gender concerns.[2]

Even so, there seem to be obvious reasons why feminists look not to Heidegger's *Destruktion* of metaphysics but rather to more recent developments in French theory, whether to Derridean deconstruction, Foucauldian genealogy, or the Lacanian psychoanalytic tradition. I mention two interrelated reasons. First, Heidegger continues to develop a hopelessly abstract, diehard apolitical, definitively gender-neutral version of ontology. Though partly nonessentialist, his ontological paradigm harbors essentializing elements as well as a marked nostalgia for the classical world. Derrida accuses Heidegger of searching for the deep truth, *logos*, or core meaning in the philosophical texts of western tradition. Irigaray exposes Heidegger's heavy reliance upon the metaphor of appropriation as bound to a masculinist relegation of feminine-earth-nature (*physis*) symbolism to the unmediated locus of truth upon which man builds his house of language (OA, 10, 19, passim). And Kristeva even more critically proclaims that Heidegger's theory is a "regressive mythological travesty" because authentic Dasein longs for a stoic retreat from social practice to a romanticized pre-Christian Roman times (RP, 129). Second, later Heidegger's view of language perpetuates these difficulties. Because largely centered on finding the meaning, truth, or *topos* of Being, a Heideggerian ontological treatment of language appears unable to provide a developed linguistic or communication theory that allows us, as does poststructuralist theory, to discuss the nature of Woman or the feminine in *critical* heuristic as opposed to *naive* ontological terms. Admittedly Heidegger's rare comments on *Geschlecht* or gender do not elevate the signifier, Woman, in any explicit manner to the status of an allegory lacking fixed meaning (Derrida). Nor does Heidegger acknowledge that the feminine operates as the keystone that bolsters, and thus is crucial for toppling, the edifice of the western patriarchal symbolic system (Irigaray).[3] In sum, Heidegger's obvious lack of critical interest in the woman-question, his often ethnocentric, stoically impersonal, and male-centered approach to philosophy, coupled with his penchant for mystification, qualify as good reasons for feminists to shy away from his thought.

It is well an unlikely prospect, then, that U.S. feminists would spontaneously turn to Heidegger as a preferred theoretical resource for addressing matters of gender. And it is no more probable that Heidegger scholars would be keen to read feminist literature in vast quantities. At first glance this book could not seem written to please either group. To paraphrase Tina Turner, feminists might ask, What's Heidegger got to do with it? Conversely, Heidegger experts might query, How can feminist theory teach us anything about Heidegger scholarship? Rather than advance the preposterous claim that Heidegger offers the most concrete and viable conceptual framework for feminist social theory, I work from a more restrained premise. Twentieth-century Continental philosophy proceeds by way of a love-hate affair with Heidegger; and, though it may be eminently reasonable to want to sidestep this affair through indifference, the *de facto* legacy of Heidegger makes such a step difficult if not impossible. At the near close of the twentieth century it has become imperative to sort out the Heideggerian legacy especially in light of his involvement with National Socialism. More to the point of this study, however, is that Heidegger's influence on French thinking has been pervasive, if also manifested in a circuitous series of transmutations. Undeniable traces of Heideggerian thought manifest in thinkers and philosophies as diverse as Lacan and structuralism, Derrida and poststructuralism, Sartrean existentialism, and, as I argue in these pages, most distinctly in Irigaray's brand of feminist theory.

As a contribution to feminist theory, this work engages a dialogue with those criticisms which regard poststructuralist theories as sophisticated versions of a neo-Heideggerian methodology that repeat his mistakes in numerous instances. Critics worry that the overly nominalist tendencies of poststructuralist theory, which claim that gender is sheerly a linguistic performance, deprive female subjects of the very agency they have been denied. They charge that transgressive and deconstructive strategies of exposure and subversion offer no criteria for differentiating between reactionary and progressive forms of transgression (as critics claim of Heidegger). And they pose serious questions about the limitations of antinormativism inherited directly from Heidegger's own maieutically focused tactics and his allergic resistance to reconstructive philosophizing. I do not intend to provide an exhaustive treatment of these conceptual issues; rather, I take up such concerns within a limited focus on Irigaray, Kristeva, and Heidegger. While demonstrating sharp advances made by Kristeva and Irigaray over Heidegger, I also recuperate Heidegger's ontology, correct his one-sided or undialectical methodology, and press his insights into the service of a social ontology. I use this critically revised ontology as a bulwark against pure nominalism as well as essentialism and biologism.

As a contribution to Heidegger scholarship, this study resists purely scholastic forms of Heideggerianism. Though these forms are important for comprehending his work, we cannot come to grips with his legacy unless we ask more concretely what Heidegger can contribute to a viable social theory able to handle the tough questions of the day. I show that an encounter with feminist theory provides unique insights into the connections between his early work, his engagement with National Socialism, and deficiencies in his latter-day philosophy. Critically engaging Heidegger against Heidegger, I extract his fundamental ontological insight—that all entities, human and nonhuman, are autodisclosive—from his peculiar and overly confining philosophical treatment of ontology in abstraction from social theory. Following Marcuse and Irigaray, I show that this fundamental Heideggerian insight can offer the basis for a social ontology that is nonessentialist. Better still, it provides justification for an ethics based upon asymmetrical reciprocity as opposed to one assuming a reversibility of perspectives. Irigaray, put directly, owes a large debt to Heidegger. We can make better sense out of her appeals to a physical reality that exceeds language when we treat them, not as residues of a neo-Freudian-Lacanian biological essentialism, but instead as renditions of the neo-Heideggerian thesis that conceptualization never encapsulates anyone or anything *in toto* because things are dynamically autokinetic and not static.

Postmodern Agents and Transgression

I begin by examining Heidegger's phenomenological shift away from epistemology-centered philosophies of consciousness to a more practical view of subjectivity as embedded in historical, cultural, and linguistic contexts. Feminist literature in general worries that voluntarist conceptions of agency lead to a moral psychology unable to handle gender differences. A significant body of poststructuralist feminist literature goes beyond critique of early modern theories to challenge existential phenomenology, arguing that even dialectical models of autonomy perpetuate gender dualisms. Judith Butler and Susan Hekman offer two representative positions.[4] Though not specifically directed against Heidegger, their

criticisms advance a strong indictment of existential and phenomenological theories in general from Hegel to Kierkegaard, from
Nietzsche to early Heidegger, and ultimately from Sartre to
Beauvoir. Like other poststructuralist theorists, they argue that
dialectical models of subjectivity (as both constituted yet self-constituting) remain caught in a dualistic epistemology that perpetuates associations of femininity with the realm of immanence, nature,
and embodiment, while assigning masculinity to conscious intentionality. Not only do these models evince remnants of transcendentalism characteristic of philosophies of consciousness, but they
valorize masculinist conceptions of rationality as an ability to
voluntaristically master meaning, historical process, nonidentity,
and the other.

It would be easy, on this interpretation, to make two presump-
tions: (i) that the theoretical ground for Heidegger's involvement in
National Socialism stems from his inheritance of an existentialist
view of subjectivity as dialectically situated; and (ii) that the
poststructuralist turn away from a phenomenologically retrograde
and masculinist model of self-appropriation resolves these dilemmas
by forswearing the episteme of the rational subject seeking to tran-
scend the realm of immanence. Even the later Heidegger criticizes
his early philosophy for failing to overcome subjectivism. I claim,
pace Heidegger, that this conceptual diagnosis is fundamentally
flawed. His engagement with National Socialism (hereafter NS) did
entail a powerful embrace of the rampant masculine ethos of the
Freikorpsmen and Nazi ideology. Ungrounded in public debate and
democratically sanctioned processes, that embrace was not simply
voluntarist but decisionistic. As Richard Wolin demonstrates, however, Heidegger's commitment to an exceptionalist logic—a logic that
exempts those with sovereign will from submission to current norms—
issues from his view of human existence as immanent not transcendent, as thoroughly embedded in historical process, as acutely aware
of the "contingency of human belief-structures." The recognition of
historical contingency and groundlessness leads to "valorization of
'radical will' or heroic self-assertion" and a voluntarist surpassing of
norms through a rejection of all of modernity (liberalism, the tech-
nological-industrial ethos, democracy).[5]

I claim that Heidegger's philosophy proves instructive for feminist poststructuralist views of agency because his embroilment in
the masculinist ethos characteristic of NS stems not from dialectics
but rather from lacking a sufficiently dialectical view of agency.
Though these decisionistic and voluntarist aspects of Heideggerian

phenomenology make no manifest appearance in feminist poststructuralist theorizing, similarities pervade their respective methodological assumptions. Heidegger's voluntarism arises because (i) he bases critique, undialectically, upon a total *negation of what is*, namely, the world of popular opinions and everyday practices; and because (ii) he grounds the recuperation of agency, undialectically, in a *transgressive dislocation* of prevailing social norms that *repudiates public accountability or normative theory in toto.* Unable to regard agency as a positive capacity for mediating social practices, the free subject emerges via stoic withdrawal from the world. Rather than retain a *transmoral* view of authenticity as cultivating critical distance on our socialized identities, Heidegger lets the transgressive moment stand in for *normative critique*, thereby sanctioning a decisionistic model of change.

Critical modernists, both sympathetic and antipathetic to postmodern theorizing, consistently charge poststructuralists with inheriting this neo-Heideggerian confusion between deconstructive methodologies (aimed therapeutically at consciousness-raising and fostering an alternative moral-aesthetic) and rejection of normative thinking about autonomy, moral decision-making, and political goals. For Wolin this inheritance unfolds in postmodern theorizing as dismantling the liberal bulwark against fascism and thus as a species of neo-Heideggerian left-fascism. Others, like Nancy Fraser, more sympathetically strive to salvage poststructuralist critiques of cultural practices—which could in principle leave the question of justification open—from their conflation of provisional critique with anti-normativism.[6] These are serious charges indeed. They imply that the quasi-apocalyptic urgency exhibited in postmodern rhetoric carries the possibility of inflaming conservative revolutionary forces; that overdramatizing the social ills of modernity obfuscates its sources for progressive social development; that conflating the nonrevolutionary nature of the era with an overdetermined view of subjectivity as hopelessly subjugated by outside forces (e.g., language and culture) undermines liberation struggle; and, finally, that tossing the baby of normative justification out with the bathwater of cultural hegemony is politically retrograde. Though not convinced by all charges, I hold that the ghost of Heidegger compels us to give them due attention.

Part 1 of this book asks how Heidegger can instruct us about the dangers of rethinking agency in conjunction with transgressive strategies of exposure. Just as Heidegger regards subjectivity as historically embedded in ways that constantly lull humans into complacent acceptance of current beliefs, much poststructuralist theory sees the linguistic construction of identity as inherently subjugating. Every name of woman represses difference and nonidentity. Critics isolate two fundamental difficulties with the nominalist position that woman is a fiction of language. First, agency appears to be a mere by-product of negating what is, rather than a productive capacity to imbue my life with new meaning and to critique false constructions of my identity. Linda Alcoff argues that these models overly determine the subject, denying "not only the efficacy but the very ontological autonomy and even the existence of intentionality." Alcoff points out that such a "wholly negative feminism," structured around deconstruction and not reconstruction, "cannot mobilize" social change without a positive vision of "a better future." Second, poststructuralists confuse transgression with critique. If all identity is subjugating, Alcoff queries, then "Why is a right-wing woman's consciousness constructed via social discourse but a feminist's consciousness not?" Similarly, Fraser points out that resignification of identity does not automatically supply justification. "Why is resignification good? Can't there be bad (oppressive, reactionary) resignifications?"[7]

As a partial response to these questions, I turn to Julia Kristeva in order to rethink intentionality as post– rather than prelinguistic. My approach is to isolate stoic consciousness as key to both voluntarist transcendence and potentially reactionary forms of transgression. I define stoic consciousness in Hegelian and Freudian terms as revolving around two premises: (i) the rational life requires abstraction from, control over, or repression of affective life; and (ii) identity-formation and society are founded necessarily upon a sacrificial loss of the purer pleasures of immediacy and immersion in nature. My own position dovetails with the recent works of Cynthia Willett and Allison Weir. These works reveal that modeling freedom on negation perpetuates a stoic and, as Weir argues, a "sacrificial logic" that has deleterious consequences for the oppressed.[8] With the help of Kristeva, I open a pathway between Heideggerian voluntarism and the postmodern temptation to do away with a theory of intentionality or willed self-regulation. That path resists both the stoic logic of affect repression which leads to a truncated moral psychology and the sacrificial logic that fails to differentiate reactionary, cathartic forms of transgression from those that lead to self-transformation and ethical investment in intersubjective relationships and social life. With the help of Heideggerian ontology, I correct Kristeva's own sacrificial theory of death drives as inherently antisocial.

Chapter 1 explores Graybeal's illumination of Heidegger in light of Kristeva's semiotic theory. Graybeal argues that, setting Heidegger's indifference to gendered aspects of identity aside, his work implicitly encourages a nondominating attitude to what French feminists call the excluded feminine dimensions of language, e.g., nonmeaning, nonbeing, absence. By transposing Heideggerian ontology into Kristevan semiotic theory, she further argues that the style of his writing cultivates the protoethical possibility of taking pleasure or finding *jouissance* in groundlessness. Graybeal connects Heideggerian authenticity, understood as a nonanxious relation to the stranger in ourselves, to Kristeva's ethical ideal of becoming subjects in process (held ecstatically between unrealized desires and metaphorical excess of meaning). I applaud Graybeal's creative rereading of Heidegger as productive and illuminating. It not only highlights language as central to *Being and Time* but also supplies Heidegger with a semiotic theory. Further, it implies that his rejection of the disencumbered self of modernity, because rooted in a transformation of attitude toward things deemed feminine, happily proves inconsistent with conventional forms of male and female social roles.

Though enhancing this strain in the Heideggerian corpus is important, Graybeal's reading overlooks another competing strain. Heidegger's appreciation of receptivity to disclosive processes, his persistent efforts to cure philosophy of hyperabstraction, and his unabashed claims that moods and attunement are central to knowledge and human understanding, all stand in profound tension with his nascent fascination with death and limit situations, his emphasis on heroic action, and most of all his brash indifference to intersubjective and interpersonal relations. Because these latter elements assume precedence in the 1930s, I suggest that we cannot make full sense out of the connection between Heidegger's philosophy and his involvement in NS without analyzing the masculinist and stoic features of authentic resolve already latent in *Being and Time*. Early Heidegger's model of agency, I submit, leads to a truncated moral psychology because it rejects a dialectical conception of the authentic subject. By dialectical, I mean a theory that treats personal identity as both constructed by its social environment and yet capable of influencing its ongoing identity-formation within that social context. The only candidate for a parallel moment to Kristeva's rich psychological analyses in Heidegger's early work could be the influence of Kierkegaard. Contrary to some received views, I distinguish Kierkegaard's dialectical and relational view of ethical authenticity from Heidegger's nonrelational postulation of authenticity as a stoic retreat from the world of social interaction and public debate.

My argument is that when Heidegger treats authenticity as the praxis of negating everyday forms of social involvement, he bases the process of reconstituting my identity on a unidirectional and rarified leap out of convention rather than a dialectical distancing from yet critical engagement with those practices. In so doing he divorces the praxis of recovering attunement to groundlessness from affective edification of the subject into a capacity for sincere and undeluded exploration of beliefs. Heidegger's allergic reaction to the social sphere drains authenticity of the rich ethical connotations found in Kierkegaard's transmoral notion of the ethical stage of development and Kristeva's subject in process. Rather than a transmoral category with connotations of developing ethical capacities for sincere engagement with normative questions, Heidegger's concept of authenticity engenders a transgressive longing for immediacy, i.e., for holistic involvement with the rarified experience that all things are autodisclosive. This nonrelational, nondialectical, and stoic breach of convention opens the door to a logic of the exception where heroic actors secure the future of (German) humanity.

Chapter 2 supplements other incisive analyses of Heidegger's political engagement by adopting a feminist angle. While I accept Wolin's charge that Heidegger's wholesale overthrow of public norms promotes decisionism and authoritarianism, an account of Heidegger's turn to NS remains incomplete, abstract, and formal without explaining his choice of a manly ethos. That choice, I maintain, was neither arbitrary nor a matter of historical coincidence; NS did not incidentally manifest the material option available to Heidegger as a vehicle for concretizing his philosophical work in political praxis. Just as Heidi Hartmann revealed that Marx's sex-blind class analysis shows that capital creates empty places to be filled by a working class yet fails to clarify why women must occupy subordinate places within the system, so too does a formal analysis of Heideggerian decisionism neglect to account for the substantive choice of manly moral-aesthetic.[9] Middle Heidegger's philosophy does not simply effectuate an anachronistic return to a premodern *Volk* mentality or wax nostalgic for an agrarian and communitarian ethos rather than an urbancentric, societal life. He draws out his philosophy not through a heroic decision for any rejuvenated and reenchanted form of life but rather for an ethos based upon a specific form of social eros. That eros is rooted in a valorization of manly respectability, harsh self-examination, a neo-Nietzschean overcoming of creative impotence, strength of will, and rejection of cowardice (SA, 29–31/SB, 9–11).

Examining that social eros, I play off Irigaray's notion of specularization and Bigwood's neo-Heideggerian critique of Nietzsche. Their works enable me to show that, like Ernst Jünger and other Freikorpsmen, Heidegger's stoic transgression of modern public conventions unearths the feminized forces of creativity, not in order to cultivate critical distance on patriarchal symbolism, but rather to ward off the emasculating effects of liberalism and supply an antidote to the impotency worked by modernity on fraternal bonding. Unlike the Freikorpsmen, Heidegger does not misogynistically treat the femininely connoted notions of absence, void, withdrawal, and concealment as irrational, disorderly, Fury-like powers. Nonetheless, his 1935 lecture course, *An Introduction to Metaphysics*, invokes a cathartic logic of transgression whereby valorous subjects violently tame the still-horrifying feminine force by limiting, channeling, shaping, and preserving it; they perform a midwifery that restores fraternal rivalry and thus binds the polis together. Following a cathartic logic, this transgression yields no transformation of male identity or German nationalism, but ignites the fire of a reactionary misogynistic chauvinism.

Pace modernist calls for a return to impartial reason as the curative for what many deem Heidegger's murky use of poetic thinking and of diffuse forms of aesthetic attunement, my analysis demonstrates that the residues of stoic consciousness in Heidegger's philosophy attest to a greater proximity between his hermeneutically embedded subject and modernist paradigms of impartial reason than his critics admit. From a feminist theoretical standpoint, masculinist biases owe as much to modernist paradigms of impartiality as they do to conventional forms of communitarianism. The issue cannot revolve simplistically around impartial reason versus a new *poiēsis*. Feminists call for both a tempered *ratio* shorn of the will to mastery and a transformation in social eros that severs the metaphorical welding of masculinity (and whiteness, European, etc.) to phallic power, agency, subjectivity, and humanity. I resist claims that liberal conceptions of individual autonomy and impartial rationality yield the strongest or the only sufficient bulwark against fascism, antiblack racism, heterosexism, and misogyny. Yet my analysis also implies that pure deconstruction, negation, and subversion of prevailing conventions prove insufficient to supply a model of situated agency that avoids a cathartic logic and complicity with reactionary social formations.

Chapter 3 argues for rethinking a dialectical model of agency. The lesson we learn from Heidegger, I suggest, is that neither willful mastery nor wholly negative strategies for fostering a critical relation to our identities via transgression completely save us from stoic consciousness or voluntarism. From Butler and Hekman I accept a definition of agency as a creative capacity to resignify meaning. But I add that this definition remains far too thin to counteract the specter of stoic consciousness when grounded solely on the slippage of meaning or plurality of discourses. Such a definition fails to specify (i) the relation of meaning to affective life and core beliefs; and (ii) the relation of affective interest in choosing particular meanings over others and investment in intersubjective and social relations. For this reason, they cannot supply criteria for differentiating stoic from ethical consciousness or reactionary from progressive resignifications. Though centered around embodiment, these theories ironically retain a strong cognitive focus when they employ interventions into discursive practices as a means of decentering identity and reforming perceptions. Echoing Weir's *Sacrificial Logics*, I locate Kristeva in a middle position between a theory of transcendental intentionality (here the rational agent masters meaning and transcends the realm of immanence) and a postmodern view of identity as inherently repressive of difference (where the subject stoically accepts lost immediacy and confuses critique with striving to attain a perpetual negation of what is). Like Weir, I find that Kristeva holds a dialectical model of creative agency. The subject in process is both linguistically constituted yet actively reconstitutes herself through enhancing the capacity to take pleasure in self-expression, shared social meaning, and communication of nonidentity.

Employing a language that is not her own, I claim that Kristeva's model of identity-formation gives a theoretical account of the emergence of intentionality. This account neither reinstates a prelinguistic notion of formative consciousness nor a voluntarist view of agential control over meaning. Without fleshing out a theory of virtuous competencies and moral respect, I show that Kristeva's contribution to a theory of agency consists of three moments. First, she clarifies that changes in linguistic systems effect transformations in identity because affect, not simply the body, forms the bridge between language and identity. Second, her work demonstrates that there is a correlation (however mediated) between a stoic inability to invest linguistic meaning with the affective desire to translate otherwise inchoate impulses into cogent self-expression and a diminished moral capacity for identification with others. Third, she grounds intersubjective relations on an intrasymbolic basis. She shows that intentionality is a kind of *parousia* which orients human desire toward inexhaustible possibilities for new meaning. This model ideally should allow us to rethink the desire for recognition on a nonantagonistic basis. Humans need not achieve recognition through a struggle to negate the other, in other words, because identity does not emerge through a necessary conflict with the (m)other but rather through cocreation of meaningful forms of life.

There are, however, competing strains in Kristeva's work. Against the aforementioned prosocial dimension, she retains a Freudian theory of drives. Even though drives are never known outside of linguistic mediation, Kristeva nonetheless fails to examine how needs are dialectically formed through material and nondiscursive historical conditions. Thus she retains an antisocial and transhistorical view of the death drive which threatens to undermine her twin theses, that creative intentionality is a social desire (not negation) and that ethical relations presuppose the nonnecessity of engaging in an antagonistic struggle for recognition. By returning to Heidegger's ontological insight that the creative impulse arises from an original intersubjective attunement, I displace Kristeva's biological foundations with a thoroughly social view of human existence. Against feminists who claim that all ontology is politically ideological, I press this Heideggerian insight into a critical social theory which begins from the premise that, because all subjectivity emerges out of intersubjectivity, vulnerability and openness to alterity need not devolve into an anxious relation to nonidentity, groundlessness, otherness, and difference. The nominalist turn to a linguistically constructed identity goes too far when it abstracts from the weightiness of ontological and existential concretion. I conclude this part by arguing that we not only can talk meaningfully about willed self-regulation without renewing voluntarism, but must do so. Any ethical theory that wishes to hold people accountable for their racialized, sexed, and gendered identities must retain something like a notion of willed ignorance or bad faith. Instead of the more voluntarist Sartrean language of willed choice, I talk about willingness as comprising only one dimension of our complex affective lives, but a dimension that plays a central role in a person's availability to those moral appeals that cut deep into her core beliefs, attitudes, and desires.

Utopia as Critical Mythologizing

Part 2 looks at agency as a socially shaped desire for recognition that is fundamentally utopian in character. Much feminist theorizing wants to demythologize modern philosophies of history. Such philosophies relate a story of history made in the mirror image of the experiences of the educated, white, propertied, male subject. They project historical development as man's linear progression toward (his) static, utopian, self-transparent humanity. Concerned to address the uneven effects of modernity on various social groups and to recover the narrative voices typically left out of history, poststructuralist feminist theory, along with Africana and postcolonial literature, has been at the forefront in questioning who exactly can and will be assimilated into this truncated white, masculinist, Eurocentric image of humanity. The matter is not simply one of expanding the category of humanity; many authors challenge the very search for a self-transparent humanity because they see it as grounded on a politically tainted and dangerous desire for mastery of reality, a desire intrinsically linked to the exclusion of various peoples from what counts as human. This fact leaves women and other oppressed peoples in the double-bind of needing, on the one hand, to yearn for utopia without, on the other hand, resurrecting a new static utopianism, projected for all times, and based upon the idolatrous, narcissistic, and solipsistic lust for perfect transparency.[10]

In chapter 4, I turn to the unique insights of Drucilla Cornell's *Beyond Accommodation* in order to demonstrate that Irigaray, following Heidegger, strives to clear a middle pathway by building a new *poiēsis* and refusing to posit a univocal image of humanity. Cornell argues that feminist interpretations of Irigaray as a strategic essentialist seriously neglect the utopian dimension in her work. At the same time that she resists idolatry, Irigaray sees no way for women to reawaken a vibrant sense of autonomy without creating artificial images of universal humanity out of their own flesh. Clearly not alone in this kind of endeavor, Irigaray forcefully unmasks how a masculinely coded humanity perverts, obstructs, and corrodes women's desire for self-expression, voice, agency. This codification deprives a woman of the symbolic resources for realizing a free mediation of her own ground, i.e., to take herself as the 'for-itself' and not merely as the 'in-itself' (ground) of man's (read: humanity's) needs, desires, and self-realizing activities (E, 107). Race, queer, and feminist theorists alike undertake noteworthy explorations into the ways that images of humanity as masculine, straight, and white twist social erotic desire for recognition into perverse sensibilities and epistemic formations that set ontological limits on the attainability of ethical relations. In focusing on the need for a transformation in cultural ethos and social eros, Irigaray argues that the marginalized and oppressed need a symbolic and imaginative basis for imaging their own humanity.[11]

Where modern philosophies of history follow a *substitutionalist logic*, electing for a univocal image of self-transparent humanity surreptitiously molded from one group's morphological features, Irigaray refuses to replace a closed patriarchal with a closed matriarchal symbolic system of meaning. Cornell argues that Irigaray replaces a *substitutionalist* with a *reiterative* model of imaginative universalism. Imaginative or reiterative universalism begins from the nonessentialist premise that 'Woman' (understood either as a universal essence or a univocal historical experience of oppression) does not exist a priori. 'Woman' as a symbol exists only a posteriori in multiple incarnations. On this reading, Irigaray's textual practice of imagining a symbolically coded humanity based upon female morphology awakens the utopian longing requisite to hope for change. Cornell's work promisingly adapts this imaginative praxis to a pluralist method able to undertake genealogies of concrete material differences across race, class, ethnicity, and nationality.

With certain reservations, I accept Cornell's proposal that the way out of the present must proceed by remobilizing the energy constitutive of current forms of social eros into a new social formation. Even though Irigaray's methodology provides no complex political strategy, its importance consists in developing a new poetic basis for imagining the possibility of nonantagonistic forms of recognition. Rather than deprive people of myth, Irigaray redirects the desire for a reenchanted world, but, as Cornell shows, through a critical rather than naive form of mythologizing. Most importantly, I suggest, Irigaray thematizes the need for a formal delimitation of all universalist images of humanity on both metaphorical (ontological) and temporal grounds. Her model breaks with a univocal image of humanity by proposing that every mediation of the sensible-transcendental is finite. Further, the practice of imagining Woman as universal is relative to the needs of the age.

Acknowledging that Heidegger works on a far less erotic and morphological level than Irigaray, chapter 5 interprets later Heideggerian thought as a *reluctant critical utopianism*. This reading shows the indebtedness of Irigaray's utopian concern with po-

etics to Heidegger, while also illuminating Heidegger's project ret-
rospectively in light of poststructuralist theorizing. Like Irigaray,
Heidegger seeks a third way between instituting a new but dreamy
static-substitutionalist utopianism and an overly austere neglect of
the mytho-poetic by advocating a purely sober rationality. If for
Heidegger modern reason carries its own mythic shadow of the
history of the metaphysical search for presence, then he too must
be cautious after the lessons of NS. Leery of political dreams, I
argue, Heidegger still fosters an ethos that opens a utopian doorway to a radically new future. Though his project to wean the West
from its instrumental ethos and insatiable desire for cultural imperialism is well acknowledged, my reading highlights Heidegger's
attempt to theorize a formal delimitation of universalism.

The poststructuralist notion of a critical as opposed to naive
metaphorical mediation of nonidentity (fleshy particulars) finds a
predecessor in the Heideggerian distinction between forms of fantasizing that fetishize others (arguably a western, masculinist social eros) and uses of fantasia that open up a space within which
others can disclose themselves without distortion. Though he does
not abandon the trope of the mirror, Heidegger delimits the will to
conceptual mastery by showing that identity never subsists in relation to a singular horizon of meaning that reflect the self's mirror
image. Instead, he argues, all transcendental-conceptual horizons
(mirrors) provide finite spheres of meaning. Thus communication
transpires within a multiplicity of mirrors, even though these
manifold conceptual horizons cannot be reduced to mere subjective
world views or to a species of relativism. I draw out the implications of his theory for intersubjective relations. His work implies
that mediating the incommensurability of conceptual-linguistic
horizons is a precondition for attaining ethically sound relationships. Mediating language as a world-disclosing medium (and not
simply an action coordinating medium of shared consensus) opens
the space for a nondistorting communication. By nondistorting I
mean interaction that neither reduces another person to the nonhuman (absolutely different) nor subsumes the other's reality as a
mere subset of my own experience (uniform sameness).

Neither later Heidegger nor Irigaray provide robust models of
community, but their works develop poetic bases for postconventional
forms of community. And they do so at two levels, substantive and
formal. Each cultivates substantive modes of poiēsis based upon
weaning western culture of the core belief that individuation must
be asserted against interdependence (Irigaray) and of the habit of

grounding philosophical thinking in the desire to conquer reality (Heidegger). Perhaps their most lasting conceptual contributions stem from their formal efforts to show that a critical relation to normatively secured social conventions will never become complete without theorizing the need for a metaphorical (or poetic) mediation of ontological sensibilities and imagined telos. This practice must become part of a critical social formation. It develops the ontological basis for letting another reveal to me that her world situation differs from and even conflicts with mine as a locus from which to interpret reality. Cognizance of this phenomenon forms a central precondition of ethical recognition, namely, an ability not to absolutize my perspective. Theorizing it contributes to founding postconventional forms of *Sittlichkeit*.

The Aporias of the Utopian Desire for Recognition

Though I provisionally argue for a new poetics, Irigaray's neo-Heideggerian method of invoking utopian images as embedded in current psychosexual notions of the feminine risks obvious dangers that make me very nervous. Like other feminists, I worry that the use of the feminine as imaginative universal risks reinforcing entrenched ideas about women, not to mention essentializing womanhood in ways that fortify heterosexist biases. Yet alternative postmodern utopian visions of proliferating sex/gender/desire constellations to the point that current configurations wither away suffer parallel difficulties. Though more appealing as a future goal, purely interventionist strategies wager a future free of sex/gender/desire ideology at the risk of sanctioning a premature celebration of difference under the current ideological rubric of sex– and gender-neutral individualism. Thus, rather than engage feminist debates over the preferability of feminine versus feminist visions of utopia, part 3 examines the aporias of utopian thinking from the standpoint of modernist critics of all postmodern endeavors.[12]

This part addresses the criticism that subversive methodologies, Heideggerian and poststructuralist, fall prey to a performative contradiction between their tacit normative commitments and their explicit antinormativism. Interventionist methodologies claim to avoid false universalism by fostering ethical humility in the theorist. By refusing to represent one's own experience as definitive for all women, such methodologies profess that they adhere to a critical awareness of the limitations of the author's own situation and perspective. Nonetheless, critics charge that much postmodern theorizing constructs its own univocal image of modernity as the adversary, yet remains incapable of acknowledging that this story is finite and often reflects the needs of a particular stratum of society. Rather than simply indict such methods as hopelessly contradictory and ideologically dangerous, my approach is to suggest that the maieutic intention of interventionist methodologies becomes ideologically tainted when the theorist assumes that such interventions offer a sufficient theoretical analysis from which to draw normative conclusions concerning the sources of oppression and strategies for overcoming them. The goal of fostering *elements* of a new moral-aesthetic is necessarily limited. To move beyond this to the normative-prescriptive level *without additional theoretical and practical mediation* makes such methodologies vulnerable to obfuscating their limits and their axes of power.

Moreover, numerous materialist thinkers claim that analyses which privilege the symbolic features of reality as the primary source of women's oppression elide problems of race and class as factors in the oppression of nonwhite, nonmaterially secure women. In keeping with my focus on utopianism, I look to Leonard Harris's challenging criticisms of specific forms of postmodern theory which valorize the present as a multicultural meta-utopia and thereby reinforce the status quo of racial and socioeconomic immiseration in the U.S. Yet unlike Hartsock, Fraser, and others, I do not toss out Irigarayan-Heideggerian type conceptual genealogies. I argue instead that these methods become race– and class-blind when they fail to theorize the need to dialectically mediate cultural change with structural transformations in political economy (though I do not develop such an analysis of political economy here). And, further, I claim that the textual practice of imaginative universalism can lead to sanctioning existing conditions as meta-utopia when that practice is not complemented by the reconstruction of an ethical theory based upon interaction and not simply imagination.[13]

Chapter 6 traces the aporias of utopianism and antinormativism to Heidegger. It presses the performative nature of Heidegger's eschatological narrative of western philosophical history, showing that Heidegger himself understood that his story did not offer a differentiated understanding of modernity but instead was a strategy employed with maieutic intent. Nonetheless, Heidegger's story reifies into a univocal and monolithic depiction of modernity because he lets his maieutic purpose stand in for normative theory. His proposal for a noninstrumental thinking thus becomes dictated as *the* social practice that will cure what ails modernity. In the name of antinormativism, Heidegger tacitly posits his utopian, poetic vision as self-validating or, better, as a historically dictated task discerned through a parochial intuitionism. I attribute the cause of this problem to Heidegger's continued lack of a dialectical approach and thus to the perpetuation of a model of transgression as total negation of what is. This false view of freedom leads him to sever the activity of meditative thinking from strategic forms of problem-solving and planning; and to uncouple the synchronic aspects of language as a reservoir of new meaning from the diachronic history of language usage. Failing to discuss the activity of mediating the linguistic sources of identity in terms of concrete empirical and social practices, Heideggerian philosophy deprives struggling groups of the resources for strategic action and disconnects symbolic meaning from social effects. Without seeing his call for a noninstrumental poetics as dialectically related to actual social and material conditions, his own theory becomes blind to its ideological interests. And his reluctant utopianism, rather than building a doorway to the future, deteriorates into a quietistic acceptance of now and a romantic longing for immediacy. This retrogressive retreat mistakenly treats now as if the material conditions for achieving social harmony already existed.

Chapter 7 reveals that Irigaray's monistic approach to the symbolic sources of women's oppression repeats these two Heideggerian mistakes in attenuated form. I engage race-theoretical concerns that the postmodern celebration of difference effaces racial immiseration; that postmodern turns to local narrative reinforce racial segregation when, as Harris puts it, they reify the nature of reality as if it were purely symbolic and fragment groups into univocal wholes; and that the postmodern focus on aesthetics treats the multicultural urban center of today as meta-utopia, again obfuscating the needs of those lost to the urban ghetto and reinforcing a morally reprehensible color-blindness in whites. Focusing only on Irigaray's unique position, I expose and challenge her foundationalist-monism. In a radical feminist vein, Irigaray holds that gender provides the paradigmatic source of all other kinds of oppression. As an empirical claim, it is outdated, blatantly false, and reductionistic. But jettisoning it does not solve all problems in her work.

Irigaray tends to treat the phallocratic symbolic sources of meaning as having a fixed synchronic structure revolving around a masculine-feminine dyad. This supposition, I argue, leads to a second kind of hermeneutical or descriptive monism. Because it places a priori constraints on genealogical analyses of women in their differences, this premise violates Cornell's more plausible position that Woman does not exist a priori. And it yields reductive descriptions because there is no reason to assume a priori that a woman is positioned primarily against masculinity and only secondarily against whiteness in her social location. Irigaray cannot handle racial difference so long as she remains committed to these two types of monism. Even so, I conditionally propose that dismantling the Lacanian assumption that masculine gender identity supersedes all other social markers in boosting ego-formation allows us to keep alive Cornell's model of reiterative universalism.

Chapter 8, however, concludes by addressing those conditions. It shows that even the utopian practice of imaginative universalism can fall prey to myopia when it takes its own practice as sufficient to foster critical self-reflexiveness and ethical humility. On the one hand, I argue that the aesthetic focus of poststructuralist theory is not inherently class or race biased. I show that the Heideggerian ontology presupposed by Irigaray distinguishes between symbolic forms of fetishization (e.g., the packaging of a multicultural harmony which ignores race-based capital exploitation) and the need to create conditions (admittedly material) that would sustain nondistorting forms of social pleasure. On the other hand, I argue that the model of reiterative universalism as a textual practice remains monological. For this reason it proves susceptible to reinforcing the current advertising practice of commodifying multiculturalism and reinforcing racial segregation. To counteract this vulnerability, I argue that such practices need to do two things: (i) address the connections between symbolic practices and material needs; and (ii) theorize an ethics based upon dialogical interaction. While recommending the former, I focus on the latter. Following Iris Young's use of Irigaray, I argue for a model of asymmetrical reciprocity and against the ideal of reversibility of perspectives.[14] Tracing the Heideggerian influence on Irigaray throughout this book supplies the ontological theory requisite to justify this model of asymmetrical reciprocity.

PART I

Beyond the Specter of Stoic Consciousness

A Dialectical View of Agency

CHAPTER ONE

Heidegger and Kristeva

Residues of Heroic Agency and
Stoic Abstraction in Being and Time

———

Heidegger's description of the human tendency to become lost in the "inauthentic" corresponds closely to a portrait of the subject given over to what Kristeva calls the "symbolic" dimension of language. To respond to the call of Care, in Heidegger's terms, entails an entry into the "semiotic" dimension of language, associated with the feminine.

Jean Graybeal, *Language and "The Feminine"*

In her innovative work, *Language and "The Feminine" in Nietzsche and Heidegger*, Jean Graybeal interprets Heidegger's concept of authenticity in terms of Julia Kristeva's semiotic theory. For Graybeal, the critical import of Heidegger's work stems from the fact that authenticity (*Eigentlichkeit*) signals a need to break with the hegemony of our "uninterrupted submersion in the symbolic" and to develop a critical awareness of the ways that discursive practices constitute our identities (Graybeal, LF, 107). Heidegger's persistent "quest for non-metaphysical ways of thinking," Graybeal argues, inaugurates a transgression of the patriarchal symbolic, God the Father, and "establish[es] new types of relations with" what she calls, following Kristeva, the feminine in language or *la mère qui jouit* (2, 19). For Graybeal, it is not incidental that Heidegger suddenly resorts to poetic *mythos* when he defines human being as care rather than as rational animal, and, further, appeals to a feminine figure, the goddess *Cura*, to justify this new name (Heidegger, SZ, 198).

An important spiritual intuition motivates Graybeal's Kristevan reading of Heidegger. For Graybeal, the paradox that humans are driven to anchor meaning in a fixed, transcendent cause (God or man) and yet are immensely attracted to negative disruptions of secure identity reveals an essentially "theological" problem (LF, 18). That problem centers on the need to cultivate a form of life that can abide well the mortality, uncertainty, and ultimate ground-lessness of the human condition. Following Kristeva, Graybeal understands the semiotic as referring to extralinguistic aspects of signification, such as gesture and intonation; the semiotic contributes meaning not simply emphasis to denotative speech. In early infancy biological impulses are organized through a liminal attunement between the infant's bodily needs and the mother's preverbal, gestural responses. For this reason the semiotic aspects of signification carry maternal associations; these associations become repressed through a social taboo against fusion with the maternal body that heralds the infant's entrance into the paternal law of symbolization. Patriarchal society censors the feminine force in language, *la mère qui jouit*; and Christian culture symbolically codified that repression, Graybeal says, in the split image of woman as both virgin "source of life" and "corrupting medium of temptation, sin, and death" (19). The theological fantasy of a God (a closed system of meaning) who secures my place in the cosmos (stabilizes my identity) rests upon this sacrificial splitting of woman. Overcoming the theological temptation thus cannot mean replacing the patriarchal God with a Goddess. Instead, it entails fostering a *jouissance* or bliss that harbors no anxious desire to turn the "human drive for meaning . . . into another 'religion' " (4).

Rather than classify Heidegger as an honorary or protofeminist thinker, Graybeal treats Heidegger's text as a philosophical parallel to the avant-garde literary figures in whose writings Kristeva finds an irruption of the semiotic, a force that "dissolves identity" and reveals "what this society censures" (Kristeva, W, 138). Without embracing Heidegger's gender-neutral project *in toto*, Graybeal explores how Heidegger's style of writing allows the semiotic to emerge in select portions of *Being and Time*. Heidegger's poetic depictions of authenticity as an ecstatic subjectivity echo the *jouissance* of Kristeva's *sujet en procès*. His style of writing "brings back into philosophy qualities and areas of concern long suppressed or ignored" (Graybeal, LF, 25). Most of all, by promoting the discovery of our self-constitution within language, Heidegger's text enables the reader to find *jouissance* in the groundlessness of human existence. For these reasons, Graybeal claims that "Heidegger's struggles to find ways of speaking after the death of God the Father, bring [him] into relation with the 'mother' in language, *la mère qui jouit*, and thus make of [him] not [a] theorist of the feminine, but its practitioner" (4).

By highlighting this maieutic dimension in Heidegger's writings, Graybeal illuminates the more radical impetus in *Being and Time*. She not only connects Heideggerian themes to contemporary gender concerns, but also accounts, in part, for the enduring and pervasive influence that Heidegger's thought continues to exercise on French thinkers as well as many U.S. scholars. Nonetheless, Graybeal overlooks competing tensions in Heidegger's text. At the same time that intonations of receptivity and solicitude for others resound in Heidegger's notion of care, we also hear a deeper, masculine, and even heroic undertone resonate in his depictions of authentic resolve. And it is this heroic tonality that bursts forth shortly after 1927 during his involvement with National Socialism. Graybeal's progressive rendition of Heidegger's writing intensifies the recent call within Heidegger scholarship to examine the relation between the socially productive aspects of his work and the regressive elements. Just as numerous scholars have questioned Kristeva's high praise for avant-garde literary works that reflect elements of reactionary misogyny, so too is it imperative to explore links between the Heideggerian notion of authentic care and his reactionary politics.

In this chapter, I wish to contribute to that task by showing that Heidegger's attempt to decenter the ahistorical, impartial— and by extension masculinist—subject of modernity shatters against his own decisive entanglement in a stoic model of resolute existence. In the first two sections, I situate Graybeal's reading of Heidegger against Kristeva's semiotic theory. Although her drive theory finally undermines her ideals, I highlight how Kristeva's early work strives to develop two ideal models: an ecstatic theory of ethical subjectivity that avoids stoic consciousness and a theory of revolutionary textual practice that resists a merely cathartic release from social constraints. In the final, more lengthy section, I will argue that, whereas the psychoanalytic basis for Kristeva's works imbues her ideal of critical consciousness with a thick psychology, Heidegger's parallel model of ecstatic authenticity abstracts from a hermeneutics of suspicion that, rightfully, he should have inherited from Kierkegaard. Heidegger fashions authenticity after a "non-relational" model that abstracts from social processes and relations to others (SZ, 263). For all the talk of overcoming abstraction and giving up myths of mastery, *Being and Time* remains shot through with an ethos of stoic resolve reminiscent of the masculinist posture of impartiality.

1.1 Kristeva: Negativity and Poetic Mimesis

In *Revolution in Poetic Language*, Kristeva demonstrates that Husserl's transcendental ego articulates a theory of the *thetic subject*, the subject capable of judgment, denotation, and representation, but not the full lived experience of the *speaking subject*. Through a phenomenology of the speaking subject, Kristeva isolates two radically heterogenous forces at work in the subjectivity of the speaker. These two forces, the symbolic and the semiotic, together comprise Kristeva's view of "the social as a signifying space" or the Symbolic order (RP, 49).[1] Understood as one aspect of signifying processes, the symbolic designates those rules and universals governing "logico-semantic articulation" (63). By contrast, the semiotic refers to a preverbal "modality of significance" that breaks out in gesture and vocal rhythm, and disrupts the presumed unity of thetic identity and the closed system of representational discourse (26). Lived experience thus reveals a more dynamic and ecstatic picture of a *sujet en procès*, split between instinctive modulations and conscious thought, biological impulses and social constraints (25–30, 49–51).

Positing the thetic subject as the origin of signification covers over the fact that the thetic position is an attainment, a "phase" synonymous with post-Oedipal ego-formation (44). Rethinking Freud's drive theory in linguistic terms, Kristeva argues that the semiotic *chora*—site of oral and anal pulsions—can be situated "diachronically within the process of the constitution of the subject precisely because *[it] function[s] synchronically within the signifying process of the subject himself,* i.e., the subject of *cogitatio*" (29). The thetic position is a "defensive construction" formed by separation from pre-Oedipal immersion in a semiotic continuum and marked by investment in the fantasy of being a unified subject positioned as master of language. Subject-object differentiation arises, chronologically, only by repressing the infant's fusion with the mother's body and, synchronically, by rejecting autoerotic enclosure in the maternally connoted space of the *chora* (49).[2]

What is central for Kristeva, and cannot be overemphasized, is that the semiotic *chora* functions as a negative dialectical force. From the thetic side, repression of the *chora* is never complete. The semiotic irrupts in speech and signifying practices as a heterogeneous force that, held in dialectical tension with symbolization, "pulverizes" meaning (51). From the other side, the semiotic *chora*, as a material drive-based force oriented toward "destruction, aggressivity, and death," simply defies full assimilation into symbolic representation (28). This irreducible and permanent negativity of the drives, coupled with the fact that the *chora* links drive processes to signifying practices, guarantees that subjectivity is never a completed, coherent state but always an ongoing process (37). As a corrective to Hegel's assimilative logic, Kristeva holds that the material heterogeneity of the drives provides the permanent basis for developing critical distance both on the production of one's identity and on the symbolic laws that rigidly structure one's experience. Negativity puts the *sujet en procès*—that is, "in process/on trial" (22, 58).

Yet before such a critical subject position can be attained, Kristeva vigorously maintains, strong thetic boundaries must be firmly in place.

> In other words, the subject must be firmly posited by castration so that drive attacks against the thetic will not give way to fantasy or to psychosis but will instead lead to a "second-degree thetic," i.e., a resumption of the functioning characteristic of the semiotic *chora* within the signifying device of language. (50)

According to Kristeva, anal pulsions mark the definitive orientation of the infant's motility. As a death drive, anality is a fragmenting and disruptive force; nonetheless, the logic of rejection (negativity) characteristic of anal processes remains a logic of excess. The rhythmic build up, excitation, and rejection of excessive matter yield an infantile *jouissance* (erotic pleasure).[3] Cases of child schizophrenia attest that the aggressivity of anal rejection is immensely pleasurable, for schizophrenia occurs in children when the body fails to defend against rejection through secondary processes of repression (152). Kristeva remarks that rejection becomes stabilized when "[i]ts tendency toward death is deferred by this symbolic [thetic] heterogeneity: the body, as if to prevent its own destruction, *re-inscribes (re-marque)* rejection and, through a leap, *represents* it *in absentia* as a sign" (171).

Thetic identity emerges through a qualitative leap that inaugurates a transposition of real relations (infant-mother fusion) into symbolic functions (represented as ego and alter). First, following

Lacan's mirror stage, narcissistic investment in the imago transposes a more liminal identification with the maternal body into a
new level of articulation; that is, into a "spatial intuition" where
voice becomes a sign "projected from the agitated body (from the
semiotic *chora*) onto the facing imago or object" (46). Second, with
the infant's discovery that the "phallic" mother is not satisfied in
their symbiotic fusion, a sense of lack (castration) disrupts the
natural *jouissance* experienced in rejection and produces the critical momentum necessary for separation. Separation establishes the
child's subjectivity as lack, that is as a desire to be, not the mother,
but rather the phallus or the symbolic Other. If we extend Chris
Weedon's explication of Lacan to Kristeva, then the defensive character of the thetic position solidifies, not simply against incest, but
also around the desire to master meaning:

> The Other is the position of control of desire, power and meaning.
> Desire is a product of language and is subject to the constant
> deferral of satisfaction equivalent to the constant deferral of
> meaning in language. To control the one would be to control the
> other. In identifying with the position of the Other, the subject
> misrecognizes itself as the source of meaning and the power that
> structures it and of which it is an effect.[4]

From this psychoanalytic perspective, the defensive construction of the thetic position is a mixed bag, both requisite for communication and yet sacrificial. All societies, Kristeva claims, are founded
upon an initial violent "murder of soma, the transformation of the
body, the captation of drives" (RP, 75). This violence, which marks
the inception of the symbolic, is displaced onto the symbolic order
and codified in a myth of an original sacrifice. But this sacralization
of murder is simply the "theologization of the thetic," the act that
brings one's *jouissance* under societal regulation (78). Kristeva holds
an ambivalent relation to feminism as a political movement, always
cautioning that feminism can deteriorate into a "jealous . . . conserving
[of] its power" while reservedly admitting that the movement is
necessary (PH, 208; W, 138). Graybeal's spiritualist reading locates
the central contribution of Kristeva's work precisely in the belief
that feminism should not become a new religion. For resisting the
fantasy of unified identity is tantamount to refusing the temptation,
as Graybeal says, "to substitute a new god for the old one, simply to
insert in the vacant space of the old Father God a Mother Goddess
with a slightly altered physiognomy" (Graybeal, LF, 20).

Decentering the fanatical position of thetic identity entails transgressing the border of sacrifice by reactivating "an asocial drive" but without lapsing into a psychotic loss of identity (Kristeva, RP, 79, 71). As Graybeal's states, in overcoming the theological temptation one must avoid "the two extreme fantasies of mastery and dissolution" (Graybeal, LF, 9). Psychosis entails foreclosure of the thetic phase or a "masochistic and jubilatory fall" toward the fantasy of the "full and pagan mother," a fall reflected in regression into infantile babble (Kristeva, Psy, 87; cf. Graybeal, LF, 14). Yet rigid adherence to the desire to master language promotes a different, but equally dangerous fantasy. By trying to make repression absolute, one elevates the thetic phase to the "theological" and hypostatizes the *thetic moment of rejection*" (Kristeva, RP, 206). Such attempts reflect a paranoid psychic structure or an inflated ego-defensive position which readily ushers in neurotic pathologies. For Kristeva, these pathologies manifest both as rigid adherence to conventional norms (conservatism) and as dogmatic reification of opposition (radicalism).

In *Desire in Language,* Kristeva characterizes an ecstatic ideal of the ethical subject as one who recovers *jouissance* without valorizing escapism. She writes:

> [I]f the overly constraining and reductive meaning of a language made up of universals causes us to suffer, the call of the unnameable, on the contrary, issuing from those borders where signification vanishes, hurls us into the void of a psychosis that appears henceforth as the solidary reverse of our universe, saturated with interpretation, faith, or truth. Within that vise, our only chance to avoid being neither master nor slave of meaning lies in our ability to insure our mastery of it (through technique or knowledge) as well as our passage through it (through play or practice). In a word, jouissance. (DL, x)

Graybeal characterizes this *jouissance* as "the agonized joy of self-relation, of self-creation, of self-observation in the bizarre and fascinating process of relating to what constitutes the self as subject" (Graybeal, LF, 17). It portrays the "double brinkmanship" of the self-divided subject, split between dissolution and law, and the ecstasy that withstands sacrifice without sacralizing it (99). But in this passage Kristeva's description of being subjected to language while playfully irreverent sounds both too stoic and too cathartic, indeed, too reminiscent of Freudian pessimism. By stoic, I mean a cognitive rather than affective change, a sort of intellectual cognizance that one is a product of both social conventions and disruptive, asocial drives beyond one's control. The stoic perhaps derives a paradoxically painful yet pleasurable sense of cathartic release because cognizant that social norms have no ultimate claim, even as he or she cannot but obey symbolic laws. Short of any real ability to transform one's drives or society, the stoic adopts an apolitical stance.

Kristeva's description of the ecstatic subject position as self-divided indicates an irresolvable tension between her ideal of a transformed *sujet en procès* and the drive basis of self-transformation which roots subjectivity in a permanently asocial pull. Still, it would be tendentious not to acknowledge that Kristeva attempts to develop an ideal model for a substantive and rich transformation rather than an episodic catharsis or mere stoic concession that one is incurably self-divided. Kristeva argues that "only the subject, for whom the thetic is not a repression of the semiotic *chora* but instead a position either taken or undergone, can call into question the thetic so that a new disposition may be articulated" (RP, 51). Based on her psychologically rich explorations of alterity, abjection, and xenophobia, we can assume that ecstatic subjectivity leads away from paranoic and rigid ego boundaries, even as the self remains bound by symbolic laws. This *jouissance* reflects a transformed disposition marked by psychological flexibility or the capacity to sustain a fallible relation to social norms while lifting repression of one's own psychic heterogeneity.

To her credit, Kristeva strives to articulate an *ecstatic*, rather than *cathartic*, model of critical subjectivity. By ecstatic, I mean a subject capable of becoming aware of the social processes involved in the constitution of her (desiring) identity but without romantically codifying the transgressive moment as a value in itself. By cathartic, I mean an uncritical valorization of the transgressive moment. Such uncritical transgressions often eroticize the pleasure felt through a violent rupturing of the signifying practices that structure desire, thereby reifying what, I believe, is mistakenly interpreted as an asocial ground of freedom. Nothing about such cathartic pleasure provides a criterion for distinguishing between transgressions that critically promote progressive social transformation and those that solidify into reactionary social formations. An adequately developed model of ecstatic subjectivity would have to articulate such a criterion and challenge paradigms that model transgression on an inherent link between pleasure, violence, and freedom. Her twin premises, that drives are asocial and that society is necessarily founded on violence, undermine Kristeva's attempt to distinguish cathartic transgression from socially productive strategies for liberation. Nevertheless, in *Revolution in Poetic Language* this intent underlies her view of poetic mimesis as a revolutionary practice.[5]

In her early works, Kristeva looks to poetic discourse for an ideal model of transgression that neither valorizes free-floating escape nor reifies opposition as an end in itself (RP, 209). The early Kristeva holds that poetic language, rather than psychoanalytic transference, affords a unique vehicle for transforming the subject's disposition for several interrelated reasons. First, poetic language does not simply shatter meaning. Rather, it transgresses the grammatical rules of the symbolic while nonetheless "maintain[ing] a *signification (Bedeutung)*" (57). Thus poetic mimesis calls into question the absoluteness of the rules that organize human experience. It brings us to see our self-constitution within the intertextuality of the Symbolic order:

> The text turns out to be the analyst of every reader and every reader the analysand. But since *the structure and function of language take the place of the focus of transference* in the text, this opens the way for all linguistic, symbolic, and social structures to be put in process/on trial. The text thereby attains its essential dimension: it is a *practice* calling into question (symbolic and social) *finitudes* by proposing *new signifying devices*. (210)

Second, rather than challenge the unicity of the thetic, it aims at "prevent[ing] the thetic from becoming theological" (58). The revolutionary potential of poetic discourse consists in its ability to reactivate repressed drives, and the affective *jouissance* associated with them, through anamnesis (60). Whereas analysis leads to "intellectual acceptance of the repressed," poetic discourse eroticizes repressed drives without sublimating the repressed into "the signified." Art holds open the dialectical "expenditure" of the semiotic drives as *"eroticized in a language"* (163–64). It reveals the prohibition and economic regulation of *jouissance* as what binds identity to symbolic practices. Recollection takes the subject not back to therapeutic acceptance of its former repression, but rather to the synchronic site of its current production (67).

Third and finally, because poetic mimesis does not rely upon direct, personified transference, it resists normalization and thus can promote ideology critique. Rather than "ossifying" the subject's newly reconstituted identity, it links the heterogeneity of drives to objective social conditions (205). Even while she praises nineteenth-century avant-garde aesthetic productions, Kristeva also critiques them for escaping into a subjectivized transgressive pleasure without questioning social conditions (82). Conversely, she attacks Marxian oppositional struggle for reifying the thetic in a kind of fanatic rejection of social norms that merely institutes a new ideology (206). Between these two extremes, Kristeva seeks an ideal textual practice that can open the subject up to its material heterogeneity and use this newly won *jouissance* to critique the sources of communal dissatisfaction with objective social conditions. Together these three qualities give poetic language a unique role in resisting the theological temptation and in making individuals capable of a new humanism, of cultivating a society that refuses to sacralize it origins.

> [M]imesis and poetic language . . . question the very principle of the ideological because they unfold the *unicity* of the thetic (the precondition for meaning and signification) and prevent its theologization. As the place of production for a subject who transgresses the thetic by using it as a necessary boundary—but not as an absolute or as an origin—poetic language and the mimesis from which it is inseparable, are profoundly a-theological. (61)

1.2 The Call of Care:
Breaking the Hegemony of the Symbolic

Graybeal reads Heidegger's *Destruktion* of metaphysics as a revolutionary textual practice that puts the subject in process/on trial.[6] Like Kristeva, Heidegger critiques the Husserlian notion of the transcendental ego for covering over the fact that humans have no *fundamentum inconcussum* (SZ, 24). For Heidegger, it is only because there is no absolute meaning that humans can find themselves naively fascinated by their world in a kind of prethematic understanding. This prethematic absorption presupposes that Dasein's meaning-context is neither reducible to human consciousness nor fixed in an absolute cause. Thomas Sheehan has shown that for Heidegger the essence of phenomena "lies in their autodisclosure":

> *Being and Time* makes one overarching point: that man is present to entities only because he reaches beyond them in the direction of his own relative absentiality: his "becoming" (*Zukunftigheit*)

and "alreadiness" (*Gewesenheit*). . . . The point is that the awareness of his own privative presence (futurity and alreadiness) allows man to know himself authentically and to know entities
properly, i.e., in terms of their kinetic intelligibility.[7]

Well before *Being and Time* (1927) Heidegger attacked metaphysical abstraction as a "hyperbolic" flight into an "absolute truth" that
takes the life out of theory and the wonder out of life (GA 56/57, 84,
90, 112–17). In 1927, he claims that metaphysics transmutes tradition into "a fixed body of doctrine" that dooms humans to a dogmatic repetition of history (SZ, 17, 20–27). Thus, as Sheehan
clarifies, critical awareness of our own constitution "demand[s] a
shift of phenomenological focus from things as disclosed to their
disclosive process itself."[8] Authenticity depicts the process whereby
Dasein breaks the twin habits of hypostatizing meaning (through
projecting a transcendent cause of reality) and conceptualizing itself as in rational control of meaning.

On Graybeal's Kristevan reading, inauthenticity and falling
(*Verfallen*) articulate total submission to the dominant symbolic
system which Heidegger names, after Kierkegaard, "publicness."
To lose oneself in the public means to conform thoughtlessly to the
"they" or *das Man*, i.e., to take for granted accepted discourses as
ways of making sense out of life. In conformity, "We take pleasure
and enjoy ourselves as *they* [*man*] take pleasure; we read, see, and
judge about literature and art as *they* see and judge. . . . we find
'shocking' what *they* find shocking" (SZ, 127). The inauthentic mode
of everyday life, in which we are all caught up in some measure,
divests us of the responsibility to think critically, i.e., to reflect
directly upon the autodisclosive nature of things (128). For Graybeal,
"it is to be limited and confined to what can be understood by all,
rationalized, universalized. In patriarchal culture, it is to belong to
the Father" (LF, 99).

Echoing Kristeva's notion that the thetic position is a defensive construction, Graybeal notes that, for Heidegger, authenticity
entails "a shattering of the pretenses with which Dasein barricades
itself against itself" (LF, 99). Authenticity resembles Kristeva's model
of the "double brinkmanship" of the ethical subject, "balancing the
pain of subjection to the law of the symbolic with the pleasure" of
a new *jouissance* (14). Graybeal explains,

> Care calls Dasein . . . into authenticity, out of the secure but
> deadened precincts of the symbolic. The effects of Care's call on
> Dasein are not comfortable but unsettling; they disturb Dasein's

condition of "fascination" by the "they"; they move Dasein into an uneasy state of not-knowing, of questioning, of awareness of its precarious and tenuous grasp on its own existence. Care's call deprives us, as Kristeva might say, "of the reassurance mechanical use of speech ordinarily gives us, the assurance of being ourselves, that is, untouchable, unchangeable, immortal." (LF, 112; quoting Kristeva, PH, 38)

Graybeal maintains that the feminine-semiotic suffuses Heidegger's own *jouissance* as a writer who wants to describe the tension between the authentic and inauthentic modes of being (LF, 100). So it seems fitting that the pull back from *das Man* answers to a summons from the goddess figure in the Latin fable of Care. Heidegger describes the call of conscience as an uncanny *"alien voice"* that disrupts feeling at home in the world (SZ, 276–77). For Graybeal, care calls Dasein to Freud's "other scene" where drive reactivation occurs and, following Kristeva, one's own and proper unconscious reveals that one is a stranger to oneself (Kristeva, Str, 183). In Heidegger's words, the call "comes *from* me and yet *from beyond me and over me"* (SZ, 275). Like the voice of the repressed, the goddess "summons" us to stray "beyond the borders of home and the familiar" (Graybeal, LF, 115). Situated on the abyss of meaning, authenticity "breaks through the hegemony of the symbolic" and puts the subject on trial (119).

Graybeal punctuates her claim that responding to Care invokes a relation to the semiotic by noting oddities in Heidegger's art of writing. Heidegger's use of fable to depict authenticity marks a "formal anomaly" in the otherwise systematic and analytic construction of *Being and Time* (LF, 111). At the juncture where he must justify the possibility of stepping back from conventional forms of theoretical speculation, Heidegger curiously turns to myth rather than to proof or argumentation (SZ, 197–98). At this "turning point," where the discussion shifts from inauthenticity to authenticity, the goddess Care (the repressed semiotic) suddenly presides over the production of meaning and challenges the absoluteness of representational discourse.

Tipping a keen ear to Heidegger's language, Graybeal further connects Heidegger's description of Dasein's everyday and inauthentic comportment as *Benommenheit* to a peculiarity in Macquarrie and Robinson's translation of the term as fascination. While *Cassell's German-English Dictionary* translates *benommen* as "confused, distraught, dazed, bemused, stupefied" but not as fascinated,

Graybeal notes, the Latin, *fascināre*, means "to enchant, bewitch, from *fascinus*, a bewitching amulet in the shape of a phallus" (LF, 97, 106). Calling this a "bizarrely contorted confirmation," she remarks that this "fortuitous translation" explicitly links Heidegger's descriptions of inauthenticity to Kristeva's view that in Christian cultures the symbolic is phallocentric, i.e., founded on a sacrifice of the maternal body (107).

Focusing on the notions of fascination and bewitchment enables Graybeal to bring forward the ethical implications of Heidegger's critique of inauthenticity.[9] Facing the call from the goddess, *Cura*, initiates a transformation of subjectivity that heals us of what Heidegger calls an "addiction to becoming 'lived' by the world" (SZ, 196). Heidegger's provocative descriptions of inauthentic life indicate that bewitchment by *das Man* is not merely a cognitive disease of mental voyeurism. Rather, the defining characteristics of inauthenticity include affective dimensions that "tranquilize" and alter the constitution of Dasein's very way of living. Idle talk refers to a kind of superficial relation to accepted ideas but one that remains assimilative. As Graybeal says, idle talk "predigests what might otherwise be up for question" (LF, 101). Curiosity, though associated with vision, issues from a holistic state of "restlessness," "distraction," and "lust" for novelty (Heidegger, SZ, 172). Finally, ambiguity indicates a "non-committal" way of surmising events in which one says what "*they*" will find acceptable and everyone avoids taking action by stipulating what "really" must be done (173). Together these "entangle" Dasein in busy avoidance of its own strangely tameless groundlessness.

What Heidegger describes as a homogenizing disease that coopts our originary wonder about ourselves and others, Graybeal diagnoses as stemming from a spell cast by the phallic amulet. Fascinated absorption in *das Man* reflects "a one-sided addiction to or plunge into the symbolic side of the situation of the subject," the desire for mastery, for control of the absolute, for God (LF, 124–25). To the extent that Heidegger's writings remedy this "addiction," they liberate the reader for a new *jouissance*. Like Kristeva's *sujet en procès*, authentic Dasein awakens from the fantasy of the phallus, the promise of a "timeless state of stasis" (LF, 17). Just as the *sujet en procès* withstands two forces—the terrifying yet exciting pull toward symbiosis with the maternal *chora* and the painful but necessary submission to the law of the father—authentic Dasein bears its "ontological anxiety" before the abyss of its being and refuses to take refuge in *das Man*. Authentic Dasein faces death,

not as its future demise, but as a jolt that shakes the security of
the thetic position and cures it of the desire for mastery (Heidegger,
SZ, 276f., 348). Here Graybeal accentuates one final oddity in
Heidegger's text: it mentions joy for the first time in connection
with this newly won sobriety. In the "face-to-face" encounter with
its anxiety, Dasein experiences an "unshakable joy"; it becomes
"armed, prepared, ready" for its groundlessness (LF, 125).

1.3 Heidegger's Stoic Valorization of Heroism[10]

Although manifold influences inform the complex vision of *Being
and Time*, Heidegger's analysis of the inauthentic and authentic
modes of life reflects a noteworthy Kierkegaardian lineage.[11] The
maieutic dimension of Heidegger's project, central to Graybeal's
reading, stems from extending the Kierkegaardian *existential* goal
of living in personal integrity (without self-deception) to include a
methodological aspect, namely, a disruption of metaphysics (the
drive for fixed meaning). John Caputo argues compellingly that
Heidegger's genius consisted in recognizing that personal authenticity must be accompanied by "methodological consciousness":

> On the existential level, authentically being oneself (*eigentliches
> Selbstsein*) is the counter-tendency to inauthentically being like
> everyone else (*das 'Man'*). On the hermeneutical level—that is, on
> the level of a thematic interpretation such as is undertaken by the
> author of *Being and Time*—an authentic interpretation of Dasein in
> terms of existence and temporality is the counter-tendency to a
> falling interpretation of Dasein in terms of presence. Our prethematic
> fallenness (as existing beings) is mirrored in a fallen ontology.[12]

Here I bracket the formal objective of *Being and Time*, to develop an ontology that reflects Dasein's temporal structure, and
focus on the practice of developing this critical awareness of the
kinetic nature of beings. Heidegger saw that Kierkegaard's ideal of
retrieving a critical self-relation must remain partial and incomplete without undertaking a radical reassessment of western metaphysics. Since authentic life does not transpire in a cultural and
historical vacuum, cultivating a critical relation to my sense of
identity is not simply psychological and interpersonal. It must include questioning the canonical heritage that is constitutive of who
I am and that structures how I represent the world (cf. SZ, 20–27).

Graybeal's interpretation stems from this methodological intuition and develops it by interpreting *Being and Time* as a book about how language paradoxically conditions and yet threatens the possibility of nonoppressive social relations. But while a hermeneutics of suspicion and a conception of the social as signifying space clearly underpin both Kristeva's ideal of the subject in process and Kierkegaard's communicative model of existential ethics, the relation of ontological groundlessness to motivated deception and to social relations is wrought with tensions in *Being and Time*.[13]

My argument is that Heidegger takes over the psychologically rich Kierkegaardian themes of anxiety, idle talk, and curiosity that, as existential equivalents to neurotic symptoms, offer a parallel to Kristeva's critique of the thetic position. But when he shifts the concept of authenticity to an ontological level, Heidegger unnecessarily divorces it from ethical critique and depletes it of psychological richness. Thus Heidegger fails to weave the existential problem of living without self-deception together with the ontological problem of fostering a nonobjectifying and nonpossessive relation to the mysterious self-disclosure of others. I locate the cause of this error in Heidegger's methodology. He mistakenly models the practical goal of fostering awareness of disclosedness after his formal, transcendental derivation of the ontological conditions of existential practices. When Heidegger's transcendentalism permeates his maieutic goal, learning a nonobjectifying way of thinking becomes a pristine activity. It is no longer a praxis that, dialectically conceived, both partially conditions *and* is partially conditioned by self-examination, social processes of recognition, and ideology critique. This truncated praxis leads to stoic consciousness and paves the way for Heidegger's reactionary politics of the thirties.[14]

The Kierkegaardian Background

Heidegger's thesis that one becomes authentic through resolute decision descends from Kierkegaard's existential reflections on the kinetic nature of human life. As temporal beings, we develop one way or another, for Kierkegaard, either naively as our society dictates or critically through active mediation of one's life.[15] In *Either/Or*, Kierkegaard depicts the ethical failure to actively take over the direction of one's self-development as an aesthetical mode of life, the life of curiosity, idle talk, and lust for novelty. But what is essential for Kierkegaard is that, through this decision, I begin to engage in a process of interior edification, a *Bildungsprozeß*.

Like Kristeva's "second-degree thetic," Kierkegaard defines ethical existence as "raising [one's] consciousness to the second power." Ultimately there are multiple stages of spiritual growth which move the self from abstract attitudes toward life choices (e.g., a stoic fatalism that hardens one against what cannot be controlled) to increasingly concrete and psychologically differentiated attitudes (e.g., sifting through the motivated attachments I have and how these keep me bound to an uncritical self-relation, to power and material position, and thus to my relations to others). Kierkegaard's authorship does not valorize the mere act of choice. Repetition holds ethical overtones only insofar as it initiates the existentially transformative process of self-exploration.[16]

In spite of his emphasis on the interior life of "spirit," Kierkegaard holds an explicitly *dialectical* view of the relation between personal autonomy (self-consciousness) and community (social context). On the one hand, Kierkegaard argues that my relation to others, to cultural beliefs, to normative discourse hinges upon my self-relation. On the other hand, since subjectivity is intersubjectivity, a critical self-relation can never be realized outside of a particular circumstance of struggling with social conditions and working out interpersonal relations. Against Hegel's tendency to subsume individual difference under Absolute *Geist*, Kierkegaard wants to isolate an irreducible moment of spiritual interiority that functions like Kristeva's negativity of the drives as resistance to assimilation. The ethical activity of developing a critical self-relation, however, is not a natural given, like the materiality of the drives, but rather an achievement that must be abidingly attained. For Kierkegaard, the logic of excess, which positions interiority in tension with existing norms, transforms *how* I relate to my world, thoughtfully as opposed to naively, honestly rather than from a motivated ignorance that enables me to enjoy social power without justification. But as a specific and irreducible activity, the critical stance is not inherently antithetical to community and public discourse. In fact, it cannot stand in for normative justification. Rather, it gives the individual free responsibility for her relation to community and societal norms; conversely, it makes the community responsible to the excess represented by individual needs and not addressed by preexisting social conventions.[17]

In *Two Ages*, Kierkegaard differentiates the modal relations, individual and crowd, from the ontological fact that subjectivity is always concretely bound up with intersubjectivity. Whereas selves never exist outside community, the terms "individual" and "crowd" designate antithetical forms of social interaction. Kierkegaard distinguishes the "crowd" from the possibility of a true community of "individuals" as "neighbors." The crowd designates a form of community that, though moralizing, maintains "en masse" a precritical relationship to its moral code and in this fashion "renders the individual completely impenitent and irresponsible."[18] Genuine community obtains only through the dialectic of interiority whereby individuals undertake a critical mediation of values and ideals. It is this mediation that brings one to awareness of individual differences. Only on the basis of this differentiation can a true communal cohesiveness be built. On the other hand, lacking such awareness,

> we have a tumultuous self-relating of the mass to an idea . . . gossip and rumour . . . apathetic envy become a surrogate of each for all. Individuals do not in inwardness turn away from each other, turn outward in unanimity for an idea, but mutually turn to each other in a frustrating and suspicious, aggressive, leveling reciprocity.[19]

Kierkegaard's concept of the individual should be confused neither with stoic abstraction nor with repudiation of community. Ethical integrity involves a pull away from the crowd only insofar as it counteracts blind adherence to convention.[20] It is arguable, then, that the birth of interiority does not lapse into antisocial, rampant individualism in spite of Kierkegaard's tendency to equate the ethical subject with a subject in exile and against his inclination to romanticize, even deliberately aggravate, his particular life experience of being ostracized. In such moments, he conflates a modal category, namely, how I relate to others, with a particular form of life. Strictly speaking, the ethical "individual" who engages in self-examination can experience isolation from the "crowd" only as a position that intensifies her engagement in society, i.e., only as repudiated by others.

For Kierkegaard, the crowd is a dangerous force not because everyone agrees with tradition, although that might be politically undesirable, but rather because no agreement can arise without first examining how one's social location, relative to others, is determined by assumptions and values. While this position does not give us ideology critique or critical social theory, Kierkegaard's point is that self-examination is a precondition (if only partial) of social and political critique. From his standpoint, how I live makes a difference. Even were I to adhere to traditional principles, my mode of action would be thoughtful and engaged as opposed to dogmatic, intolerant, and disingenuous. While interiority will not justify my moral or political choice, it will prepare me to engage in critical discussions about normative issues.[21]

Heidegger's Abstraction from Interior Life

Heidegger anchors the aesthetical (inauthentic) and ethical (authentic) modes of life in ontology and this anchoring shifts the Kierkegaardian concept of mode from an intersubjective, *existenziell* level (existence in its concrete determinations) to an ontological, *existenzial* level (the universal structures in every concrete act of existing). Modes (the *Existenzialien*) denote temporal rather than static neo-Kantian structures; they designate the conditions of possibility for intersubjective and historical forms of life.[22] For Heidegger, all forms of lived self-alter relations presuppose that "Others" are already "with" me as part of the modal structure of Dasein as a projected Being-in-a-world. Heidegger's discussion of Being-with advances one key claim: that ontology logically precedes psychology and actual intersubjective relations. In Heidegger's words, "[t]his Dasein-with of the Others is disclosed within-the-world for a Dasein, and so too for those who are Daseins with us (*die Mitdaseienden*), only because Dasein in itself is essentially Being-with" (SZ, 120). Yet when Heidegger says that others are with me a priori, he does not mean that they are actually present. Rather, "[t]he Other can *be missing* only *in* and *for* a Being-with. Being-alone is a deficient mode of Being-with; its very possibility is proof of this" (120–21). Because my sense of being the kind of entity I am is embedded in a sense of others, I can experience aloneness and, moreover, I can be alone even when another is present in the room (124). For Heidegger, psychologically based phenomena—such as relating across individual differences, getting to know another's interiority, developing sympathy or hatred, empathy or indifference—rely upon an a priori ontological, albeit prethematic, understanding of others as humans like me.

At an ontological level, we encounter ourselves as both an entity in the world and the very ec-static site of disclosure of the world. In his 1929 lecture "What is Metaphysics?" Heidegger calls human being a transcendence because humans are "held out into the nothing" or non-Being (BW, 105/W, 12). Because we touch this groundlessness in certain moods, the world recedes from us and entities come into view as autodisclosive. In Sheehan's language, only because our own absentiality is a question for us, can we contemplate the kinetic process of all things. This prethematic ability to contemplate our own presencing and absencing enables us to differentiate the various modes of disclosure peculiar to different kinds of entities. Being-with specifies the particular prethematic recognition that Daseins have with one another. We encounter other Daseins not as entities first objectified and separated from us (present-at-hand) nor as things for manipulation and use (ready-to-hand) but rather as those with whom I share the world and who co-constitute the site of disclosedness of all things (SZ, 118).

At this point, Heidegger's ontology *appears* consistent with Kierkegaardian dialectics. Heidegger uses the term *Fürsorge* or solicitude to depict the specific form of care Dasein exhibits in its prethematic comportment toward other humans. Thus *Fürsorge* denotes the ontological basis for adopting both inauthentic relations of domination and intersubjective relations that free individuals up to be together authentically. Echoing Kierkegaard, Heidegger says that authentic care "helps the Other become transparent to himself *in* his care and to become *free* for it." Similarly, Kierkegaard's crowd resonates in Heidegger's comment that, even when engaged in a common undertaking, humans often "mistrust" one another (122). Formally anchoring inauthentic and authentic care in Being-with does not seem to posit an inherent contradiction between becoming an authentic individual and engaging in productive social relations.

In spite of this promising strain in *Being and Time*, Heidegger ultimately pits the practice of overcoming objectification of others against psychological and interpersonal development. On the one hand, Heidegger's formal claim that the process of understanding the psychical life of others presupposes an original prethematic sense of being like one another is sound. On the other hand, Heidegger's practical claim that becoming authentically "free" for one's care cannot occur through empathy seems highly questionable. This latter claim severs the awareness requisite for authenticity from a hermeneutics of suspicion. Although Being-with is the formal possibility of either "opening oneself up" or "closing oneself off" to others, Heidegger's comments on empathy confuse formal claims with practical ones. Heidegger says,

> This phenomenon [opening oneself up to another], which is none too happily designated as *'empathy'* (*"Einfühlung"*), is then supposed, as it were, to provide the first ontological bridge from one's

own subject, which is given proximally as alone, to the other
subject, which is proximally quite closed off. (124)

In this discussion, Heidegger argues that the psychological view
of empathy as personal disclosure reflects false ontological presuppositions, namely, that we are first separate individuals who can
only subsequently cross over to one another. Such a viewpoint cannot
account for how humans can disclose themselves to one another
because the "Other would be a duplicate of the Self," a mere projection of one's own identity (124). As a formal argument, Heidegger's
conceptual point is sound: empathy is possible only because Being-
with is part of Dasein's ontological constitution (125). Still, the
status of Heidegger's claim remains unclear. While a descriptive
psychology of human behavior and popular psychological conceptions may not yield fundamental ontology, it remains specious to
assume that the science of psychoanalysis cannot provide a sound
theoretical foundation that accounts for the preobjectifying basis
for self-alter differentiation and thus for processes, not simply of
bonding, but also of explicit reconciliation of the self to others in a
social whole.

More important still are the implications of Heidegger's comments for specifying the nature of the practical relation between
empathy (or other existential and therapeutic processes) and examining one's ontological suppositions (methodology) in fostering
critical consciousness. Heidegger claims that "welfare work" (121)
and empathy (125) get their "motivation from the unsociability" of
inauthentic intersubjective relations. We could take this to mean
that empathy counters inauthenticity at a lived, *existenziell* level,
but does not provide an explicit formal account of its own ontological foundation. Such a claim would be sound. Yet in analyzing that
foundation, Heidegger strictly rejects the notion that empathy is
an explicit manifestation of the ontological structure of Dasein (one
of the *Existenzialien*). Rather than depict empathy as a positive
existenziell and explicit unfolding of our implicit prethematic and
ontological solicitude for others, Heidegger rigorously demarcates
Fürsorge from empathy.

We can interpret this demarcation in two ways: (a) either
empathy initiates a countermovement to inauthenticity but remains
partial and incomplete without the critical moment of "methodological consciousness" wherein we break through our static,
essentializing suppositions and reach awareness of the autodisclosive
nature of beings; or (b) empathy-based relations necessarily rein-

force false ontological assumptions and so perpetuate an inherently truncated and misguided effort to counter objectification. Two features of Heidegger's discussion lead to the second interpretation (b), that interpersonal disclosure is an impediment to genuine awareness of the autodisclosive nature of human life. First, Heidegger subsumes his discussion of empathy under not simply the everyday horizon of self-interpretation, but inauthentic ways of existing. Second, he implies that psychological analysis is inherently linked to treating others as numbers, as objects.

For example, Heidegger's claim—that understanding others "depends *only* on how far one's essential being with Others has been made itself transparent"—is replete with ambiguity in that he conflates everyday forms of discourse with inauthenticity (SZ, 125, emphasis mine). Heidegger could mean that interpersonal disclosure of interiority constitutes a necessary but insufficient condition of nondominating relations. Awareness of the other's irreducible absentiality would then provide the sufficient condition that enables me to revel joyously in the fact that I can never know another transparently; it would transform my everyday engagements. Or he could mean *"only"* correct ontological vision yields understanding, whereas empathy never breaks with everyday falsehoods. Does Heidegger consider empathy part of the masquerade of *das Man*, a superficial role-playing in which the effort to listen to others hides the fact that I really project others as "duplicates" of myself? Must empathy shipwreck on this superficial pretense at hearing?

The text is full of gaps, but Heidegger's second move settles the question by implying that, no matter how valuable as an *existenziell* practice, empathy cannot overcome "'inconsiderate' Being-with." On the tail end of his formal call for an ontologically grounded hermeneutic of empathy, he suddenly launches a discussion of calculation. He says that we can only think of intersubjective relations on the model of a bridge between separate subjects because "the Others who are concerned proximally in their Dasein-with are treated merely as 'numerals' (*Nummer*)" (125). At this point, Heidegger ties empathy to inherently objectifying and deficient ways of treating one another. My reading accounts for seemingly ancillary comments made throughout *Being and Time*. Flush with disdain, these comments elevate the authentic subject above "that Self which inertly dissects its 'inner life' with fussy curiosity" and "that Self which one has in mind when one gazes 'analytically' at psychical conditions and what lies behind them" (273).[23] In his

theoretical effort to differentiate the *formal* science of phenomenological ontology from a Husserlian focus on interiority, Heidegger
throws the baby out with the bath water. He severs the process of
existential edification and psychological growth from the *practical*
endeavor to learn to face the ontological groundlessness of human
existence without anxiety.

Attunement without Empathy

Heidegger's preliminary and gap-filled analysis of Being-with
forms the backdrop for his subsequent treatment of inauthentic
falling as a kind of fearful flight from the self's primordial anxiety
before the groundlessness of existence. It prepares another excessively austere demarcation between moods and feelings. Moods
designate prevolitional and prethematic modes of attunement to
the disclosedness of the world; they are constitutive of Dasein's
ontological structure as the site of disclosure. Joy, anxiety, boredom
comprise moods (*existenzial* notions) that reveal the totality of one's
world in specific and unique ways, whereas feelings are secondary,
ontic phenomena for Heidegger, *existenziell* reactions that one may
have to this disclosure. Feelings presuppose an ego-based conception of self that already abstracts from the prevolitional basis of
the self's comportment. Authentic resolve decenters thetic consciousness by stilling the emotive-based flight from anxiety—the most
primordial mood that we cannot escape and which delivers us to
the groundlessness of existence.

Moods certainly are not synonymous with feelings. Heidegger's
central insight holds that accepted intellectual and popular discourses literally detach us from a more original contact with the
autodisclosive nature of phenomena. Since, as linguistic beings, we
rely upon some current discourses, Heidegger constantly reiterates
that we are always partially inauthentically related to one another.
This insight into the autodisclosive irreducibility in ourselves and
others gestures toward the foundations of a theory of social recognition that, following Kierkegaard and Kristeva, enables one to
take joy in mutual understanding without suppressing individuated difference. Heidegger's point—that vulnerability before the
uncontrollable absentiality in ourselves and in others contributes
to conformity and to taking refuge in discourses that distance us
from our vulnerability before one another—is well-taken. This insight could, in principle, enrich social theory. But, whereas Kristeva
focuses on how rigid identification with accepted signifying prac-

tices serves to objectify and oppress some groups, Heidegger advances a transcendental analysis that locates flight from anxiety before the absentiality of beings as the singular cause of objectification and social conformism.

Although ontological anxiety makes an irreducible contribution to perverse social relations, Heideggerian transcendentalism fashions contemplation of absentiality or attunement to disclosedness as a lived practice that must precede, in fact work against, 'mere' psychological grappling with fear and 'mere' intellectual disagreements that do not modify false ontological suppositions. This transcendentalism unravels what otherwise could have been an intricate fabric, weaving threads of psychology, the hermeneutics of suspicion, and critical ontology into a rich view of critical self-awareness. That model could have reflected a multifaceted practical mediation of the psychic mechanisms, symbolic and discursive appeals, ontological vulnerabilities, and material conditions that together comprise sources of anxiety and alienation. Such a model would fit with a theory of social recognition that does not fall prey to an assimilative logic that reduces the other to a mirror reflection of myself.[24]

Heidegger's rigorous effort to formally differentiate ontology as a foundational science from the nonfoundational discourses of psychology, philosophy of consciousness, historicism, and existential philosophy leads him to split the practice of becoming attuned to disclosedness from other dimensions of personal and social analysis. As a consequence, *Fürsorge* and Being-with wane into formal abstraction. Even as these reflect moods of attunement to others, they are stripped of any definitive relation to the complex attitudinal life that humans develop, not simply as fearful reactions or from naiveté, but through critical assessment of their concrete interpersonal relations and concrete social conditions. Whatever maieutic intent we can distill out of Heidegger's concept of anticipatory resolve, the import of learning not to objectify other humans and oneself seems set adrift, dislocated from actual attunement to other people. The formal project, of bringing Being and Dasein's ontological structure transparently into view, rather than presupposing a hermeneutics of suspicion and ideology critique as its lived prerequisites, displaces a dialectic between theory and praxis. Both as a potential lived relation to one's kinetic structure and as a theory of kinesis, ontology displaces social theory; social theory comprises a secondary discourse about 'mere' ideological disputes. Heidegger's purified contemplative notion of praxis dilutes his con-

ception of wonder and attenuates his vision of attunement, rendering these sorely inadequate 'foundations' for establishing a critical
relation to social conventions, symbolic or material.

The Retreat into Stoicism

A significant consequence of Heidegger's transcendentalism is
that his picture of authentic subjectivity dwindles into a narrow
and truncated subject, reminiscent of Hegel's stoic consciousness.
In sharp contradiction with Heidegger's insistence that the authentic self is not "removed, purified, isolated," Daniel Berthold-Bond
argues, the actual descriptions of authentic resolve present an
abstract "dislocation . . . of the self from its absorption in the world
of the everyday" that renders Dasein "utterly *alone.*" Like Berthold-
Bond, I hold that *Being and Time* labors under the difficulty of an
inadequate distinction between the public realm *per se* and the
"publicness" of *das Man.*[25] Failing to develop this distinction,
Heidegger articulates authenticity not only as a lived, *existenziell*
counterpoise to uncritical and inauthentic forms of sociality, but
also as a reified counterposition to existing social relations. Allegedly Dasein is ontologically "for the sake of Others" (SZ, 123). Yet
authenticity is grounded in an ontological breach, a moment of
"non-relationality," that literally cuts off Dasein's relations to others and to the world (125).

In discussing kinds of knowing, Heidegger takes pains to present
"non-relational" as a technical term, indicating the specific kind of
understanding that corresponds to the disclosedness of entities.
Representation, by contrast, objectifies entities and covers over
disclosedness; it breaks things apart into separate objects because
"there still lurks a relation character" (225). On this definition, the
"non-relational" moment signifies a distinctive kind of awareness
which, rather than sever my relations to others and the world,
should prepare me to truly cultivate them. Discovering the beauty
inherent in the distinctly autodisclosive nature of things should
dispel my attachment to socially learned fears about the groundlessness of life. It should free me from the sway of rote discourses
that, like the lens of prejudice, constantly distort my perceptions
and impede my ability to touch another. Or, better, this awareness
should enable me to witness others reveal their uniqueness at least
without completely misinterpreting them.

Yet Heidegger's descriptions of how anxiety before death individualizes Dasein and pulls it out of immersion in *das Man* rely

upon an overly categorical distinction between two kinds of knowing, specifically, witnessing the disclosedness of Being and representation. His descriptions of anxiety fail to differentiate between dominating and nondominating forms of objectification. The individualizing moment of anxiety severs Dasein from worldly representation. In Heidegger's words: "the 'world' can offer nothing more, and neither can the Dasein-with of others; anxiety thus takes away the possibilities of understanding itself, as it falls, in terms of the 'world'" (187). Anxiety individualizes me as "Being-possible," as abstractly oriented to possibility, rather than as facing specific possibilities in relation to others (189).

Heidegger does claim that being individualized into awareness of kinesis "bring[s] [the self] face to face with itself as Being-in-the-world" (188). And he implies that there is a dialectical relation between recovering this awareness and engagement with others: "But if concern and care fail us, this does not signify at all that these ways of Dasein have been cut off. . . . these have an equal share in conditioning the possibility of any existence whatsoever" (263). In spite of these gestures toward dialectics, his reductionist view that all objectification is domination leads him to postulate authentic care, here understood as witnessing disclosedness, as uniquely distinct from pragmatic forms of concern. Heidegger says that care and solicitude "will fail us" because they necessarily bind us to inauthentic viewpoints (*das Man*). Thus, recovering awareness of disclosedness resists not simply disingenuous relations but all forms of concerned engagement in worldly affairs.

Heidegger's methodology requires these falsely categorical distinctions because he argues that an authentic fore-sight, which brings us to awareness of our constitution, can only be projected from the individuated Self. We might simply ask why. Why wouldn't he fill out the problem of decentering subjective perceptions and naive submission to tradition through an intersubjective paradigm? The twin claims that Dasein is both *Mitsein* and groundless seem to warrant such a conclusion. If we cannot transparently know another's situation, then why wouldn't authentic fore-sight be an ideal that could only be approached as a kind of verisimilitude through an interactive model of knowledge? And if we take seriously the finitude of Dasein, would we not come to see that material and social location influence one's perspective? Instead of taking this fruitful turn, Heidegger's methodological solipsism leads him down a pathway to stoicism. As Berthold-Bond says,

The stoical consciousness, for Hegel, is motivated by a yearning for freedom, but a yearning which despairs of having its freedom acknowledged in the social and political world, a world in which its feels forsaken, just as the Heideggerian analysis of the experience of anxiety portrays Dasein as feeling lost and "not-at-home" in its everyday world. Hence the stoic practices the movement of withdrawal, and turns inward into the freedom of *thought*. In thought, the stoic achieves his or her freedom because "in thought . . . I am not in an *other* but remain simply and solely in communion with myself"—words which are echoed in Heidegger's portrait of the radical individualization and "non-relatedness" to others which occurs in anxiety, being-towards-death, guilt, conscience, and resoluteness.[26]

Without pretending to represent the old Stoic doctrines, stoic consciousness after Hegel and Freud has come to refer in general to two things: (i) the practice of eliminating the irrational and mastering passions; and (ii) a conception of the virtuous "man" as unattached to what is fated in the external world. Heidegger holds a holistic conception of Dasein that rejects mind-body, affective-cognitive dichotomies. Nevertheless, I am arguing that once Heidegger severs attunement to the autodisclosure of beings from a hermeneutic of desire and motivational life, his concept of authenticity indeed does shrink into a more restricted cognitive achievement, devoid of a certain affective breadth. Authenticity takes on the contours of a practice that, while not exactly suffering from a commitment to impartiality and value-free objectivity, still retains elements of the truncated psychological, affective, and attitudinal development associated with Euro-masculinist conceptions of impartial rationality.[27]

Whereas for Kierkegaard authenticity calls me to strive without terminus to close the gap between how I actually live and how I represent my motives and actions to myself, for Heidegger it calls me to witness the temporal nature of all things. But, unlike Kierkegaard, Heideggerian authenticity gives no indications that this praxis could never be merely a stiff cognitive achievement. Brilliant philosophical insight has never been a guarantee of a well-rounded psychology. Further, the formal ontological practice of seizing upon and making explicit the kinetic nature of beings hardly promises the ethical sensibilities for sincere engagement with others characteristic of either Kristeva's or Kierkegaard's ideal of postconventional subjectivity.[28]

An Emergent Heroic Ideal

Heidegger's insistence that authentic choice is concretely realized in social situations shipwrecks on the fact that, as Karsten Harries puts it, "resolve calls man to a form of life, not to a particular life."[29] Just at the moment that Dasein heeds the "call of conscience," what Graybeal claimed was the "voice from the other side," it discovers emptiness and indeterminacy but no guidelines for engagement (SZ, 258, 274). Clearly resolve is not entirely empty insofar as it recovers awareness of the kinetic nature of beings. But I am arguing that the call of conscience fails to deliver the self to the life of motivational analysis. Without this therapeutic moment, authenticity yields no development of the competencies requisite to assess my complicity with conventional ideologies. The transgression of tradition proves an absolute breach and a search for a kind of contemplative purity. Once this contemplative praxis is dislocated from social relations, Heidegger opens the door to a heroic breach of tradition that valorizes willfulness for its own sake and offers no accountability to public discourse, existing norms, or others. The solipsistic standpoint from which authentic Dasein gets the true vision of reality stands dangerously close to an authoritative refusal to accept the very finite character of individual perspective his theory supposedly proclaims.[30]

In the end, Heidegger fails to develop the genuine possibility of a theory of social recognition intimated by his kinetic view of human being, namely, a theory which need not ground intersubjective relations in a *trial by death*. Instead, facing death removes Dasein from others. Worse, this transcendentalism finally undercuts the possibility of understanding care as a nonauthoritative relation to others. To come full circle to my initial reflections on *Mitsein*, Heidegger's descriptions of Being-with as care are undoubtedly beautiful and suggestive. Yet they remain seductive.

> [S]olicitude has two extreme possibilities. It can, as it were, take away 'care' from the Other and put itself in his position of concern: it can *leap in* for him. . . . In such solicitude the Other can become one who is dominated and dependent, even if this kind of domination is a tacit one and remains hidden from him. . . . In contrast to this, there is also the possibility of a kind of solicitude which does not so much leap in for the Other as *leap ahead* of him [*ihm vorausspringt*] in his existentiell potentiality-for-Being, not in order to take away his 'care' but rather to give it back to him

authentically. . . . it helps the Other to become transparent to himself *in* his care and to become *free for* it. (122)

Heidegger's comments suggest the possibility of nondominating relations to others. Yet a genuine ability to let others be in their
differences would seem to require the capacities of tolerance and
empathy as well as a highly attuned sensitivity to material conditions. When Heidegger fails to flesh out the intersubjective and
material conditions for authentic care, his concept of helping others
become "free" wavers. Once rooted in the "non-relational" break
with ordinary discourses, nothing guarantees that help is not simply a new form of Socratic paternalism. For the early Heidegger,
letting something be seen, *"etwas als etwas sehen lassen,"* connotes
taking control of one's fore-sight (32). The authentic thinker "lets"
beings reveal themselves by wresting phenomena from dominant
interpretations which obscure their self-revelation (37). Heidegger
offers no explicit theory of consciousness raising, no paradigm of
communication, not even a therapeutic or pedagogical paradigm
that distinguishes between detrimental and nondetrimental ways
of educating. How, we might ask, does Heidegger envisage the
relation between fore-sight, true disclosure, and "leaping ahead" to
help others realize their own freedom as care? Should the authentic person decide to "strip away" (in a sort of intellectual rape?)
what he perceives as the other's false conceptions? Can authentic
Dasein assume that he has the true insight into my inauthenticity?
Or must he, like the analyst, first let me ask for his help and,
second, validate my self-disclosure? Arguably Heidegger resorts to
an indirect form of communication through his own writing and in
this way avoids problematic forms of direct, personified transference. But it is also true that his descriptions of authenticity support the self-proclaimed authority of authentic persons and that
his powerful, often mystifying rhetoric has seduced many a reader
into uncritical devotion to the presumed authority of his vision.[31]
    Sadly, Heidegger's asocial, and thus falsely oppositional, model
of freedom cannot avoid a certain valorization of the heroic individual and his alleged authority. Having collapsed the isolation of
the authentic person into one of *ontological* distinction, as compared with Kristeva's and Kierkegaard's respective *dialectical* and
exilic views, Heidegger slurs the boundary between a *qualitative*
and an *essentialist* view of excellence. Kierkegaard holds that natural talent never distinguishes us, but only the ongoing process of

self-transformation that divests us of righteousness and self-certainty.[32] Kristeva critiques the authoritative personality as paranoic, inflexible, and obsessed and advocates that we become more flexible, less xenophobic persons. But Heideggerian authenticity invokes a Greek sense of an ontologically or naturally grounded elitism: Humans are distinguished by virtue of pregiven personality traits and abilities, not by the egalitarian principle that each is capable of cultivating for herself the most supremely developed self-awareness and critical relation to her life conditions. It is not, then, surprising that during the thirties Heidegger valorizes special heroes—"creators, poets, thinkers and statesmen"—and spiritually superior nations, such as Germany (IM, 62, 38/EM, 47, 29). These "creators" and creative entities are born to a superior authority to see and embody what the public cannot: the higher purpose of humanity.

CHAPTER TWO

Heidegger, Irigaray, and the Masculine Ethos of National Socialism

Or, How to Tame the Feminine

In our eyes, the ideal German boy should be slim and trim, quick as a greyhound, tough as leather and hard as Krupp steel.

Adolf Hitler, Speech 1936

When the Other falls out of the starry sky into the chasms of the psyche, the "subject" is obviously obliged to stake out new boundaries for his field of implantation and to re-ensure—otherwise elsewhere—his dominance. Where once he was on the heights, he is now entreated to go down into the depths. . . . But how to tame those uncharted territories, these dark continents, these worlds through the looking glass? How to master these devilries. . . . Perhaps for the time being the serene contemplation of empire must be abandoned in favor of taming those forces which, once unleashed, might explode the empire. A detour into *strategy, tactics, and practice* is called for, at least as long as it takes to gain vision, self-knowledge, self-possession, even in one's decenteredness. The "subject" sidles up to the truth, squints at it, obliquely, in an attempt to gain possession of what truth can no longer say.

Luce Irigaray, *Speculum*

Ernst Tugendhat suggests that there is a "missing link" between Heidegger's concept of authenticity and a publicly verifiable (i.e., nonauthoritative) criterion for political praxis.[1] Richard Wolin and Reiner Schürmann represent two sophisticated responses to Tugendhat's challenge. Wolin argues that Heidegger's *Seinspolitik* (politics of Being) collapses politics into the historical process of overcoming metaphysical conceptions of Being; rather than supply the missing link, this reduction of politics to ontology embroils Heidegger in decisionism. Schürmann, conversely, suggests that Heidegger's politics between 1933 and 1936 betrayed the deeper egalitarian and anarchic political implications of his lifelong critique of metaphysics. This betrayal stemmed from Heidegger's failure to posit the "symbolic difference" as the missing link connecting his reflections on the impossibility of absolute grounds to a critical social praxis. When juxtaposed, Schürmann and Wolin sketch two extreme tendencies inherent in Heidegger's antifoundationalism. One tendency moves toward a dangerous antinormativism; the other fosters an ethico-deconstructive corrective to postulating normative principles as absolutes without critically examining the cultural fantasies invoked by such ideals.[2]

In this chapter, I will cast a different angle on the now many fine analyses of the theoretical foundations for Heidegger's turn to National Socialism. The particular historical and theoretical juncture from which I will examine the 1935 lecture course, *An Introduction to Metaphysics*, is signaled by Heidegger's embrace of the virulent manly ethos valorized by numerous conservative reactionary thinkers. Between 1929 and 1935 Heidegger's thought coalesces into a strange weave of philosophical, ideological, and reactionary mechanisms. As a partial contribution to untangling this weave, I want to highlight how Heidegger seamlessly inserted his theory of authenticity into the masculinist vision of the strong-willed nation paraded by reactionaries, like Ernst Jünger, and Nazi propagandists alike. Under the influence of protofascistic ideas, Heideggerian thought centers ambiguously around an elitist and masculinist belief that he and his generational cohorts are the chosen heroic midwives to the future destiny of Germany and western humanity.[3] This centering of a manly ethos of creative mastery brings Heidegger's thought into the province of German chauvinism and ethnocentrism.

In the preceding chapter, I argued that Heidegger's twin aims—to decenter the Cartesian-Husserlian subject and to break with the ethos of liberal humanism—shatter against his stoic model of authenticity and lead to a reassertion of the very ethos of mastery his work promised to overcome. Here I demonstrate that Heidegger's stoic breach of public accountability leads not simply to a decisionistic paradigm of transgression, as Wolin argues, but to a specifically masculinist ethos. Wolin is right that Heidegger's undifferentiated critique of modernity leads to a wholesale rejection of public norms and, further, props up his commitment to an authoritarian *logic of the exception* which exempts visionaries from public accountability and grants them sovereign authority in determining Germany's future. Yet Wolin tends to classify all *Existenzphilosophie* and all philosophical versions of antihumanism (i.e., poststructuralism) as virtual extensions of Heidegger's overthrow of 1789 that threaten to erupt into "left fascism."[4] His formal analysis of Heidegger's antihumanism, while key to deciphering the relation of Heidegger's transgression of modernity to authoritarian politics, fails to fully diagnose the substantive basis, in the stoic model of authenticity, for Heidegger's choice of a manly *Gemeinschaft* as Germany's future destiny.

If Wolin does not differentiate between transgressions which lead to authority and those which promote critique of oppressive forms of life, Schürmann, by contrast, attempts to compensate for Heidegger's authoritarian turn by linking theoretical antihumanism to symbolic critique. Schürmann's proposal encourages a nonauthoritarian public sphere, but offers little by way of a concrete, substantive critique of patriarchal or other prejudicial cultural values and their institutionalized grounds. Set in the historical context of the thirties, the Heideggerian concept of Being—first identified in 1927 as the call of the goddess *Cura* and variously named in 1935 as *phusis*, *logos*, and the goddess *dikē* or justice— becomes transfigured into an anthropomorphized and virtually feminized figure of destiny. Great visionaries preserve the manly spirit of German Dasein and ward off the emasculating effects of liberalism by tapping into and bringing forth the creative power granted by the *Geschick* (destinal sending) of Being. Later when, with political aspirations exhausted, he recounts his official story, Heidegger continues to project an image of himself as the gallant suitor who strove to guide a dangerous but promising movement to its authentic "inner truth and greatness" the way one might educate a wanton but powerful woman to respectability.

I want to argue that we cannot understand the problem of decisionism in Heidegger's thought in purely formal terms but must examine how it is substantively tied up with a failure to critique the patriarchal fantasy of Woman as man's origin. With the help of Carol Bigwood and Luce Irigaray, I will interpret his 1935 lecture course as caught in a phallocentric logic, even though the text makes no explicitly misogynist claims. Similarly, I appeal to Klaus Theweleit's study of the misogynistic dimensions of the fascistic imaginary of the Freikorpsmen, including Jünger, to historically substantiate this reading.[5] Although the early decentering of the male Cartesian subject of thetic mastery allows the repressed feminine to rise up from the depths—in the figure of the goddess of Unconcealment—Heidegger's transgression of metaphysics is insufficiently critical. Borrowing Irigaray's words, we could say that he risks the "uncharted territories" and "sidles up to the truth" of the feminine. But his "detour" beneath the realm of rational representation, instead of transforming his desire, effectuates a new "practice" of retaming the female forces of destiny (SP, 136–37). Lacking material criteria for action, Heidegger turns to the feminized force of destiny to smuggle in a ground for the tiresome patriarchal discourse of mastery.

Ecofeminists, like Bigwood, find the later Heidegger's nonviolent ethos of receptivity a promising curtailment of his earlier manly ethos; other feminists rightly argue that early Heidegger's ontology supports a Kristevan ethics of difference (McAfee); still others explore fruitful dimensions of the notions of care and mood (Graybeal, Bartky). Many of these authors note that even the early Heidegger's thinking marked an incipient feminization of Being which partially broke with misogynistic fears and staunchly negative views of the femininely connoted notions of absence, void, withdrawal, and concealment (Bigwood, Graybeal). Where other malestream thinkers find only lack, Heidegger finds productive conditions of disclosure. I agree that elements of Heidegger's ontology can be used in fruitful ways, but only when his insights are developed in ways that correct his one-sided formulations. My argument is that, if theoretical usages of Heidegger (feminist or otherwise) are to move beyond the traditional apologetic strategy of claiming anomalous status for the clearly chauvinistic works of the middle period, then they must ask why Heidegger found no clear disconnection between his early positive rendition of absence and concealment and his decisive adoption of a masculinist ethos during the mid-thirties. And they must correct for the methodological and substantive deficiencies which allow for problems of decisionism.

2.1 Missing Link I: Heidegger's Decisionism

Wolin insightfully argues that the notion of historicity provides an immanent criterion against which to examine Heidegger's work in its historical context and, more importantly, links Heidegger's existential theory of authentic resolve to the problem of decisionism.

One key implication of Heidegger's concept of historicity is that philosophy itself proves historically determined. It follows that, in spite of Heidegger's nominal privileging of ontological analysis, the existential dimension (embodied choice) provides the real transcendental condition for realizing a proper ontology (overcoming metaphysics), not the reverse. Wolin points out that Heidegger's *Existenzphilosophie* did not occur in a cultural vacuum, but rather presupposed a "generational crisis" rooted in the widespread sentiment that there had been a "total devaluation of traditional meanings and inherited beliefs." Thus, the "Heideggerian variant" of *Existenzphilosophie*, which rejects as inauthentic all existing institutions for legitimating a moral or political course of action, "tends to be inherently destructive of tradition." Polemical against public discourse per se, authentic resolve devolves into a species of decisionism, that is, the view that authority is embodied in a sovereign will.[6]

The concept of historicity, articulated at the end of *Being and Time*, presages Heidegger's leap into a revolutionary ontic practice. Heidegger never tires of saying that one can only know authenticity by living it. That authenticity comprised a theoretical abstraction in need of its practical a priori condition of fulfillment was manifestly clear in Heidegger's 1928 lecture course, *The Metaphysical Foundations of Logic*. There he claims that fundamental ontology, i.e., "the analysis of Dasein and of the temporality of being," can only be fulfilled in the ontic (FL, 158/GA 26, 202). This describes Heidegger's early notion of the *Kehre*: "But the temporal analysis is at the same time the turning-around (*Kehre*), where itself ontology expressly runs back into the metaphysical ontic in which it implicitly always remains. . . . [T]he aim is to bring ontology to its latent overturning (*Umschlag*)" (158/201). Once the *Destruktion* of traditional metaphysics must be accomplished as a practical condition of authenticity, individual Dasein's possibilities prove subordinate to a broader collective situation and resolute decision takes on historic (read: destinal) proportions. The radical deconstructive aim of fundamental ontology entails nothing short of forging, as Wolin puts it, "a pathway of deliverance from the contemporary cultural crisis—the 'decline of the West'."[7]

Heidegger's adoption of *Existenzphilosophie* presupposed a generational crisis (Wolin) or prewar capitalist anxiety (Kristeva). Germany's rapid and troublesome transition to an industrialized economy in the late nineteenth century fueled worker sympathy for socialist ideas. Worker sentiments triggered fears of anarchism or communism and spurred an antimodern yearning for authoritarian control among the middle and lower-middle classes. Germany's cultural elite professed a fervent apoliticism which, rather conveniently, proclaimed the authority of the dominant classes against what they saw as the Enlightenment corrosion of German tradition and culture. Like his fellow reactionaries, Heidegger lumped modern nihilism, Enlightenment rationalism, industrialization, and liberal individualism together into a undifferentiated bundle and spurned the whole. The crisis mentality of Heidegger's generation fostered a reactionary yearning—reactionary because an uncritical, atavistic departure from modernity that sought an escapist return to immediacy through instinct, nature, or essentialist notions of indigenous races. Whether they longed for a return to a pretechnological *Volksgemeinschaft* or reconciled the antimodernist notion of *Volkgeist* with technology, reactionaries agreed that German culture could only be saved from its spiritual demise by a fundamental overthrow of the leveling forces of liberal democracy.[8]

Heidegger's search for a complete rupture with past philosophy congeals under the influence of conservative revolutionary thinkers, like Oswald Spengler, Möller van den Bruck, and Jünger. The initial shift to a collectivist view of destiny at the end of *Being and Time* evolves in 1929–30 into a Spenglerian preoccupation with boredom as the defining mode of attunement (*Grundstimmung*) in modern liberal democracy (Heidegger, FC, 70). Even more greatly influenced by Jünger's Nietzschean views, Heidegger formulates his theory of *Seinsgeschichte* which views so-called rational progress as the cause of a vapid emasculation of spirit. Taking Nietzsche as their "spiritual godfather," Spengler and Jünger "based their hopes for a revitalized German Reich on the protofascistic vision of a militant, expansionist, authoritarian state." While Heidegger did not definitively accept this militant vision, Wolin demonstrates that, when set in this chauvinistic context, two pillars join Heidegger's thought to conservative revolutionary *Kulturkritik*. These include: (1) a *heroic* ethicopolitical valorization of will (decisionism); and (2) a "shared disposition, mood, or *aesthetic sensibility*" that embraced a "general fascination with 'limit-situations' " for their ability to restore vitality to life through "shock, disruption, experiential immediacy; an infatuation with the sinister and forbidden."[9]

The concept of decisionism derives largely from Carl Schmitt's legal theory. Schmitt posits the *authority* of decision as providing the final justification for a course of moral, legal, or political action; he links authority to dictatorship because pure decision overrides

public discourse, existing systems of law, or procedures for legitimation. Wolin, following Strauss, links existentialism to decisionism.
According to Wolin, the notion of historicity, indebted to Dilthey,
placed Heidegger's work within a *logic of contingency* that rendered norms relative to history. What is central for Wolin, however,
is that Kierkegaard and Nietzsche supplied Heidegger with the
twin axes of a *logic of the exception*. These axes claim: (i) that the
exceptional person overrides the norm (Kierkegaard's teleological
suspension of the ethical) and (ii) that only the power and abun-
dance of radical will establishes truth, not what one wills (Nietzsche).
Faced with the historical contingency and inauthenticity of bourgeois norms, Heidegger adopts a decisionistic stance. For only a
will purified of conventional norms could free one from existential
contingency and the sham character of normalcy.[10]

Such a total and unnuanced rejection of modernity, Wolin argues, displaces normative theory in favor of a Nietzschean
justification of life in aesthetic terms. And this aestheticization of
the political, a noted feature of numerous forms of fascism, brings
Heidegger's work into the proximity of an aesthetic of horror with
its emphasis on the "shock-laden structure of temporal experience":

> Thus, whereas the "They" (*das Man*) experiences time helplessly
> ("un-ecstatically") as a serial succession of empty "nows," authen-
> tic Dasein is elevated above this routinized temporal stasis in the
> "moment of vision" (*das Augenblick*). . . . The "moment of vision" is
> a type of secular epiphany that both explodes and transcends the
> "fallen" character of routinized, inauthentic temporality, which
> Heidegger refers to as "world time" or "public time."[11]

Unlike Jünger, Heidegger does not explicitly esteem the horrors of
war as a paradigmatic experience that breaks with immersion in a
routinized, everyday life. Nevertheless, Wolin rightly suggests that
Heidegger's descriptions of authenticity encourage an ethos that
prizes disruption, partly for its cathartic shock value in lifting one
abruptly out of mundane affairs, and partly for its revitalizing
influence in delivering one to a revelation of one's cultural destiny.
But, as Wolin fails to address, Heidegger also prizes disruption in
large measure for its hardening and purifying effects in strengthening a *Volk's* will.

Wolin keenly details the structural logic that links *Being and
Time* to right-wing and fascist politics. Heidegger faced two interrelated problems after 1927: (i) he had to reconcile the emptiness

of a total breach of society with a social conception of humans as intersubjective; and (ii) he had to supply some quasi-objective principle that could justify a path of action allegedly without appeal to mere subjectivism and voluntarism. As Wolin incisively shows, the 1927 concept of authentic resolve threatened to advance a radically private individualism. Seeking to avoid this solipsistic, narcissistic, and voluntarist conception, which would bring his thought too close to the modern Cartesian subject, Heidegger develops the concept of destiny as both a collective notion and an allegedly quasi-objective ground for action. Heidegger thought he could obviate the empty, indeterminate, nonrelational character of an individual breach of tradition by transposing it into a "moment of vision" about the supposedly objective destiny of the collectivity. Heidegger's answer to decisionism is fatalism; he treats action as nonarbitrary if Being provides the pathways of decision (*Ent-scheidung*) that place a people on their proper path (IM 168/EM, 128). Wolin rightly claims that the 1927 call to "choose one's heroes" transmutes in 1932 into the view that "the National Socialist movement presented itself as a plausible material 'filling' for the empty vessel of authentic decision." In Heidegger's brand of *Existenzphilosophie*, the *Führerprinzip* represents no debased voluntarism that unfolds into a dangerously cultlike, quasi-mystical sense of belonging, but rather the gateway to authentic national rebirth.[12]

Again, Wolin plainly deciphers Heidegger's theoretical tendency to presume that the recuperative effects of the "moment of vision," in counteracting Germany's cultural anemia, outweigh the need for public discourse and accountability. Crucial to Wolin's analysis is that the Heideggerian concept of destiny provides "a material point of orientation that serves to intensify the inchoate, existential bond of Dasein in its everyday Being-with-others. It gives existential meaning and direction to the otherwise lax Being-with of Dasein in its everydayness."[13] I find this analysis interesting. Yet in his effort to note dangers in Heidegger's work, Wolin both makes his case too strong and not strongly enough. By falsely assuming that every existential rejuvenation of a vibrant cultural ethos leads to decisionism, he makes his case too well. And, outside noting the external chauvinistic context, Wolin does not fully account for the theoretical foundations of the specific choice of a *manly ethos* that forms the substance of Heidegger's vision of a tightly bonded *Volk*. During the thirties Heidegger does not simply praise the disruptive moment for granting releasement, he binds releasement to a substantive effect, that is, to producing manly respect and a strong-willed nation. The promise of radical transgression is, minimally, twofold. It not only restores an intense and originary state of co-belonging (because rooted in forces of Being deeper and greater than any individual), but this vitality redeems German *Volk* by clothing them in manly respectability. Even though Heidegger rejects war-exalting renditions of Nietzsche, his adoption of this manly ethos forms a key ingredient for weaving his philosophy seamlessly into the protofascistic, neonationalist rhetoric of his day.

The *Rektoratsrede*, for example, talks of the need for the "harshest self-examination" (*härteste Selbstbesinnung*) and willful self-assertion before the "creative impotence" of modern knowledge (SA, 29–31/SB, 9–11). His student address, invoking the hero Schlageter, calls German students to "let the strength of this hero's native mountains flow into your will!" (PS, 41). In another address during 1933, Heidegger emphatically proclaims, "*University study must become a risk [Wagnis],* not a refuge for the cowardly" (45). Rather than seek mere knowledge and information, students are called to face the unknown, the abysmal groundlessness of human existence, and thereby to preserve Germany's spiritual essence and secure its destiny. In this address, his employment of the term *Geschlecht*—which means at once race, nation, gender—transforms the academic schoolyard into a battlefield on which to forge a new manly humanity:

> A hard race (*Geschlecht*) with no thought of self must fight this battle, a race that lives from constant testing and that remains directed toward the goal to which it has committed itself. It is a battle [*Kampf*] to determine who shall be the *teachers* and *leaders* [*Führers*] at the university. (45)

Though he denounces "blind tyranny" and resists biological race theory, the 1933 language of "hard race" supports the notion of a special Graeco-Germanic destiny, conjures images of the idealized muscle tone, heroic strength, and chiseled features peculiar to the fascist aesthetic soon paraded about at the 1936 Berlin Olympics, and endorses a national mobilization of Germany's youth. The will to true community, he declares, is "the awakening of the young who have been purified and are growing back into their roots" (50).

Heidegger's vague and unspecified references to purification stem not from biological race theory, but rather from his indictment of *Seinsvergessenheit* (forgetfulness of Being) as the source of the emasculation of the German spirit. Courage is fostered through a thinking that attunes one to the "abysses of existence." He says, "For us, questioning means: exposing oneself to the sublimity of things and their laws; it means: not closing oneself off to the terror of the untamed and of the confusion of darkness." By breaking with the "all-too-cheap answers afforded by artificial systems of thought," questioning preserves a "a people's will to know" and secures its "self-responsibility." Contact with the abyss cleanses German Dasein, one can assume, of the imposition of foreign ideals of democracy and the shallow soullessness of utilitarian rationality. Heidegger links ethnocentrism to patriarchy in that contamination by foreign elements causes Germany to suffer emasculation. The process of purification welds a people's will into "*one* single resolve," preserves national autochthony, and thus guarantees "peace among nations" by binding a *Volk* to "the basic law of manly respect and unconditional honor" (51–52). In contrast to Wolin, I maintain that Heidegger's student addresses praise, not general release from alienation, but a specific masculine revitalization of collective identity. This talk of clear boundaries between nations pulls his philosophy into the sphere of a masculinist national chauvinism and an ethnocentric politics of difference.[14]

Heidegger's talk of a hard race-gender-nation (*Geschlecht*) is of Jüngerian persuasion; yet the immanent ground for adopting this manly vision stems from his stoic concept of authenticity. His antifoundationalism grounds ashore on antinormativism, as Wolin claims, because he subordinates political autonomy to a collective fate that receives specious justification by appeal to the special insight of the elect. But rather than imply that all existential philosophy, all radical critics of the liberal ethos, or all models of transgression inevitably lead to decisionism (as Wolin would have it), it is more helpful to identify how a stoic ethos supports fantasies that open the doorway to decisionism. The stoic concept of authentic resolve, articulated in *Being and Time*, readily evolves into the logic of the exception because it presupposes a categorical, nondialectical separation between the praxis of contemplating Being and psychologically or socially transformative processes. The stoic stance makes the authentic person incapable of assessing either the epistemic effects of social location on psychic processes of thought and fantasy or, conversely, the influence of personal fantasies on political choices. Lacking such examinations, Heidegger's critique of modern reason offers an inadequate standpoint from which to assess the masculinist image of brotherhood he so heartily espouses. The rigid psychology of the authentic person, devoid of relational and communicative dimensions, exacerbates rather than alleviates the masculinist bias of western philosophy.[15] This becomes evident in his poor effort to resuscitate a social theory after positing authenticity not only in abstraction from a *Bildungsprozeß* but also as a radical dislocation from existing social relations. By positing individual authenticity as pure transgression, the Heideggerian notion of authenticity reifies a despairing and alienated subject. Unable to feel any sense of communal belonging, the authentic subject is vulnerable to the fanciful victim mentality of conservative revolutionary movements. Indeed, many of the reactionary thinkers who influence Heidegger, while drawing upon a genuine experience of alienation, falsely proclaim extreme oppressed status for those who suffer no material disadvantage. Moreover, once transgression is severed from critique of social location, it is not incidental that the spiritual autochthony of Germany must be won from the duplicitous power of destiny, a power whose duplicity will be figured in *feminine* terms. Heidegger can only recuperate a social ontology through a romantic yearning for glory that exempts himself and others like him as the unique and exceptional group; this group overcomes its emasculation through reigning victorious against a "feminized" power of Being which wraps destiny in concealment. Heidegger's stoic logic attains fulfillment in a grandiose fantasy of great and steadfast leaders who, like warrior-midwives, deliver Germany back to its rootedness in a singular willed, honorable, and manly *Volksgemeinschaft*.

2.2 Missing Link II: The Symbolic Difference

In an insightful attempt to save the deconstructive from the profascist Heidegger, Reiner Schürmann proposes that we judge the works from 1932 to 1936 from the standpoint of the mature later philosophy. Only a *retrospective hermeneutic* can trace the enduring strain in the corpus, thereby enabling us to judge what type of political theory truly fits Heidegger's defining problematic. Schürmann observes,

> The hermeneutical dilemma is remarkable: reading Heidegger forward, from the Fundamental Analysis of Being-There to the Topology of Being, one is left with the evidence of an "idealization of unity at the expense of plurality," that is, ultimately of the *Führer* principle. Reading Heidegger backward, from the Topology

to the Fundamental Ontology, the picture is quite different: instead of a unitary concept of ground, the Fourfold; instead of "the hard will" (the main theme of Heidegger's eulogy of the Nazi hero Schlageter), releasement; instead of integration of the university into the "fields of construction" (Heidegger's article in the student newspaper of June 1933), protest against technology and cybernetics; instead of the identification between the *Führer* and the law (Heidegger's article in the student newspaper of November 1933), anarchy.[16]

Taken together Wolin and Schürmann isolate one difficulty with transgressive strategies. For Wolin, deconstructing the distinction between theoria (ontology) and praxis (political theory) leads down a slippery slope to decisionism; it elevates a retrogressive ethico-aesthetic form of life above the very moral principles and democratic procedures designed to protect the individual and preserve pluralism; it marks an atavistic retrenchment to a premodern *Gemeinschaft* (i.e., community) and conjures the ghastly specter of Auschwitz. For Schürmann, the singular thread woven throughout Heidegger's lifelong query is his antifoundationalist conception of Being as an-archic. Since Heidegger's deconstruction of metaphysics reveals the impossibility of providing certain foundations for moral and political action, it decenters, not recenters, authority in both the personalist forms of premodern societies and the modernist forms of procedural justice.[17]

Since Heidegger's antifoundational ontology offers no unmediated directive for political praxis, Schürmann argues that the "missing link" is the "symbolic difference." Heidegger's critique of metaphysics rests on the insight that Being is not univocal and subsisting, but rather polymorphous and duplicitous. As duplicitous, "Being" reflects the twofold movement of a process of unconcealment that always remains partly in concealment. That twofold movement means that finite, historical Dasein can never have a perfectly transparent grasp of reality as a whole, for it cannot step outside the historical process. "Being" manifests to humans in plural ways that depend upon how we classify beings under unifying categories and by analogical similarity. But these forms of classification, while they exhibit generational sensibilities, provide no hierarchy of Being from entities to the One final cause nor do they yield a macronarrative like a Hegelian processional of history that marches in logical sequence toward full transparency. The ontological difference between Being (the referential context of interpretation) and beings (a particular way of representing entities) can be metaphysically or speculatively construed as a relation of cause to effect, of particulars subsumed under a universal One. Yet, phenomenologically understood, Being is not a cause. Rather, Being is the epochal process that we experience prethematically as a kind of generational sensibility; and we articulate this experience conceptually by designating our locus as differentiated from previous conceptions of Being.[18]

Schürmann argues that the symbol is unique in that it "thematizes explicitly this simultaneity of concealment and unconcealment." From a metaphysical standpoint, the symbol represents "*what* it manifests and occultates at the same time." But from a phenomenological standpoint, the symbol reveals "*how* it signifies." The shift to a phenomenological way of seeing means that we focus on the symbolic nature of existence as such; Heidegger's "moment of vision," properly understood, simply dissociates our experience of having no final ground from "myth and metaphysics."[19] Rather than do away with metaphysics, it surpasses it without destroying its sphere of use; for this reason, it desacralizes rather than resacralizes Hitler on the atavistic totem of Being. Schürmann's argument is that Heidegger misunderstood the kind of lived praxis his insight delineates because he failed to develop the symbol as the middle term between thought and action.

According to Schürmann, the "symbolic difference" exceeds Heidegger's ontological difference because it calls us to a *specific* praxis, rather than an arbitrary choice of ethos to fill the empty vessel of deconstructed traditions. The symbolic difference guides us onto a specific pathway of interpretation that shifts away from ontotheological constructions (metaphysical hierarchies) to a capacity to live without *archē* or telos. This reading echoes Graybeal's Kristevan interpretation of Heidegger which holds that reenacting the rituals that sacralize symbolic conventions brings us to abandon the felt need for secure origins by helping us to see the very structure of symbols and how symbolization, as a reflection of the polymorphous and historical character of modes of existing, constitutes "an ever new event rather than . . . a subsisting origin in a sequence of causation." Had Heidegger taken seriously the radical implications of this de(con)struction of metaphysics, Schürmann claims, he could not have embraced a cathartic, allegedly wholesale transgression that inevitably proved an uncritical mimetic recovery of the authority of tradition (*Gemeinschaft*). Transformed into symbolic consciousness, the Heideggerian *Umschlag* or overturning of tradition would not digress to a premodern nostalgia for unity, but instead offer up a postmodern, anarchic resistance to "fixed social constellations" and "central authority."

> [Heidegger's] thought, if it yields this political dimension, would thus introduce radical fluidity into social institutions. . . . Political thinking as *Seinsdenken* would be as critical of utopian constructions as of central authority. In either case it would denounce an underlying static ideal. Such ideals, together with extrinsic legitimation of power, have been destroyed by Heidegger's phenomenology.[20]

Schürmann offers a fruitful beginning for distinguishing Heidegger's retrogressive nostalgia for the past from more productive postmodern strategies better able to address contemporary problems even as they critique Enlightenment reason. Even so, the problem of the missing link is far more aggravated than his meta-level principles for decentering absolute principles allow. Critics of the avant-garde show that even an explicit mimetic appropriation of symbolic practices does not necessarily lead to a progressive critique of objective social conditions. Nothing in Schürmann's abstract approach to the symbolic difference addresses the specifically gendered, racialized, or ethnocentric aspects of Heidegger's middle vision of German culture. His ideal of living without why, while rejecting absolutes, does not grapple with the thick symbolic, psychic, and material foundations of oppression. Later I will show how Schürmann's Heideggerian notion of the symbolic difference remains far too abstract to clarify the oppressive social effects of specific symbolic practices and provides neither compensation for the masculinist bias of the middle period nor for the methodological privileging of ontology over social analysis. In the next section, I turn to Carol Bigwood's Irigaray-based critique of Nietzsche in order to prepare the basis for situating Heidegger's 1935 lecture in relation to the fetishized presentations of women found in the war-exalting, Nietzschean, heroic ideal of his generational cohorts.

2.3 Heidegger and the Feminization of Being

In *Earth Muse*, Carol Bigwood argues that later Heidegger breaks with a phallocratic conception of Being and develops a poetic ethos rooted in receptivity rather than mastery. While her Heideggerian ecofeminist concerns are insightful, I want to use

Bigwood's critique of Nietzsche as a foil against which to examine Heidegger's work of the mid-thirties. Bigwood likes late Heideggerian thought because it breaks with the "neo-Nietzschean underpinnings" of both his middle works and other postmodern critiques of foundationalism (EaM, 6). She contrasts the "phallocratic metaphysics" inherent in Nietzsche's will to power with a Heideggerian meditative ability to "muse on the simple 'that it is' of being, on wondrous reasonless emergence itself" (29). Rather than strive to master concealment, meditative thinking recognizes the exiled feminine movement of absencing within presencing, thereby encouraging a non-nihilistic relation to those things, like women, nonwestern peoples, and nature, cast as Other to western *ratio*.

Bigwood borrows Heidegger's holistic and historical view that Being is not "a being, not God, an absolute unconditional ground or a total presence," but rather "the living web within which all relations emerge," the epochal "constellation of art, science, politics and religion within which an historical people dwells" (EaM, 3). And, following Irigaray, she ascribes sexual morphology to Heidegger's key names for unconcealment, *phusis* and the goddess *alētheia*. The reclining movement of withdrawal in unconcealment holds feminine connotations while the uprising movement into presence is linked to masculinity (Heidegger, EGT, 113/VA, 262). Since only the latter lends itself to rational re-presentation and encapsulation, metaphysical systems suppress the former. As Bigwood clarifies,

> In western metaphysics, difference is not allowed to be *as* difference, but, rather, the one term, unconcealment, is constituted as the privileged ground by whose differentiation the other term, concealment, may be. . . . In our contemporary age, concealment, whose cluster of characteristics are similar to those historically associated with the feminine, is suppressed, feared, and understood as that which must be overcome and brought into the light of unconcealment. (EaM, 80)

Bigwood can be interpreted as using Irigaray to introduce a gender corrective to Schürmann's interpretation. For she does not claim that gender-neutral reflection on the nonunivocal polyvalence of unconcealment suffices to break the habit of dwelling in an earth exploitative and dominating relation to nonmasculine and nonwestern ways of life (4). Bigwood, like Graybeal, more carefully associates the achievement of this nonviolent mode of dwelling with learning to appreciate the repressed feminine element which is co-constitutive of all things and every form of life, including conceal-ment, darkness, recession (37). Because the double movement of unconcealment carries sexuate associations, Bigwood argues, learn-ing to accept the groundlessness of human existence encourages us to cultivate a critical relation to those spheres of activity (e.g., the kitchen, the earth, the household) or ways of life traditionally as-sociated with the irrational Other of the European, male subject (e.g., the feminine, the bodily, blacks, the third world) (103).

The problem of the missing link is not Bigwood's theoretical concern. Yet her Irigaray-based ascription of gender to Heidegger's Being implies that a critical mediation of the sexualized imaginary underlying a social form of life constitutes an essential determi-nant in breaking with reactionary misogynistic formations. For Irigaray, conceptualizations of Being—how subjects and objects are designated in a world—are permeated by imaginary dimensions. I would say in contrast to Heidegger that Being reflects not simply a peculiar historical formation with its attendant withdrawal of other possibilities, but rather a sexuate economic organization supported by a sexuate fantasy. The notion of phallocentrism offers an ideal typical way to isolate how variations in metaphysical conceptualizations of Being are not simply sexuate, or modeled after bodies, but sexed in a specific way, that is, modeled after the mor-phological marks of the male body. Metaphysical depictions that reify Being as transcendent principle, first cause, absolute spirit, or powerful God evince a consistent privileging of phallic attributes. This symbolization produces a socially regulated economy of desire that revolves around particular cultural fantasies. In the West, these fantasies comprise what Irigaray calls a masculine imaginary; they center around the drive for unity, noncontradiction, and fullness of presence at the expense of the inassimilable particularities of things.[21]

While Heidegger uses the name concealment to designate the 'origin' or 'condition' which supports the "systematicity" of western forms of representation, Irigaray identifies it as the suppression of female sexual morphology and its imaginary associations (TS, 74). In her doctoral thesis, *Speculum of the Other Woman*, Irigaray argues that the canonical texts of western philosophy follow a *specu-lar economy* which breeds a very specific construction of the ratio-nal subject as male and narcissistic. By *specular economy* she means conceptual systems that suppress sexuate difference by assuming that the world is a "mirror" reflection of male experience (SP, 21, 32–33, 133). Toril Moi explains,

The philosophical meta-discourse is only made possible, Irigaray argues, through a process whereby the speculating subject contemplates himself; the philosopher's *speculations* are fundamentally narcissistic. Disguised as reflections on the general condition of man's Being, the philosopher's thinking depends for its effects on its specularity (its self-reflexivity); that which exceeds this reflexive circularity is that which is *unthinkable*. It is this kind of specul(ariz)ation Irigaray has in mind when she argues that Western philosophical discourse is incapable of representing femininity/woman other than as the negative of its *own* reflection.[22]

Although Heidegger and other philosophers have shown that the self-transparent subject of modern western philosophy is a truncated abstraction, Irigaray takes this line one step further. She argues that, in a phallocratic economy, the desire to achieve self-transparency rests upon a masculine imaginary that relegates the feminine to the netherside of reason and situates 'Woman' symbolically outside representation. Becoming rational thus entails freeing oneself of all things deemed feminine—impurity, flux, groundlessness, or, in Heidegger's vocabulary, the mysterious, inassimilable recessiveness in things.

Western speculation has posited rationality in abstraction from bodies in general, but a more liminal basis for this abstraction consists in the suppression of female morphology, female erotica, and female autonomy. For this reason, not all versions of decentering the self-transparent rational subject are successful in uprooting its support system, namely, the phallic drive to reduce all difference to the same, to male desire and the male subject's mirror image. Irigaray's concept of *specularization* provides a framework for interpreting Heidegger's asocial and uncritical version of an ec-static breach of tradition as embedded in the logic of the same. This transgression does not, thus, transform one's desire or open the possibility for new forms of collective eros. The conservative revolutionaries, Heidegger among them, despised speculative rationality and sought precisely to ground politics in a return to an original connection with the lifeworld and thus with embodied subjectivity. Nonetheless, especially in the works of reactionary modernists like Jünger, one finds an irrationalist romanticism reconciled to a valorization of a heroic ethos. In the epigraph to this chapter, I note Irigaray's commentary on this phenomenon. She says that, when it loses its foundations, the male subject of discourse "is obviously obliged to stake out new boundaries," to delve into "the depths" and "tame those uncharted territories, these dark continents." But the "really urgent task is to ensure the colonization of this new 'field,' to force it, not without splintering, into the production of the same discourse" (SP, 136–37). The feminine—defined as patriarchal representations of woman as man's other—becomes sublated into a new telos, a new, albeit decentered, projection of himself (TS, 95–105).

One thing that Heidegger shares in common with conservative reactionary thinkers is the masculine fantasy of co-opting the female power of birth. The unruly feminine forces of life need not be projected as a future, static utopian state of completion (see chapter 4 below). Instead the teleological projection of Woman appears in Nietzsche and Heidegger as desublimated into a kind of ateleological eternal now, a present and ongoing achievement of ecstasy. But, with respect to the patriarchal symbolic, these paradigms exhibit a truncated or uncritical mediation of origins. They romanticize immediacy as a heroic process of creative midwifery produced by confronting limit-situations. Yet this transgression is effectuated through confrontation with his specularized Other: a fetishized feminine power that symbolizes the limit of the male psyche and allegedly thrusts man outside hearth and home into the uncanny region beyond his ordinary self-representation. Rather than promote a critical relation to patriarchy, this recovery of creative virility, subsumed under the rubric of Socratic midwifery, feeds off the so-called inchoate, irrational, unstable, or duplicitous feminine forces of life.

Nietzschean Ecstasy as Masculine Virility

Understood as a philosophical effort to decenter rational abstraction and "resuscitate the earth and the body," Bigwood suggests, "the Will to Power would [seem to] be an ontological letting-in of the feminine" (EaM, 82). To the contrary, she argues, Nietzsche's purported resuscitation of the earth—figuratively understood in feminine terms—is a deception. Zarathustra does indeed "love" the earth and the sensuous. But, Bigwood shows, this "love" is truly an "unrestrained assault" on the earth (85). Nietzsche criticizes the sterile, super-sensuous rationality of the metaphysicians for being "'castrated,' 'severely mutilated,' 'emasculated,' and 'effeminate'" (90).[23] Zarathustra's counsel to love the earth has but one aim: to regain virility and harness the sensual power requisite for command over the earth.

Bigwood demonstrates that Nietzsche's notion of "gift-giving love" is rooted in domination. Unlike the "'emasculated leers' of the impotent mooning metaphysicians who gaze benumbed at the earth, Zarathustra, like a virile lover, takes command of the situation, penetrating the earth with his 'sun-love'" (87). Love of earth is a twofold movement of, first, penetrating the earth by sowing your seed and, second, taking command by leading the earth to its true telos, will to power. Creativity is a manly virtue through which Zarathustra lovingly gives meaning to the otherwise inchoate earth. This love, however, has a specific narcissistic structure that fosters a particular desire. On the one hand, the will to command "is not simple domination, for in loving the earth, man becomes a gift and sacrifice, venturing himself." Yet, on the other hand, "this venturing of himself is only for the sake of the heightening and strengthening of *himself*; not, for instance, for the sake of opening himself to his lover, the earth" (87).[24]

Bigwood links Nietzsche's ethical-aesthetic of virility to an eco-destructive ethos.[25] I am more interested, however, in the specific desire embedded in this narcissistic virility. Nietzsche's embodied subject, while transgressing speculative reason, does not break with the logic of specularization. Rather, this transgression reveals how the masculine imaginary fashions creativity and life-feeling out of the co-optation of female powers. Bigwood says,

> Human beings, moreover, who take up Zarathustra's teaching do not respond to the enigmatic earth and life itself with respect. On the contrary, although Zarathustra wants to preserve the enigma of life and not impose thinkable truths on life, he teaches that one must command that "damned nimble, supple snake and slippery witch" with one's will and whip and thereby stamp a human meaning on her deep mystery. Unlike previous suitors, Zarathustra manages to finally fathom the unfathomable mistress, Life. The romance ends with this marriage to Life, whom he renames "Eternity." With Life's secret nature revealed, the earth is reduced to a flat table on which the gods play dice games, games in which mortal "men" can now participate. (88, quoting Nietzsche, *Zarathustra*, 226 and 229)

On this reading, a Nietzschean return to earth is not only narcissistic (since it strengthens only him), but also sacrificial (heroic) and exceptional (pure). Zarathustra's teachings advocate venturing deep into the hidden, mysterious, feminine earth principle, and this venture is great because it is dangerous. For the decentered male subject could fail to conquer and tame the mistress 'Life'. Unless he succeeds in channeling feminine life forces into masculine vision, all things lapse into meaninglessness. If, on the other hand, he succeeds, then he emerges with restored hypermasculinity, having broken with the emasculating effects of abstraction. His renewed creative possibilities arise from harnessing life origins (the mistress) into an eternal now. Having expurgated the demon, abstraction, and ventured the witch, Life, the new breed of man engages an originary praxis of venture and renewal that only the exceptional few, newly purified, can sustain.

In the later Heidegger, Bigwood finds a diametrically opposed view of *phusis* which encourages, not an assault on, but rather respect for, the feminine earth principle. By elevating the rising-masculine movement above the reclining-feminine, western metaphysics inaugurated "a power struggle between two polarized forces" (EaM, 80) that established the war between the sexes on an ontological plane. This struggle, rather than having abated, appeared in Nietzsche ever more virulently through his pressing of *phusis* into the service of male conquest. The later Heidegger sees the relation of these two movements as one of mutual interdependence, whether thought as *alētheia* or *phusis*. Heidegger calls this relation a "reciprocal favoring" in which each, "mutually inclined" toward the other, "bestows upon the other its proper nature" (EGT, 114/VA, 263). What is crucial for Bigwood is that, in later Heidegger's vision of *phusis*, neither the feminine-reclining nor the masculine-rising movement cancels the other out (EaM, 29–38, 94–103). Their reciprocal relation of *philia* stills the symbolic war between the sexes and for this reason later Heidegger does not plunge us into a nihilistic relation to groundlessness. Neither swallowed up by abysmal feminine forces nor forced to tame the nonrational witch, we are encouraged to embrace difference, to become healed of the drive to conquer with its misogynistic and imperialistic ramifications.

We can now recapture Schürmann's hermeneutic dilemma as complicated by these questions of gender. In his 1943 lecture on Heraclitus, Heidegger discusses *phusis* in conjunction with *philia*, love or reciprocity, but in his 1935 lectures, "The Origin of the Work of Art" and *An Introduction to Metaphysics*, we find *phusis* or *alētheia* depicted as strife (*Streit, Kampf*). When we read Heidegger chronologically backwards, we can isolate how the focus on "letting be" eventually overcomes the heroic and masculine rhetoric he freely adopts in accord with Nazi ideology in the 1930s. Especially during his 1932–33 *Rektoratsrede*, but still present in the 1935 lecture, *An Introduction to Metaphysics*, we hear talk of "rank" and "power," harshness, "blood and soil," "self assertion," and most significantly of "creative" willing of the "spiritual mission" of the German *Volk*. Not only do we not find the later nonviolent tonality, but when we read Heidegger chronologically forward, we see that this aggressive tone was not entirely anomalous. From 1919 onwards Heidegger indicated a preference for militaristic metaphors; he consistently valorized the experience of the soldier in exemplifying his phenomenological points; and his linking of Heraclitus's notion of *polemos* to the German struggle (*Kampf*) in order to creatively countermand the decline of the West reflected these values (IM 46/EM 49).[26] In 1935 *polemos* consists, not of dwelling respectfully in the mystery of Being, but of a violent struggle to tame the overwhelming forces of Being.

2.4 Heidegger's Brand of Reactionary Thought

Just as Jünger was no official party member but proved utterly instrumental in the rise of Nazi ideology, so too Heidegger's student addresses, public speeches, and philosophical works from 1929 to 1935 prepared the basis for increased popular reception of protofascistic ideals. It is a well-known fact that the customary and mundane cultural prejudices against Jews supplied the "necessary historical precondition for the racial-biological anti-Semitism" of Hitler's Germany.[27] Heidegger's 1935 lecture course, *An Introduction to Metaphysics*, makes no widespread, let alone overtly, misogynist usage of the feminine imagery that is so clear in Bigwood's reading of Nietzsche. Yet just as his rejection of biological theories of racial superiority did not prevent him from holding his own variety of Graeco-Germanic ethnocentrism, so too he voices no essential misgivings over the masculinist ethos pursued by his fellow reactionary thinkers and their often explicit misogyny. Although this ethos operates at two different levels in their works, I compare the phallocratic logic of Heidegger's 1935 lecture to Klaus Theweleit's object-relations diagnosis of the misogynistic dimensions of the fascistic imaginary of the Freikorpsmen.

War: Paradigmatic Masculine Form of Ecstatic Transgression

Jeffrey Herf notes that "the leading figures of both the conservative revolution and National Socialism" were "generational cohorts." The first World War "taught them a contempt for bourgeois society, accustomed them to violence," and gave them an intense yearning for "the masculine community of the trenches, recreated in paramilitary groups such as the *Freikorps*." This war experience "provided the reactionary tradition with its concrete utopia" imaged as "a fully up-to-date masculine alternative to bourgeois society, one preferable to the so-called effeminate and escapist fantasies of previous generations of less daring conservatives."[28] In his disturbing work, *Male Fantasies*, Theweleit explores the unconscious fascistic fantasies of the Freikorpsmen. Many of these men, having fought during the postwar period between 1918 and 1923, eventually formed the core of Hitler's SA or else, like Jünger, played a pivotal role in preparing the widespread popular reception of Nazi ideology even as they condescended to join Party politics. Central to their fantasies is an intense hatred of women and contempt for all things effeminate and unmanly.

The men in Theweleit's study all fear and resist actual sexual contact with women, regarding the marital chamber as a seduction away from two key virtues: real love and real pleasure. Real love can only be found in love of country and love for the leader, while real pleasure can only be derived from extreme acts like "vengeance" (killing the enemy) and in extreme situations like "war and revolution." In Theweleit's words: "These men look for ecstasy not in embraces, but in explosions, in the rumbling bomber squadrons or in brains being shot to flames."[29] Drawing on object-relations theory, Theweleit decodes the influence of the mother-son relation on the fascist imaginary. The Freikorpsmen replace fear of being engulfed by the mother with rigid defenses against their own sexuality and feminine vulnerabilities. Desexualizing relations to their wives, they displace aggressive erotic feelings onto the arena of war. The repressed image of 'Woman' reappears as an imaginary fetishized symbol for everything they fear in themselves and which thus invokes horror—everything that moves, that does not stand still, that threatens to engulf one, everything associated with blood, menstruation, and fluid bodies. Rigidly unable to feel any normal sense of intimacy or societal belonging, they venture the threatening life force, Woman. By prevailing against her, they emerge heroic, potent, gathered up into a newly formed, manly *Gemeinschaft*, i.e., a community that reestablishes clean, uncontaminated boundaries between men and thus supersedes all feminine lack of form, clarity, and orderly beauty. In short, this defines an emergent authoritarian community and a hypermasculine model of ecstatic subjectivity. We must distinguish this kind of transgressive and erotic bonding from a relational notion of ecstatic subjects bound by asymmetrical forms of recognition.[30]

For the Freikorpsmen, the fetishized symbol 'Woman' is ambiguously cast as split: Woman is at once productive condition of
and threat against salvation. Woman represents the portal to the
hidden (sexual) force of life otherwise covered over by decadent
bourgeois culture; but Woman also appears as the social and political forces that, in the reactionary mind-set, threaten to emasculate
Germany's spirit (e.g., Jews and the proletariat). The neo-nationalist
idea of Germany as the nation "in the middle" was clothed in feminine metaphorics. For example, Theweleit notes that W. von
Oertzen's report on the Baltic situation in 1918 issues a warning
about Bolshevism in the rubric of flooding, tides, and waters that
threaten "not only to swallow up the republics of Estonia and
Latvia . . . but also to inundate the eastern border of Germany."
Commenting on Theweleit, Zimmerman clarifies that, among other
images, the flood and the "red tide" were associated with fear of the
"indeterminate and insatiable female."[31] Red women, symbolizing
the external threat of communism and the internal fear of class
conflict, were cast as sexually aggressive whores seeking to engulf
the Freikorpsmen and against whom they must defend themselves.
Heidegger's oft-quoted comment, about how Europe "in its ruinous
blindness . . . lies today in a great pincers, squeezed between Rus-
sia on one side and America on the other," certainly reflects a neo-
nationalist German heritage (IM, 37/EM, 28). But it should also be
situated in the unique coalescence of anticommunist and antiwoman
rhetoric into a vision of Graeco-Germanic *Volk*. Although Heidegger
talks not of whores and Red floods, his remarks exhibit a heightened paranoia similar to that of the Freikorpsmen in that he projects
actual social conditions in phantasmic terms but without any concrete referent isolating the causes of this spiritual anesthesia.

The Freikorpsmen long for releasement from their vital anemia (impotence) and social alienation and this makes them both
repulsed by and attracted to the boundless feminine forces of life
(water, blood, menstruation). Theweleit continues, "[t]he powerful
metaphor of the flood engenders a clearly ambivalent state of excitement." Flood waters denote limit-situations that deliver one to
his psychic border. Because floods forebode the real possibility of
being overrun by forces greater than any single man, they promise
the adventitious dissolution and propitious refashioning of a new
race (identity). Floods and Mother Earth. These are names that
Heidegger, too, will use in 1935 to depict the "overpowering" (*das
Überwältigende*) character of Being. For the Freikorpsmen, the
image of Mother Earth describes not simply the experience of the

trenches, but the hidden force of history throwing off encrusted social values. Commenting on Dwinger's words, "my body, which snuggles so trustingly up against its [the earth's] coolness," Theweleit notes:

> [T]he anthropomorphized body of Mother Earth is presented as the cauldron that is threatening the soldier's body with scorching floods. . . . In this "grenade fire," the tension isn't between the opponent who shoots and the victim who seeks cover; at the heart of the experience is the tension between the soldier's body and the surface of the earth he presses himself against. The surface feels human (skin) and it reacts (to feelings such as "trust") in a human way. . . . He is "snuggled" up against it; short of penetration, no greater intimacy is possible.[32]

Dwinger's language resonates in striking ways with Irigaray's descriptions: even in its "decenteredness," she says, the male subject "sidles up" to truth—the virgin womb "veiled in her nakedness" upon which masculine ratio depends—and tames those "uncharted territories" (SP, 136).

Psychic and real space melt into one, since the thrill of war consists in the "potential for physical, and not simply hallucinatory, dissolution." Total dissolution is tied to an essentialist logic of authenticity. Before the "deluge" the soldier slips into his fear and passively lets his ego boundaries dissolve through the active agency of the earth. The distinction between inner psyche and outer social processes disappears. Almost miraculously, the soldier suddenly "*experience[s] himself.*" Through the dissolution of his ego boundaries, he makes contact with the "*underlying*" colossalness of his own socially unacceptable interior desires. Yet because these desires, he believes, were forcefully checked by the outside sociopolitical order, that order must be indicted as having prevented him from realizing authentic selfhood and genuine community.[33] The discovery of authenticity provides 'material' justification for a wholesale overthrow of the existing social practices as inauthentic and oppressive. More importantly, authenticity, on this model, is clearly devoid of any critical self-examination, any *Bildungsprozeß*. One simply is his underlying desire. Transgression supposedly delivers up a real self when, in fact, one's previously socialized and repressed desire is simply released and serves to reify preexisting patriarchal values.

Four pivotal moments define the range of vision of the Freikorpsmen. First, alienation, though projected as a collective sociospiritual problem, is severed from critical examination of material and psychological causes alike. Second, alienation finds its "authentic" counterpoise in activities that supposedly deliver the subject to an ec-static transgression of the social order. This *specific* ec-static locus, however, can only be induced by withstanding horror, where horror is aroused by effeminate powers (women, Jews, the proletariat, earth, fluids) that symbolize the hidden agonistic force of life itself. The needed contact with these powers is squelched by chaotic dissipation induced under the liberal (democratic, Jewish capitalist) ethos. Third, this ec-static rejuvenation of virility radically dissolves one's (already tenuous) bonds to society, thrusting one out of "home" into the uncanny. Fourth, it is only in the isolation of this un-canny status as a-polis (i.e., homeless) that one finds one's true (pre-Oedipal) selfhood, true generational bond in manly recognition, and true mission.

An extremely repressed stoic psychology undergirds the logic of the exception that exempts these conservative revolutionaries from social accountability and reifies their repressed desires into an illusory redemptive experience, illusory because it is only pseudoecstatic and really offers no affective or cognitive transformation of self and others in a community of recognition. This war-survivor mentality has strong affinities with the *völkish* ideology of conservative romanticism which emphasized the subjection of the individual to destiny, "encouraged a preoccupation with a world of hidden powerful forces," and invoked apocalyptic visions of a complete and sudden overthrow of "degenerate *Zivilization*." But rather than nostalgic return to a preindustrial, effeminate, romantic life, this exaltation of war found one of its greatest proponents in Jünger's reactionary modernism. Jünger sought to reconcile modern technology with "*Kultur*—community, blood, will, self, form, productivity, and finally race"—and to thereby rescue Germany from its engulfment in the "chaotic postwar reality" of liberal democracy.[34] Rather than return to an older, pastoral life, he strove to bring Germany into a primordial relation to ontological forces in the present age.

For Jünger, whose work enabled Heidegger to develop his notion of *Seinsgeschichte*, the First World War "presaged cultural renewal" as it had provided a welcome "relief" from a "boring middle class obsessed by a need for security."[35] War symbolized a fate granted his generation. Dissolution through the limit-situation of war simply revealed the deeper will to power that stamps a particular *Gestalt* on each epoch and its generation. In Jünger's words:

> No—war is not a material matter. There are higher realities to
> which it is subject. When two civilized peoples confront one an-
> other, there is more in the scales than explosives and steel. . . .
> Values are tested in comparison with which the brutality of the
> means must—to anyone who has the power to judge—appear
> insignificant. A strength of will, all-embracing and concentrated to
> the last pitch in the highest untamed expression of life asserting
> itself even in its own annihilation, is brought into play.[36]

Having passed through the crucible of war, Jünger felt he had
been dissolved, transfigured, and chosen: "[the individual soldier]
has melted into everything," says Jünger, yet an incomparable
"manliness [of courage] bursts" through him, "the blood boils as it
surges through the veins," surges "like a raging storm." Nietzschean
overtones are clear. Contact with the elemental force of the will to
power points one onto the destined pathway to lead Germany (and
thus the rest of humanity) out of chaos into a new race.[37] In his
illuminating comparison of Heidegger and Jünger, Zimmerman
explains, "For reactionary thinkers such as Jünger, the key was not
to get rid of the flood but to channel it . . . 'to stand with both feet
and every root firmly anchored in the soil . . . to stop, and dam up,
those floods'." Jünger celebrates a new race of men who fear not
death, but instead adopt a "disinterested or even depersonalized
attitude" before the "gruesome" abyss. Here the *stoic* posture makes
a virtue out of the "pain-defying" adventurer who can withstand
the deluge of will to power and, chiseled by the onslaught, let his
virtue become strengthened into a steely courage. Steely men,
Zimmerman continues, "combine fire with ice, volcanic passion with
cold precision, blood with steel."[38]

Rather than a cultural *Bildungsprozeß*, we find a reactionary
yearning for steel-like romantic-modernism that does not require
actual engagement with and recognition of others, but instead
transfigures stoic psychology into a falsely utopian community based
upon the delusion that it has permanently overcome the alienating
contradictions of modernity. For Jünger, the technological era found
itself at first necessarily caught beneath a "sham" liberal moralizing about progress. Like all organic processes, a preliminary phase
of historical change ushers in destruction and chaos. Thus, bourgeois liberalism effaces the distinction between war and peace but
lacks "the spirit" to inaugurate the "total character of battle" that
alone can mobilize the *Gestalt* (historical configuration) of technology. Jünger envisages the new "type" of humanity, which attunes

one to the hidden *Gestalt* of technological nihilism, as a society of worker-soldiers who successfully complete the transition from passive to active nihilism. "[P]urification of the technical creative will" calls for total mobilization—a state of domination founded upon permanent readiness for war—as the means to overcome the contradictions of modernity. This overcoming is no fleeting change, but rather a permanent and stable "domination (*Herrschaft*)" that would deliver Germany from chaos to a structured, clean, orderly, and imperial social hierarchy. That form of life would derive its stability and completeness, not from human artifice, but from the fact that it perfectly mirrors the epochal constellation destined by Being. Subjugation to the "immovable center" of will to power would liberate the polity. For Jünger power equals liberation: "*Imperium et libertas.*"[39]

Heidegger's Masculine Ecstasy: Not War but 'Auseinandersetzung'

Central differences separate Heidegger's notion of ecstatic subjectivity from other right-wing thinkers whose works he regarded as superficial because they reflected a choice of value without piercing through to the deeper ontological cause of Germany's spiritual decline: *Seinsvergessenheit* or forgetfulness of Being. It would be overly zealous to accuse Heidegger of the war-survivor psychology that, others claim, led Jünger to "elevate war into a metaphysical abstraction" as a compensatory mechanism that transmuted Germany's defeat in WWI into a redemptive experience.[40] Heidegger's more strictly spiritualist, less instinctual view of Germany's decline offers a cleaned-up notion of struggle; he turns to the Greeks, not the trenches, for his paradigm of greatness. Yet even as they resist Jünger's glorification of war and evince an anemic acceptance of technology, the texts of the middle period (1932–36) nonetheless exhibit Heidegger's own reified conception of struggle as a battle for redemption from *Seinsvergessenheit.*

Similarly, Heidegger's works do not reflect the deep xenophobia and dramatic misogyny of the Freikorpsmen in Theweleit's study. Yet there are disturbing parallels: Heidegger's free appropriation of the Nietzschean jargon of emasculation, his clothing of violence in beauty, and the sacrificial logic by which visionaries are exempted from social bonds only to heroically return as the redeemers of an authentic community. In a more tempered and attenuated form, we can trace the four defining moments of the *Freikorps* mentality: (i) the view that political conditions are but epiphenomenal manifestations of deeper ontological forces; (ii) phantasmic presentations of Being as an overwhelming and horrifying force; (iii) a correlative tendency to split Being into a force that both exerts a dangerous feminine allure on man[41] and conditions renewal of spirit; and (iv) above all a disquieting glamorization of violent types who wrest Being from shimmering appearances, thereby performing a sacrificial midwifery to Germany's spiritual rebirth as a nation.

(i) *Being is logos*. Middle Heidegger's lectures are not replete with phantasmic projections of Life as a formless feminine power, like menstruation or blood, that engulfs everything and causes all to melt together. Gregory Fried argues that Heidegger's 1934–35 lecture course on Hölderlin's hymns, "Germania" and "The Rhine," borrows the notion of chaos from Hölderlin, not Hesiod for whom it constitutes an unordered mass. Chaos, in the sense of "the undifferentiated," is, for Heidegger, "only the degraded and contrary essence to what 'chaos' means. Thought as 'nature' (*phusis*), chaos remains that gaping apart out of which the Open opens itself and by which this Open grants truth to each undifferentiated thing in a bounded presencing."[42] In his 1935 lecture, Heidegger connects *phusis*, the power by which beings as a whole emerge, to *logos*, where *logos* depicts Being as the "steady gathering, the intrinsic togetherness" of all things (IM 130/EM, 100).

Shorn of "explosions" and "red spots increas[ing] on the map," Heidegger's account retains a sharp likeness to Jünger's battle to find order in chaos.[43] For the ordering power of Being stands diametrically opposed to the vapid leveling of everything into undifferentiated equality and sameness that Heidegger finds appalling in the modern, technological age. And, without directly invoking the ideal of *Imperium*, he nevertheless claims that *logos* distinguishes entities, following Nietzsche, in terms of "rank and domination" (IM, 133/EM, 101). This gathering that orders things harmoniously by rank endows existence with "the greatest beauty" (131/100). Taking his cue from Sophocles, Parmenides, and Heraclitus, Heidegger adopts the Greek figurative representation of *logos* as the goddess *dikē*. He argues that *dikē* should not be interpreted in superficial juridical terms as "justice" because the goddess is the originary "governing order" that brings things into harmony (160/123). Like Jünger, he relegates social values and norms to epiphenomenal considerations that either reflect or obscure the power of *dikē* to rank things according to their intrinsic differences. Subsumed under a logic of essentialism, a just social order would mirror this essential granting. We land dangerously close to an authoritarian adoration of social hierarchy.

(ii) *Being is polemos (strife, war).* When Heidegger thinks *phusis*, *logos*, and *dikē* in conjunction with harmony, beauty, and order, he attributes an intelligible core to the feminized figure, *dikē*. Though the image of *dikē* does not describe an irrational and boundless principle, neither do we find a peaceful rendition of the reciprocal play of masculine-revealing and feminine-concealing that Bigwood sees in the later Heidegger. The fundamental meaning of *phusis* in the texts of 1934 and 1935 centers on the violent, agonistic manner by which presencing occurs. *Logos* is *polemos*, an inherently strife-ridden, metaphysical relation between concealment and revealment. In a clear attempt to differentiate his thought from Jünger's glamorous portrayal of the trenches, Heidegger proclaims that, *polemos* is "not a war in the human sense" but rather the "*Auseinandersetzung*," the setting apart requisite to bind things together into a differentiated yet unified constellation of presencing (IM, 62/ EM, 47). Still, he intones, "being dominates" (138/106); it is "the terrible in the sense of the overpowering power which compels panic fear, true fear"; it is power, *Gewalt* (149/114).

Unlike Jünger, Heidegger does not turn to actual war to find a *Grenzsituation* (limit-situation) that discloses the deeper metaphysical will to power governing human history. Heidegger's own quasi-transcendental view of *polemos* as a pristine spiritual event, not laden with physical and instinctual overtones, nevertheless reflects all too well the militant, war-exalting ideology prevalent in his day. Heidegger, like Jünger, seeks to mobilize Germany into a unified state that elevates it out of forgetfulness and alienation into authenticity and collective belonging. It would not be far-fetched to claim that Heidegger retrogressively projects the prevalent imaginative representation of Germany's ontic circumstance (caught in a pincers under foreign theories of liberalism that atrophy its unique creative powers) and adult preferences (like his respect for warriors) onto his descriptions of a so-called originary experience of unconcealment as an essential antagonism. Moreover, it is not clear that an originary, prethematic experience of human finitude manifests, in child psychology for example, as enthrallment to the essential life and death antagonism ontologized by Heidegggger.

(iii) *Being is destiny.* Even given the positive rendition of *logos* as a beatifying principle, Being still assumes an anthropomorphized form as an overwhelming yet duplicitous force with which men must grapple. As the "supreme antagonism" Being brings a world into existence and grants Dasein its fundamental pathways of historical choice (131/101). Yet we find traces of an ambivalent, imaginary splitting of Being into both the measure and cause of man's fallenness. Being is both a productive condition (an event that grants historical options) and a dangerous mystery that lulls man into complacency and forgetfulness. Heidegger says, "Struggle is the power of the generation of beings. . . . And where struggle as the power of preservation and standing true falls off, there begins standstill, compromise, mediocrity—and harmlessness, atrophy, and decline" (GA 39, 125–26).[44] Elsewhere he reiterates, "Where struggle ceases, the essent does not vanish, but the world turns away" (IM, 62/EM, 48). Though not without some responsibility for their future, humans do not cause their condition. Consistent with the notion of falling in *Being and Time*, the thrust of destiny (*Geschick*) simultaneously tosses humans into their historical situation and seduces them into inauthentic fascination with superficial appearances.

Heidegger is right that we do not create our finite historical circumstance by fiat. Social customs and mainstream discourses do exert an ideological pull on us often before we are old enough to recognize these forces. But rather than critically examine the material and human causes of our social conditions, Heidegger projects historical forces onto a quasi-transcendental power of Being, thereby fatalistically disavowing human responsibility equally for oppressive social conditions as for their remedy. Accordingly, the fatalistic character of *phusis* takes on a fetishized form as duplicitous, as both deceiver and ground, both seducer and gateway to the greatness of one's will or even desire (109/83). *Phusis* grants an intelligible core to history, otherwise it could not grant Dasein its "pathways of decision" amidst the leveling forces of the modern age. But like Nietzsche's feminine lover 'Life,' the shimmering presencing of *phusis* deceives, thereby making it difficult to distinguish authentic self-assertion from distraction by superficial and ordinary perspectives. "Every decision," Heidegger says, "bases itself on something concealed, confusing; else it would never be a decision" (BW, 177/H, 44). "Because being, *physis*, consists in appearing . . . it stands, essentially and hence necessarily and permanently, in the possibility of an appearance which precisely covers over and conceals what the [unconcealment] in truth is" (IM, 104/EM, 79). While not an insatiable female, the goddess *dikē*, transfigured into *phusis*, nevertheless exerts an unnoticed pull on modern man, imperceptibly engrossing him in errant ways.

(iv) *Being needs special heroes to limit it.* Heidegger's text does not make use of overtly misogynistic metaphors, like Nietzsche's notion of whipping earth, the 'slippery witch', into place. Yet *phusis* needs to be captured and subjugated (157/120). Heidegger belabors the point that "creators, poets, thinkers, statesmen" must become a countermeasure to the emasculated spirit of Germany in order that an authentic historical existence can emerge (62/47). Since Being is *logos*, Heidegger attributes this decline to an emasculation of intelligence (spirit) which leads thinking into superficiality and not, as do other conservative revolutionaries, to a loss of contact with instinctual life forces. For Heidegger, when thinking becomes the mere cleverness, knowledge, technique, calculation, utility, and problem-solving characteristic of ordinary politics, morality, and even science, then "hatred and suspicion of everything free and creative" has set in. Overcoming this "creative impotence of knowledge" and indifferent complacency of modern man, great visionaries must bring thought back into touch with Being (38/29; SA, 31/SB, 11).

How treacherous could this call to converse with Being, to hold a little *Auseinandersetzung* or intellectual confrontation with history, actually be? Even though Heidegger rejects Jünger's steely paradigm of the new breed and Nazi visions of an Aryan race, his picture of the hero is hauntingly violent. In a gesture parallel to Jünger's fatalistic modeling of the new breed as the perfect reflection of the technological *Gestalt*, Heidegger too seeks to fashion Dasein into a mirror image of Being's epochal manifestation. The "fitting" (just) response is to think and will what destiny grants. When Heidegger discusses this intimate relation between Being and man, he adopts a tone far removed from the positive nurturing and enabling connotations of his later vision of the fourfold and of *Gelassenheit* (letting-be), and instead names the basic trait of man *to deinotaton*—the terrible or the horrible. Since Being is violent power, *deinon* or *Gewalt*, man, correlatively, is and must become the violent one. Given the context in which he chooses this metaphor, his 1935 vision, allegedly cleansed of barbarism, disturbingly sanitizes the emergent fascist state and its aesthetic fascination with horror.

Just as Heidegger dissociates the power of Being from actual warfare, so too he claims that the violence of man is not "mere arbitrary brutality" (IM, 150/EM, 115). The Heideggerian model of violent reciprocity between man and Being refrains from praising actual war as a unique situation in which the terrifying Mother Earth dissolves ego boundaries, releases asocial instincts (erotic longing for the mother), and smelts a newly hardened steely man, complete with restored boundaries, from out of its cauldron. Still, in contrast to rich forms of sympathy, Heidegger conceives heroic types, albeit on a less psychic and more symbolic plane, as mid-wives who must undergo a violent dissolution of bonds to society. Heidegger finds his paradigm for the reciprocal relation of Being and man in the choral passage from Sophocles' "Antigone" which names man "*deinotaton.*" Since the Greek, *deinon*, literally means terrible, Heidegger calls Being a terrible power that man can only violently hold "in check" (149/115). But he quickly goes on to justify his translation of *deinon* as *unheimlich*. Man is the strangest, Heidegger says, because Being, the overpowering, is the uncanny, the *Unheimliche*: "the supreme limit and link of man's being," that which "casts us out of the 'homely,' i.e. the customary, familiar, secure" and "prevents us from making ourselves at home." The uncanny call of Care appears transfigured into a call from destiny that fosters a yearning in man to venture "into all realms of the essent, of the overpowering power." And "in so doing he is flung out of all paths" (151/116).[45] Expelled from the polis and exposed to the abyss of existence, the exceptional one finds his genuine selfhood and, by becoming a passageway for the power of Being, restores authenticity to the polis.

Zimmerman offers a superb account of the key difference between Heidegger and Jünger. Both Heidegger and Jünger work within the scope of the fascist view that the goal of life is to transform the world through art. For Heidegger, the modernist "one-dimensional disclosure of entities" had to be countermanded by an "authentic producing" that would let things be in the poetic, artistic, and monumental creations of the State. Yet as early as 1935, Zimmerman shows, Heidegger begins to differentiate his own philosophy of technology and art from that of Jünger. He resisted Jünger's utopian view of the *Übermensch* as "the iron-hard, hot-blooded worker-soldier" who surpasses cultural deca-dence. For Heidegger, such a view remains caught in the anthropocentrism that debases thinking man by turning him into a clever animal. Zimmerman clarifies, "[f]or Heidegger, the overman is the artist who is called upon by the overpowering to limit the overpowering. For Jünger, by way of contrast, the over-man is the worker summoned by the will to power to overpower all entities." Heidegger regards great art not as a product of individual will and personality, but rather as "a preserving, a measuring, a shaping (*Gestaltung*) of entities as a whole" (GA 43, 105). The artist is "claimed by entities as the site through which they can achieve the limit necessary for them to manifest themselves."[46]

While we can concede that middle (and not just the late) Heidegger resists the way of will to power as domination over entities, precisely his tragi-fatalistic perspective leads him to glorify man as "the violent one, the wielder of power" who heroically ventures against all odds to limit an unmasterable force in order to win a pathway of deliverance for his people. Heidegger claims that the polis—the Open site of the belonging together of a people— becomes truly political only when an elect few, the chosen ones, are called by Being to bring its overwhelming power to stand revealed in their creations:

> [The *polis*] is political, i.e. at the site of history, provided there be (for example) poets *alone*, but then really poets, priests *alone*, but then really priests, rulers *alone*, but then really rulers. *Be*, but this means: as violent men to use power, to become pre-eminent in historical being as creators, as men of action. Pre-eminent in the historical place, they become at the same time *apolis*, without city and place, lonely, strange, and alien . . . without statute and limit, without structure and order, because they themselves *as* creators must first create all this. (IM, 152–53/EM, 117)

Great creators "break past [the] boundaries [of the polis]"; they penetrate, capture, and subjugate the very source of the polis, thereby letting each entity attain its proper place, as what it essentially is, "*as* sea, *as* earth" (157/120).[47]

But again, creators subjugate Being through "originary speech" and "the violence of knowledge," not actual war, since the word "opens up the essent [Being] in the structure of its collectedness" and is "the primordial poetry in which a people speaks being" (165, 17–72/ 126, 131–32). His *violent one* is not the rendition of Nietzschean man as the virile animal who carries whips, conquers the earth, or dams up red spots. By making the thoughtful person rather than the barbaric warrior a true creator, Heidegger shifts the arena of *Kampf, polemos,* or *Auseinandersetzung* to academia, to philosophical life, to art and poetry, and of course to those politicians who themselves are artistlike and have beautiful hands (Heidegger's quip about Hitler). *Auseinandersetzung* constitutes not sterile intellectualism, but the spiritual battle of confronting the works of the great thinkers of western metaphysics (49/37). This confrontation, as Fried clarifies, "is a gesture of the most profound respect," a kind of honorable rivalry with one's adversaries that forces a self-confrontation "with one's faith, ideas of nature or ideals of political belonging."[48]

Yet rather than critique the teutonic, masculinist warrior mentality for resisting psychological and moral transformation or for failing to undertake the humble but difficult work within ordinary life to alleviate social oppression, Heidegger reifies the desocialized, uncanny moment into an arguably falsely sacrificial and redemptive experience. For "those who ground the abyss (*jene Gründer des Abgrundes*) must be immolated in the fire of what is brought to endure as truth" so that humans can be "saved" and "undergo a restoration in the Open of the strife between Earth and World" (GA 65, 7).[49] Elsewhere Heidegger calls the great artist "a passageway which destroys itself in the creative process for the sake of the emergence of the work" (BW, 167/PLT, 40/H, 29). Creators, defined as those who think Being in abstraction from real social relations, have special powers that enable them to preserve the meaning of a people's destiny. Without the word of these creators a people would have no way to face the decisions of history. Creators, not just any person, are the sites of the *polemos*. And, like Heidegger's idols, they may well be destroyed in the service of their fate: Oedipus had an eye too many; Hölderlin committed suicide; Hitler went astray; Van Gogh shattered against the Dasein he could see; Nietzsche went insane.

Even if Heidegger does not transmute hatred of the feminine into a fraternal community, his vision adheres to a sacrificial logic that is elitist, stoic, and phallocentric. Rather than envisage the transgression of the polis in transformative terms, he reifies the stoic breach of society and narcissistically elevates the vision of those who face the abyss into the very essence of Being; hence, we can only infer that creators by nature enjoy a fate that grants them special vision, "an eye too many." Moreover, Heidegger's tragic perspective equates midwifery with heroic glory. Because man cannot truly master the Overpowering and yet great men are called upon to battle with it, these men must "shatter against being" and sacrifice themselves to the point of being violated (IM, 177/EM, 138). In a startling and perverse imaginary reversal of actual gender roles, Heidegger at one point characterizes their sacrifice as risking violation or rape by Being, where Being represents a power clothed at times in female garb. "[O]mnipotent being (literally) violates [*vergewaltigt*, to do violence to, to rape] being-there" (178/ 136, translator's brackets).

What is important about *phusis* for the Heidegger of the thirties is that great men win their people's destiny from the errancy built into Being's duplicitous self-concealment. Heidegger's romantic view of fatalism reinforces patriarchal sentimentality. A hallmark of patriarchy is its production of a sentimental attitude toward manly acts of false bravado, toward so-called heroic feats of running headlong and recklessly into life without principle and measure. Since patriarchy produces subjectivity as male, we identify first with men, we deck the male warrior (intellectual or physical) in medals and pity him his burdensome task. The desire deployed in middle Heidegger's depictions of authentic self-assertion is a masculine desire for glory and hardness, combined with a healthy dose of narcissism. The felt need to bask in glory by passing through the fire of pain comprises part of the specular matrix of patriarchy in which the world revolves around the European conception of the male subject and his imperial conquests. It promotes the belief that reality mirrors European man's greatness back to himself and exports the ideology that he deserves sympathy from the nonmale, nonwestern others who presumably need to be saved by his willingness to give meaning to their lives. Like Nietzsche in Bigwood's reading, Heidegger, too, engages in flamboyant acts for his lover: Germany's world-historical destiny.

2.5 The Missing Dialectic

The enormous influence exerted by Heidegger on deconstructive methodologies (especially Derrida and Irigaray) makes this excursus into his political *engagement* instructive. Both Wolin and Schürmann admit that Heidegger's antifoundationalism does not of logical necessity lead to the *Führerprinzip* (decision for the leader). Wolin consistently argues that not all critiques of modernity but rather Heidegger's total critique leads to antinormativism, while Schürmann inveighs that a deconstruction of modern *ratio* does not abdicate reason but only decenters it. The debate between Wolin and Schürmann reflects broader modern-postmodern disputes about antihumanism. If traditional ways of grounding practical action have become insufficient to contend with the complexities of our world, then are we doomed to find ourselves caught in a Heideggerian aporia, an antithetical either/or? Either decisionism or liberalism, authority or preexisting norms? Do we either accept a relativistic logic of historical contingency in choosing an alternative poetics, or retain liberal notions of procedural justice and impartial moral judgment with their proven inability to address the cultural and liminal bases for racism, sexism, and imperialism?

The task of distinguishing neoconservative reactionary from progressive revolutionary paradigms is more complicated than either Wolin's tendency to classify *Existenzphilosophie*, deconstruction, and other oppositional theoretical strategies as politically retrogressive attempts at finding a third way, or Schürmann's defense of Heidegger. While I share Wolin's concern over antinormativism, there are good reasons why feminists, race theorists, and manifold others groups have sought to rethink both materialism and idealism, to draw the lines between theoria and praxis differently than do many modernist thinkers, and to find new pathways beyond the limitations of modern political theories in both their liberal and Marxian variations.

Even given this goal, numerous feminists have disputed the value of strategies employed by Kristeva and Irigaray that center around the transgressive force of signification. Where some authors find rich resources for moving beyond the limitations of traditional modern moral paradigms (Meyers, Young), others hold that Irigaray and Kristeva desocialize and reify signification in ways that correlate to reactionary formations in advanced capitalism (Hennessey, Leland, Fraser). While I do not offer a solution to these debates, I have undertaken this excursus in order, first, to flesh out the gender dimensions of Heidegger's politics and, second, to bring the ambiguous influence that Heidegger exerts on contemporary philosophy to the fore. The deficiencies often criticized in transgressive strategies are in significant ways of Heideggerian vintage. Examining that legacy helps to isolate the ways that deconstructive, mimetic, and transgressive strategies mark advances over Heidegger and, thus, may be far more congenial to integration into a developed moral or political theory. But it also shows how those strategies may continue to exhibit residues of Heideggerian problems that a viable social theory would have to resolve.

I traced the ramifications of *Being and Time* by showing that Heidegger's stoic logic of authenticity has a twofold outcome. First, it produces a truncated moral psychology that severs contemplation of the disclosure of beings from the ethical and humanistic dimensions of relating to one another through disclosure. Thus Heidegger's notion of authenticity offers no standpoint from which to critique the heroic masculinist ethos of Nazism. Second, the stoic logic proves methodologically reductionist in that it displaces social theory with a critique of metaphysics developed in abstraction from an analysis of symbolic conventions and the material causes of alienation. So understood, the project of developing a critical ethos or poetics of life desocializes the moment of authentic transgression. Transgression thus yields a flattened and unvariegated critique of culture and society for impeding the (depersonalized) disclosure of Being. Heidegger's nondialectical methodology is what embroils his theory of authenticity in stoicism and produces the falsely critical logic of the exceptional person (or the pseudoecstatic one) and his authoritative vision of society. Focusing on the difficulties implicit in Heidegger's stoic and apolitical methodology leads to several implications.

First, in contrast to Wolin's approach, this focus provides an angle of critique from which to simultaneously resist the limits of impartial reason and its stoic, i.e., unnuanced, transgression. Heidegger's transgression of Enlightenment rationality abstracts from examining the epistemic effects of social location. Thus, it mimetically reproduces key aspects of preexisting ethical conventions, specifically patriarchy and modern nationalism. Kristeva's poststructuralist and Kierkegaard's existential moral psychologies are far richer than Heidegger's paradigm of authenticity. Numerous feminist efforts to develop a nonstoic moral psychology manage to critique impartiality without lapsing into antinormativism. Moreover, even though most existential philosophies and deconstructive methods do not offer complete political theories, they do not necessarily fall prey to the logic of the exception characteristic of Heidegger's decisionism. One reason for this may be that they often consider the problem of developing critical consciousness as a supplement to social, moral, and political theory, rather than as its replacement.

Taken as a precursor to postmodern attempts to situate the ethical-ecstatic subject of existential philosophy in the realm of the linguistic and cultural construction of desire, Heidegger's stoic dislocation of transgression from social relations leads to a "category mistake." Heidegger's transmutation of Kierkegaard's existential philosophy slurs over the boundary between an existential *mode* of action (*how* I act, what motivates action, what desire and fantasy move me to act) and the *substantive* choice one makes in action (*what* I enact).[50] Even though his authorship lacks an explicit critical gender consciousness, Kierkegaard's model of the ethical subject offers resources for articulating the relation between psychological growth and a critical relation to norms. Because he strives to maintain a sharp distinction between the how and the what, his authorship follows a *logic of supplement* or *qualification*. Instead of displacing questions of normative theory with the *Bildungsprozeß* of ethical consciousness, he claims that ethical life (sincerity of motives) qualifies my capacity for social critique and normative evaluation (justification for a course of action).

For this reason, Habermas has stressed that the complement to Kierkegaard's ethical individual in the realm of group-identity could only be an intersubjective model for "communication among different, equally entitled and coexisting forms of life." Habermas clarifies, "[t]he weight of the 'decision' . . . stress[es] the autonomous and conscious character of the act of taking hold of oneself. The only thing that can correspond to this on the level of the appropriation of intersubjectively shared traditions, is the autonomous and conscious character of a publicly conducted debate." Ethical consciousness does not of itself provide the sufficient conditions requisite to justify moral and political decisions. This point highlights the nature of the category mistake, since the ethical problem of developing a critical relation to my motivational and desiring life, while it may prepare me for moral discourse, cannot be confused with prescribing moral content. I would add that Kierkegaard's ethical consciousness remains incomplete as well. Without an interactive model for developing a political consciousness able to assess the effects of material conditions of disempowerment on perspective and communication, one's critical self-relation remains undeveloped.[51]

Understood as an ontological category, the Heideggerian notion of modality or *how* one exists cannot be located in interiority, that is to say, the psychosomatic site where world and self intersect, where reflective mediation of motivational and desiring life and the formation of habitus occur. Rather, the temporal-modal concept of being expands to encompass a people's basic, historical way of life which Bigwood aptly describes as "the living web . . . of art, science, politics and religion within which a historical people dwells" (Bigwood, EaM, 3; Heidegger, BW 168/H 31). This historicized notion of ontology appears to be a transmoral, supplemental concept like Kierkegaard's ethical inwardness. Our prethematic form of life is chock full of phonemic associations, symbolic presentations, linguistic markers that form the cultural matrix of our perceptual life and create an erotic foundation of collective belonging. What people in exile, for example, readily love in finding others who speak their native tongue is an immediate, prethematic level of understanding, an intuitive grasp of the nonlinguistic dimensions of communication, and the sheer ease felt in communication. Had Heidegger followed a transmoral logic of the supplement, he could have shown that a critical relation to these aspects of human identity is central to a critical ethos. He could have expanded Kierkegaard's inwardness to incorporate the linguistic, cultural, and symbolic influences on identity-formation. In effect, he could have tied his critical ontology to a critical social theory that would extend the problem of pluralism beyond the limited individualist focus of liberalism to include questions of symbolic practices and the erotic organization of cultural (gendered, racialized, ethnic) or national identity.[52]

But Heidegger's methodological reductionism, which severs ontology from ontic relations, violates the logic of the supplement. Instead of weaving culture critique into self-examination and vice versa, Heidegger bypasses self-examination and further grounds 'how' a people live in a quasi-transcendental, epochal event of Being. Since Being grants 'how' a people live, preexisting social conditions are only secondary manifestations of this deeper granting. Rather than prepare a critical relation to how I am acculturated, Heidegger reifies an apolitical model of transgression and, in a tendentious effort to avoid treating its cathartic effects as inherently dictating a critical form of life, he justifies a choice of life in an ahistorical process. A form of life is grounded, not in ontic cultural practices (parole), but rather in the ahistorical disclosure of Being that 'pure' language reveals. The historical, allegedly epochal notion of Dasein devolves into an essentialist ontological politics of cultural difference.

Even though Kierkegaard posits a disjunction between the critical life of inwardness (the ethical) and the social and moral claims society places on me, this does not elevate the individual above social norms. Without the possibility of ethical life, humans could undergo no separation of personal conscience from blind adherence to and internalization of the rules of society. By contrast, Heideggerian authenticity abstracts from ethical self-transformation and then posits the 'moment of vision' as antithetical to all past metaphysical systems. Heidegger denies the validity of measuring and legitimating a political course of action on the basis of the material past and present, while nonetheless demanding practical realization through a revolution in cultural ethos (mode of life). Here we witness a slippage in Heidegger's transmutation of Kierkegaard from an ethical concept—cultivating a critical relation to existing social practices—to one that supplants altogether normative criteria for action justified through public and democratically conceived procedures.

Heidegger's holistic approach to situated existence contributes to the devolution of his historical notion of Dasein into an essentialist logic because it tends to flatten the complexity of human existence into an undifferentiated whole. A Heideggerian analysis of the collective ethos of boredom in post-War Germany regards all social causes of alienation as epiphenomenal manifestations of forgetfulness of Being. Actual economic conditions, subcultural tensions, international relations merge into an undifferentiated whole. That is to say, bourgeois culture, alienation as boredom—the *mood* of post-war Germany—reflect a fundamentally ontological problem of failing to ground our existence in the deeper event of Being. Instead of a supplemental, reworked ontological basis for a fallibilist conception of social theory, we find a logic of purity and dislocation. Heidegger's overly austere and falsely oppositional distinction between ontological and ontic discourses devalues empirical and social science and cuts off the dialectical relation between one's desire to be and a critical awareness of the symbolic and material context within which one acts.

Second, it follows that any effort to develop a Heideggerian notion of critical ethos must compensate for Heidegger's tendency to essentialize cultural differences and, further, it must show a definitive relation between symbolic conventions and material conditions. Schürmann's recommendation—that Heidegger's seemingly arbitrary political decision for an alternative *Volksgemeinschaft* can be corrected by connecting his ontology to symbolic practices—is inviting because it promises to overcome Heidegger's ahistoricism and to connect Heidegger's view, that finite humans cannot stand behind history and know that a single principle organizes all life into a hierarchy of Being, to a critical social praxis. Yet Schürmann's proposal fails to touch Heidegger's methodological desocializing of language (the referential context in which beings disclose themselves). Thus, Schürmann abstractly derives guidelines for political action directly from contemplating the difference between what a symbol manifests and how it signifies, rather than additionally measuring symbolic practices in terms of their concrete ideological functions.

Heidegger's transgression of metaphysics can be completed, Schürmann argues, by extending his antifoundationalism into a set of meta-ontological guidelines for institutionalized politics. Schürmann derives five guidelines: (i) learn to live without teleology, "which suspends ontological justifications of domination by depriving the political deed of exterior grounds for legitimation"; (ii) focus on respondence rather than responsibility; (iii) inaugurate protest as openness to new constellations of truth rather than as calculated action; (iv) emphasize "the Now" as the time of political conduct; and (v) develop an anarchic rejection of utopian dreams and authority. The first unsatisfactory implication of Schürmann's proposal is that ethical life replaces political action altogether. In addition, Schürmann's theory has aggravated problems within its self-defined scope: His rendition of the symbolic difference reflects Heidegger's own peculiar abstraction from intersubjective and social relations; and it lacks a material point of reference for political action.[53]

Unlike Kristeva, who views religious symbols and rituals as maintaining oppressive social structures, Schürmann claims that symbols and rituals have no external goal, but only enjoyment of festivity. While this may be partially true, it is also partially false and so continues to support a notion of transgression that posits value in escaping or abstracting from social conditions. The phenomenological contemplation of symbolic structures, far from bringing us to question specific social practices, leads to the pristine and rarified contemplation of "the origin of Being and language." Schürmann describes this ethics of responsiveness not in intersubjective terms, but simply as thinking the "Difference" between Being and beings proper. To "exist originarily" does not pertain to the epistemic effects of social location; it does not prescribe traveling to another's world as central both to critical self-awareness and moral judgment. Similarly, protest, he claims, resists calculative rationality through a "detachment" from metaphysics; and it is this detachment that alone shows "which path is aberrant."[54]

On this model, noncalculative thinking remains connected to a stoic psychology of detachment, rather than a critical relational and expressive engagement with others. Self and cultural transformation are reductively dictated by criteria that derive abstractly from contemplation of Being, and thus independent of an analysis of the psychic and social effects of symbolic and material practices. It is hard to see how Schürmann's Heideggerian notion of symbolic meaning compensates for the problem of decisionism, since it locates the measure for what constitutes the greater good of society in the abstract insight gained through noncalculative contemplation of how things signify in general and not in our world. This is arguably a solipsistic moment because Schürmann develops neither a concept of intersubjectivity nor grounds the moment of critique in an interactive paradigm of communicative recognition. The path of protest, understood as "openness to new constellations of truth," remains deeply apolitical and largely asocial; contemplation of the end of metaphysics is the historical destiny of the age of technology. Since "the future is not a matter of human powers," our only posture can be disinterest in the future (Heidegger's Nietzschean Now). This hardly offers a thick enough model to promote activities aimed at alleviation of suffering.[55]

Even as he strives to overcome Heidegger's authoritarian politics, Schürmann does not address Heidegger's methodological reductionism, namely, that Heidegger measures social analysis against a transcendent principle. To the contrary, Schürmann himself leaves social theory and political analysis as derivative of critical ontology. He fails to recognize a dialectical relation between these levels of analysis. Schürmann's "symbolic link" fails to give equal weight to critical ontological and ontic practices in proposing a social theory. His approach remains methodologically uni-directional in that he links the autodisclosure of Being to the abstract, synchronic conception of the "symbolic difference." Even if symbolic ideals take on a life of their own and thus have synchronic dimensions, they nonetheless originate in as well as influence the diachronic transmission of culture and social practices.

The key implication of my analysis is that Heidegger's insight, that human being is ec-statically held out into the nothing, begs for a concrete theory of an ecstatic, yet ethical subject capable of social recognition in order to avoid the related problems of stoicism (individual) and decisionism (social). But developing a critical theory of social recognition would entail a significant modification of Heidegger's nondialectical methodological privileging of ontology over ontic science, of historicity over historiography, of Being and language over culture and parole. Schürmann's theoretical anarchy interestingly suggests continuity between the later quietism and the early voluntarism. For Heidegger's stoic logic of abstraction from sociopolitical conditions rears its head in the thirties as a rarified, cathartic praxis of purgation to make "the world safe for the flourishing of Being."[56] And in the later works, residues of this stoicism reappear when later Heidegger prescinds from politics. That act at best offers a partial contribution to developing an alternative ethos. At worst, as Schürmann's work shows, Heidegger's methodology reduces politics to a detached version of the ethos of learning to live without why; this, in turn, leads to a much worse result, a studied indifference to concrete suffering.

Rather than implicate all existential theory, deconstructive methods, and appropriations of Heidegger's work as reactionary rejections of 1789, it is better to base critique on the degree to which any work fosters flat and undifferentiated analyses of social relations, desocializes meaning as ahistorical, or reduces political theory to fostering a poetic ethos *independent* of its relation to objective social conditions. There is a marked difference between critically analyzing the concrete effects of symbolic practices on perception, moral judgment, and political exclusions, and Schürmann's largely asocial guidelines for a critical poetics of living without why. Heidegger's later nonviolent ethos is appealing and can make a partial contribution to ecofeminist critiques of modern forms of domination. Yet even as these appropriations of Heidegger tacitly fill out his deficient model of sociality, they do not necessarily redress the methodological abstraction of the linguistic origins of identity from their embeddedness in material conditions.

For this reason, I agree with Bernard Dauenhauer who argues, against Schürmann, that a second link is necessary to connect Heidegger's thought to political theory. He claims that "political decision is significant only if it is *discernibly* indebted to the past and places a lien upon the future." But even this second link requires us to first qualify that the notion of the symbolic as well must be developed as specifically related to concrete social practices, and this Schürmann does not do. Moreover, we would still need some ontic criteria for responsible action since the past and future do pertain to political action. Dauenhauer's definition of the political allows us to defend a deconstruction of acontextual or transcendental grounds without accepting that Schürmann's proposal of theoretical an-archism gives us as a viable and complex political strategy. That there is neither an ontological, a priori ground of action "nor an independent goal against which action can be assessed," Dauenhauer notes, does not mean that there is no ontic ground for action and its legitimation. As Dauenhauer says:

> Whatever the second middle term refers to is the ontic *archē* and *telos* of all action. Now one of the things we learn from the first middle term [Schürmann's symbolic difference] is that this second middle term cannot refer to anything which stands outside the realm of political action. But this fact does not preclude the founding of the realm of political action by and on specific political performances.[57]

CHAPTER THREE

Agency, Affect, and the Postmodern Subject

Overcoming the Logic of Sacrifice

Theories that postulate the inevitability of sacrifice never manage to distribute the burden of that sacrifice evenly.

Cynthia Willett, *Maternal Ethics*

Feminists have long been leery of voluntarist conceptions of agency which, they contend, promote a truncated portrait of the moral subject. When these conceptions encourage purging oneself of lesser passions, self-appropriation diminishes critical awareness of one's desiring and fantasy life, and thereby allows one to project 'irrational' impulses onto marginalized groups. Yet early Heidegger's peculiar lapse into stoic consciousness, with its accompanying voluntaristic ethos, is instructive because that lapse stemmed neither from the pessimistic assumption that humans harbor antisocial, animalistic desires (which they must learn to rationally control) nor from grounding subjectivity in transcendence of the corporeal, natural, and immediate dimensions of existence. Given that he begins instead with twin premises, that subjectivity emerges out of *Mitsein* (intersubjectivity) and that thinking arises from affective attunement (*Stimmung*) to the world, I locate the source of his voluntarism not in the fact that he attempted to delineate an existentially situated notion of willed self-regulation. Rather, the latent voluntarism, which erupted in the middle period, stemmed from his methodological failure to see a *dialectical* relation between his ontological premise, that identity emerges out of attunement to the disclosure of beings, and the existential fact that we never know that *attunement in itself* as if we interpret 'the totality of what is' independently of social location.

Whereas my critique of Heidegger effectuates a return to dialectics, feminist critics charge that dialectical conceptions of subjectivity—conceptions ranging from Hegel's speculative dialectics to Sartre's and Beauvoir's respective existential philosophies—are haunted by a Cartesian ghost in that they continue to posit a prelinguistic locus of intentionality. In order to dispel the concept of "a doer behind the deed," numerous poststructuralist feminists develop a notion of agency as resignification.[1] Here agency denotes a linguistic competency defined as the creative capacity to rewrite the script of our discursively constituted identities. In this chapter, I want to accept a linguistically based notion of agency as creativity while addressing the difficulty that notions of creative resignification often fail to specify what makes one kind of performance nonstoic and another stoic.

Locating creative resistance in the slippage of meaning or in the plurality of discourses in competition for my identity retains an extremely cognitive approach to the attainment of a critical standpoint. While important, such an approach offers at best a thin explication of the creative, agential impulse; it effectively drains the motivation to alter meaning of its rich affective dimensions.[2] Rather than indict every theory of dialectical mediation as voluntaristic, I want to recuperate a view of dialectical praxis as the ability not simply to alter meaning but to critically mediate and intensify one's affective investment in particular meanings. In this endeavor, I turn to Kristeva and borrow from Allison Weir's interpretation of her work as notably occupying a middle position between traditional existential theories and poststructuralist thought. Although a borderline figure, at times valorizing transgression in itself, Kristeva points to a connection between overcoming stoic consciousness and a capacity for critique.

My first aim in this chapter is to demonstrate that Kristeva strives, although not with complete success, to delineate a post-Beauvoirian theory of intentionality which is grounded in language rather than in a paradigm of consciousness. In part 3.1, I outline key feminist critiques of Beauvoir's existential and dialectical theory of agency and accept Weir's charge that these feminist critics fail to overcome stoic consciousness. I explore Kristeva's theory of intentionality in 3.2. What is significant about her project, I argue, is that it recognizes the need to explicate the relation between affective life and language. Kristeva realizes that the existential intention to transform meaning denotes a particular kind of affect, namely, a prosocial desire to express oneself coherently in terms of shared meanings. Weir defines this prosocial desire as an *existen-*

tial striving to deliberately harness the tension between identification with the social whole and the heterogeneous aspects of one's nonidentity with the social whole.[3] Against the thinner view that agency arises from slippage in meaning, Kristeva demonstrates that affect forms the bridge between meaning and identity. The ability to invest linguistic meanings with affective force binds the work of altering meaning to psychosomatic or self transformation. It follows that there is some relation between effectuating critical rather than naive self change and a capacity for nonrepressive ethical relations.

My second, more critical aim, however, will be to reground Kristeva's theory of existential desire in a critical social ontology rather than, as she does, in a Freudian drive theory. In 3.3, I argue that Kristeva's reliance upon Freud's drive theory has, minimally, two seriously undesirable outcomes which undermine the contribution she makes to developing a linguistically grounded notion of intentionality. First, drive theory undercuts her effort to treat affective life as genuinely social, rather than partially antisocial. Second, the idea that intentionality is a transmutation of drive cathexes also encounters, if not difficulties supporting a notion of free agency, then a similar inability to treat intersubjective relations as sympathetically grounded rather than as desperate longings to compensate for repression of asocial pleasures. This compensatory view leads Kristeva to a dangerous valorization of an arguably patriarchal ideal of romantic love as hysterical collapse into another person. I aim to correct these two deficiencies. Using Heidegger against Heidegger in 3.4, I reclaim his ontological insight, that creative longing arises from an original, affective attunement to others, and use it to supply what is missing in Kristeva's notion of *parousia*: an original protosocial basis for human existence.[4] I conclude in 3.5 by showing that regrounding intentionality in a social ontology need not reinvoke the specter of voluntarism. Instead of a notion of willed-mastery, I propose that we isolate willingness as one dimension of our complex attitudinal and desiring lives, but a dimension which allows us to ascribe ethical responsibility to both attitudes and actions.

3.1 The Dialectical Subject and Its Critics

Hegelian phenomenology and existential philosophies share in common the view that, to borrow Cynthia Willett's words, the "individual is embedded within a sociality whose origin in the material and cultural forces of history is incommensurate with powers of the individual to conceptualize or to control."[5] Dialectic means that the terms one seeks to conceptualize, like individual and society, cannot be grasped purely analytically because they are internally related. Yet against Hegel's speculative logic, existential thinkers from Kierkegaard to Beauvoir objected that dialectical reasoning does not yield a higher synthesis. Speculative logic abstracts, in other words, from the very conditions of embodied existence when it assumes that one can resolve the irreducible particularities of individuated subjects under a final system. Although this delimitation of Hegel's logic of identity should evoke their sympathy, poststructuralist feminists have advanced sharp critiques of existential philosophies including that of Beauvoir. Critiques of dialectical models, which regard the self as both *constituted* by the world yet partially *self-constituting*, center around two focal points. First, they charge that existential theories of intentionality posit a prelinguistic, Cartesian core of subjectivity which gives the subject voluntaristic control over meaning and signification (cultural forces). Second, because reliant upon the premise of an innate core, the dialectical subject remains conceptualized as divided or caught in a bad dichotomy between its masculine-transcendent agency and its passive-feminine socialized body.

In this part, I want to set the backdrop for my critical use of Kristeva to recuperate a notion of the existential capacity to regulate one's behavior which does not rely upon a prelinguistic theory of consciousness. By, firstly, reviewing critiques of existential dialectics, I take seriously the poststructuralist call to theorize creative-existential capacities as products of language. But, secondly, I discuss Allison Weir's recent work in order to support my argument that the problems of stoicism are not automatically alleviated by taking a linguistic turn away from paradigms of consciousness. I take the problems of stoicism to be two: either stoicism issues in a sacrificial model of society as founded upon an initial loss of pleasure or it siphons off responsibility for one's affective life, thereby depleting subjects of key ethical competencies. Weir tracks the thread of stoic logic, rooted in the assumption that all identity is inherently repressive, from Beauvoir's existential philosophy to poststructuralist feminist theory. Her work enables us to identify those aspects of Kristeva's work that offer resources for delineating a model of existential agency as a capacity for nonstoic, nonsacrificial, and nonrepressive forms of socialness.

Against Dialectic: The View of Agency as Creative Resignification

Judith Butler forcefully claims that existential theories posit agency as a "capacity for reflexive mediation" which transcends cultural influences. "On this model," Butler continues, "'culture' and 'discourse' *mire* the subject, but do not constitute that subject."[6] Similarly, Susan Hekman attributes this problem to Beauvoir's existentialist epistemology which harbors an irreconcilable dichotomy between two antithetical notions of subjectivity, one autonomous and the other determined. Because she assumes that the episteme of self-knowledge resides in a rational self-constituting capacity, Beauvoir subscribes to a masculine view of freedom as transcendence of the situated realm of immanence traditionally associated with women and femininity. Whereas Butler charges Beauvoir with presupposing "an agent, a *cogito,* who somehow . . . could, in principle, take on some other gender," Hekman extends this line of critique to encompass more recent efforts, by Linda Alcoff and Teresa de Lauretis, to rethink nonmasculinist, dialectical views of the self using pragmatist resources. Hekman contends,

> [T]hese theorists presume that the only way to avoid a conception of the subject that is wholly determined is to retain some key elements of the Cartesian subject. Thus they do not wholly deconstruct the conception of the Cartesian subject, nor do they reveal this subject to be itself a discursive formation.[7]

Butler and Hekman concur that the epistemology of the *constituting subject* denotes an innate rational core that precedes linguistic socialization. Every dialectical conception amounts to a bad paste job wherein feminists desperately try to glue an inner, transcendent self-reflexiveness onto the subject of linguistic and social determination.

Even granting significant differences in their respective Foucauldian and Kristevan influences, Butler and Hekman share two central views in common. First, they assume that every attempt to give a normative definition of woman's oppression, though perhaps practically necessary, inevitably establishes new discursive forms of subjugation. And, second, they adumbrate a conception of agency as the *capacity to creatively rewrite the script* of our discursively (rather than epistemologically) constructed identities. The first assumption leads them to embrace methodological strategies which appear to many as wholly negative or purely antinormative, aimed at negating preexisting symbolic and social practices rather than reconstructing normative ideals. Though largely interventionist and often positioned against normative theorizing, their strategies are not wholly antireconstructive. As Hekman clarifies, they reformulate agency through *displacement or deconstruction*, rather than through dialectic. In lieu of the dialectical activity of self-constitution, Butler portrays agency as "the possibility of a variation of [the] repetition of the signifying practices that constitute my identity"; and Hekman follows suit, stating that *"[a]gency* here is a product of discourse, something that language provides us in discursive formations, not an innate quality located in 'inner space'."[8]

I read Butler and Hekman as holding a normative concern. They claim that it is both descriptively more accurate and prescriptively preferable to depict the exercise of agency as a performative capacity to "resist, mutate and revise" the discourses which comprise our identities. This model breaks with the very language of dialectical mediation which they believe invokes a politically dangerous epistemological, even ontological dichotomy between active agent/passive determinant, inner reason/outer circumstance. Far from reducing women to passive dupes of signifying practices, it acknowledges that critical skills and creative forms of expression result from socialization. Although Hekman and Butler adeptly reveal that there is no inherent contradiction in claiming that subjectivity is discursively produced yet not on that account passive, I nonetheless disagree that all talk of dialectical mediation inevitably erects false dichotomies, projects a prelinguistic interiority, and idealizes an unhappy subject divided against itself. The concept of deliberate mediation intends not simply to describe the conditions, discursive or nondiscursive, which enable humans to actively participate in the ongoing process of identity-formation. More importantly, it specifies that agency is a normatively thin, even vacuous category if not specifically linked to critique, i.e., to the activity whereby humans reach critical distance on their identities and social locations.[9]

Let me be clear. Critical evaluations of symbolic systems and popular discourses do contribute to personal-psychological transformation in that they encourage awakening to the ways that norms and classification systems suffuse our ideational and corporeal lives; moreover, they show that such ideal-typical representations of group identities tend to solidify into fixed notions which harbor potentially damaging political consequences for oppressed groups. While helpful strategies for critique, such indirect methods of reconstructing critical self-development (via displacement rather than dialectic) yield at most a theory of the *minimal, linguistic conditions of possibility* of agency. Here critical consciousness emerges as a possible effect of largely negative resistance to the subjugating effects of discursive practices. Yet the nature of the deliberate, self-regulating moment in this positive and productive activity, whereby we critically differentiate between nondominating and repressive, feminist and masculinist forms of adopting an alternative script among those in competition for our identities, is left unspecified.

Treating agency as creative resistance to the effects of socialization places a fairly strong taboo on thematizing, in ideal-typical terms, the positive and deliberate activity of consciously cultivating nondominating attitudes. This taboo implies that it is unnecessary to undertake a depth analysis of the 'inner' psychic dynamics of self-transformation. Efforts to displace such an explication generally focus on the corporeal aspects of desire and performance, but this focus does not suffice to clarify how humans exercise deliberate influence over their affective lives. Granted the idea that inner psychic space has a physical topos is sheer fantasy. Yet humans do develop a relatively stable set of 'core' attitudes which enable them to exercise, with success, influence over their continued growth. Competencies function not only in negativistic terms, as resistance to social forces, but as the positive activity of evaluating those forces and choosing to incorporate some of them. The effects of such culturally learned competencies are real, i.e., efficacious. To the extent that theories of performativity undertake neither a depth psychology of the formation of affective (not simply corporeal) habits nor an existential analysis of willed regulation of those dispositions, they cannot provide a model of agency robust enough to explicate how resistance to social practices produces subject-formations which effectively overcome rather than ineffectively reproduce stoic and defensive forms of consciousness.[10]

My approach is to isolate stoic consciousness as what leads to a voluntarist paradigm of agency, rather than to make the blanket assumption that all talk of willed mediation leads down a slippery slope to the ghost of Cartesianism. Understood as a transcendent will in control both of one's emotions and of one's cultural embeddedness, the specter of stoic consciousness is not eradicated by throwing the baby of disposition out with the bathwater of psychic topos; nor do dilemmas of voluntarism evaporate by rejecting the notion of willed mediation in favor of that of performativity. Much as in Heidegger, associating rich analyses of affective dispositions with inauthentic discursive practices tends to lead back to overly cognitive models of oppression (as epistemic effects of language) and, correlatively, to overly negativistic approaches to agency (as negation of what is, rather than production of more ideal forms of life). These approaches provide at best thin resistance to the stoic assumptions underlying voluntarist notions of willed freedom. The feminist goal of making people and theory accountable for the affective dimensions of thought, perception, and action can still be served by discussing the value in existentially striving for a certain coherence in the narrative one tells about oneself, one's affective life, and one's deeds. Similarly, it may be ethically important to develop ideals which could guide us to reconcile selves in a social whole, even though there are no perfect classification systems and we must delimit the ideal of an absolute Hegelian system which aspires to sublate all difference.

Kristeva's Alternative Dialectic of Existence

Two central points in Weir's *Sacrificial Logics* echo my concerns and open the way toward a post-Beauvoirian model of dialectical autonomy. First, she demonstrates that Butler and Beauvoir are united in their common assumption that identity follows a "sacrificial logic" and thus necessarily entails stoic repression of difference or nonidentity. Second, Weir emphasizes that, in spite of the limitations of her theory and politics, Kristeva's work is significant because of "the stress she places on the existential and ethical dimensions of affirming and living an identity of self" and because she seeks to theorize "the basis of a social identity which is not purely repressive." Weir traces the "sacrificial logic" of theorists as diverse as Judith Butler, Jessica Benjamin, Nancy Chodorow, and Luce Irigaray back to Beauvoir. Each, she reveals, violates the logic of dialectic which locates identities as embedded in history, culture, and material circumstance. What unites these thinkers is the common, yet reductive, assumption that all identity is inherently repressive of nonidentity. No matter how great their differences, each finally equates the development of the reflexive capacity to posit oneself as a speaking subject with stoic acceptance of an inaugural loss of immediacy. Due to this assumption, Weir continues, "feminist theory has become caught in a series of impasses, produced by a failure to theorize nonoppositional, nondominating relationships between identity and difference."[11]

Weir salvages the concept of dialectic from its ties to Cartesianism by clarifying that Beauvoir's notion of freedom derives from a Kojèvean dualistic ontology rather than a genuinely dialectical model of self-expression. Following Kojève's definition of freedom as "negation of what is," Beauvoir transmutes subject-object relations into a fixed dichotomy where "the subject is defined by negativity, and the object by mere positivity." By subscribing to this dualist ontology, Beauvoir develops not a dialectical model of selves attuned to one another as embedded in a social world, but rather a theory of subjects doomed by their inability to fully negate the immanence of the body and essentially opposed to one another in seeking their individual transcendence. In a move parallel to my claim that Heidegger's nondialectical methodology collapses into a stoic and repressive psychology, Weir shows that Beauvoir's dualistic ontology leads to Hegel's "Unhappy Consciousness." Hegel defines stoic consciousness as developing an awareness of being free without finding a connection between the freedom exercised in thought and one's concrete conditions. Stoic consciousness solidifies into "Unhappy Consciousness" at the point that the subject becomes enmired in the view that it is a divided being, self-identical and immutable, on the one hand, and embodied and changing, on the other. Embroiled in this dualistic legacy and its unhappy logic, the poststructuralist premise, that identity is solely repressive, cuts short the possibility of reconstituting an ideal of mutual recognition rooted in "self-expression, self-completion, rather than negation."[12]

By contrast, Kristeva's work implies that notions of creative alteration of meaning cannot be adequately theorized when we assume that identity-formation via language is solely repressive of nonidentity. The motivation to change must harbor an element of a productive, i.e., self-originating desire to make sense out of oneself and the world. The central contribution of Weir's interpretation stems from her argument that Kristeva has a double conception of language. Weir demonstrates that, unlike other poststructuralists, Kristeva differentiates between two conceptions of language: (a) language as a metaphysical law of identity that represses nonidentity and (b) language as the medium of self-expression. These views of language correlate to two distinct approaches to subjectivity: (a) corresponds to the view that self-identity is a defensive form of mastery manifesting an ambivalent conformity to existing norms and fear of one's own nonidentity or difference; while (b) fits with a conception of self-identity as a productive capacity for communication and self-expression of nonidentity via integration into shared meanings.

On this view, Kristeva's work offers a middle position between an overdetermined Cartesian agent (capable of willfully squelching his passions and muscling his way out of social conditions) and an affectively underdetermined creative agent (whose affective desires oddly do not stem from productive, self-directed motives but arise as effects of negating preexisting meanings, thus leaving us to question what enables us to negate). Kristeva moves beyond the sacrificial logic underpinning interventionist strategies of critique, Weir argues, because she locates agency not in "negation of what is" or constant resistance to how discursive practices bind us viscerally to ideologically tainted perspectives. Rather, she regards negativity as "a force of production that is open to change." Neither willed mastery nor simply negation of what is, creative agency manifests as the dialectical and transformative possibility of taking pleasure in symbolic communication of nonidentity. Instead of "a lonely, isolated self who lives forever fighting against the slide back into primal pleasure—fighting against, that is, the thing he most desires—in order to preserve himself," the self emerges as "a capacity for *participation* in a social world."[13]

Later I intend to claim that Kristeva's middle position unravels because she cannot reconcile her view that affective life originates in antisocial drives with her effort to posit subjectivity, and thus intentionality, as an unsullied prosocial desire to communicate. In the next part, however, I advance the claim that Kristeva strives to delineate a post-Beauvoirian account of existential intentionality. The central merit of Kristeva's work stems from two insights. These are that (i) the impetus for self-change must itself exceed the total effects of socialization of desire; and, moreover, that (ii) this impetus stems from developing a rich affective investment in the linguistic capacity to translate otherwise inchoate feelings and impulses into meaningful desires. These desires, in turn, can be articulated, represented, communicated, and disclosed as well as critically evaluated in relation to social conditions. It is not enough to talk about this agential impetus as deriving simply from the tension or energy produced by slippage of meaning. For Kristeva, the linguistic possibility of generating new meaning is itself vacuous unless connected to the substance of one's identity, i.e., one's affective struggle to make one's biopsychic processes meaningful within a shared form of life.

Although critique and the expression of one's felt-alterity are not synonymous, Kristeva's work teaches us that there is some relation between the psychological desire to express nonidentity (i.e., to overcome stoicism) and the development of the existential capacity to critique as well as agitate for social conditions which allow heterogeneity to flourish. Sometimes her work confuses simple alteration of meaning with an inherently desirable outcome. But I will press another side of her work. That side reveals that overcoming the psychological aspect of stoic consciousness entails not simply a release of repressed desires, but rather a transformation of outlaw desires into a prosocial force. If unable to intentionally direct affective investments in meaning, then we could not differentiate between action which stems from critique and that which simply reactively alters what is. This side of her work implies that an efficacious notion must equate creative agency with a distinctly critical competency: a deliberate mediation of our affective responses to socialization.

3.2 Toward a Post-Beauvoirian Theory of Intentionality

We can read Kristeva's explorations of pre-Oedipal identification as a theoretical account of the birth of intentionality. Here intentionality denotes a qualitatively different level of motivation than the infant presumably has in its rudimentary immersion in the flux of its own (allegedly) chaotic drive processes. Kristeva, following Freud, calls this existential level of motivation a "new psychical action." According to Kristeva that intentionality emerges, first, on the basis of linguistification of drives at the semiotic level in the pre-Oedipal phase and, second, through an additional preparation for transmuting drives into meaning, a transmutation which effectuates a qualitatively new level of affective desire. Intentionality emerges as a capacity to transform libidinal cathexes into a desire to communicate.[14] I wish to stress that Kristeva is right to recognize that, in order to account for processes of self- and social change, we need to theorize a level of intentionality which exceeds libidinal drives and promises a kind of autonomous self-regulating capacity. For the same reason, she rightly depicts creative intentionality in terms of *parousia*. Social change presupposes that this psychical formation channels human desire toward an inexhaustible possibility of realizing ever new forms of meaningful social praxis which exceed preexisting social norms and symbolic ideals.

In contrast to critics of existentialist thought, I argue that Kristeva's developmental theory has the advantage of giving an account of the origin of intentionality which is not prelinguistic.

She shows that intentionality emerges as a preverbal transfer of affective desire to an ideal proto-object, that is, language. This affective investment reflects the emergence of a *positive desire to be*; that is, a *protoexistential desire to enter the real* (= world of shared meanings). The desire to be, while incorporating the dynamics of libido and repression, cannot be reduced to the negative effect of what has been repressed by societal regulation. Nor does it emerge simply through an act of negating inchoate drive processes. The existential desire to express one's own nonidentity constitutes the activity of becoming a self; it denotes the self-striving whereby I continually search to make meaning out of my identity and to coproduce meaningful forms of social praxis with others. Kristeva realizes that the possibility of mutual recognition necessitates that there be a level of intentionality oriented toward surpassing societal regulation of desire. Though that intentionality is not prelinguistic, never manifests outside intersubjective relations, and relies upon psychosomatic energy, it also is not an uncontrollable eruption of the repressed.

In this context, I use the term existential to denote dimensions of *desire (affect) and attitudinal motivation (willingness)* which exceed, at the very least, three aspects of subjectivity assumed by Freudian-influenced psychoanalytic theory: (i) the Oedipalization of desire which binds one to conflictual relations between self and alter, relations characterized by conflicts rooted in romantic identification and transference; (ii) the total effects of the early formation of the psychic agencies which comprise one's individuated personality; and (iii) those biopsychic impulses Freud calls drives, aggressive and libidinal cathexes, which lie beyond the full control of the will. This definition is commensurate with what Sandra Bartky calls existential motivations when she points out that Freudian ontogenesis fails to fully address the sociogenic sources of identity, i.e., the ongoing nature of continued changes in identity which adults undergo as a result of their actions and choices. That process, while informed by one's initial Oedipalization within the family, is definitively bound to social and material location both during Oedipalization and after. As Frantz Fanon points out, the *causes* of psychic alienation for extremely oppressed groups bear no necessary correlation to the proximate influences on one's psychosexual development which arise within the family.

Given the complexity of sources of identity and desire, the continued process of self-transformation presupposes a form of striving which, as productive, exceeds simple reaction mechanisms, the return of the repressed, and the effects of discursive and social conditions even as it finds an outlet only within the parameters of such conditions. Kristeva theorizes the foundation of these extrafamilial and extralinguistic sources of identity as a kind of *parousia* or ec-static orientation toward the production of meaning. In order to account for how subjects mediate their disease, she argues that the existential desire to be is oriented beyond the effects of such processes. This foundation makes it possible for humans to recover a preference for health and thus to find satisfaction in seeking harmonious intersubjective connections.

I find Kristeva's basic intuition sound, that we cannot account for processes of self and social change without analyzing two fundamental things: (i) how affective life is related to language (meaning) and (ii) how the desire to make meaning together (intersubjectivity) exceeds the total effects of individuation via socialization (and supplies the intrasubjective foundation of intersubjective relations). Before criticizing her for failing to provide an adequate ontological foundation for her existential theory of intentionality, I will draw out her view that affective life plays a central role in developing nonstoic identity-formations.[15]

Affective Investment in Language: A Condition of Nonstoic Identity

From *Revolution in Poetic Language* (1974) to *Tales of Love* (1983), Kristeva is preoccupied with showing both that identity emerges as the active capacity to make an affective investment in the reality of shared meanings and, moreover, that intensifying this affective identification through *critical rather than naive mediation* is a fundamental precondition of loosening stoic or rigidly narcissistic identity-formations. Thus, her analysis in RP of the advantages of poetic language over therapeutic analysis hinges on two premises which she does not entirely explicate until later works like TL. The first premise is that subjects can and do exercise the *existential capacity* to harness and shift drive energy in various ways, indeed subjectivity emerges precisely as this capacity. The second premise is that *intrasubjective processes*, which simultaneously ground the emergence of subjectivity and intersubjectivity, condition the possibility for transforming *intersubjective relations*. What enables subjects to develop critical distance on their highly socialized identities is not simply the fact that the semiotic harbors a reservoir of possible slippage in meaning not contained within any finite sociosymbolic order. Rather, because the unconscious and preconscious aspects of psychosomatic life are affectively linked to social meanings, debates over ideology can evoke deep-seated aspects of our motivational life and psychology, thereby challenging us to undergo change.

For Kristeva, intentionality is not rooted in a consciousness which is severed from the corporeal; it is not an abstract cognitive ability to express and lord over desires and needs, but instead a biopsychic capacity to concretely transfer libidinal energy to linguistic communication and thus to take pleasure in speech. That we deliberately mediate such processes of transference, either naively or critically, links the impetus for self-change to a desire to increasingly shift one's pleasure (meaning) from the quasi-autoerotic enclosure of narcissism to those social pleasures achievable only by virtue of becoming open, vulnerable, and fluid subjects. Stoic consciousness thus refers to any identity formation which does not merely repress asocial drives but stifles the very development of an affective desire to communicate one's nonidentity and to take pleasure in the qualitative process of growth involved in such a communicative praxis. The rigid, thetic subject, who stoically grounds his identity in the want of total control over his desiring and motivational life, has but a truncated intentionality and a diminished capacity for affective identification with others.[16]

Already in RP, Kristeva claims that directly attaching drive energy to an object or addressee depletes the negativity of the drive-laden semiotic sphere of its transformative force. Efforts to decenter and transform self-alter relations directly, without a third moment of critical mediation of one's desire, fail. For example, she argues that fetishism is a form of transgression in which the subject tries to decenter the overly rigid thetic identity by dissociating itself from symbolic meaning. Nevertheless, this dissociation is not psychosis because it does not destroy the subject but rather transfers narcissistic investment (ego-ideal) in one's thetic subjectivity to objects, to the fetish (object-ideal). Fetishism, she says, entails "imagining the thetic at the place of an object or a partner"; it involves telescoping the thetic capacity for symbolization by displacing it onto a body part, "one of those instinctually invested stases" (RP, 63–64). This kind of transfer results in an incomplete second-degree thetic shift; it does not issue in a critical mediation because the purposive intention aims solely at inducing an episodic and transitory ec-stasis, i.e., a pleasurable release from the position of responsible actor. Fetishism momentarily intensifies the influx of drive energy (the return of the repressed) but without integrating its decentering effect into a transformed critical perspective, an examination of the relation of one's desiring life to social conditions.

Similarly, Kristeva's respective critiques of the avant-garde and of Marxism reflect alternative ways that we can existentially harness and fix drive energy. By using poetic techniques which shatter meaning, the nineteenth-century avant-garde literary figures valorized the subjective experience of feeling one's thetic identity dissolve, but they did so, Kristeva argues, at the expense of harnessing the tension between semiotic reactivation of repressed desires and critique of the existing sociosymbolic contract. By contrast, the subject of revolutionary praxis does connect subjective experience to objective social conditions in the form of ideology critique. Yet, she claims, in taking the object of critique to be *only* material conditions and not the subjects of social praxis, the revolutionary subject reifies its desire. Lacking critical self-examination, revolutionary subjects, whether conservative reactionaries or radical progressives, dangerously adopt the position of being a justified and transcendent will in control of the very force of negativity which effectuates social change.

I am not concerned to evaluate Kristeva's conceptions of either the avant-grade or activist-oriented social movements, though I find her account, especially of the latter, narrow and overly simplistic. For now, I wish to highlight two aspects of Kristeva's analyses of the central role that the dynamics of affective life plays in persons either successfully becoming critical social agents or not. First, these analyses—of how we direct our desires toward specific objects or kinds of pleasure and toward truncated outlets—presuppose that humans ultimately derive greater pleasure from overcoming narcissistic gains and stoic identity-formations. We could interpret the main thesis of RP to be that the most complete and enduring (i.e., least repressive, least episodic, least truncated, and thus least dangerous) expression of human desire is the inexhaustible process of becoming edified into critical subjects. How subjects develop critical capacities but also desire to do so, Kristeva acknowledges, if not a matter of teleological orientation toward a specific end, is then a matter of human existence being oriented to surpass uncritical forms of life. Even though the existential desire to be emerges as an open-ended orientation toward possibilities for new meaning, the structure of this desire places a premium on developing critical and harmonious forms of social interaction.[17]

Second, Kristeva's analyses imply that there is an irreducible dimension of attitude which is crucial to bring about self-transformation: either one is willing or unwilling to become a subject in process. While never divorced from either bodily and unconscious impulses or social conditions, the dynamics of affective life also never appear in her work as simple one-to-one effects of either discursive practices, bodily habits, or material social conditions. During the shift in meaning produced by poetic language, then, one has to be *attitudinally predisposed* to undergo a transformation of awareness, fantasy, and desire, a transformation that fosters the capacity for ideology critique and strengthens the ability to communicate nonidentity in the form of social critique. Presumably, then, there is a relation between wanting to bring one's own alterity out through dialogue and willingness to assess those ways in which it reproduces or potentially challenges questionable social norms. The significance of her analysis is that this attitude is freely adopted, albeit grounded in our initial identification with language as a medium of self-expression. That is why Kristeva claims that only by making language the penultimate object of one's desire can the subject intensify its engagement in the world and reach a level of affective intentionality able to support transgressions of preexisting norms without valorizing either the dizzy fall into the dissolution of meaning (and identity) or the temptation to posit oneself as master of meaning. To intensify the desire for the real is to be *willing* to become edified into a capacity to derive greater pleasure from socialness than from dissociative escapes from reality. This Kristevan model anticipates her subsequent effort to delineate a theory of intentionality able to support harmonious self-alter relations.

Intentionality as Second Mediation of the Need for the Real

Although the later works ascribe a privileged role to transference love over poetic discourse in fostering ethical interaction, this shift in focus does not uproot but rather extends her original premise that intrasubjective processes ground intersubjective possibilities for harmony. By the time she writes *Tales of Love*, Kristeva has realized the need to theoretically fill out her explication of the linguistic foundations for developing nonantagonistic forms of intersubjectivity. Subjectivity emerges as an intentionality directed toward an ideal metaphoricity (or inexhaustible desire to produce meaning); this intentionality both exceeds the preexisting symbolic order and sets up the need for the real (communication). Thetic identity, while partially rooted in a defense against dissolution and the narcissistic desire for masterful agency over language, thus belies an incipient social orientation to surpass this mastering posture in the direction of the real. The real denotes establishing productive connections to other humans within a shared set of meanings as opposed to remaining enveloped in various pseudoprivate worlds, attained either through quasi-psychotic forms of dislocation or by indulging neurotic fantasies which enclose the subject in a stoic inability to experience social relations in an open, vulnerable, and affectively rich fashion. On this basis Kristeva models love, which neutralizes narcissistic identification, after a dialectic between socialness and responsibility. Developing an increasingly stable predisposition to intensify one's affective investment in the real is to ground the meaning of one's life in intersubjective human relations (as opposed to finding release solely through cathexes which promote the fantasmatic distortions peculiar to stoic consciousness, whether fetishistic or paranoic).[18] At the same time, intensifying one's rootedness in intersubjective relations cannot, dialectically speaking, simply transfer meaning from self (narcissism) to alter (hysteria). One must strike a balance between hysteria and narcissism, between the pleasures of socialness and the need to assume ethical responsibility for one's needs for meaning.

Following Freud, Kristeva hypothesizes that autoerotic drives are originary, "there from the very first," whereas "something must be added to autoeroticism—a new psychical action—in order to bring about narcissism" (TL, 22, quoting Freud). Presupposing that the autoerotic state is one of chaos, Kristeva claims that this pre-Oedipal psychic formation literally produces spatiality, the structure of emptiness. The protosubject emerges as the tension between emptiness and narcissism:

> the *emptiness* that is intrinsic to the beginnings of the symbolic function appears as the first separation of what is not yet an *Ego* and what is not yet an *object*. Might narcissism be a means for protecting that emptiness? But against what?—a protection of emptiness (of "arbitrariness," of the "gaping hole") through the display of a decidedly narcissistic parry, so that emptiness can be maintained, lest chaos prevail and borders dissolve. Narcissism protects emptiness, causes it to exist, and thus, as lining of that happiness, insures an elementary separation. (24)

Here Kristeva identifies the protoexistential activity of producing organized space as the intrasymbolic foundation for taking pleasure in the real in two senses: it prepares the infant for the ability to represent the world in terms of shared symbolic meanings; and it prepares a proto-intersubjective connection between the infant and the (m)other without basing that connection upon a desire to eliminate the (m)other's alterity.

First and central to Kristeva's account is that primary "narcissan" identification establishes the protosubject both through a defensive repression of immersion in the autoerotic, chaotic immediacy of drives and by setting up a qualitatively new desire. That desire, which effectuates thetic identity via separation, marks a qualitative change of mere drive pulsions into an affective need for the real: "The child, with all due respect to Lacan, not only *needs* the real and the symbolic—it signifies itself as a child, in other words as the subject that it is, and neither as a psychotic nor as an adult, in the zone where *emptiness and narcissism*, the one upholding the other, constitute the zero degree of imagination" (24). Second and more important still, pre-Oedipal identification structures this emergent desire around a ternary structure: protosubject, proto-(m)other, ideal metaphorical Other. This triadic structure makes possible nonpossessive intersubjective relations; although, according to Kristeva, the triadic basis of selfhood collapses into an imaginary dyadic configuration with the solidification of thetic identity, through the Oedipal drama, into a narcissistic or mastering position which entails "denial of otherness."[19]

Extending the premise that the condition of possibility for attaining harmonious intersubjective relations is an intrasymbolic basis, Kristeva claims that the ternary structure of primary identification contains the seed for realizing that there is no inherent conflict between individuation and affective bonding to another person. The capacity for adult amatory identification, or "the assimilation of other people's feelings," stems from the first identification characteristic of the oral phase, a "nonobjectal identification . . . that sets up love, the sign, repetition at the heart of the psyche" (25). Love is possible because primary identification entails reduplication of a pattern without needing to cathect the pattern as an object, i.e., as completely separate. "When the object that I incorporate is the speech of the other—precisely a nonobject, a pattern, a model—I bind myself to him in a primary fusion, communion, unification. Identification." The pleasure found in "chewing, swallowing, nourishing oneself . . . with words" lays the foundation, not simply for the pleasures of speech acquisition, but for a genuinely social pleasure (26).[20]

Because the relation of the infant (protosubject) to the (m)other emerges through identification with a third (metaphorical Other), primary identification channels desire toward the metaphorical Great Other; this fact makes possible a social desire in which self-other relations are neither possessive nor repressive (29).[21] By hypothesizing that the metaphorical nonobject is the ground of intersubjective desire, Kristeva undercuts the Lacanian view that metonymic desire founds subjectivity in a set orientation toward phallic control over meaning. Here she decenters the Lacanian and Sartrean tendency to reify desire around an antagonistic struggle against others for control over meaning. She argues,

> Metonymic object of desire. Metaphorical object of love. The former controls the phantasmatic *narrative*. The latter outlines the *crystallization* of fantasy and rules the poeticalness of the discourse of love. (30)

Kristeva depicts pre-Oedipal identification with the alterity, not of another, but of meaning as an *original parousia* which suffuses all intersubjective possibilities. The intentionality which sustains personal identity is, thus, oriented toward the intrinsic alterity of language as something which brings nonmeaning into meaning. In this psychical action, drives become sublated in a fundamentally productive orientation toward nonmeaning such that the polysemic nature of metaphoricity provides the condition of creative self-realization.

Yet during pre-Oedipal identification as well as throughout Oedipalization, two levels of affective desire are conflated in the individual psyche: the *intrasubjective desire to be*, as a productive orientation toward expressing one's alterity in meaningful ways, and the *intersubjective desire for recognition*, as love or the desire to exist for another as wholly present and thus to exist for oneself as complete. These two levels of desire are *analytically separable* as well as *psychologically differentiable*; indeed, the goal of therapy can be defined as bringing about their separation in the individual consciousness. The psychological condition of surpassing antagonistic forms of self-alter interaction is learning to differentiate the desire for self-expression from the felt need for idealized collapse into another person. The discourse of love is, in the final analysis, the discourse of the fantasy of the ideal loving Other which enables us to come to terms with the real.[22]

Following Freud, Kristeva treats harmonious loving relations as a "secondary, mediate identification" that recovers this "primary, direct identification," thereby resolving the conflictual Oedipal struggles that ensued and were marked by a felt conflict between covetous identification and a taboo against fusion with the maternal body (TL, 27, quoting Freud). Mediately recovering the moment of primary identification does not necessarily mean that I remember when "I" chronologically came to be; instead it means that I engage the activity first set up as the "zero degree of imagination." In therapeutic adjustment, the analyst provides the occasion for the analysand to merge the idealized identification with the metaphorical object of one's forgotten primary process with a love object (an actual person). But, by showing that s/he is fallible, the analyst indirectly allows the analysand to see that "idealizing distance [is the] condition for the very existence of [her/his] psychic space" (31). "[S/h]e creates the space of transference," wherein the analysand could separate "the emergence of a *metaphorical object*" from its previously truncated outlet in the desire for a "narcissistic merger with the maternal container" (31).

In this space, the analysand can come to terms with primal repression because the initial "splitting that establishes the psyche" is now recovered by "bend[ing] the drive toward a symbolic other" (31).[23] Put otherwise, the analysand comes to terms with the groundlessness of her identity, with the fact that her subjectivity is the border between nonmeaning and meaning (zero degree of imagination), hangs over the vortex of death and life forces, and comprises a tension between alterity and identity. All that we could be is not expressed in our present identity; accepting ourselves as "works in progress" means to become capable of loving the stranger in ourselves and, on this basis, to differentiate between the desire for creative growth (exploration of one's nonidentity or unrealized possibilities) and the need for a beloved other to supply me a total and immediate sense of completion (*parousia*). The joys of creative dialogue must come to surpass the demand for ideal recognition which is, finally, an impossibility given that all subjects are incomplete works in progress. The desire for intersubjective recognition then shifts away from demanding that we be ideal mirror reflections to sharing in each other's respective processes of creative growth.

3.3 Tipping the Scales against Death or Social Attunement?

The Kristevan premise that *parousia*, or an intrasubjective orientation toward language, makes possible harmonious intersubjective relations is compelling. Something akin to a *parousia*-like orientation toward alterity must uphold intersubjective desire, otherwise social relations would be doomed to collapse into antagonistic struggles unto death. Yet Kristeva's Freudian assumptions impede her effort to break with a sacrificial logic. At a foundational level, drive pulsions, though organized through semiotic intonation and symbolic meaning, nonetheless retain a transhistorical structure for Kristeva. Rather than characterize the existential desire for the real as an unfolding of a more original prosocial desire, she assumes that an autoerotic state is foundational, and thereby posits an original asociality at the root of human existence. I want to show that due to this supposition, the weft of her prosocial conception of existential intentionality unravels on its biological warp.

First, Kristeva cannot fully maintain the hypothesis that the existential desire for the real marks a radical, qualitative transformation of rudimentary, asocial libidinal cathexes into a decisive preference for social pleasure.[24] Given that subjectivity emerges as an ambiguous defensive/productive bending of the death drive into the service of life, the existential desire for the real appears to be an ambiguous curtailment and redirection of a an original antisocial pleasure and not its complete qualitative transformation. It follows, second, that the ability to live with this tension between life and death impulses, while refusing to transfer it onto self-other relations, can only occur through a psychic activity weighty enough to counteract the death drive. Kristeva posits this counterweight as *idealized identification* with another person, as the hysterical seed of love.[25] These Freudian underpinnings lead Kristeva to reify historically specific conceptions of romance as necessary features of psychosexual development. And they undermine her justification that harmonious forms of intersubjectivity are preferable to antisocial pleasures. In the end, I believe, she can only account for why humans should develop an existential preference for socialness on biodeterminist grounds, i.e., as an effect of the natural tendency of matter to reproduce itself in qualitatively higher forms of life.

The Hysterical Orientation of Love

Particularly worrisome is the fact that Kristeva reifies romantic love as a necessary and universal vehicle for outweighing the desire to lapse back into either the psychotic world of relatively private meanings or the borderline world of vertiginous pleasures such as those found in fetishism. Because our bonds to other human beings within *the real world of shared meanings* are ambivalent, idealized identification simultaneously harbors the seed of sympathetic interaction and reproduces the very hysteria she attributes to border cases where separation is incomplete.[26] Romantic love thus refers to the activity of fusing one's idealized orientation toward metaphoricity to idealized identification with another person. Kristeva's love ethic, which moves toward an ideal of balancing narcissism (inability to be loved) with hysteria (an impossible demand for immediacy), may offer an exacting account of how many people divest themselves of their Oedipal baggage. But it is less compelling as an account of a necessary stage in the development of social orientation as such.

The strength of Kristeva's account consists in her demonstration that affective investment in the real (metaphoricity and shared meanings) is simultaneously affective attachment to a peopled reality (to other subjects). Yet only because she assumes that infancy begins in an autoerotic state must she demonstrate that the idealized orientation toward metaphoricity is not a solipsistic or individualistic pathway. The premise of autoeroticism places undue burdens on her theory of intentionality. The inaugural birth of the intention to communicate not only must be so miraculous that it compensates for psychic digressions back toward the vertiginous pleasures of dissolution, but it should somehow win back the vertiginous pleasures of immediacy in the face-to-face encounter with the other.[27] Otherwise even the pleasure of speech might not sufficiently bind me to harmonious interaction with others.

Thus, the Freudian assumption—of an original devouring state—precludes claiming that our ideal orientation constitutes a purely prosocial outlet for the innate desire to devour. The ego arises through partial repression of the cannibalistic drive to devour the (m)other: "my libido had to be restrained; my thirst to devour had to be deferred and displaced to a level one may well call 'psychic'" (26).[28] This deferral of cannibalism which maintains emptiness must fuse the subject to another person. As a defense against the (allegedly) primordial state of chaos (vortex of drives), identity shifts autoerotic pleasure into a new level of ambivalence, i.e., fearful love of plunging into the disorienting, vertiginous pleasures experienced in rushing back toward chaotic immediacy. Idealized identification with another person, via transference or romantic love, sublates these joys of death by catapulting me back into this disorientating vertigo and promises a recovery of immediacy in the face-to-face encounter.

What makes this account disturbing is not its failure to descriptively resemble the actual pathway of many people's lives, but instead its inability to differentiate between a historically specific structuring of desire and valorizing submission to another as a necessary stage in psychological maturation.[29] Admittedly this state of disorientation can be productive therapeutically and existentially. Yet because intentionality (desire for the real) is posited as a secondary development, it manifests not as creative longing for a mediated return to an original social pleasure but instead as idealized collapse into another person, into loss of self. Instead of interpreting this idealized dissolution as a failure to develop a preexisting social orientation—a failure based upon psychological immaturity within a specific set of cultural, familial, and material expectations of the adolescent—Kristeva reifies the desperate longing for idealized identification as a necessary compensatory mechanism for loss of immersion in corporeal and libidinal immediacy.

The idea that psychological development must pass through a phase of self-abandonment stems from two false assumptions. These are (i) that autoeroticism is our original way of being and (ii) that idealized love reflects a compensatory phase in transforming asocial pleasures into socialness rather than a misguided attempt to realize an original social yearning. Both these assumptions make Kristeva unable to factor the gender-differential into her analysis of romantic notions of idealized identification because love must bend the death drive in the service of life. Rather than see such cultural notions as ideological, she simply accepts the hysterical element in idealized collapse as a necessary occurrence. Instead of criticizing such ideals for placing an uneven burden on women in relationships and in their psychological development, she treats idealized identification as a therapeutically productive phenomenon and not simply a therapeutically requisite clean-up job.

Kristeva's genius is evident in that she recognizes the need to show how our orientation toward self-expressiveness entails affective investment not simply in language but also in others; thus, one could not abstractly and individually move toward self-realization while stoically related to others. We become increasingly autonomous within intersubjective relations by becoming edified in the capacity to critically mediate our intentions, desires, and needs. Even so, both the idea that drives are innately cannibalistic and the view that idealized identification must be structured around a complete and massive transference of all pleasure to an, admittedly imaginary, ideal person promote rather than challenge patriarchal fantasies about woman. The former lends itself to mythic images of man's emergence from out of a state of nature into a civilized form of fraternal bonding and codifies abjection of the mother as primary object of need as the condition of achieving fraternity. As Kristeva says, I can only calm the vortex of emptiness, the possible slip back into nonexistence or autoeroticism, by strengthening "the defense of the narcissistic ego" (43). This feat is accomplished by absorbing the mother and, in her place, creating the "whole contrivance of imagery, representations, identifications, and projections" which create the imaginary idealized object of my desire (42). And this latter idealized fantasy life inadvertently sustains the sacrificial logic of patriarchy which encourages women to give themselves up to an idealized yet real Other and not to their own creativity.

Allegedly the orientation toward the metaphorical Other promises women agency. Separating the ideal relation toward self-expressiveness from the felt need for an idealized lover promises to give women an autonomous role as cocreators of meaning. Yet this account fails to address how this ideal of romantic love has been historically correlated to an unequal burden distributed to males and females in heterosexual patriarchal relations. Rather than see idealized identification as an effect of specific cultural conditions, Kristeva proposes it as a prescriptive cure for the asymmetrical development of men and women resultant from the fact that both men and women tend to value themselves solely through the eyes of men. The root cause of this problem in Kristeva's work is that she assumes that our ontological or original way to be is autoerotic rather than protosocial or proto-intersubjective. This is, I think, a problematic holdover from Freud's theory of psychosexual development. And it impedes addressing the extent to which not only our romantic ideals but also our assumptions about death and the void reflect patriarchal social practices. Both the premise that humans necessarily experience the groundlessness of their existence as a vertiginous and deathlike slide into the vortex of chaos and the assumption that idealized identification is a necessary counterweight to the death drive reproduce, rather than critically challenge, the patriarchal socialization of desire.[30]

Kristeva's Biodeterminism

Kristeva's tale depicts how love wins against the tragicomic struggle with the death drive (TL, 31). It is a story about how humans can tip the balance of life and death slightly in favor of the excessive pleasures found in language over against a theologization

of the original murder of somatic autoeroticism requisite to found
the social order. Instead of theologically reifying the founding
sacrifice, we open the pathway to love. And yet this is a story, I
believe, which can only partially account for why I should be motivated to find greater pleasure in tipping the scales against death
through love. There are other ways to tip the scales, after all.
Kristeva's partially convincing answer is health. Yet how can one
measure the pleasures of health against the thrills of psychosis if,
indeed, there is a form of pleasure more original than social pleasure, a pleasure that stems from autoerotic enclosure rather than
from an original socialness between two or more beings?

Kristeva does argue that the infant needs the real. Certainly
we can all grasp that there is a kind of relief in psychic health
which is absent in less healthy pursuits. My point is that Kristeva
cannot account for why this *existential need of the real* would promote nonhysterical forms of identification as its best possible outlet
unless the need for the real stems from a more original and primary ontological orientation toward socialness. There are numerous ways, after all, to recover the vertiginous pleasures of
cannibalism, dissolution, and rejection. If socialness is compensatory for loss of a more original asocial yet primary orientation, why
should we prefer more sober pleasures of shared communication
and of striving for mutual understanding? Why not, for example,
simply prefer fetishism? Why not take pleasure in regressing toward vertiginous pleasure without on that account lapsing entirely
into psychosis? Or why not, rather, simply give in to death either
through psychosis or sociopathic behavior or hatred?

Without developing an alternative ontology of social desire,
Kristeva can only invoke the specter of the material basis of drive
impulses to account for why humans prefer the existential desire
for the real and for psychic health over other more phantasmic
pleasures and states of being. In RP, Kristeva appeals to a kind of
Freudo-Leninist theory of matter to develop an answer to this
question and I believe she never abandons this foundation. Following Freud, Kristeva holds that all psychic energy follows the basic
principle governing matter, namely, to seek to arrive at a state of
equilibrium. This material principle manifests in higher-order processes, like psychic health, as an equilibrium. The psychologically
normal person has achieved a balance between the transgressive
pleasures dictated by the drives themselves and adjustment to
reality, i.e., the fact of interdependence dictated by necessity or
survival. Measured in this way, love appears to offer the most

fruitful possibility of reconciliation or health because it rests upon rejecting the intrinsic antagonism between life and death. In love, one's nostalgia for an original autoerotic immersion in the maternal body is resolved in favor of being subjects in process, subjects who bend death in favor of life and thus balance hysteria (death) with life (sober social pleasures).

But, in order to clarify what gives force to the existential desire to supersede the purer pleasures of death drives, Kristeva's work must fall back on a deterministic theory of matter which propels this movement toward equilibrium. Without a transhistorical and transcendental notion of matter, it remains unclear why the logic of renewal, which, like Freud's life drive, reproduces tensions on a qualitatively new level, should supervene over the pleasure at a prior level, i.e., over the pull of the death drive back to a lower stage of development. It seems that Kristeva is somehow claiming that life drives, which press matter to evolve into higher-order processes, are structured so as to win out over death drives. But, like Freud, she must also maintain that "Thanatos is pure while Eros has, since the beginning been permeated by Thanatos" (31). Kristeva must claim that the fundamental organization of all drive processes is death oriented in order to sustain the very negativity which exceeds socialization and thus accounts for the motivation to self- and social change as well as cuts off any false and static utopian belief that there can be a perfect sublation of drives into the social order.

Kristeva needs the notion of negativity in order to explicate that there are sources of motivation which exceed every form of life and thus enable critique. While I agree that desire must exceed the effects of socialization, this deterministic theory of matter leaves Kristeva with this dilemma: either she adheres to a biodeterminist model in which matter exceeds itself by its own principle, thereby effectively excising the existential sources of motivation; or the existential orientation toward metaphoricity must stem from an original socialness of human nature. Since the former material foundation collapses motivational life into drive impulses and their naturalistic evolution, talk of existential motivations as critically mediating one's drive-based and affective life, although not rendered meaningless, is depleted of much of its significance. Free agency proves a largely inexplicable outgrowth of natural development. Beyond a certain threshold drive-based impulses miraculously transform into deliberate capacities via their linguistification.

It does not suffice, I think, to account for existential agency as a quasi-naturalistic impulse. This drive-based view threatens to conflate mere return of the repressed with critique, mere eruption of semiotic modifications of meaning with critical and free opposition to social conditions rather than naive, even nondeliberate resistance. I suggest that the force of negativity must stem from an original protosocialness of human being, rather than the ambivalence of life and death drives presupposed by the Freudian-Lacanian tradition in which death reigns as the purer principle. The very ability to harness destructive impulses in favor of life processes presupposes a form of desire which itself cannot be reduced to a drive. A Freudian residue of material pleasure outside sociality reflects not simply a latent individualism but also a tacit determinism in Kristeva's works.

3.4 Toward a Social Ontology

Kristeva depicts the metaphorical relation as inaugurating the possibility of forms of socialness which exceed the dynamics of transference and countertransference (Oedipal dynamics); and she names pleasure, not simply defense, as an original motivation for developing metaphorical capacity and a sense of subjectivity. Yet because she erects identification with the metaphorical Other on an ambivalent foundation, she can account for the striving to prefer social pleasures only on evolutionary grounds. Ontogenetically, individuals in present-day societies, through therapy and existential edification, stretch toward the capacity to decenter and mitigate the effects of their drive impulses and socialization. Kristeva has it backwards, I suggest: it is not that we evolve the ability to behave in non-narcissistic ways and, indeed, to even enjoy doing so. Precisely an original socialness accounts for how humans arrive at a sustained capacity to enjoy forms of pleasure which exceed, even as they allow for, the dynamics of transference and thus develop these original possibilities for nontransference-based forms of social bonding. Because such a socialness is real, even in infancy, alternative forms of socialization are possible in the here and now.[31]

More importantly, her Freudian assumptions keep her working within a somewhat reductive account of social pleasure. Here social pleasure looks like a barely attainable ability to decenter narcissism rather than a rich love of alterity. There is some validity, for example, to her ethical notion that overcoming fear of one's own alterity contributes an important ingredient to relating well to others. Nonetheless, this model brings us only to the capacity *not* to resist projecting alterity onto others (Kristeva's mediation of separation) without *in addition* addressing how humans develop the capacity to understand perspectives for which they lack all personal experience to grasp. The capacity to bridge horizons or, as María Lugones calls it, to engage in "world-traveling" into another person's horizon presupposes that humans have a fully productive, rather than ambivalent, orientation toward alterity. Although I may benefit from world-traveling in that it may expand my understanding, the value of recognition for each party need not be reduced to ego-gratification. The desire for recognition and to give recognition extends beyond the difficulties of Oedipal crisis; that is, it extends beyond the therapeutic need to come to terms with one's memories and personal biography. There is a level of creative expression which exceeds Oedipalization and which allows us to give creative attention to others and to bridge horizons. This creative attention is a social pleasure which cannot ultimately be reduced to psychological needs, even as it might incorporate, mitigate, or become subverted by psychological difficulties.[32]

While the capacity to move beyond amorous identification may occur chronologically late in psychological maturation, I suggest that the basis for developing this capacity originates from an ontological possibility which is logically prior to the dynamics of narcissistic structuration and thus allows for a decentering of Oedipal-based needs to a higher degree than Kristeva's model affords. A better model of *parousia* stems from Heidegger's intuition that human existence is ontologically based upon a relation to the absentiality or the excess manifest in all things as what is not yet present and thus has not yet achieved meaning (i.e., been articulated in language). If becoming an idealized Other for myself (internalizing a loving gaze toward myself) is a developmental necessity in the process of relating to other humans in nonstoic ways, then it also cannot provide the sufficient condition for relating to others in nonpossessive and non–ego-centered ways. Instead of reifying idealization as a counterweight to autoeroticism, we need to recognize that the critique of dominating forms of intersubjectivity presupposes a memory of a more original protosociality; it presupposes original forms of sensual pleasure which are broader than libidinal gratification (i.e., drive cathexes, sublimation of drives into affective investment in language and other people).[33]

In his 1929 inaugural lecture at Freiburg, Heidegger defines the ontologically ecstatic basis of human existence as a form of "creative longing." Because humans are held out toward the absentiality in all beings, human and nonhuman, their primary connection to all things stems from wonder; they can question and reflect; they implicitly experience their own existence as a kind of excitement which stands "in secret alliance with the cheerfulness and gentleness of creative longing" (BW, 108/W, 15). I find Heidegger's insight, that human existence obtains as an ecstatic relation to the dynamic presencing of all things, a fruitful and plausible thesis. This insight can ground the Kristevan account of affective investment in the metaphorical process of creating new meanings without structuring desire as hysterical. The Heideggerian notion of attunement enables us to work toward a social ontology in which intersubjectivity and intrasubjective relations to meaning are co-original. Moreover, because alterity proves an ontological facet of all being, humans need not experience alterity in ambivalent terms. This foundation allows for a richer possibility of recovering a critically mediated relation to alterity as an adult. It allows for a form of love which finds repose in difference rather than merely derives narcissistic ego-gratification from another, even from letting the other be different from me. It encompasses and includes the transference dimensions of relationship, without reducing relationships to transference love.

Heidegger's notion that there is a fundamental attunement of Dasein to all beings articulates the idea that humans could never develop reflective capacities had they not an original awareness of the basic alterity or nonidentity held back in every modal presencing of a particular being. Although Heidegger, like most existential thinkers, fails to provide an ontogenetic account of identity-formation, this ontological insight leads to an alternative, non-Freudian developmental theory. It implies that the infant, although not yet a self-reflective subject who can symbolically represent itself, begins with a rudimentary social attunement which precedes processes of identification, i.e., the process of developing subject-identity via identification with an alter (= via language acquisition and through intersubjectivity or *Mitsein*). This rudimentary attunement suggests that, contrary to Kristeva's view, humans begin neither in a state of autoerotic enclosure nor as simple bundles of libidinal cathexes. To the contrary, this attunement presupposes a rudimentary awareness of difference, of the dynamic revelation of things as protodistinct from one's own protosubjectivity. More important still, it establishes the development of reflexive capacity as occurring from out of an original protoawareness of intersubjectivity.[34]

Thus, we can talk about "creative longing" as a desire for creative self-expression, yet this would be potentially misleading since it implies an individualistic natural orientation. For Heidegger, our ecstatic orientation toward alterity is simultaneously an orientation toward the absentiality in other things and in ourselves. Translating this insight into Oedipal terms means that creative longing manifests as a dynamic orientation toward discovering the possibilities of proto-others and in that manner discovering the possibilities of the protoself. The desire for creative expression is not inherently narcissistic (not self-centric) because it operates prior to the development of reflexive capacity and is intimately bound up with the disclosure of other things. The awareness that I cannot know myself transparently is co-original with grasping the impossibility of capturing anything *in toto*. Not only do I discover what I am capable of becoming actively through developing competencies, but I make meaningful sense out of my possibilities in part by exploring how other things and other people develop differently than do I. In the end, Heidegger's insight leads to the view that intersubjectivity grounds subjectivity both because we develop in a world of shared meanings and because we discover our individuated possibilities for identity through engagement with the ontological disclosure of other beings.

By setting Kristeva's model of ecstatic orientation toward metaphoricalness back onto a social ontology, we can avoid several Kristevan difficulties. (1) We undercut the need to describe the inexhaustible movement toward new possibilities for meaningful forms of life as a hysterical transfer of libidinal drives. To the contrary, because humans begin with a sense of repose in relation to alterity, sympathetic attunement rather than hysterical identification proves foundational in human existence. (2) By thinking *parousia* in ontological and linguistic terms, we postulate that a proto-intersubjective attunement to beings is co-original with a protolinguistic orientation toward metaphoricalness. This double foundation corrects the individualistic basis of Kristeva's theory implicit in her notion of autoeroticism. Thus it accounts for the rich ways that humans not only escape but transform narcissism and hysteria into social pleasures; it explains why humans prefer socialness to transference love; and it allows that, with alternative patterns of socialization, humans might not need to valorize culturally specific ideals of romance. (3) Finally, by postulating an attunement to (proto)beings as an original affect, we retain the thick affective investment in language which Kristeva theorizes while avoiding the biodeterminist implication of grounding affective life solely in biology. By showing that language and ontology, that creatively altering meaning and developing dispositions, are intertwined, we need not slip into a thin, overly cognitive model which locates agency in the slippage of meaning. We can show that affective investment in language stems from a rich, protosocial investment in real beings.

I want to be clear. I am using Heidegger against Heidegger. I have argued that it is Heidegger's great failing to divorce his articulation of the ontological relation to absentiality from intersubjective relations. In *Being and Time*, Heidegger gives us a false either/or choice: either fall into average intersubjective modes of communication or discover your individuated self-expression alone before death.[35] Repose in Being proves largely antithetical to intersubjective relations. Heidegger reifies ambivalence at an existential level when he posits the achievement of self-transformation in stoic abstraction from socialness and identifies the self's voluntaristic appropriation of alterity independently of developing a critical relation to social formations. Still, there is nothing in Heidegger's fundamental concept of creative longing, as rooted in an ecstatic relation to the dynamic presencing of oneself and other beings, which is inherently antisocial or individualistic. Where early Heidegger posits a voluntaristic view of will as categorically transcending (in a radical act of appropriation) the effects of psychology and society, Kristeva offers rich explorations of the complexity of desire and the difficulties of self-transformation. Yet Heidegger supplies the insight that our relation to alterity is original and thus grounds forms of existential desire which exceed libidinal and psychological pleasures of ego-gratification.

When Heidegger misnames the activity whereby I recover distance on accepted narratives a "non-relational" moment before death, he posits the creation of new, critical meanings as a lone, maverick praxis of defying shared meanings (SZ, 263). Instead, this "non-relational" moment should have been called the second mediation of an original social attunement, an overcoming of narcissism rather than of socialness. Despite what Kristeva maintains, when we are able to delimit narcissism and our ego-based projects, we recover, not the crisis of emptiness (death drives) and the necessity of abjection, but rather the simple creative desire to be, the dynamic movement toward self-unfolding within communities of shared meaning. Yet also in contrast to early Heidegger's formulation, recovering awareness of the irreducibility of one person to that of another does not stem from a "non-relational" moment before death in which I break with intersubjective relations. It marks, instead, a preliminary breaking with one's own socialization into a narcissistic ego or rigid identity. Developing a sense of one's unique creative orientation can only occur through interaction with others, through modes of engagement that draw alternative possibilities out of me, that enable me to develop capacities, as well as allow others not to be like me yet to be with me. Yet even this process stems from a pleasure that exceeds its benefits for me. The desire to "be" rather than to have is, as the later Heidegger says, without why, without utility.[36]

I am arguing that what comes later—the ability to revel in social attunement—presupposes the original possibility that human intentionality does not originate with ego-formation and the felt need for idealized identification. Social attunement, its rudimentary form as well as latent possibilities for development, precedes identification. The very language of transference and identification is ego-centered and renders socialness a developmental compensation for an original disconnection or autoeroticism, i.e., an inability to reach others. Identification counteracts disconnection by satisfying a primary need. The notion of attunement, by contrast, suggests that fears of emptiness (loss of meaning) emerge through socialization; our ability to be vulnerable before others and before our own creative possibilities without anxiety implies that such fears are not ontologically necessary. Rather than root socialness in the abjection of chaos—a thesis which leaves anxiety about chaos intact—the possibility of harboring no anxiety about difference, of experiencing no sense of loss or emasculation in being interdependent and connected, of finding value in the pleasures of social attunement for their own sake, requires an ontological theory that places inquisitiveness, wonder, and repose at the base of human existence. This repose does not rest on the premise that the abyss is necessarily experienced by humans as vertigo, as a vortex which causes ambivalent repulsion and attraction. This view reifies the shadow of the self as the incorrigible longing for the rush of dissolution with its attendant fear of being devoured by maternal space. While attributing to patriarchal symbolic systems responsibility for mythic figurations of the feminine as devouring, Kristeva leaves abjection of the maternal intact because she assumes that identity-formation rests upon rejection of fusion with the maternal body. Thus, she erects the abyss as a Nietzschean vortex which permanently evokes vertiginous pleasure.

Heidegger's basic and enduring insight, that humans are ecstatically oriented toward the simultaneous presencing and absencing of all beings, supplies precisely the protosocial, ontological foundation that is missing in Kristeva's work. Rather than postulate that protosubjectivity emerges in tandem with terror before the chaos of emptiness, we can only account for the fact that humans do attain harmonious relations by assuming an alternative hypothesis. We must assume an original repose before the void, a productive desire to realize possibilities, in order to account for the fact that humans do not simply learn to manage psychological anxiety but indeed find beauty and repose in their *inability* to master the disclosure of others. This is a fact that moves us beyond a concept of love rooted in being grateful that the other does not abuse my idealized identification with her or him.[37] Early Heidegger and Kristeva alike use the wrong language and the wrong experiences to depict creative self-longing as facing death. I recast Heidegger's insight not in terms of ontological anxiety before the abyss, but rather as an ontological vulnerability and openness to alterity. This interpretation finds confirmation in his later shift to the language of proximity and nearness, to that of repose.

3.5 Willingness Not Willed Self-Appropriation

Locating the origin of creative longing in a Heideggerian social ontology need not wed us to a species of voluntarism. Humans do not have unmediated access to this longing independently of socialization into language and material conditions. To the extent that a concept of willed self-appropriation (a) implies that humans can muster up a radical decision that sharply and instantaneously breaks with psychosomatic habits, (b) renders the epistemic and psychic effects of material circumstance inconsequential, and (c) thoroughly overrides the unconscious, it traps us in voluntarism and a stoic logic, theoretically and practically. Yet intentions are often efficacious even as their efficacy does not protect fully against the unpredictable operation of the unconscious nor simply melt those core dispositions solidified into identity. A better depiction of intentionality can be had by reinterpreting the existential theory of self-choice (Sartre) or willed self-appropriation (early Heidegger) as pointing to an attitude of willingness to undergo change.

Here willingness refers to one of manifold factors constitutive of a person's complex motivational and desiring life, and not a will which can de facto override complex dispositional tendencies. That humans can relatively freely adopt an attitude of willingness by no means negates the habitual momentum of desire or the complex epistemic effects of social conditions. Yet adopting an attitude of willingness to critically examine the sources of one's motives, fantasies, and identity is a difference that makes a difference. Willingness funds the intention requisite to foster the often long-term process of transforming desire, perception, and identity; it fosters the ability to recognize one's fallibility by anticipating that one's unconscious could be operative in unforeseeable ways. Its ethical import lies in that it provides some kind of immediate check against questionable tendencies in my behavior and allows me to factor my fallibility into decision-making processes. Critically anticipating that I could be wrong may curtail my actions or at least predispose me to change if, indeed, all does not turn out well.

The enduring significance of existential thought consists in an admittedly overzealous effort to isolate the fact that such an attitude is freely adopted. I say overzealous because existential thinkers often imply that we can willfully transform the entirety of our complex fantasy and desiring lives, and by extension our complete attitude, on a dime. By contrast, psychoanalysis indicates that no human can call every aspect of her identity into question at a given point in time. The human psyche relies upon a core set of competencies; these core habits, even if instilled later in life through the laborious process of replacing original convictions with critically informed ones, nonetheless can be impediments to ethical action in novel situations just as much as they often promote a readiness to meet up to the unexpected ethical appeal of other persons. In addition, lived social conditions can drain humans of much of the emotional energy requisite to retain an attitude of psychic flexibility and openness to challenge. Nonetheless, we can and should hold ourselves ethically responsible for such failures of attitude because there is a relative degree to which we can freely question some aspects of our identity from within extraordinarily oppressive situations. While that recognition neither alleviates my social situation nor miraculously breaks the weighty shackles of my identity, it isolates the fact that, under most conditions, humans have some psychic resources for influencing their desires.

The necessity of retaining a concept of willingness is at least twofold. First, we cannot account for agency solely as an effect of drives. Second, I want to reassert the importance of keeping alive the issue of ethical responsibility in any contemporary social theory attempting to deal with deeply entrenched phenomena, like misogyny and antiblack racism. An exclusive focus on subjectivity as the *site* rather than the *subject* of discourse may eclipse the productive role we play in our mimetic identifications. I want to highlight the ever-present possibility of motivated deception thereby implicating us, ethically, both in our early formative and ongoing development. Although children do not have the same awareness of the world that adults do, my analysis presupposes that young children do strive in tandem with and struggle against the process of identity-formation. Moreover, young children do discern power hierarchies and negotiate these in ways they perceive as advantageous. Normal levels of adjustment and normal ranges of desire thus result not solely from onto- and phylogenetic development but from what Fanon, following existential insights, called sociogenic choices which are ongoing.

My first point, then, is that socialization is not a purely top-down process; discursive practices are not simply imposed upon some unformed raw matter called the protosubject or a bundle of biochemical drives. Identity is not simply the total effect of a culturally determined sublation and modification of the infant's pregiven and individuated biochemical composition. Even the infant or protosubject exercises a certain amount of positive willingness or unwillingness to undergo identity-formation and thus to become formed in specific ways through socialization. That willingness is not simply a reaction based upon biological impulses, but already reflects a rudimentary awareness that the infant is a source of potentiality. Kristeva clearly recognizes this when she claims that pleasure must motivate development. Yet she locates this productive source of movement and its positive role in the formation of identity in the excessive energy of drive impulses. I have criticized this view for threatening to collapse agency into a biodeterminist materialism. More to the point, it presupposes that a certain psychic agency, a desire to be, operates prior to primary identification; but this presupposition conflicts with her assumption that infancy begins in a state of fusion. Though inclusive of biological processes, the excessive creative movement must stem from an original orientation, rather than secondary development, of human being.

That creativity arises from the fact that, ontologically speaking, human subjects are temporal, i.e., always oriented metaphorically toward absentiality or possibility. *Pace* Kristeva, this ontologically grounded notion of existential desire implies that, while infants certainly have no self-reflexive ability to posit themselves as speaking subjects, they do begin with a rudimentary awareness, at least by the first few weeks after birth, of their differentiation from other proto-things. Certainly infants and small children are naively related to attitudinal postures and do not have a developed critical relation to culture, social location, and ideology. They nonetheless exercise an element of freedom in adopting attitudes; while reactions to environment, these attitudes cannot be called simple one-to-one effects of environment. Temperamental predispositions to defiance or acceptance are dialectically formed, we could postulate, on the basis of tensions between one's ontological orientation toward creative development and the constraints of social circumstance. The locus of existential resistance arises out of one's fundamental creative orientation, an orientation which exceeds any given form of life even though we only discover our possibilities for identity within a preexisting form of life. Perhaps what we call willfulness in children is a relatively prereflective effort to protect that creativity against felt limitations of its social world.

Secondly, I am arguing that we need to keep alive the existential notion of *willed ignorance* while rejecting voluntarism. In order to avoid voluntaristic implications, I call this a kind of *(un)willingness* rather than *willed choice*. Willingness comprises a definitive and special component informing the formation of existential and habitual dispositions. These habits denote a core repertoire of corporeal-behavioral tendencies but also of creative modifications of one's repertoire; they manifest as active perceptual ways of organizing reality; and they include general patterns of fantasy and emotional reactions even as they allow for the possibility of harnessing outlaw emotions in critical oppositional ways. Such habits may or may not reflect the effects of critique. But in order to theorize the active dimension involved in habit-formation, we must accept that one among numerous elements characteristic of adopting attitudes is deliberate and thus bears ethical import.

Let us take the adoption of racist and misogynistic attitudes as an example. The simple refusal to actively oppose such social formations certainly reflects numerous factors which are constitutive of identity. Education, social values, symbolic matrices, socioeconomic location, and so forth all contribute to, e.g., my inability to see my racial social location as 'white'. As numerous poststructuralists have argued, deep-seated core features of identity are often formed before we have the psychic ability to make critically informed decisions about the influences which lead to their formation. Although in agreement with this claim, I think it would be fundamentally mistaken to confuse lack of an informed adult perspective with innocence. Small children exhibit rudimentary sensibilities which enable them to assess influences. Thus, we must assume that one element contributing to the cognitive and affective distortions constitutive of identity, in addition to the seductive power of culture, is a preferential want to become this (white) rather than that (black) identity, to perform this (pure) as opposed to that (tainted) mode of self-presentation, to assume a particular narrative construction of self (as white).

To become socialized as 'white', Lewis Gordon has argued, is to become identified with the light and goodness. This identification clearly reflects the seductions of an antiblack symbolic system which gives birth to a fantasy life that equates whiteness with moral innocence, purity, and goodness; indeed, the symbolic value of 'white' structures desire as the drive for purity. As Gordon's *Bad Faith* insightfully portrays, these seductions are perverse and they literally pervert one's desires.[38] Upon discovery, as an adult, that I indeed have such perverse desires, it is not false to indict my society, even my family, for the respective roles they played in coercing my early identity-formation. But it would be ethically irresponsible not to acknowledge that, admittedly from a child's-eye view, I contributed to the process because I (must have) wanted, and in many cases continue to want, the recognition associated with, or the material rewards promised by, becoming purity and lightness incarnate.

Just as poststructuralists argue that competencies are ambiguous—both binding us to existing social values and enabling us to critique those values—so too do children learn racial values before they grasp their broader significance. But this ambiguity does not mean that they are not partially free agents who grasp their immediate significance from a child's standpoint. The poststructuralist view of agency as critical re-deployment of socialized competencies presupposes this thick existential view that self-identity, grasped as an ongoing process, entails an element of 'free' acceptance of or resistance to socialization and social location. 'Free' in this context is a qualified term. It suggests that, while I never simply create values by myself or in a vacuum, while I never experience my desires outside the constitutive work of socialization, I am not simply a passive raw material in this process of desire and development. Even as my reactions to and interpretations of social location demonstrate that my desires have been constituted by that location, an element of freedom is evident in my attitudinal life in my preferences, likes, and dislikes. Rather than invoke the specter of

voluntarism by claiming that humans simply will their own ignorance, we can draw out the import of such existential claims by
isolating the active element which coalesces with a variety of factors as co-constitutive of our identities and choices. Humans, then,
are complex social actors, working under material and symbolic
influences as well as already solidified attitudes and habits constitutive of identity and desire and formed in childhood before one
was able to perceive the world in critical ways. We can further note
that the early adoption of attitudes toward racial values by children may not necessarily indicate malicious intent. But it points
nonetheless to a positive striving for social pleasures and for becoming a subject valued by the broader social world. Thus, even
where development occurs by way of a certain naivete about the
broader, adult-governed social and political struggles surrounding
race relations, children nonetheless exercise a certain deliberate
embrace of their possibilities.[39]

It would be profoundly mistaken, then, to confuse naivete with
innocence. That I was naively raised as white does not imply that
I do not share responsibility with my society for my identity and
my desiring life. To operate on the view that I am a largely rational, sincere, and innocent white gal who simply had little chance
before age twenty to encounter black folk and assess false information disseminated about black folk, reflects precisely the element of
freedom involved in motivated deception. Better put, I relate to my
habituated racial beliefs and socially defined fantasies either as not
my fault or as my responsibility. Willingness to assume responsibility for who one is and what one does exceeds the effects of socialization and social location even though those effects are not
eradicated by a feat of will. We can, for this reason, ascribe culpability for who we are, even though we reject institutionalized pun-
ishment of such attitudes and even though we allow for the naivete
of youth as a factor mitigating degree of responsibility.

In this light, we can reinterpret the Kristevan notion of a
"second-degree thetic" as pertaining to the existential desire to be.
In some cases it may be existentially and psychologically difficult
to differentiate between willed ignorance and deeply internalized
patterns of white solipsism. Yet we can analytically differentiate
such factors. Further, we can claim that this is the ethical task: to
strive to differentiate the existential desire for meaning from whatever deeply incorporated desires for whiteness one may have. Willed
ignorance may coincide with a rigid psychic inability to deal with
the limitations of my false beliefs. Still, humans often exhibit both

psychic immaturity and lack of willingness to explore dimensions of their identities. Though counterproductive to attack someone who is psychologically unprepared to see that she is racist, there always remains the next step that any person's psyche can withstand. In lived practice there may be no clean distinction between willingness and fantasy. But we can posit attitude—willingness or unwillingness—as an irreducible dimension of a person's response to the next step in the growth of critical awareness. Racist attitudes may reflect deep-seated, unconscious beliefs, irrational fantasies, and lack of moral development. But we cannot rule out that an element of deliberate, albeit prereflective choice is involved in such processes. Willed ignorance often exhibits a deliberate dimension which exceeds the limitations of psychic immaturity. Critique of identity and ideology is possible because we cannot posit psychic rigidity as the cause of wanting to remain ignorant, any more than we can reduce the complexity of psychic processes to simple effects of willingness to change. There is a dialectical relation between willingness and core dispositions.[40]

There is a difference, however slight, between the person who is willing to entertain the idea that she may be racist and the one who categorically denies it. As I age, I realize that the effects of patriarchy on my psyche more than likely will not be totally transformed in my lifetime. Through a gradual process, however, the psyche can become prepared to abandon habits and to grow sufficiently fed up with its own suffering to become prepared to embrace alternative self-images and cultivate alternative habits. While we may have to wait upon the desire to change, I am suggesting that this waiting indicates an existential willingness that, finally, is a function of attitude. We either are or are not willing to grow and be challenged. Even as that willingness does not make me automatically prepared to have the very ground of my psychology uprooted, it orients me productively toward that possibility. This willingness is funded by an original lack of fear before the creative possibility of transformation and an original sympathetic intersubjective orientation. Willingness, then, is an existential basis for exchanging one set of habits and beliefs for another, one narrative for another even though that exchange is not instantaneous and simply achieved through a macho choice. The possibility of differentiating between critical and naive consciousness stems from this willingness, though a critical relation to society reflects much more than that willingness. It reflects not simply the results of much self-examination but those of systemic analysis of political economy and social institutions. The latter make crucial contributions to the development of newly internalized psychological habits, new competencies, perceptions, and attitudes.

Whatever chemicals we mix into a curative for racist and other entrenched attitudes (e.g., developing multicultural education, cultivating open-ended communities of tolerance, fostering an alternative value system, and transforming political institutions) necessarily remain incomplete and partial. No magic potion can completely cure me and society. By virtue of the finite yet free character of human being, overcoming racist attitudes must entail an active existential dimension to which no past development, no formula, no yogic aesthetic, no Kantian principle, not even the momentum of character can deliver me. That existential dimension refers to the need to renew our attitude toward possibilities and conditions presented to us; this is the element of freedom that requires ethical responsibility for both the affective and reflective aspects of my identity.[41]

PART II

Utopia as Reiterative Universalism

A Poetics of Recognition

CHAPTER 4

A Critical Mimetic Recovery of Origins

Reading Heidegger with Irigaray and Cornell

Psychoanalytic discourse on female sexuality is the discourse of truth. A discourse that tells the truth about the logic of truth: namely, that *the feminine occurs only within models and laws devised by male subjects*. Which implies that there are not really two sexes, but only one. A single practice and representation of the sexual. With its history, its requirements, reverses, lacks, negative(s) . . . of which the female sex is the mainstay. . . . So there is, *for women*, no possible law for their pleasure. . . . Women's enjoyment is—for them, but always according to him—essentially an-archic and a-teleological. For the imperative that is imposed upon them—but solely from the outside, and not without violence—is: "enjoy without law." . . . But men insist that women can say nothing of their pleasure. Thereby they confess the limit of their own knowledge. For "when one is a man, one sees in the woman partner a means of self-support, a footing on which to stand (oneself) narcissistically."

From this point on, does not that ineffable, ecstatic pleasure take the place, for men, of a Supreme Being, whom they need narcissistically but who ultimately eludes their knowledge? Does it not occupy—for them—the role of God?

Luce Irigaray, *This Sex*

Heidegger and Irigaray undertake searches for the 'origin' of metaphysics and of patriarchy, respectively. Each tells a story or mythos about the fall of western thought into a nihilistic historical formation. While their stories differ, each holds that this fall stems from the way that metaphysical systems of categorization institute a world encapsulated in a static conceptual economy governed by

119

a logic of identity; accordingly reality appears as controllable by and accountable to the desire of the knowing (male) subject. Such appeals to a static, ahistorical, and univocal transcendental principle produce subjects with and forms of life based upon truncated sensibilities. Heidegger's story is gender-neutral. It is the story of the synchronic and discontinuous aspects of being historical. For Heidegger, human history inevitably produces formations which are qualitatively greater than the sum total of collective intentions of all human agents. Heidegger tells the story of the fall of human beings into forgetfulness that they do not master meaning, that all reality is shot through with dimensions which cannot be brought under a first principle or final cause. His story suggests that the very compulsion to ground historical life in a final cause and by extension a static utopia of perfect transparency depicts a historically specific and limited ethos binding western humanity together as a collectivity. The felt need to project and represent a foreseeable end of humanity produces a nihilistic ethos; it closes humanity off from the genuine possibility of harmonious coexistence.

Irigaray's story, by contrast, centers on sexuate identity or the social organization of eros, rather than Heidegger's gender-neutral yet passional notion of ethos. She tells a myth about how the libidinal organization of a phallocratic symbolic economy excludes females from having unique sexual desires, independent of the structure of male pleasure. The metaphysical-symbolic foundations of patriarchy, by equating subjectivity with masculine desire, rest upon matricide, i.e., an explicitly sexuate annihilation of an autonomous female desire/sexuality. Phallocratic symbolic systems co-opt female sexuality, manipulate female pleasure, and twist female erotic drive into the service of male pleasure. 'Woman' thus is modeled symbolically as the object of man's satisfaction, his telos, his mythical utopian dream of desire fulfilled, and finally the mirror image of his own desire. If, in Hegelian terms, utopia denotes the historical formation wherein every 'I' will finally become reflected in the 'we', then Irigaray argues that within a phallocratic metaphysics woman's difference must be excluded from the economy of desire defining the meaning of the collectivity. Accordingly, the identitarian dream of symmetrical recognition sets history on an assimilative course which can only be described as nihilistic and dystopian from the standpoint of those who represent difference. This history is doomed to reduce woman to man's image, to exclude all difference, to remain caught in a monotonous cycle of various transmutations of the same erotic subordination of woman (Irigaray, TS, 72–78, 87–100).[1]

Intriguing as these stories are, we might ask, does not every methodology of mimetically recovering origins itself prove an obstacle to overcoming the Hegelian dream of symmetrical recognition? Would not every conception of origin lead back to a fixed telos or final vision of utopia? Every story of the fall, we are told, presupposes an origin from which we fell; this origin contains the hidden seeds of the end to be recovered, the future state of innocence, the lost paradise which overcomes the fall. And would not every search to recover original possibilities, supposedly lost through the fall, not clothe the groundlessness of human existence in a new fantasy about true origins, thereby creating a dangerous new historical yearning for communities whose immediacy spontaneously and transparently proves their validity? Heidegger's involvement in National Socialism led him to desire a community purely transparent to itself and in touch with the original autodisclosive nature of other beings; this yearning inaugurated recovery of communal immediacy as a historical task and clothed this destinal recovery of origins in the idolatrous figure of German humanity's radical other, Woman. Do not, then, Irigaray and late Heidegger simply foster yet additional phantasmic utopian projections of a perfect, ideal, harmonious community in which we get our Eden back? Would not their archeological projects enact new fetishes of the lost (m)other of our current humanity?

In this chapter, I press a reading of Irigaray which stresses the nonessentializing side of her work as a backdrop for a similar reading of Heidegger. There are, minimally, two moments of this reading. First, I emphasize that each demonstrates the necessity of learning to critically mediate the desire for immediacy as central to developing nonviolent forms of social life, rather than pretending that rational ideals could sober up from fantasies of origins once and for all. Whereas Heidegger can readily be charged with essentializing his view of history and Irigaray has often been attacked for essentializing the feminine, I will stress the importance of their focus on mediating origins in fostering alternative sensibilities, affective bonds, and an ethos able to break with a logic of identity.[2] Second, I will show that each contributes to envisioning post-Hegelian ideals of recognition primarily by emphasizing the need for utopian thinking in fostering such models of recognition. This means that, although each continues to work at the most abstract and quasi-metaphysical level of analysis, their works strive to critically delimit evocations of divinity, rather than to pretend that thinking ever occurs without invoking a transcendental that structures desire and utopian ideals.

Although I will later criticize various limitations in Heidegger and Irigaray, my primary objective in this chapter is to use Irigaray's psychoanalytic assessment of utopianism to lay the groundwork for interpreting later Heidegger as breaking with his earlier masculinist vision of utopia. Masculinist utopias are static rationalizations of some objectified lost origin that, projected as the future, symbolizes the possibility of man's self-transcendence. As Irigaray argues, such utopias are romantic and dangerous; they envision peaceful coexistence as a *substantive state* of transparency which, though mediated, no longer entails a radical effort to achieve a critical relationship to what might be completely foreclosed in this way of existing and thinking. Harmonious coexistence, while dynamically mediated in some ways, nonetheless has a static transcendental dimension, since the community attains to its divinity, its final, *formal principle,* which has been and will remain normative for all times. I will explore how Irigaray's thought, though critical of masculine utopianism, retains what Drucilla Cornell calls an "unerasable trace of utopianism" but without lapsing into an uncritical reification of origins and ends.[3] On the basis of this reading, I will demonstrate in chapter 5 that later Heidegger attempts to wake up from the (masculine) fantasy of transcendence, earlier enacted in his reification of the feminine as destiny, by achieving a critical relation to utopian ideals.

Some might still question, how can Irigaray help Heidegger to give up his lust after the lost (m)other-feminine—who functions as the ecstatic transcendence of the male subject either through God or through finding the rational telos of history—when she, too, searches for lost origins? Can Irigaray truly get beyond the sheer fantasy of a new feminine symbolic or matriarchal utopia? To these questions, I give a provisional yes answer. Yes, firstly because we can comprehend the status of an origin neither as some merely relative play of meaning nor as a static or "virginal a priori," but rather as whatever constitutes the suppressed economy of desire supporting a symbolic system (Bigwood, EaM, 24, 34–38). More to the point, however, is the second question whether or not a critical relation to origins can be sustained within any form of utopian thinking. Against the project of critically imagining women's ideal autonomy, many feminists prefer metonymic strategies precisely because, as Cornell explains, they expose the "power of the discourses that form women, but not in the name of authentic Woman."[4] In order to steer beyond a logic of identity, should not feminism rest content with the *deconstructive* work of unmasking the subju-

gating effects of discursive practices, while rejecting any reconstruction of a univocal ideal of woman's autonomy?

Much is at stake in feminist debates about utopian thinking.
For many, every attempt to imagine a normative ideal of women's
liberated sexual autonomy inevitably leads to essentialism on both
substantive and formal grounds. Substantively, the foundationalist
search to depict the singular contours of woman's gender oppression (across race, class, ableism, and such) has proven falsely universal and essentializing. There simply is no universal womanhood,
no single kind of gender oppression, nor consequently a univocal
ideal of woman's autonomy which would correct for women's manifold forms of oppression. Rather than try to derive a utopian vision
of a new womanhood by mimetically embracing repressed feminine
sensibilities, thinkers like Judith Butler argue that people should
proliferate their sexual/gender identities and create a future in
which all current language about sexual and gender identity would
no longer be applicable or necessary. Formally, then, the very discourse of woman's oppression, feminine sexuality, or autonomy
employs the logic of the master's discourse; every attempt to define
woman's sexuality keeps us bound to preexisting concepts of womanhood and, worse, invokes a logic of identity with its subjugating
effects. Those effects include placing strong taboos on the range of
accepted sexual/gender identities by continuing to measure identity against a univocal norm.[5]

Like Butler, I think Irigaray's method sometimes fuels as many
preexisting myths about woman as it challenges. But there are two
important ways that Irigaray's work can help us grasp the role of
utopian thinking in moving toward a world which will free us from
the need to employ systems of sexual categorization that measure
identities against a univocal norm. Irigaray, first, assumes that we
cannot achieve a sufficiently critical relation to our current forms
of desire by a too-early return to the warmed-over substantive vision
of liberalism which treats pluralism in gender-neutral terms. For
Irigaray, we can only begin the historical process of change by
moving beyond metonymic deconstruction to metaphoric visions of
alternative ways to be, ways which include women as women, i.e.,
which can sustain difference. Even if we are committed to a different future ideal than Irigaray invokes, her work compellingly suggests that we cannot achieve even a substantive life beyond sex/
gender as we know it without re-metaphorizing the feminine. This
means that women need their own images of the divine, a transcendental metaphor of their possible universality, precisely in order

to awaken alternative sensibilities, forms of desire, and thus an intentionality which will no longer be defined as man's counterpart, as privative of his universal mirror image.

Irigaray's turn to *mimēsis* shares with other deconstructive methods a moment of *via negativa*. But she does not stop with metonymy or a genealogy designed to demonstrate the limits of our current locus. Negativistic strategies of exposing the limitations of the patriarchal symbolic do not suffice, according to Irigaray, to yield a rich critical relation to the present. We reach a critical pose only by imagining positively how things could be different. We need to undergo a process of metaphoric transference, whereby we recover the ability to imagine something that breaks with the past logic of the same and hold this new dream out as a future possibility. Secondly, and more important still, Irigaray recognizes the formal need to prevent the process of re-metaphorization from deteriorating into a static and univocal normative ideal. I will argue that Irigaray elevates the feminine to the quasi-transcendental status of a metaphoric ideal (i) in order to foster new erotic sensibilities and (ii) so as to effectuate a formal delimitation of this and all utopian ideals. Working from Drucilla Cornell's illuminating reading, I argue that Irigaray decenters the univocity of a metaphoric ideal without abandoning utopian thinking.

My main purpose, then, will not be to offer a full interpretation of Irigaray's various utopian images, but rather to explicate the two functions of the utopian moment in her work. These include (i) her strategy for effectuating some type of transformation in the attitudes, habits, and fantasies that support patriarchy; and (ii) her formal model for delimiting all paradigms of utopia. By exploring these two strains in Irigaray's strategy, I lay the basis for interpreting later Heidegger as employing a parallel double-sided effort to move toward a critical recovery of origins aimed at a transformation of ethos as opposed to longing for the immediacy of lost origins; similarly, he overcomes metaphysics by breaking with a univocal ideal or perfect future which allegedly will mirror man to himself (chapter 5). Before I can advance such a reading, I must not only explicate Cornell's interpretation of Irigaray but also examine Irigaray's critique of topological thinking. Technically, later Heidegger's methodology is a version of topology. Adopting Irigaray's psychoanalytic notion of 'origin' as the social imaginary, I argue that later Heidegger goes beyond topology and recovers his own critical utopian moment. His work can be read as offering a parallel therapeutic practice that awakens the ability to wonder again, not just at present but in such a way that possibility (which Heidegger always associated with the future) returns.

4.1 Toward a Critical Mediation of Origins

Drucilla Cornell offers a cogent and insightful discussion of the relation between metaphor and metonymy in feminist critiques of the logic of identity. By logic of identity, I mean systems of categorization which seek to organize the plurality of things under unifying concepts and ultimately to resolve all unifying categories into a single, first principle. Iris Young notes two central features of the logic of identity. First, it "tends to conceptualize entities in terms of substance rather than process or relation"; thus this method treats substance as the natural given that "underlies change" and which forms the basis for classification. Second, "the logic of identity represses difference" or "flees from the sensuous particularity of experience," thereby reducing the "differently similar to the same."[6] When Irigaray claims that a phallocratic symbolic system follows an identitarian logic which equates humanity with maleness, she focuses on both these moments: woman's sexual identity is naturalized and locked into the service of male (humanity's) desire. Whatever other factors contribute to identity formation and the regulation of desire, the metaphorical connotations associated with the divine (first principle) delimit the substance (nature) of desiring subjectivity. Irigaray claims that in a patriarchal symbolic system, the phallus occupies the metaphorical position of the divine or a fixed transcendental signified. Since the masculinely connoted phallus forms the mirror of humanity in which individuals find their autonomous desire constitutively imaged, the substance of the phallus as metaphor has asymmetrical effects on male and female agency/desire. To desire to be human, to participate in the utopian search for universal meaning, means to desire to be male (Irigaray, SP, 133; E, 97–115).

The first difficulty that writers like Irigaray face, then, is that any attempt to symbolically give body to feminine sexual difference risks lapsing back into a logic of identity. To image Woman's difference risks essentialism (naturalizing her sex) and reinvokes the fixed metaphors of humanity by simply substituting one religion for another, i.e., erecting Woman, instead of the phallus, as the new transcendent image of humanity. Many feminists thus interpret Irigaray's work, which explores the metaphoric excess in the patriarchal signifier 'Woman', as undertaking a metonymic strategy of unmasking the ways in which 'Woman' has been constructed. Such interpretations regard essentialism as a necessary strategic risk that inheres in techniques of exposure. But, as Cornell points out, because the idea of strategic essentialism leads to a paradoxical tension, it is vulnerable to critique:

> The tension, simply put, is between the postmodern deconstruction
> of rigid identity structures and the very idea of identity itself, and
> the attempt to specify the feminine, even if only as a subversive
> force against the symbolic. As we have seen, this tension has led
> some feminists sympathetic to the postmodern critique of identity
> to conclude that the very attempt to embody the feminine through
> metaphor is a mistaken retreat to phallogocentrism.

Stating the critique otherwise, if feminists offer an alternative metaphorization of the feminine instead of pure metonymic exposure, then they reassert a masculine strategy of identity which ties women to a single, unitary, homogeneous, and exclusionary notion of womanhood. Such efforts "reinstate the divide between masculine and feminine" and so cannot break with the binary logic which treats woman as man's other. Moreover, they reinforce the naturalistic, metaphysical "'myth' of full presence by claiming to *show* us what the feminine *is*."⁷

Against suspicions that re-metaphorizing the feminine will reestablish woman's natural place, however, Cornell argues that feminists need both metonymic deferral and metaphorical transference. Cornell rejects literal readings of Irigaray which claim that she holds an essentialist conception of women's sexual pleasure and strategic essentialist interpretations which neglect Irigaray's commitment to utopian thought. For Cornell, Irigaray offers a third way, a model of critical mythologizing. Following Irigaray, Cornell claims that a critical mimesis or a mediated recovery of origins cannot be sustained sheerly by exposing the limits of current discursive practices. Rather, a central tenet of Irigaray's work has been that women need to invoke their own imaginative universal, to rethink intimacy and rename feminine sexual desire. Invoking a kind of feminine-transcendental is central to displacing the mediation of women's desire, and thus women's intersubjective relations to one another, through the phallus or the competitive drive for recognition by the normative gaze of masculinity. Cornell argues that Irigaray's method is not mere strategic essentialism aimed at challenging patriarchal conceptions of woman's nature. Instead, Irigaray utilizes metaphor. Metaphoric transference entails evoking new images of women's autonomy from the "surplus of meaning" of the metaphor "Woman" as represented in patriarchy. Although such images have a utopian or transcendental status, they reawaken sensible forms of desire and agency no longer defined in terms of man.[8]

Irigaray's point is that we cannot break with the logic of identity simply by sobering up from imagination and abandoning all utopian thought. If women do not envision their possibilities for transforming their sensible, incarnate, embodied, and reified natural desires by establishing a truly feminine-universal, then their lives will continue to be dictated by the reigning, singular universal of maleness (E, 95–115). Cornell clarifies that we need a critical relation to myth and metaphor, not simply their abandonment, because all metonymic strategies are "contaminated by . . . metaphors" and rooted in the continuity of language and history. Whereas metonymic strategies wish to shift focus from the old utopian vision of the static future to the imperfections of the present or past, Cornell argues, we cannot give up envisioning the future in substantive utopian terms as a way beyond current gender formations. Still, if the only way to move beyond stereotypical repetitions of past metaphors is to re-metaphorize the feminine from out of that which was suppressed within patriarchal discourses, then Cornell also admits that this re-metaphorization of the feminine cannot form "a replacement of the phallus as the primary metaphor of desire."[9] Cornell's reading enables us to treat Irigaray as employing a dialectical methodology whereby she first supplies women with the formal link to divinity missing in phallocratic symbolism and then decenters the status of this quasi-transcendental by showing that it is one of many necessary but critical forms of fantasizing humanity. The feminine utopian moment, though concerned with the future, does not erect the 'feminine' as a new transcendental signified (primary metaphorization) supporting an alternative matriarchal or female symbolic as opposed to the male symbolic.

For Cornell, Irigaray's critical mimesis resides on the border between not abandoning the dream of the future (metaphorical transference) but also not absolutizing this dream (metonymic critique) as if ahistorical and universal. Critical mythologizing thus emphasizes two simultaneous practices. First, those rejected as radically Other to existing symbols of humanity need a substantive dream (metaphor) of the future that radically breaks with the identitarian logic of the present and past. What metonymic strategies overlook, in their retreat to the present perfect, is that static utopias are reifications of our present forms of existence and thus truly lack a futural moment. While metonymy criticizes static utopianism for lusting after the illusory dream of the perfectly real (transparency), it offers no way to move toward a different future. It can delimit but not transform the imaginary projection of female difference as lack and the continued drive toward universality which assimilates female difference to the same, thereby closing off the new. Second, feminist-dynamic conceptions of utopia tie into what is suppressed in the past and present in order to cultivate genuinely new sensibilities, while accepting that utopian ideals must be revised as history and societies change. As Cornell says, the formal-critical delimitation of these ideals, which prevents their lapsing back into a static vision, lies embedded in the fact that this kind of utopian moment challenges the divide between the literal and the metaphorical, the real and the imaginary.[10]

In order to clarify Cornell's two points, let me briefly contrast her view with other readings of Irigaray. Allegedly Irigaray does not wish to replace the male with a female symbolic, and yet she offers metaphoric depictions of intersubjective relations based on female anatomy. In "When Our Lips Speak Together," she uses women's "two lips" to imagine a fluid, tactile, nonrepresentational form of intimacy wherein two touch without merging but also without division. The two lips of the woman's body image this relation: they are two but not distinct or atomistically divided; they are together but not fused:

> We live by twos beyond all mirages, images, and mirrors. Between us, one is not the "real" and the other her imitation; one is not the original and the other her copy. . . . Our resemblance does without semblances; for in our bodies, we are already the same. Touch yourself, touch me, you'll "see." (Irigaray, TS, 216)

And further on, she continues, "You? I? That's still saying too much. Dividing too sharply between us: all" (218).

Widely divergent and conflicting interpretations of such metaphoric passages exist. Literal interpreters claim that Irigaray reinforces naturalistic and essentialist views of women's sexuality, while others argue that the risk of essentialism is necessary to any strategic effort to break up the exclusionary logic of identity. The latter suggest that her work is not referential because it does not depict the "truth of female sexuality or the make-up of the world" (Grosz) but rather the way in which 'Woman' is imaged in patriarchy. Even so, these manifold views of her work stress the strategic function of imaging a world in terms of female morphology. The female imaginary could be said to reveal that there is no "unmediated body available outside the symbolic order" (Gallop); or to operate as a "reversal and displacement of Lacan's phallomorphism" (Fuss); or to formulate the deconstructive moment which refuses to give priority to one polarity within dualistic discursive paradigms, thereby rendering meaning undecidable (Grosz). Moreover, some suggest, this is a strategy of turning to the margins to find alternative ideals for humans in general.[11]

Although metonymic strategy comprises an important aspect of Irigaray's methodology, I agree with Cornell that such readings "neglect the utopian moment" in her work. Cornell's argument, as I understand it, is that for Irigaray the futural moment counteracts both the failures of strategic essentialism and those of purely metonymic strategies. Simply replacing the logic of identity (the unicity of the phallus) with that of difference (the plurivocity of the vagina) would produce a new "closed circuit" of metaphorical substitutions. Even when strategic, this method operates according to a substitutionalist logic and thus postulates a female symbolic in static and fixed terms. If strategic re-metaphorization involves a conservativism that threatens to invoke the real truth about women's natural sexuality, Irigaray perceives an equally strong threat from the opposite side, namely, that sheerly *metonymic* strategies cannot move beyond the existing *substitutive* metaphoric system. They remain too formal and contingent, and thus do not cultivate an alternative eros (cf. Irigaray, TS, 76).[12]

By *metonymic* strategy, I mean challenging a metaphoric or symbolic system through circumscribing the limits of its economy. Whereas primary metaphorization produces identity and a closed system of meaning by virtue of the key signifier that unlocks all other meaning (e.g., the phallus), metonymy refers to the underlying logic of combination and association in that system which reveals that any systemic code is rooted in the possibility of an alternative metonymical syntax or economy.[13] The latter strategy strives to unveil the origin of a given metaphoric economy as contingent and not fixed, as the activity which binds meaning into its stable form. Nevertheless, Irigaray does not stop with a critical *topology* of origins because she does not think that metonymically circumscribing the borders of a given *symbolic* economy, by locating its *imaginary* claim to eternal truth, delivers us to the *real*. Here the real denotes possibilities for social change that move beyond the present by transforming the character of the suppressed erotic economy sustaining our intersubjective forms of life. Irigaray rejects metonymy as a species of topology because the mythos of phallocentrism is not obviated simply because we sober up and expose its limits. We do not develop alternative identities and desires by seeing that the myth is a myth; in fact, we do not truly know how mythic our naturalized state is until we begin to move beyond it. We wake up from the mythos of patriarchy and curtail its operation in mediating our identities only when we *can* imagine an alternative mythos, thereby critically mediating and changing preexisting relations to our habits, desires, and fantasies.

Only by invoking a quasi-transcendental utopian dream, then, can we rejuvenate a future that is not a mere extension of the present, on the one hand. On the other hand, in order to sustain this critical mediation of our erotic form of life, it does not suffice to envision *what* a different future could be. We must also develop a critical relation to *how* we fantasize about change. This is the force of Cornell's point that the utopian moment in Irigaray poses a challenge to the rigid divide between the symbolic and the imaginary. Revealing that a hidden and suppressed metonymic economy of fluidity (female morphology) underlies the metaphoric and substantive economy of solids (male morphology) might destabilize the phallocentric symbolic. But, even if it critically suspends the imaginary projection of woman as man's radical other (*what* we imagine), it will not yield a critical relation to imaginary processes as such, i.e., *how* we imagine. If, indeed, all rational depictions of reality implicitly appeal to the fantasy of another future world, then we cannot sustain critique simply by positing the underlying metonymic economy as the new "ahistorical truth" about patriarchy. As Cornell says, "[t]he origin that is lost is resurrected as fantasy, not as an actual account of origin. When we remember the origin, we remember the future of a feminine irreducible to the castrated other of the masculine imaginary."[14] Irigaray's recovery of origins refuses to stop with topology or metonymy because it entails a pure *via negativa*. It is the moment of *metaphoric transference* that allows her to challenge the stability of *any* primary metaphorization (phallic or vaginal) by no longer positing a rigid divide between the metaphorical and the literal, the symbolic and imaginary, the metaphoric and the metonymic.

Although I later (4.4) address Irigaray's repudiation of univocal ideals, here I want to highlight Cornell's point that we do not transgress the phallic symbolic as a moment of purely sober critique, for this metonymic strategy retains the formal goal of finding the 'real' in a transparent form of life; and, even as it uproots the substitutionary logic of static utopianism, it collapses the future back into the present. For Irigaray we do not circumscribe the real solely by showing the logic of the symbolic to rest upon a male imaginary. Instead, we generate the possibility of a new poetic-erotic form of life through fantasizing a positive alternative. Accordingly, we recover the ability not to absolutize the patriarchal economy by imagining something beyond it, by invoking possibility, and not simply through a noting that something is missing in the present. I want to stress that this unerasable utopian moment cannot be taken as the totality of the real. Indeed, there is no real independent of fantasy, no literal without its metaphorical support. Instead of seeking critique in pure sobriety, as if reality exists transcendent to human imagination, it is paramount that we cultivate a critical relation not only to *what* but to *how* we imagine. We must learn to critically dream the future without taking it as a univocal or absolute ideal for all people and times. Only this way of critically mediating origins refuses to absolutize the future's utopian aspect. In this way can we break the tendency of symbolic practices to reify and naturalize our desires (origin). We must cultivate the capacity to inhabit the tension between the transcendental (metaphorical) and the sensible (literal), thereby fostering a way beyond both the substance of our current desire and all reified forms of understanding sex, nature, and desire.

4.2 The Critique of Topology

Irigaray's critique of methodologies that stop with metonymic transgression or a *via negativa* stems from her critical analyses of Freud and of Lacanian topology. Irigaray resorts to psychoanalytic theory because it promises to provide a gendered paradigm of social and personal identity-formations as compared with traditional ontology and anthropology. Yet while Freud revealed "*the sexual indifference*" of western discursive practices, his work nonetheless remains subject to the "economy of the logos" (Irigaray, TS, 72). He gives "*a priori* value to Sameness" by defining female sexuality in terms of masculine desire, since her organ is a small version of his penis (TS, 69). By reducing female sexuality (and female identity) to lack of man's sexuality, Irigaray claims, even Freudian theory perpetuates indifference toward sexual difference. In her words, "the fact that Freud—or psychoanalytic theory in general—takes sexuality as a theme, as a discursive object, has not led to an interpretation of the *sexualization of discourse*" (73).

But this indifferent and uncritical relation to gender identity is not sustained simply through a failure of critical rationality to take women into account. To the contrary, it is a produced indifference rooted in a particular fantasy which supports a vision of reality. In chapter 3, I noted that for Irigaray the economy of the same (*logos*) is governed by a specular symmetry which fashions reality in the image of a male speaking subject (74). Punning on the French 'homme', Irigaray demonstrates that the libidinal economy of the western symbolic order "depends upon a hom(m)osexual monopoly" that privileges men's desires (171). That economy (where homme = man and homo = same) maintains itself through the exclusion of female sexual specificity, i.e., her autonomy (77). What Freud treats in anatomical terms she identifies as the collective unconscious or the male imaginary underlying the western symbolic (75, 94). The fantasy of the same supports the coherence of the phallic organization of the social order.

In comparison to her treatment of Freud, Irigaray recognizes that Lacan attributes this taboo against desire for the (m)other to a discursive as opposed to anatomical basis. For Lacan, the child obtains coherent identity via language acquisition but at the price of *loss* or exit from the sphere of "maternal desire." Through castration of this desire, the child acquires the "phallic emblem" that makes it like the father who is more desirable to the mother than the child. Yet since the father functions as the symbolic law prohibiting fulfillment of desire for the mother, sexual pleasure is delimited and a *"hiatus between demand and satisfaction of desire"* obtains (61). Having the phallus, which means gaining control over signification, rests upon loss of being the phallus, i.e., enjoying fulfilled incestuous pleasure with the maternal-body. As a result of symbolic castration, then, "it is only in fantasy," Cornell clarifies, that the child can "call her back and have her satisfy his desires." The paternal law codifies the maternal-body as a "lost paradise." This lost pleasure is resurrected in the utopian fantasy of desire-fulfillment. Here utopian desire manifests as the nostalgic and impossible dream of recovering an immediate, symbiotic relation to origins.[15]

The Lacanian shift to a structural as opposed to anatomical basis for castration acknowledges the differential positionality of men and women in relation to the phallus—she *is* the phallus, while he *has* it. Lacanian psychoanalysis reveals that there is no prediscursive reality or unmediated access to the maternal-body; instead, Woman is a product of the masculine imaginary which associates having a penis with having the power of the phallus. As Cornell clarifies, masculine subjectivity harbors a libidinal investment in the illusion that he "can regain what he lost," namely, the power "to satisfy the mother's desire."[16] Whereas men find their individuated desire through the (admittedly elusive) promise of having the phallus (elusive because control over meaning is impossible), women lack the phallus and can only 'be' the passive, unknowable, unrepresentable body, and mysterious origin of his subjectivity (Irigaray, TS, 62). Kaja Silverman notes that, for Lacan, the phallus is "a signifier for the cultural privileges and positive values which define male subjectivity within patriarchal society, but from which the female subject remains isolated." This means that the male subject "will derive validation from [the current symbolic order] at a psychic if not an economic or social level. In other words, he will 'recognize' himself within the mirror of the reigning ideology, even if his race and economic status place him in contradiction to it."[17]

Yet in spite of Lacan's recognition that Woman operates as a discursive function, Irigaray critiques him for failing to distinguish between the signifier Woman (i.e., the fantasy of a real or unmediated relation to pleasure, nature, the maternal-body) and women's actual oppression in society. This failure leads him to relegate women to the same old "penis envy" postulated by Freud, since women are left to yearn for autonomy by lusting after the phallus (62). Lacan at once unearths the symbolic *matricide* supporting western culture and reburies the possibility for women to have a self-governed sexuality. When he claims that women's *jouissance* is less mediated by symbolic practices than male sexuality, Lacan confuses the necessity of developing the capacity for symbolic representation with the mistaken view that we have to accept the existing symbolic order. In holding that phallic castration has to occur, he glosses over the destructive ramifications of patriarchy for women, here noted by Margaret Whitford:

> [Men] can relate to the phantasied mother as to an object, without their own subject-position being put into question. If women learn their identity in the same way, the results are disastrous for that

identity: "The woman cannot reduce her mother to an object without reducing herself to an object at the same time, because they
are the same sex" [Irigaray, Par, 210]. If women take the mother's
body as phantasied object, and at the same time a woman *identifies* with her mother, she is forced to take herself as an object
too. . . . Using language then presents a woman with the choice
between remaining outside the signifying system altogether (in
order to stay with her mother) or entering a patriarchal genealogy
in which her position as object is already given.[18]

By leaving women's struggles for identity caught in this false ei-
ther-or, either passivity or the quest for the phallus, Lacan prevents female specificity and autonomy from ever surfacing.

What interests me in Irigaray's critique of Lacan are the implications for thinking beyond the logic of identity. In "Così Fan
Tutti" Irigaray demonstrates that Lacanian psychoanalysis remains
stuck in a "negative theology." Lacan locates the *topos* of the femi-
nine-other of patriarchy; "female sexualization" is the excluded, the
"unconscious," the "lack" in man's discourse (Irigaray, TS, 89, 94).
As such Woman both threatens male identity and symbolizes the
ec-stasis of his potential self-transcendence. She challenges his
sexual impotence—his lack of fulfillment, his lack of mastery over
representation, his rootedness in the economy of the *logos*—and
yet, as sublated into the object of his desire, she guarantees his
imaginary potency; she functions, like his God, as a mirror reflecting
his mastery to himself. Even though she threatens his identity, he
"seek[s] her out," but *only* in order to keep her in the locus of the
spatiality, the nothing, the silence that sustains masculine desire.
Hence, Irigaray queries: "Might psychoanalysis, in its greatest logical rigor, be a negative theology? Or rather the *negative* of theology? Since what is postulated as the cause of desire is lack as such"
(89). In the end, Lacanian topology keeps Woman in her proper
place as the nonsubject by denying that her sexuality is mediated.[19]

Rather than recognize that women's sexuality is mediated by
phallocratic symbolic practices, Lacanian topology presupposes a
rigid divide between the symbolic and the imaginary. It locates
female pleasure outside the law of the phallus: "enjoy without law"
(96). This alleged outside, however, functions inside the phallic
symbolic: "Their exclusion is *internal* to an order from which nothing escapes: the order of (man's) discourse" (88). Irigaray objects
that having "utter[ed] the truth about the status of female
sexuality . . . [psychoanalysis] stops there" (102). Certainly Lacan
shows that sexual relations *as such* do not exist but rather subsist

as effects of a hom(m)o-sexual symbolic economy; nevertheless, Lacanian psychoanalysis reduces the 'not-all' of symbolic discourse to the "Other of the Same" (99). Lacan thinks Woman only in relation to the speaking subject as his male imaginary. So "[c]ircumscribing the abyss of negative theology," he continues to "submit the real to the imaginary of the speaking subject" (103). And women's specificity remains lost: "Women's enjoyment is—for them, but always according to him—essentially an-archic and a-teleological" (95).

To summarize, Lacan locks us into the logic of metaphoric substitution, whereby we enter the mediated realm of language through a break with the real. For Irigaray, Lacan posits the real as an absolute transcendental, i.e., as the impossibility of unmediated relations to sex, nature, pleasure. Yet by positing a rigid divide between the real and the symbolic, he ironically institutes the necessity of conflating the fantasy of the lost Other with the real, namely, with the imaginary desire for immediate and prediscursive fusion. This conflation forecloses an alternative grasp of the real as the possible. Here possibility has a both a temporal and a collective connotation. Real thus denotes the genuine future understood as critically mediating origins (the imaginary) and ends (utopia). Such a mediation of the mortal-divine, sensible-transcendental dissolves the rigid divide instituted by Lacan's literalistic rendition of the real, that is, the divide between the natural (lost origin) and the transcendent (future possibility) (cf. Irigaray, Par, 127–49; E, 97–115).

At this point, I can draw together three implications of Irigaray's critique for getting beyond metaphysics and phallocentrism. First, Irigaray's critique of Lacan's topology leads her to reject other negativistic strategies on the grounds that these lock Woman into an ahistorical or transcendental truth. The claim that Lacanian topology is the negative of theology implies that the desire to stay in the position of transgression absolutizes the (feminine) other as the foundation of (phallocratic) discourse. The very activity of projecting an infinitely deferred real comprises the mechanism which absolutizes present and past forms of thinking and being. By absolutizing Woman as outside, as the 'not all', the lost *archē* and unattainable telos, Lacan avoids coming to terms with the fact that Woman is a function of a specific, male imaginary that is partial. His delineation of the discursive structure of the patriarchal symbolic thus sets up a fixed, ahistorical truth. This is tantamount to claiming that Lacan's theory still suffers the delusion of hoping to find the real in a transcendental moment or noumenal reality.

Irigaray is critical not only of Lacanian topology but also of deconstructive strategies which she argues colonize the feminine. To Irigaray's mind, strategic methods for critically excavating the role of the feminine as ground of the symbolic, instead of focusing on the need for actual women to gain voice and autonomy, either leave the feminine in the fantasized locus of the transcendental signified (in the manner of Lacan) or, as Whitford notes, take over the privilege of speaking like woman (as in Derrida).[20] Critique, then, remains incomplete without imagining a better future for women.

Second, to say that Lacan wants to find the truth of castration in an ahistorical moment implies that he fails to challenge the necessity of castration or the rigid imaginary/symbolic divide. As Irigaray puts it, in revealing that sexual relation cannot be *"posited* as such," outside the logic of representation and discursive reality, Lacan mistakenly infers that this implies "there is no exit from the *logos*," i.e., from castration (TS, 99). Lacanian theory lapses into a form of *symbolic fatalism* when it collapses the fact that there is no prediscursive reality into the conclusion that the acquisition of identity necessarily occurs within the preexisting phallocratic symbolic order. Locking Woman (the imaginary) out of the symbolic locks us into phallocentrism. From Irigaray's perspective, this means that Lacan reifies the male imaginary as ahistorical and irreducible; this reification collapses his distinction between the real and the "imaginary of the speaking subject" (Irigaray, TS, 103). For Irigaray, by contrast, the real denotes not the final metonymic exposure that Woman comprises the imaginary support of a phallocratic symbolic order. Rather, the real "includes, in large measure, a *physical reality* that continues to resist adequate symbolization" (106). This claim lends itself to the essentialist interpretation that Irigaray believes there is a natural basis for women's specific sexual pleasure. But I interpret it more broadly as pointing to a neo-Heideggerian notion of possibility, namely, that we are always more than we represent and embody at any point in time. The real denotes those sensuous pleasures of ecstatic human interaction which are not yet realized, yet which metaphorically promise new erotic possibilities for poetic forms of life.

When Lacan reduces this metaphorical excess, latent within any configuration of a cultural imaginary, back into the metonymic glue binding the existing logic of the symbolic order together, he undermines the possibility for symbolic and by extension social change. He cuts off the temporal dimension of metaphoricity, namely, that as linguistic beings we stand in relation to possibility (new meaning), to our own poetic or sensuous excess. This excess is neither an absolute opposite nor a mirror image of what we are now, but a genuine possibility of transforming ourselves (read: the real) from within. As Whitford incisively notes:

> Any particular organization is taken to be reality in an imaginary operation, since the world cannot be grasped without the framework of a set of categories. However, if one takes the imaginary to be equivalent to reality, and implies for example that reality is coextensive with the categories of discourse, then of course the only possibilities for change will be permutations within the same set of categories; no totally different reorganization would be possible.[21]

Irigaray argues that Lacan leaves us stuck with our respective male and female roles because there is no prediscursive sexual relation. She rejects any such identitarian logic that collapses the social imaginary (collective unconscious) into the pregiven symbolic, thereby reducing the future, or the genuine utopian moment, to the imperfect present or past. If masculinist utopian visions fetishize woman as an excuse *not* to change, then metonymy perpetuates matricide by catapulting society into the throes of symbolic fatalism. Irigaray, by contrast, takes seriously the implication of Lacanian theory that reality—taken as including the excess, the possible, the unthought—harbors the seeds of genuine social change, or in Cornell's words, a " 'way out' of our current system of gender identity."[22]

This brings me to my third, final, yet related point. Somewhat paradoxically, the act of positing the real as transcendent to fantasy fetishizes Woman as absolute Other, collapses the distinction between the real and the male imaginary, closes off temporal possibility, and locks us into permutations of the same (nihilism, matricide). For Irigaray, finding the real, understood as the concrete possibility for a new poiesis, depends upon fantasy and imagination. I would claim that Irigaray, reflecting Heideggerian influence, differentiates between (a) fantasies which lapse into fetishizing the real and (b) those which open productive pathways to richer forms of sociality or a richer eros binding humans together collectively. This marks the substantial difference between static and dynamic, masculinist and feminist, substitutive and critical forms of utopianism. Because Irigaray associates the repressed feminine with the excess out of which we could imagine alternative forms of intersubjectivity, she must methodologically resist the substitutive logic that replaces one primary (static) metaphorization of the symbolic around the phallus with another organized around vaginal lips. Yet, since we do not reinvent the future in a vacuum as if we can simply abstract from patriarchy, she turns to the marginalized feminine in order to open the doorway to a novel future.

Her method of mimeticism or mimicry, whereby she dramatizes female sexuality as conceived by the male imaginary, opens this doorway in at least three ways. (1) It unloosens the latent, excess meanings out of the phallocentric symbolic system. (2) It recuperates specific forms of fantasy and imagination which are depleted, suppressed, and literally drained off by the reigning fetishization of Woman. This depletion is central to perpetuating the status quo of patriarchy. We reinvent the real by giving symbolic form to that which is latent within but cannot symbolically coexist with phallocentrism: the possibility of a female imaginary. This moment is left unsymbolized and thus unthought, according to Irigaray, by purely metonymic strategies. A basic condition for women to conceive themselves as free agents and coauthors in the production of meaning is to imagine a world (a system of meaning) which breaks the identitarian logic that equates subjectivity with maleness and posits control over meaning as having the phallus. This is why Irigaray argues that women need their own divine or a world interpreted through female morphology rather than the phallus.[23] Only by giving new form to the signifier Woman can we demonstrate that there is no inherent contradiction between the signifier Woman and humanity, the feminine and the speaking subject, the maternal-body and meaning.

(3) Nonetheless, in order to prevent this symbolic fantasy of equating Woman with the universal from solidifying into a static matriarchal utopianism, Irigaray must delimit her invocation of new goddesses. The problem of delimiting ways of re-metaphorizing Woman and utopian ideals revolves around two poles. In order to develop a critical as opposed to naive form of utopian thinking, it does not suffice to treat alternative substantive utopian visions as historically relative to the present stage in cultural evolution, as opening new doorways to the real instead of presenting a totalizing utopian vision for all times, peoples, and places. The very logic of fantasizing must become critical. We cannot simply call on humans to adopt a critical attitude toward all fantasies by regarding *mimēsis* as therapeutic rather than regulative or temporally restricted rather

than eternal. Something within the formal-logic of the transcendental invoked in metaphoricity must encourage a critical relation to utopianism or to metaphysics proper.

Here Cornell's interpretation of Irigaray proves immensely helpful. Cornell argues that Irigaray develops a model of mythologizing which is inherently self-critical because it moves away from a substitutionalist to a reiterative logic. By reiterative logic, Cornell means that the status of the universal is non-univocal. Rather than delineating a single, substantive vision of women's future state of liberation, this universal is imaginative; it provides a formal way for different groups of women to give voice to their plural and diverse situations and to rejuvenate their manifold imaginary visions of the future (I return to this point in 4.4). Many criticize Irigaray's project, claiming that her limited therapeutic goal cannot provide a complex political strategy for social change.[24] Though sympathetic to these charges, I find Cornell's argument persuasive. Her argument implies that the reiterative logic of Irigaray's universalism is therapeutic at two levels, one interpersonal and centered on the recovery of agency, the other systematic or formal. It is the latter which comprises the more extensive contribution that Irigaray makes to social theory.

The logic of Irigaray's feminist utopianism is therapeutic at the substantive level of envisioning a new poetic form of life. Against striving to assume the sober pose of the stoic-rational witness to the limits of the patriarchal symbolic, Irigaray employs a mimetic practice aimed at reconstituting women's autonomy and the eros binding sociality proper. More significant, to my mind, is that she avoids resurrecting a form of metaphoricity governed by substitutive universalism. This second therapeutic goal aims at a formal delimitation of philosophizing understood as the fantastic search for first principles and apodictic foundations. Closed symbolic systems operate according to a substitutionalist logic because based upon a new transcendental signified (objectified as the lost and final telos for all times). Irigaray thus displaces the notion of the phallic mother as the signified, and replaces it with the view that Woman is a signifier like all other signs.

Cornell suggests that Lacan "recognizes the status of the phallus as metaphor" for difference; however, he fails to recognize that the phallus is not necessary but only the referent that "establishes [woman's] lack as a *fact* of sexual difference."[25] In other words, Woman operates within an identitarian logic as the transcendental signified by which we make real female lack of sexuality and male codified autonomy. Whereas Lacan ignores the potential metaphoric slippage implicit in his own discourse, Irigaray not only recognizes that metaphorical transference is necessary to social change but also uses this insight to propose a critical model of universalizing based on metaphoric transference as a way to break the logic of identity. Irigaray provides a formal model of critical universalizing in which none of the universals that organize systems of meaning are treated as first principles. Woman, then, is not a unified category under which all particular women's identities fall and into which they could be resolved without excess. To the contrary, Woman is a formal signifier that lends itself to proliferation; it gains substance only through the manifold ways that specific women interpret their actual and dissimilar lives.

Although the largely abstract focus of Irigaray's work does not provide a concrete, thick, and interactive model of reciprocity and recognition, her formal delimitation of utopianism does avail us of a model of thinking which contributes to that project because it opens the way to thinking beyond the binary logic of identity. In the end, then, critical *mime¯sis* entails not simply a cure or a process of awakening to the possibility of a different, more healthy world. It transforms the status of universals, not by striving to abandon metaphysics but rather by delimiting metaphysics. At a substantive level, Irigaray's critical utopian moment shifts our perception away from the nature of castration toward possibility. Since the futile struggle to get over castration or the desire to define oneself against castration entangles us in castration, nihilism, and pessimism, Irigaray emphasizes healing through rejuvenating the depleted capacity to imagine an ecstatic kind of intersubjectivity which avoids dualistic thinking. Her image of the two lips shatters the poetic dynamic of being caught between fear of castration (loss of atomistic identity) and the deluded desire for an undifferentiated state of innocent being (i.e., instead of fusion which is bound to domination, the lips remain two). And at a formal level, Irigaray shows that we cannot simply swap metonymy for metaphor; we need to critically mediate metaphoric transference as a means of coming to a non-dysfunctional relation to origins (desire for immediacy) and to universal visions of social harmony (desire for stasis and apodictic certainty), the sensible (essential), and the transcendental (univocal).[26]

4.3 Heidegger on Awakening To versus Overcoming Metaphysics

Many feminists might balk at the prospect of reading later Heidegger as undertaking a parallel attempt to get beyond castration or the logic that equates subjectivity with maleness. After all, even later Heidegger's turn to language does not clearly explicate the nonontological status of 'Woman' as a signifier within the discourse of patriarchy. Later Heidegger views the origin of human existence as the groundless play (the *es gibt*) which, by granting the conceptual horizon peculiar to a specific topos in history, binds the ethos defining a historical form of life. Nonetheless, he never critically questions Woman as the social imaginary underlying these conceptual horizons. Indeed, both Irigaray and Kristeva challenge that Heidegger, like Lacan and Derrida, cannot get beyond a reification of the 'nothing' or the groundlessness of human existence. In *L'Oubli de l'air*, Irigaray criticizes Heidegger for leaving Woman in the locus of the "earth" or *physis* (OA, 10, 19, passim). Using Woman as the material body and solid foundation upon which men build their house of language, Heidegger provides no way out of the logic of metaphoric substitution which codifies dualistic divisions, like that between the feminine-carnal and the masculine-rational. In a similar vein, Kristeva argues that Heidegger ossifies the "nothingness" underlying western discursive practices (RP, 131).

Like Irigaray's critique of Lacan, these complaints charge that Heidegger's topology of historical forms of life can do no more than leave the trope 'Woman' in the locus of the nothing, the necessary lack, the opaque, empty, unrepresentable hole in man's discourse. He can isolate the ways that western thought suppresses awareness of this nothing, but he offers little by way of critique of its association with femininity. This omission seriously limits the value of his work for providing a substantive utopian vision of social transformation.[27] As serious as I take these charges to be, Irigaray's own work is heavily indebted to Heidegger's methodology and his efforts to prepare western humanity for an alternative poiesis or substantive form of life. Admittedly Heidegger approaches metaphysics and western nihilism from a masculinist perspective, yet what distinguishes the later from the early Heidegger is precisely his attempt to articulate not only the substantive vision of a particular way of life, but also a critical relation to all forms of *poiēsis*. There is an element of metonymic sobering up in later Heidegger's turn to a topological recovery of origins (the event of Unconcealment). His methodology moves beyond topology to include an unerasable utopian moment. Transposing Heidegger's thought into psychoanalytic terms, I suggest that later Heidegger begins to give up the myth of castration or at least to awaken from it.[28]

Briefly tracing the course of his thought, it is not off the mark to claim that Heidegger always dreamed his work would influence social change or open the possibility of an authentic new existence for western Dasein. His early work arguably sketches the contours of a form of existence that yields greater heterogeneity than naive socialization allows. In his early period, humans are to find meaning by developing a critical relation to average everyday beliefs and practices (*das Man*). Yet because Heidegger regarded his early model of individual authenticity as lacking historical specificity, he adopts a collective view of human existence in his middle phase. This shift strove to decenter the epistemic subject by recognizing its dependence upon language and history for effectuating its truths or principles of social change. Still, this collectivist shift was not enough to bring Heidegger to his sought-after break with metaphysics and the identitarian (anthropocentric or subjectist) logic which re-centers men as the masters of historical processes of social change. Middle Heidegger projects a static utopian truth as a destiny fashioned in man's image.

Even though he thinks Being (the totality of what is) as finite, Heidegger's middle work suffers the metaphysical desire to conquer reality and this leads him to reify Being as destiny. Instead of finding a way out of the past in the future perfect—the lost possibilities that come toward us from out of what 'has been'— Heidegger's situated view of the future-perfect collapses back into masculine utopianism and false universalism (permutations of the past). The claim that humans only know Being in finite ways as their destinal or historical possibilities (and not as God or an absolute telos) does not save Heidegger from interpreting destiny from the standpoint of his mystical view of National Socialism. The feminine (destiny), who continues to secure even the finite and immediate telos of man's being, is but his projection of what he needs to conquer.

Only with the later turn to topology do we find Heidegger beginning to articulate the fact that, as historical, humans have no God's-eye view over the totality of what is, but without reifying that totality (Being) into an entity or a destinal agency that guarantees the validity of human action. For this reason, Being stops functioning in his analyses as either a solid ground or fetishized telos. Later I will argue that Heidegger is not entirely successful in this endeavor. Here I highlight that Heidegger's shift to marking off our topos in history brings him to a method that at least begins to offer a way beyond metaphysics. He reins in his earlier attempt to get out of history by overcoming (*überwinden*) metaphysics—a strategy that merely entangled him during the thirties all the more deeply in the desire for mastery. We could add that this was a struggle against castration or an imaginary male impotence before the overwhelming nothingness of unconcealment (Being). This struggle creates the vicious circle of the male imaginary, whereby recognizing the groundlessness of human existence leads to projecting a future as freedom from anxiety about groundlessness. Since Woman (nothing) is what scares man, the struggle must transpire as conquest over Woman.

Heidegger's delimitation of the *topos* characteristic of our current locus in history approximates what Irigaray calls "negative theology" to the extent that this methodology evinces two things. These include that (i) he relinquishes all direct forms of political activism (which he now regards as effectuating social change by conquering history) and, by extension, that (ii) he forsakes the agonal dream that men forge their utopia by wrestling with the feminized forces of destiny. What saves Heidegger, however, from resting content with a *via negativa* (complete fatalism or quietism) is that he does not entirely abandon his silent dream of change (though he clearly offers no definitively political strategy for human action). He alters course. He casts aside the assumption that we can get to a novel future by surmounting our present and instead paves the way toward the future by questioning how such a strategy binds us to the old belief that humans have mastery over history and thus closes us into the perpetuation of our current patterns of thinking.

From one perspective, Heideggerian topology thoroughly relinquishes the definitively political goal to fashion a future society through human power and action. This, however, is only partially true. For later Heidegger carries out his restricted and moderate task of delineating the *topos* of western humanity's current situation via a critical practice aimed at changing modernist sensibilities, the general ethos or habits and fantasies that pervade, define, and limit us to our current form of historical embeddedness. Heideggerian topology proves a creative mediation (metaphorical transference), not merely a delineation (metonymic deferral) of the excess in the present. To be historical, as humans are, means for

Heidegger that history emerges in formations that, qualitatively speaking, yield more than the sum total of all of collective human actions, i.e., of human intentionality. Being, then, refers to the fact that humans experience their own historicalness as the synchronic and discontinuous event whereby certain possibilities fade from memory and no longer govern our habits and perceptions; and other habits emerge. Being is Heidegger's name for the netherside of our own historicalness. Heidegger's notion, that Being contains the unthought, unrepresented, and unsymbolized dimension of our present historical topos, functions in his later work in a manner parallel to Irigaray's view that metaphoric transference is possible because the imaginary opens out on the excess unrepresented in a finite symbolic system. What finally distinguishes his later from his middle period is that, instead of projecting the unthought outward as a substantive future utopia, he uses the method of topology to foster concrete transformation from within our current technological epoch. Without a notion of metaphorical slippage, he relies upon the ontological view that, to borrow Irigaray's words, a physical reality exceeds every finite system of conceptualization, every historical horizon of existence. And later Heidegger, much like Irigaray, argues that humans must indirectly imagine and foster an alternative poiesis rather than strike out toward some unknowable future (static utopia). The latter, in point of fact, unwittingly promotes a nostalgic yearning for origins and a naive repetition of (Greek) beginnings.

My argument is that later Heidegger can be read as carrying out his critical transgression (*via negativa*) of metaphysics through an unerasable utopian moment. That utopian dimension is, as with Irigaray, therapeutic (personally and collectively) rather than static because he invokes this utopian moment through a critical mediation of the poetic origins of western rationality. Further, Heidegger's utopian thinking twists free of metaphysics on two levels, formal and substantive. The former centers on Heidegger's critique of representational and instrumental forms of reason, and marks his formal effort to delimit metaphysics or philosophy. The latter I equate with the delimited utopian project to foster a new ethos and vision of a heterogeneous and nonviolent mode of "belonging-to-gether" (EGT, 88/VA, 233). Each aspect, however, contributes to transforming our collective ethos. This commentary on Heidegger's methodology enables me to advance a reading of his later thought as engaged in a form of critical utopian thinking. Although I will examine his actual utopian thought in the next chapter, here I summarize the methodological contours of that practice.

First, Heidegger's critique of representation, though broached from the side of the masculine, can be read as a curtailment of masculinist utopianism or fantasizing. His break with projectionist forms of thought that encapsulate the world in man's image, reins in fantasy in its fetishizing form. Restricting fantasy is a logical move, from a masculinist perspective, requisite to give up lusting after lost origins and perfect utopias. More interesting, however, is that Heidegger implicitly recognizes that this restriction on fetishization cannot overcome calculative rationality without relying upon an alternative mode of imagination. According to Heidegger, all ontological sensibilities and modes of thinking are historical forms of *poiēsis*. They constitute productive ways of imaginatively bringing forth possibilities. In order to break with modern *technē*, or calculative forms of rationality, he resists both his earlier nostalgia for a return to classical origins (a pristine immediacy) and the perpetuation of modern anthropocentrism. Instead, he cultivates a critical transformation of the poetic basis of rationality from within modernity.

This mimetic focus indicates a therapeutic orientation roughly equivalent to metaphoric transference. As opposed to striving to overcome metaphysics, later Heidegger rests content with healing western humanity of its desire to master reality. Even so, we do not awaken from the dream of mastery in abstraction. Rather we awaken to an alternative. Heidegger encourages a metaphorical shift whereby our sensibilities move from conquest to releasement, from *Überwindung* (overcoming) to *Verwindung* (awakening). Despite Heidegger's quietist inclinations, awakening is not complete passivity since it engenders the ability to think beyond making the world over in man's image (anthropocentrism). It is releasement to the possibility for a nondominating ethos.[29]

Second, Heidegger's conception of the project of overcoming modernity during the thirties represented destiny (our future telos) in a way that collapsed the social imagination into the phallocratic symbolic system. In Heidegger's language, he reduced the genuine future (possibility) to an image of the past, that is to say, to the present-perfect (actuality). Though already critical of historiography, he nonetheless molded the future out of the ethos or desire to conquer man's historical being; this desire comprises the male imaginary underlying western rationality. Western *ratio* absolutizes a symbolic horizon by conflating possibility (future) with the male imaginary and relegating the feminine to the libidinal support for their discourses. Attempts to effectuate change from the desire to conquer fail to tap into the broader social forms of imagination that are irreducible to male desire. For this reason, masculine utopianism cannot break with the logic of identity or with substitutionary metaphoric matrices that mirror man in his image. Even the effort to create a new future cannot get out of the vicious circularity of masculine utopianism, since possibility—the surd in being or the excess in the 'real'—becomes conflated either with the actual past (as in historiography) or with the 'origin' (the unconscious or excess in being) but imaged in terms of man's drive to conquer.

In 1946, Heidegger rejects historiography. With this rejection, I propose, he implicitly mitigates the vicious circularity of masculine utopianism:

> All historiography predicts what is to come from images of the past determined by the present. It systematically destroys the future and our historical relation to the advent of destiny (*Ankunft des Geschickes*). Historicism has today not only not been overcome, but is only now entering the stage of its expansion and entrenchment. (EGT, 17/VA, 301)

It is important not to see later Heidegger's turn to topology as a pure retrenchment to the present, which Irigaray argues is Lacan's mistake. Instead we can read this as a formal chastening of utopian thinking, again similar to Irigaray's move to reiterative universalism. While later Heidegger continues to use the term *Geschick* (destiny), he more successfully keeps to its strict meaning than he did in the thirties. Destiny denotes the structure of historical existence; as a historical category, it functions as a collective equivalent to the individual-based concept of facticity (finding ourselves thrown into a world not of our making) in *Being and Time*. Thus, *Geschick* names the fact that humans do not think or desire in a vacuum but rather inherit cultural, linguistic, and historical presuppositions. Like Irigaray's conception of the real, however, Heidegger's *Geschick* is complex, since it retains the sense of *es gibt* (there is)—the event (*Ereignis*) whereby we are cast into a locus and orientation in history—without being completely severed from that which remains unthought within a historical horizon. Just as the social imaginary is not so very unconscious that we do not know it, so too Heidegger's destiny harbors possibilities for change. Yet the later Heidegger no longer links destiny to a substantive political vision (a material filling). We prepare our own future by transforming our current ways of dwelling.

Later Heidegger gives us a less pernicious notion of destiny because he treats it as a formal structure which orients us toward possibility and enables us to achieve metaphorical transference. But instead of projecting the future as a kind of gift mysteriously allotted from outside our present situation (which inevitably reduces the future to man's imaginary), he holds that the excess within our current historical topos proffers concrete possibilities for enhancing our humanity now. He no longer seeks an eternal greatness achieved for all times. This move anticipates Irigaray's methodological premise. I take that premise to be this: recognizing that the feminine does not lie outside the masculine symbolic but rather is a keystone, internal to it, proves essential to challenging the myth of castration and to rethinking the feminine in ways that offer a way out from within. Like Irigaray, later Heidegger neither gives up on the future nor fashions it in man's image. He, too, seeks a way between erecting false utopias and a critical mediation of origins that delivers us to the possible, to what is concretely possible for us now.

In both Heidegger and Irigaray we encounter a version of antinormativism that rejects abstract universals for all times, while recovering concrete normative possibilities which, though contained within the present, introduce correctives into our historical circumstance. Heidegger engages his own method of re-metaphorizing not 'Being' per se but western technological existence; and precisely this, in a manner analogous to Irigaray's thinking the female imaginary, provides an image beyond the logic of identity. It relinquishes conflating all that could be (Being) with thinking or reducing the social imaginary to a function of the masculine symbolic economy. For the later Heidegger as for Irigaray, the way to foster resistance consists in refusing to collapse the future into the present by cultivating, concretely from within our topos, the way beyond it.

Third, although Heidegger does not speak of his work as an alternative kind of utopian thought, neither in terms of *metaphoric transference* nor *reiterative universalism*, I will develop this interpretation in the next chapter. I will show that his substantive vision of *Gelassenheit* as an ecstatic mode of 'belonging-together' both enacts a new poiesis and thematizes a critical as opposed to naive mediation of origins. Just as Irigaray must introduce a formal mechanism for modifying the status of the utopian ideals she invokes, so too Heidegger thinks that we delimit the logic of identity not by abandoning universals but rather by imaging these ideals as non-univocal. The Heideggerian concept of the fourfold counteracts traditional utopian discourses by showing that we can always mediate our self-understanding through manifold, incommensurable, yet universalistic conceptual horizons (PLT, 150, 179/ VA, 144, 172). Rather than hope to fashion a final state of humanity transparent to itself, we should give up the naive and romantic longing for immediacy while retaining the belief that we can be humane. Irigaray and Heidegger hope for peaceful coexistence; however, they see this prospect as something that will require constructive effort, not effort *against* Woman or to wrest the hidden from unconcealment, but rather *for* noncompetitive relationships (Irigaray) and a nonhierarchal relation to difference (Heidegger). Harmonious social recognition will necessitate adopting a critical and nonromantic relation to origins and ends that is grounded in fallible and limited efforts to take only that one step toward change which is offered to us now. Still, this step must be taken.

4.4 Unhappy Consciousness Revisited

By thinking Heidegger with Irigaray, I have been proposing that there is a complementary relation between ecstatic subjectivity (part 1) and critical utopianism (part 2). The ethical goal of developing a nonrepressive relation to alterity (my own and that of others) requires the support of an asymmetrical form of recognition. Admittedly working primarily at the most abstract level, Heidegger and Irigaray contribute to this endeavor by showing that the possibility of asymmetrical reciprocity is at least partially conditioned by the practice of utopian thinking. This practice must relinquish direct efforts to overcome metaphysics and instead work indirectly to prepare a delimitation of all metaphysical ideals. This, indeed, is the paradox of breaking the logic of identity. That paradox is that we can only relinquish hierarchical equations of the universal (God or humanity) with one aspect of the social (man for Irigaray, whites for Lewis Gordon) by developing critical forms of utopianism. Those who have been marginalized need ways to desire their humanity without the perversities of masochism which are rooted in the fact that, symbolically speaking, one cannot be both female (or black) and autonomous. Cornell's reading of Irigaray argues that universalizing women's ways of being is a necessary factor requisite to engender ethical relations among women. Until woman's identity is not mediated by the phallus, it will be impossible to dissolve competition for recognition. Whatever other factors are necessary to eliminate a competitive-based society, a central dimension of social and political change must include unshackling the stronghold of a conception of Woman that reduces women "to 'their' vision of us."[30]

Nonetheless, feminist critics of strategies that offer a re-metaphorization of female relations charge not simply that we cannot replace a patriarchal with a matriarchal symbolic; more difficult is the challenge that all definitions of woman erect a new false universalism. Because any woman's oppression reflects the experiences of some (e.g., white, middle class) women, such a re-metaphorization inevitably hierarchizes women's experiences, attributes "a special status [to] one vision of Woman," and threatens to valorize one group of women as the vehicle of social emancipation. In concluding, I want to return to this problem in more detail. Cornell admits that a paradox pervades Irigaray's re-metaphorization of the feminine. On the one hand, because the feminine is associated with the metaphorical "spillover" or "surplus of meaning" in the patriarchal symbolic, metaphorical trans-ference links what "is" (man's representation of Woman) to the "is not" and the "not yet." Cornell calls this utopian element "imagining, not describing" the feminine, because it moves beyond present specification(s) of woman. On the other hand, every specification of woman, even if an imaginary future and not an actual description of woman's essence, risks becoming essentialist and falsely universal: "Woman *as* still implies Woman *is*."[31]

We can interpret one dimension of this paradox to be the inverse problem of unhappy consciousness. The unhappy consciousness has freedom in thought (the truth) but cannot conceive how to enact it in reality. Here, by contrast, the affirmation of this paradox of women's situation appears to issue in a kind of bad faith; we postulate a concept of women's oppression (identity) in order to ground women's political liberation, while we reject the truth of Woman. The paradox or double-bind consists in that, without re-thinking the feminine-transcendental, women cannot disrupt the identitarian logic of masculine rationality; yet in order to avoid reproducing the master's logic of false universalism, women must disclaim the very identity they postulate as exclusionary. Feminists then are left to dream without taking their dream very seriously either in the present or as a final stage of evolution (since all such ideals are limited, if not wholly inadequate).

But doesn't this leave feminist theory vulnerable to Hegel's criticism of Kant? Hegel accuses Kant of being involved in "dissemblance or duplicity" in his articulation of a universal regulative ideal, not because Kant defers the attainability of harmonious and peaceful coexistence when presupposing the very drive of rationality toward this end as a real possibility. Rather, Hegel argues,

> Action, therefore, in fact directly fulfils what was asserted could not take place, what was supposed to be merely a postulate, merely a beyond. Consciousness thus proclaims through its deed that it is not in earnest in making its postulate, because the meaning of action is really this, to make into a present reality what was not supposed to exist in the present.[32]

We can interpret the feminist paradox as a Kantian dilemma of duplicity. Feminist theory must propose an ideal, so as to orient social change, while at the same time infinitely deferring its attainability and even desirability because no concept of woman's autonomy could be truly universal. I have already enumerated several ways out of this paradox which are being sought within poststructuralist circles. First, we might rest content with interventionist strategies that have no positive reconstructive goal beyond critique of our contemporary forms of life. Second, we could follow the school of strategic essentialism by accepting that there is no way out of the paradox and learning to live with it. Third, Cornell argues, Irigaray resolves the paradox and avoids duplicity both ethically and formally.

By rejecting the label strategic essentialism for living with the paradox, Cornell refuses the ethical dilemma of the unhappy consciousness and the quasi-stoic logic implicit in assuming that we must simply accept the paradox. Cornell considers the dichotomy, between strategic essentialism and metonymic exposure, to be false. I suggest that the dichotomy proves false because each strategy presupposes that we cannot get beyond the stoic logic that all identity and every representational system is repressive. On this premise, we are left either to risk essentialism even though all identity formations are inherently repressive, or rest content with practices of exposure because all identity is repressive. For Cornell, the latter falls into a cynical assumption that there is no way for women to dream a way out of their present oppression; and the former misrepresents itself as stuck with duplicity, as erecting ideals of women's final liberated state to govern emancipatory practices while denying the universality of such ideals. Strategic essentialism falsely implies that humans are caught between an irreconcilable either/or: either the duplicity of postulating a context-free "blueprint of an ideal society" for all times; or the bad-faith refusal to dream at all. This is not really to live with paradox, but only to succumb to historical despair.[33]

By contrast, Cornell works toward a critical theory of gender. The language of strategic essentialism belies a confusion. It assumes that all references to social context are essentialist, while nonetheless implying that every effort to identify and specify some woman's situation risks essence. Cornell argues,

> [T]here is a difference between an appeal to essence and the illumination of feminine specificity as an explicit ethical and political position. Spivak, in other words, is right to claim that not every "context" involves essence. Her mistake is that we should even adopt the word "essence" when we are indicating specificity. It is precisely the confusion of essentialism with any writing of the specificity of feminine difference that leads to the belief that we risk either "essentialism" or indifference to the suffering of women.[34]

A critical theory of gender, which depicts women in their local and complex sociohistorical situations, rejects the premise that all identities are exclusionary. Cornell helps us move in this direction through her formal suggestion that we can differentiate critical analyses of gender-identities from the logic of identity.

Representing women's historical contexts need not invoke either essentialism or false universalism. Here I analytically restrict the meaning of essentialism to two things, the view that there is an "original femininity, a female essence," and historical depictions of a "universal female oppression." I employ the term false universalism to denote univocal ideals of women's liberation.[35] The problem, according to Cornell, with both essentialism and false universalism is that each invokes a univocal concept of Woman (woman's oppression or woman's liberation). The logic of identity inevitably derives utopian ideals from one female group experience of oppression, e.g., middle-class white women. Arguably, Cornell's theory implies that there is no contradiction between local identity politics (based upon conceptions of women's specificity) and rejecting the logic of identity as a species of false universalism, since the latter postulates a single ideal for change that abstracts from the very contextual oppression and specific needs of various groups. We can flesh out the body of various women's specific group situations without essentializing the signifier, Woman. And we can specify futural ideals without presupposing a univocal concept of Woman.[36]

The notion of *reiterative universalism*, which Cornell adopts from Michael Walzer, provides a non-univocal universal. Reiterative universalism assumes that analyses of what woman have been and normative ideals for what women want to become are context-dependent and not abstractly universalizable for all women or for all times. Against the logic of identity which substantively subsumes concrete particulars under a unifying category, Cornell rejects every notion of free-floating universals. The signifier Woman only acquires meaning a posteriori in its various localized manifestations. When rejecting the categorical distinction between fantasy and reality, Cornell adopts the nominalist view that there are no real universals. Rather than regard entities as particular instantiations of real universals, she rejects the identitarian logic of universal-particular altogether. Instead, there are only women's specificities. The feminine must be understood as an *imaginative universal* that does not commit us to a univocal, transhistorical concept of woman's oppression.[37]

Two points clarify Cornell's reading of Irigaray. First, Cornell claims, imaginative universalism is "self-consciously an artificial mythology." Since there is no real truth of woman as she was or is, Cornell argues, images of the feminine are critical myths, dreams, and ideals. Critical mythologizing overcomes Kantian duplicity because it produces dreams that are attainable in the near future; they are connected to real needs emergent from within the historical specificity of people's situations. As artificial, moreover, these myths indicate that the very substance of feminine specificity always needs to be revised and envisioned anew with the passage of time and the alteration of circumstance. In Cornell's words,

> Feminine writing . . . does not so much try to reach the truth of Woman through metaphor. Instead we are trying to discover the possibility of the "way out" from our current system of gender identity in which "her" specificity opens up the unknown, in which sexual difference would not be re-appropriated. Through Irigaray's *mimesis*, we move within what has been prefigured so as to continually transfigure it. We not only affirm Woman, we continually re-metaphorize her through the "as if."

The "as if" refers to the utopian breach of the present and past which resurrects a possible future while recognizing the limits of all such dreams. But, Cornell quickly reminds, "to recognize the limit [of the imagination] is not to deny the imagination."[38]

Second, because mythical universals are tied to the very contexts they intend to correct, their body or substance must be retold. Not only at different times but also currently in diverse circumstances, the myth assumes plural shapes. The feminine-universal is told differently or reiterated in diverse ways, for example, by white, middle-class women and poor, working women. One hears in Cornell a tacit theory of oral tradition, wherein the telling of myth, as the vehicle for transmitting historical possibility, necessarily involves metaphoric slippage. Through this slippage, myth adjusts to the changing needs of a society and proliferates to give voice to various subgroup narratives within a society. The practice of "imaginative universalism" strives to curtail false universalism, while nonetheless alleviating unhappy consciousness through dream. Following Derrida's double-gesture, Cornell's third way strives to develop a critical as opposed to naive *mimēsis*. This critical practice requires that we learn to dwell within the border between metaphor and metonymy, critically traversing the space between dreaming the future and knowing that we create possibility *as* dream. As a critical practice, imaginative universalism aims to collapse the hierarchical thinking which subsumes particulars under universals. It strives, not to surmount, but rather to divest humans of universalistic patterns of thinking which mask, as Iris Young says, "the ways in which the particular perspectives of dominant groups claim universality and . . . justify hierarchical decisionmaking structures." Rather than tacitly postulate one group as the harbinger of historical change, the reiterative logic of Cornell's imaginative universalism aspires to cultivate change by enabling the marginalized to enter into the historical process of cocreation of meaning.[39]

4.5. Poetic Contours for Ecstatic Communities

Irigaray and Heidegger share in common the notion that the real is the concretely possible. Thought in concrete, contextualized terms, the possible refers not to abstract, speculative, or logical possibility as if all things can be realized in all times, in every way, for every human. A critical as opposed to naive *mimēsis* dreams a concretely possible future by avoiding the assumption that there is a noumenal or transcendent reality which we asymptotically approach as a static regulative ideal. To dream the future is to assume responsibility for changing our current world, not to lust after a final state of transparency. Analogously, to fill out substantive views of feminine specificity is not to delineate what women essentially are; rather, it is to offer an ethical image of a better way to be given present circumstance. Whereas Cornell finds a precedent for her reading of Irigaray in Derrida, Irigaray shares with Heidegger an explicit concern to provide a poetic-erotic sensibility that divests us of cynicism and nihilism.

What connects Irigaray and Heidegger is their shared view that learning to live *without why* (i.e., without final ground, cause, telos) requires not collapsing, at an attitudinal level, into skepticism about the need for utopian thinking. Settling for topology and transgression would be to lapse into quietism if not full-blown cynicism, and, finally, to relegate the future to a nihilistic reproduction of the same old past. I find Krzysztof Ziarek's comparison insightful. Ziarek contends that neither Irigaray nor Heidegger care simply to analyze systems of difference in the manner that Derrida demarcates the undecidability underlying all fixed systems of meaning. As a counteraction to "the abstract and disinvested nature of thought," Ziarek emphasizes, each cultivates "a new economy of thinking based on nearness and proximity rather than difference and postponement":

> [B]oth Heidegger and Irigaray eventually attempt in their own ways to de-emphasize and displace the economy of difference, and argue the need for a new discursive mode: one attuned to nearness rather than difference, to the interval rather than the opposites, and to the fold rather then the dialectic of otherness and sameness.

Where Heidegger wants to edify western humanity into a capacity for recognition based upon ecstatic proximity rather than struggle, Irigaray cultivates the communal capacity to partake of an "amorous exchange" rooted in *giving* rather than "incompleteness and undecidability." Rather than a cognitive focus on challenging the logic of identity, their respective projects bear ethical import, Ziarek well argues, because they strive to transform the passional dimensions of thinking. Their newly envisaged economies create sensibilities which make possible communities rooted in valuing heterogeneity, rather than remaining based upon the passional confusion between unity and homogeneity. They encourage the development of this new sensibility, not through pure critique of the logic of identity, but by encouraging forms of social attunement that could support a heterogeneous community.[40]

For Heidegger, we attain a productive relation to heterogeneity not directly by focusing on difference in oppositional terms, but rather by realizing that there is a nonhierarchical proximity between beings (all things) and Being (the totality of what is). Humans stand in a nonhierarchal proximity not only to other humans, but also to other beings and spheres of interpreting beings such as gods, mortals, earth, sky (PLT, 150, 179/VA, 144, 172). This vision allows for differences to coexist without reducing various entities to lesser versions of God, man, Nature, or Divinity. Mortals, for example, are not subsets of an absolute measure, a transcendent universal, a final Being, a God. Mortals and gods abide their difference as the proximity which enables each to see what it is. With Irigaray these nonhierarchal relations are more sexual, material, and bodily than in Heidegger. But the economy of the two lips similarly rejects the dichotomy between difference and sameness, since the lips are two yet one, touching without merging but never atomistically distinct.

Like Heidegger, Irigaray dissolves oppositional hierarchies by turning our attention to the space of proximity between the two sexes. Kelly Oliver clarifies,

> For Irigaray, desire *is* difference. This difference is not Lacan's lack, which always leads to opposition and hierarchy, and in which one sex becomes a mere reflection of the other. Irigaray figures desire as "the interval," "the residue," "the between," "a dynamic force," "wonder," as "angels." [Irigaray, Diff] So, if for Lacan desire is the gap between need and demand, for Irigaray it is the wonder-full excess between two sexes.[41]

Overcoming oppositional constructions of desire does not occur by demonstrating the undecidability of an economy built on lack, but rather by thinking sexual relations differently and in this way altering all relations. Irigaray says,

> The link uniting or reuniting masculine and feminine must be both horizontal and vertical, terrestrial and celestial. As Heidegger, among others, has written, this link must forge an alliance between the divine and the mortal, in which a sexual encounter would be a celebration, and not a disguised or polemic form of the master-slave relationship. In this way it would no longer be a meeting within the shadow or orbit of a God the Father who alone lays down the law, or the immutable mouthpiece of a single sex. (Diff, 127)

Irigaray's vision of amorous exchange "re-interpret[s] the whole relationship between the subject and discourse, the subject and world, the subject and the cosmic, the microcosmic and the macrocosmic" (119). It links "*matter* to *form*" and thinks the "interval *between* the two." The interval is "desire," "attraction," "nearness," not an empty void or opaque space (120).

The critical practice of utopianism, which mediates the transcendental-sensible and decenters hierarchy, provides a basis for rethinking recognition and community sustained by a new communal pathos. Irigaray wants to base sexual relations on an ethical demand that I not fill in the space between myself and another with "greed, possession, consummation." Instead this space should vibrate with "wonder." Irigaray claims, "man and woman, woman and man are therefore always meeting as though for the first time since they cannot stand in for one another" (124). She envisions a "communion" or *parousia* that is at once thoroughly bodily (connected at the level of touch, flesh, fluids, mucosity, fertility) and yet so ethical that it is divine (never reducing the other to an object, a "corpse," an inert "body deprived of mucus," or a passionless distance). An intimacy that mixes two together without possessiveness, Irigaray calls "a sexual or carnal ethics" in which "both angel and body" can be found together (127).

What brings Irigaray closer to Heidegger than to Derrida is her sustained concern not to relegate woman, in a nihilistic gesture, to the undecidable. Irigaray and Heidegger, like Kristeva, seek a locus between utopia and anti-utopia, between foundationalism and antifoundationalism, between reifications of ground and nonground alike. They reject both cosmos and chaos theory, univocal truths and pure transgression (the truth that there is no truth). Like Kristeva's *jouissant* subject they seek a position in-between, capable of not absolutizing origins and living without why, on the one hand, but willing not to evade the weightiness of historical circumstance, on the other hand. People need to bind themselves to some 'ground' in the positive and enabling sense of developing alternative bases for nonrepressive forms of social recognition.

Later Heidegger would not refer to his project in terms of metaphoric transference and reiterative universalism. Yet he offers a critical theory of *poiēsis* rooted in a sober form of imagining the future. And, without explicitly addressing the carnal side of this new form of communion, his concept of *Gelassenheit* fills out the contours of a new social pleasure. Instead of criticizing the specular optics of a phallic economy and its lack of carnality, as does Irigaray, he fashions an alternative ecstatic form of wonder. He refigures, I will argue, the trope of the mirror as multiple rather than dichoto- mously organized around self and the position of masterful control over meaning (Other). We always reside in a fourfold, mirroring play wherein the interaction of different beings cannot be reduced to the normalizing gaze of the (masculine) subject. By dreaming up a renewed basis for nonrepressed forms of intimacy, Irigaray and Heidegger dissolve the nihilistic bonds that solidify recognition around an antagonistic struggle and deprive us of the passionate efficacy of imagination.

CHAPTER FIVE

Gelassenheit: Heidegger's Reluctant Utopia

To think Being without beings means: to think Being without regard to metaphysics. Yet a regard for metaphysics still prevails even in the intention to overcome (*überwinden*) metaphysics. Therefore, our task is to cease all overcoming (*vom Überwinden abzulassen*), and leave metaphysics to itself (*überlassen*).

Martin Heidegger, *On Time and Being*

Through a confrontation with Nietzsche's concept of will to power in his lectures between 1936–40, later Heidegger identifies the nihilistic element in western metaphysics as a *desire to overcome*. Heidegger's analysis links the epistemic search for certainty to an ongoing ontological crisis over human mortality and historical finitude. The desire to overcome denotes these two interrelated activities. Striving to secure knowledge in a first principle by overcoming sensuous particularities finds its ontological correlate in the struggle to surmount historical process and bring it under rational organization. But, Heidegger warns, the very desire to overcome rests on a flawed premise, namely, that there is a fundamental symmetry between human reason and reality. Because humans can no more stand behind and conceptually contain reality than they can engineer and perfectly calculate historical progress, this faulty premise heralds a dangerous anthropocentrism; it threatens to foreclose possibilities for achieving forms of recognition based upon heterogeneity and for effectuating historical changes that discontinue our present form of life. Breaking with the premise that reason mirrors reality thus holds implications for fostering sound ethical relations (the former) and for engendering a more utopian future, a future that will be worth living (the latter).

159

Heidegger wants a postmetaphysical world. But, like Irigaray, he believes that the anthropocentric impulse to reduce reality to an image of human being pervades both traditional metaphysics and modern reason's efforts to overcome metaphysics. The effort to get beyond metaphysics, Heidegger submits, cannot be accomplished through a direct assault against metaphysical representation. Every attempt to overcome metaphysics reinforces, if not the premise that we govern history, then the economy of desire which binds us to the logic of identity. Similarly, every effort to circumscribe the desire underpinning metaphysics may destabilize the modern subject of reason and the Enlightenment assumption that history is progressive, but it offers no alternative ethos or poetic desire. For Heidegger, the only way out of metaphysics is to cultivate an alternative attunement to the totality of what exists. Only by relinquishing the desire to overcome can we wean ourselves of the anthropocentric and, I would add, Eurocentric myth of mastery. This new attunement restores and makes explicit an awareness that human reason cannot contain the sensuous nature of things and, moreover, it engenders a poetic or ontological sense of belonging together based upon heterogeneity rather than symmetry.

Later Heidegger envisions this new *poiēsis* in both practical and theoretical terms. His vision of this *poiēsis* as *Gelassenheit* has a double connotation; it means both *letting be* and *releasement*. Reiner Schürmann clarifies that *Gelassenheit* first "appears as an attitude of man" (letting be) in Heidegger's 1944 dialogue, "Conversation on a Country Path about Thinking," yet later becomes articulated as "Being's way to be" (as the *es gibt* that releases us to our world).[1] The practical side of *Gelassenheit* denotes a collective attitude, a mode of comportment *(Gebärde)* toward reality that refuses to reify the world into a containable totality; it resists transforming awareness of the dynamic nature of things as self-showing into a re-presentation of things as static substances or objects. This nonrepresentational form of meditative thinking keeps its conceptual grasp off the self-disclosive character of things and others. It lets things be in their self-showing dynamism and their sensuous particularities.

Heidegger's theoretical strategy for preparing a change in ethos entails demonstrating the *ontologically asymmetrical* and *nonanthropocentric* relation between Being (the totality of what is) and human thought. For Heidegger, Being denotes the linguistic, social, cultural, and historical matrix of meaning into which we are born and thinking is a holistic activity, not simply cognitive but also passionate. Thinking refers to a basic attunement we have to the specific, historical matrix of meaning into which we are born and which orients us to perceive reality and to relate to one another in specific ways. The second connotation of *Gelassenheit* as Being's way to be refers to the structural condition of our historical embeddedness, which is that every constellation of meaning and every lived form of attunement is finite. Heidegger discusses the structure of human finitude by talking about Being as the *es gibt* or the event wherein a particular matrix of meaning emerges through the withdrawal of a surplus of alternative meanings. The *lēthē* in *alētheia*, the absencing in every historical constellation of presencing, introduces an asymmetry that breaks up the logic, best theorized by Hegel, which posits an identitarian relation between Being (meaning) and thinking.

While Heidegger shies away from direct interest in ethics, I want to harness this ontological asymmetry for ethical and moral relations of social recognition. Later I argue that Heidegger's phenomenological ontology contributes to my argument for asymmetrical reciprocity (along with Young) and a concrete model of interactive universalism (with Anzaldúa, Lugones, Gordon). Although the ontological asymmetry between Being and human existence does not suffice to develop an ethical model of asymmetrical reciprocity, it provides a crucial level of justification for such a model. I find it productive to read Heidegger, against his own antinormative predilection, as undertaking an intervention into modern western culture that is both therapeutic and utopian in a normative sense. Heidegger's admittedly abstract and quasi-mystical meditations on Being or the *es gibt* guide us into an experience of our own historical embeddedness and lack of access to a final truth for all times. So interpreted, later Heidegger's corpus seems less a systematic account of the essential human condition and more a series of meditations designed to loosen our ensnarement in the metaphysical assumption of identity. It appears purely nominalist, largely strategic, and fundamentally antinormative. Reading Heidegger against Heidegger, however, stresses the normative ideal of postmetaphysical thinking implicit in the rejection of the logic of identity invoked through these interventions.

In this light, Heidegger's critique of representation marks the first, therapeutic moment in his pedagogical effort to wean westerners of anthropocentrism and an ethos of willful domination. Yet Heidegger's critique goes beyond therapy to a formal delimitation of models that base critical capacities on self-reflexivity. In lieu of self-reflective consciousness, Heidegger's analysis implies that the synchronic and discontinuous aspect of history is the structural condition of possibility for decentering our identities. To experience Being as unrepresentable is not simply to acknowledge that reason is fallible; it is to step-back before the mode of attunement (desire) sustained by our current locus in history, language, and culture. Being designates not simply that reality is always more than mortals can know at any given time, but that the desire for rational closure guiding our historical projects itself poses dangers and needs to be critically mediated.[2] The strategic and therapeutic aspect of Heidegger's meditations yields a second, critical utopian moment. The pedagogical practice of unlearning the myth of mastery culminates in his positive vision of an alternative postmetaphysical mode of existence. Thus, Heidegger's antinormativism (his attacks on valuative systems and modern universalism) implicitly, pragmatically, and performatively projects a normative ideal.

In this chapter, I advance a reading which shows that Heidegger's *theoretical antinormativism*, because worked out as a performative and critical retrieval of an alternative form of life, delineates what Drucilla Cornell calls the *"unerasable trace of utopianism."*[3] Derridean deconstruction and Irigaray's critical mythologizing are thoroughly indebted to Heidegger on this point. Were it not for this unerasable trace in Heidegger's method, we would not be able to salvage the critical Heidegger (who gives up longing for the purity and innocence of lost origins) from the romantic Heidegger (who wanes into quietism and fatalism). Heidegger's method for invoking a utopian vision is both substantive and critical. Like Irigaray, Heidegger understands his substantive vision as a modest corrective to the ethos of modernity and not as a static normative ideal for all times. Even so, by uprooting the drive for a static vision of the fully self-realized humanity, Heidegger introduces a formal delimitation of all static utopian ideals into his substantive notion of *Gelassenheit* as a playful and nondominating engagement with other human and nonhuman beings.

Letting be proves historically relative because what needs to be decentered in modernity is the ethos of mastery. Yet the formal structure of *Gelassenheit* symbolizes the temporal structure of historical existence proper and the dynamic character of phenomena. By depicting critique as an active mediation of the sensible economy of desire peculiar to an historical age, Heidegger models a new kind of normativity with respect to utopian ideals. Since Heidegger lacks a name for this normativism, I propose that Cornell's notion of *reiterative universalism* is applicable. Every age must flesh out its substantive corrective to its one-sidedness; but to approach historical process as unrepresentable already adopts a postmetaphysical ideal. This critically mediating side of Heidegger pertains equally to our origin as to our telos. It anticipates the poststructuralist idea that systems of meaning tend to naturalize a sensible, ontological given and to reify univocal utopian ideals. After using Irigaray's concept of the imaginary as a backdrop (5.1) against which to advance this reading of Heidegger as a utopian thinker (5.2), I show the relevance of his thought for uprooting the logic of identity (5.3) and for ethics (5.4).

5.1 The Relation of the Imaginary to Heideggerian Ontology

I want to establish a link between Heidegger's critique of representational thinking and Irigaray's concept of the imaginary. The notion of the imaginary has a complex and generally not well-clarified usage in Irigaray's work. Rather than address the imaginary in Lacanian terms as part of the psychosexual development of the individual, Irigaray treats the imaginary as a broader notion that operates on a conceptual cum ontological level. In reference to psychosexual fantasy, the imaginary comprises a central element of identity-formation; when the ego posits itself reflexively as consciousness through repression of drives, the self emerges with an imaginary sense of unity. In psychosexual terms, the imaginary identifies the fact that the self's rational sense of coherence is a misrecognition shot through with the unconscious fantasy that it has perfect control over its needs and desires. Although she utilizes a psychoanalytic paradigm, Irigaray is not primarily analyzing psychosexual development. Margaret Whitford suggests that in Irigaray's work "[p]athology is transferred from the individual to the symbolic; it is the symbolic which is sick."[4] Irigaray equates the male imaginary not with a faculty of the individual ego but rather with the sociosymbolic practices that condition identity-formation. The nature of individual fantasy life presupposes this social imaginary, since the child does not develop ego-identity in a symbolic vacuum. Methodologically, then, we cannot account for the symbolic system in terms of adding up the collective sum of male fantasies. To the contrary, Irigaray psychoanalyzes the construction of western rationality as a discursive practice that gives rise to a specific formation of the social imaginary as male. Even though perpetuated through the individual fantasy lives of all who participate in this imaginary, symbolic practices are not first caused by individual imagination.

In her important commentary, Whitford traces three major strains in French thought contributing to Irigaray's broad conception of the imaginary. As opposed to deriving her concept directly from Lacan, Irigaray draws on and combines (i) phenomenological views of imagination (largely derived from Merleau-Ponty but also represented in Sartre), (ii) Bachelard's approach to art, and finally (iii) the union of the political and psychoanalytic treatments of cultural fantasy found in Castoriadis (also in Althusser). Whatever differentiates the first two models, Whitford argues, they share a common view of the imaginary as a "faculty of the mind which alters the images provided by perceptions and *distorts* them" in artistic production. Both Sartre and Bachelard distinguish perception from imagination. This distinction leads Sartre to define the "imagining consciousness" as intentional and to equate the imaginary with its object, whether an object internal to the mind (daydream) or an external "product of imagination" (art, myth, poetry). Bachelard extends this view to include two additional hypotheses. He claims, first, that the imagining mind functions solely in terms of the basic elements of earth, air, fire, and water; and, second, that "creative writers" generally "feel most at home" in one basic element.[5]

Largely speaking, Irigaray displays little interest in Sartre, is more sympathetic to Merleau-Ponty, and never mentions Bachelard; yet Whitford detects both a phenomenological and a Bachelardian influence in her explorations of how the imaginary manifests in artistic, especially literary, productions. Though she shares with Sartre and Bachelard the assumption that myth and poetry reflect the passions out of which they are constructed, Irigaray rejects Sartre's theory of intentionality. Because she "conflates in a single term" Sartre's imagining and perceiving minds, Whitford emphasizes, her view of the imaginary moves "fluidly" across the boundary between "the phenomenological definition of imaginary (the conscious, imagining, and imaging, mind) and the psychoanalytic definition (the unconscious, phantasying mind)." This fluidity, I suggest, marks a clear extension of her claim that our perceptions already reflect unconscious fantasies which stem from society, not the individual intention. The Bachelardian influence appears in Irigaray's *Amante marine* and *L'Oubli de l'air*. There she psychoanalyzes the operation of the social imaginary in Nietzsche's resistance to water and Heidegger's fixation with earth as indicators of the diseased symbolic of western culture. Whereas her conflation of the imagining and perceiving minds anticipates her view of the imaginary as arising from social-symbolic practices, her analyses of Heidegger and Nietzsche attribute their preference for one element not to artistic temperament but rather to a cultural organization of the symbolic in terms of male morphology. "[T]he four elements," Whitford explains, "are subtended by a more basic schema than Bachelard's, namely the male/female division" or the sexual imaginary that grounds western rationality on the exclusion of the feminine.[6]

The third strain influencing Irigaray thus forms the most basic and fundamental aspect of the imaginary and can be traced to Castoriadis's critique of Lacan. Whitford clarifies,

> In *L'Institution imaginaire de la société* (1975), [Castoriadis] proposes a definition of the imaginary which (a) argues that there is an imaginary more primordial than that conceptualized by Lacan, an imaginary of which the mirror stage imaginary would be but a secondary derivation, and (b) deploys the concept of the imaginary in an explicit attempt to understand the persistence of social formations and the possibility of changing them.[7]

Because this definition unites the notion of a *primordial creative source* (which Castoriadis calls magma) with the economy sustaining a *social formation*, Whitford argues, it best captures the rich associations assembled in Irigaray's view of the imaginary. But we must also note Whitford's caveat that Irigaray supplies a sexual dimension to the imaginary not included in any of these influences.

Immensely helpful for clarification, Whitford's analysis also provides a venue into my comparison of Heidegger and Irigaray. I suggest that associating the imaginary with a *primordial creative source* implicitly links symbolic meaning to an ontological residue and not simply a metonymic reservoir of possible slippage in meaning. The imaginary, then, is a *primordial creative source* never reducible to a given social formation or personal appropriations of these social images. Since the imaginary cannot be a metaphysical entity, a reified reservoir of meanings, we must consider it an effect of a given metaphoric economy of symbols but an effect that is greater than the mere inverse of that economy. On the one hand, the imaginary comes into existence as the shadow or excluded dimension of a social formation with its specific symbolic structure.

On the other hand, the creative reservoir offers broader possibilities for imagination than those images which are structured by a symbolic system as its excluded antithesis. If the imaginary did not harbor such excess possibilities, then we could not explain processes like metaphoric transference and reiterative mimesis as means to effectuate a cultural transformation of ethos. Neither could we explicate how humans can understand perspectives that defy their experience through interactive dialogue and asymmetrical reciprocity.

But this brings me to my point. I propose that this *primordial creative source* refers to more than slippage of meaning. Just as for Kristeva metaphorical slippage transforms the psychology of the individual only because meaning is linked to an affective-drive life that exceeds signification, so for Irigaray mimetic reiteration can effectuate a new *poiēsis* only because connected to a physical reality that defies symbolic categorization. That physical reality, I suggest, refers to the fact that sensible particulars defy neat containment in any referential totality (primary metaphorization) and its underlying syntax (metonymic economy of combination). This assumption connects language to a notion of *parousia* which comes very close to the Heideggerian view that all beings are auto-disclosive.[8] As autodisclosive, things have ontological possibilities which never appear to us outside language but which exceed language. While this interpretation appears to press Irigaray dangerously close to an ontological reification of the primordial source as an empirical given, this is not a necessary implication. We need not infer that the creative source has a fixed structure (set of archetypal elements), but it also houses more than the inverse set of images excluded by the phallocratic symbolic as its opposite. For this reason, it cannot be exhausted by generating multiple imaginary concepts of humanity based upon the diverse standpoints embedded in the manifold social locations of all the marginalized in a society.[9] Such an expansion of the imaginary would not add up to the final objective picture of reality. More important, positing reality as harboring sensuous possibilities not contained in any system of meaning and its abstract slippage does not entail a return to empiricism, biologism, or positivism. Instead, it suspends our tendency to assume that there is a given (a static empirical referent) and a got (a total picture of reality, including its shadow).

In this light, Irigaray's notion of physical reality counters the *naturalizing* thrust of the logic of identity which treats entities in terms of substance rather than process. Associating the real with possibilities for disclosure (Heidegger's ontology) and desire (Irigaray's *poiēsis*), Irigaray treats reality as inherently resistant to not only the limitation of the current symbolic system but representation as such. Whitford warns,

> Irigaray would argue that rationality in the western tradition has always been conceptualized or symbolized as male. She adds a psychoanalytic dimension to this . . . by making a connection between the morphology of the body and the morphology of different kinds of thought processes. It must not be assumed here that the body is the empirical body; symbolism (or representation) is selective, and it is clear from *Speculum* that Irigaray is talking about an 'ideal morphology' [Irigaray, SP, 320], in which the relationship to anatomy is metaphorical, somewhat schematic, a 'symbolic' interpretation of anatomy.[10]

What falls outside western rationality—the primordial source—ultimately points to the Heideggerian tenet that no system of representation can contain the real. In a phallocratic symbolic, this outside is imaged as feminine. What guarantees the male subject his freedom deprives the female of autonomy by locking her into unmediated bodily affectivity (she is his body, she is body). Because the feminine is associated with the irrational residue that defies symbolic law, Irigaray sees the male symbolic as nihilistic and destructive; it is totalizing and prevents female anatomy from being mediated metaphorically.[11]

In order to break the *totalizing* tendency of the logic of identity, it does not suffice, however, to multiply the imaginary sources of symbolic meaning. Though necessary, this multiplication can only dissolve the logic of hierarchical subordination and exclusion when we realize that it will not add up to reality. We must foster critical awareness that sensuous particulars (similarities) defy assimilation under unifying categories (sameness). Ending the reign of one primary (phallic) metaphorization will require a poetic form of life that allows multiple mediations of anatomy within the social body, thereby opening up a nonrepressive relation to fantasy and the imaginary. But we can only sustain this cure for the diseased symbolic by instituting a form of metaphorization that makes us cognizant of the asymmetry built into human rationality, for we cannot know reality as a totality. Irigaray's notion, that physical reality subtends social formations, introduces asymmetry at a critical ontological level. It indicates that humans have an ecstatic orientation toward their own inexhaustible and unrepresentable possibilities for developing new forms of life. Happily we can never attain transparency.

Rather than psychoanalyze the Heideggerian imaginary, as I did in my analysis of his involvement in National Socialism, I wish to advance an interpretation of his later view of representation as a critique of a destructive form of imaginative thinking. Heidegger's notion of Being, though not nearly as complex as Irigaray's conception of the imaginary, performs a structural function in his work that parallels the role of the imaginary in Irigaray's work. Being depicts the fact that human existence is historical; the epistemic subject can never stand behind history and see reality as such or find a guarantee that historical actions will yield pure progress. Heidegger staunchly maintains that Being is not an entity or a metaphysical substratum, while also rejecting any facile reduction of Being to a specific sociohistorical configuration. Without elevating it to the status of a symbolic and its imaginary, we can minimally claim that Being—an inclusive term covering both our epochal mode of life and its excess—roughly parallels Irigaray's notion of the imaginary in, minimally, these ways:

1. Being, understood as the event (*Ereignis*) that opens up the historical existence of a particular culture, constitutes an equivalent to the *primordial creative source* which grants our basic possibilities for thinking (rationality) and for interaction (poetic attunement to one another). Far too often Heidegger speaks as though Being were some kind of preexisting reservoir of possibilities independent of human existence. Yet he means to designate the fact that the cultural text of western humanity is always greater than any social formation or historical epoch reveals. Like Irigaray on the imaginary, he postulates *Ereignis* as having both a synchronic moment (the excess that conditions change) and a diachronic moment (a specific sociohistorical formation). Moreover, the synchronic moment depicts more than the mere inverse or excluded aspects of the diachronic unfolding of human history.

2. All modes of thinking, including calculation and meditation, are imaginative ways of bringing-forth (*hervorbringen*) a totality of beings into view; thinking is *poiēsis*. As the excess of any historical mode of rationality, then, Being designates the condition which enables and orients thinking (similar to the way the imaginary funds thought).

3. Thought and imagination are not mere faculties of the mind. Heidegger's holistic view of thinking, as rooted in and arising out of the excess in Being, recognizes no distinct border between conscious and unconscious production, just as Irigaray's view of the imaginary links rationality to fantasy life.

4. Whereas forgetfulness of Being produces destructive effects as do repression and closed symbolic systems, awakening from forgetfulness no more annihilates the necessary structure of absence in Being than becoming cured of repression wipes out the unconscious and than a nonexclusionary symbolic domain eliminates every social imaginary. The difference between health and disease in each case entails a transformation in mode of life that reflects not simply a change in the type of social ethos or erotic distribution of the symbolic economy (what we do), but also a change in *how* we relate to historical processes as such or to symbolization per se.

Just as the imaginary never exists independently of a specific social formation and yet remains irreducible, so too Being never subsists as a force independent of the possibilities latent in an epoch but proves an inexhaustible source of historical possibility. Being is always *our* excess, the excess to our historical-material existence; and yet we experience our being-historical as greater than the mere shadow or unconscious inverse of our current form of life and its diachronic genealogy. We encounter Being, our own synchronic historical excess, as an originary source that, like the social imaginary, carries new possibilities that are disjunctive to our present and past history. Focusing on history as the cumulative effects of human agency in diachronic history ignores those synchronic discontinuities with the past which harbor possibilities for radical change. When transmitted in the mode of forgetfulness, those discontinuous elements prove destructive like the haunting specter of the repressed.

5.2 Heidegger's Tacit Curtailment of the Male Imaginary

Without explicitly isolating gender specific biases, Heidegger's delimitation of modern *ratio* tacitly implicates western rationality in an uncritical form of fantasizing that fetishizes reality. Heidegger's critique of *Vorstellen* (representational thinking) begins from the premise that modernity did not offer a radical break with metaphysics. To the contrary, Heidegger argues, the conceptual shift to modernity simply made explicit the very foundational impulses underlying the classical, metaphysical ideal of rationality. Commenting on Hegel's work, Heidegger defines western metaphysics as "onto-theo-logic" in *Identity and Difference* (ID, 59/126). Metaphysics, he claims, is the activity whereby we account for the totality of beings through giving grounds or reasons until we reach the universal explanatory principle for beings as a whole (58/125). The logic of metaphysics presupposes a fundamental symmetry between Being and thinking; it assumes that Being is *logos*, i.e., thought, reason, and ground. When positing Being as the ground (highest cause) of all that exists, reason "gathers itself toward Being as its ground, in the manner of giving ground and accounting for the ground" (57/124). Metaphysics is onto-theo-logical because it accounts for the totality of beings (ontology) in terms of the highest being (theology) by using logic. Here logic means the science of the total "nexus of grounds" that allows objects to appear in light of their first cause (Being) (59/126).

Heidegger regards the logic of the *logos* as identitarian because, in bringing the totality of what exists under a single, unifying, and ultimate explanatory principle, human reason suppresses the asymmetrical difference between what it can know (thinking) and what exists (Being). It represses critical awareness of its own finitude. By interpreting the concept of Being as the sensible excess in all things which defies categorization, we can translate Heidegger's point, namely, that failing to think the difference between Being and beings suppresses discontinuity and reduces historical process to an anthropocentric projection of the epistemic subject. In Heidegger's words, "[i]f we try to form a representational idea of [this difference], we will be misled at once into conceiving of difference as a relation which our representing adds to Being and to beings. Thus the difference is reduced to a distinction, something made up by our understanding (*Verstand*)" (62/129). When the Enlightenment replaces a suprarational first cause with human reason as the ground of reality, Heidegger finds not a break with the past but rather the culmination of the metaphysical view that human *ratio* attains to its own rationality by mirroring Being and finding Being mirrored in reason.

Interestingly, rather than simply challenge the identitarian assumption that Being (reality) and thinking are symmetrical at a strictly cognitive and formal-conceptual level, Heidegger directs his critique to the *desire* and ethos he believes actuate representational thinking. At the height of his mature thought, in his 1956 Bremen lecture *Der Satz vom Grund,* Heidegger identifies the fundamental ontological anxiety humans experience before their historical finitude as a *compulsion to ground.* Though he prefers the language of will to that of desire and addresses this anxiety in gender-neutral terms, his description underscores that this specific, compulsive passion suffuses western rationality:

> The understanding demands that there be a foundation (*Begründung*) for its statements and assertions. Only founded statements are intelligible and intelligent (*verstandlich und verständig*). Yet understanding requires reasons not only for its statements, but human cognition (*das menschliche Vorstellen*) is already looking for reasons as soon as it dabbles in those things about which it might make statements. In all that surrounds and concerns it, human cognition seeks reasons (*Gründen*), often only the most proximate ones, sometimes even the more remote reasons, but in the end it seeks first and last reasons (*Gründen*). (PR, 3/SG, 13)

He punctuates the compulsive character of representational thinking as a "ubiquitous quest for reasons" that "*pervades* human cognition" (*Vorstellen*) and thrives on "getting to the bottom of what is encountered" (3/13).

According to Heidegger, it took a lengthy 2300-year period of gestation before western *ratio* rendered explicit its ubiquitous desire in Leibniz's famous dictum, *nihil est sine ratione.* With this dictum western thought becomes cognizant that its basic mode of comportment (*Verhalten*) toward reality "stand[s] and fall[s] in the train of the principle of reason" which is "the motive of its conduct" (*Beweggrund seines Verhaltens*) (4/14). Western rationality *is* this desire to provide reasons; it is a 2300-year-old "cognitive habit" (*Gewöhnung des Vorstellens*) (9/22). Nonetheless, Heidegger quickly declares that cognizance is not critique. What interests Heidegger is that Leibniz's explicit theorization of the principle of reason does not bring modernity to see this cognitive habit *as a habit, a passion, a mode of comportment,* indeed the way we dwell among things and approach reality. Though this principle enables significant gains, we inherit the practice of seeking grounds as a specific *poiēsis;* our compulsion to ground proper is a customary way of in-habiting life without actively questioning that habit (9/22). The German term used by Heidegger, *Gewöhnung,* means not only habit or custom but also *addiction.* "It is clear," Heidegger says, that "we adhere to [fundamental principles] without reflection" (*befolgen sie ohne Besinnung*). More accurately rendered, we follow (*befolgen*) the direction in which custom points us; we obey (*befolgen*) without deliberation (*Besinnung*) (20/42).

This discussion of habit as orienting thinking in a particular direction rests upon Heidegger's theory of history. Defining historical process as the *Geschick* or destinal sending of Being, Heidegger claims that to be historical is to find ourselves thrown, sent, born into a finite historical epoch (61–62/108–9). Since Being denotes, not an entity or first cause, but rather the structural condition of our own historicalness, we experience Being, our epochal location, as a synchronic slice in history which Heidegger terms *Ereignis*. *Ereignis* names the event (the *es gibt*) whereby a specific economy of meaning arises, a gathering of all things into a particular set of relations and conceptual possibilities that are partially discontinuous with past configurations of meaning. To be historically situated, then, is not simply to find ourselves neutrally placed in a location but rather to be impelled in a direction. Being historical casts us into a basic comportment toward reality. For example, the technological era gives us a certain set of ontological sensibilities and epistemic possibilities peculiar to the age. To be cast into history is to be released toward a historically finite interpretive horizon and a collective disposition to perceive reality in a specific way. The life of thought—enacted by individuals within a specific culture, language, and historical space—moves within the medium of the historical sensibilities of the age; thinking is a way we dwell among things.

Being historical, from a Heideggerian standpoint, is a double-faced phenomenon. It conditions wonder; we find ourselves embedded in a specific historical constellation that opens up possibilities that are not one-to-one effects of human agency. Yet the very momentum of this historical throw weights us down in an unacknowledged ethos. Precisely by being thrown into fascination with the unfolding of diachronic historiographical venues, we lapse into ontological laziness and forgetfulness. We fail to question the basic habitus of the age and its economy of meaning; we forget to question what transpires behind our backs, that is to say, the particular way that history constructs our sensibilities, desire, thought—our compulsiveness. As in his earlier position, later Heidegger continues to depict modernity in one-dimensional terms and to persist in his dismissive attitude toward other methods of philosophical critique which have their own edifying effects. If careful, however, we can isolate what is of value in Heidegger's critique without jettisoning all of modernity. Rather than conclude, with Heidegger, that we attain no critical relation to our age without acknowledging in a radical way our historical finitude, we can instead claim that critique remains incomplete without examining the basic ethos of western rationality and the assumption that history is the progressive unfolding of reason.[12]

Heidegger teaches us that developing a critical relation to historical process comprises one main ingredient in nourishing nondominating forms of life. History provides those concepts, ideas, and beliefs that together congeal into a legacy. That legacy orients our historical epoch and forms the foundational conceptual knowledge for speculative reasoning about how to tackle new historiographical problems and how to compensate for our continued shortcomings in the struggle to become a more fully rational humanity. But history also narrows our vision and channels our primary motivations into a set of habits, historically old and regularly modified, yet nonetheless solidified in ways that restrict our ability to imagine the new. In order to recover a deep sense of wonder that might enable us to develop alternative ways of thinking and perceiving, we must counteract the momentum of our habitual patterns of thought and the ways we conceptually approach problems. Ultimately, Heidegger argues, counteracting the weighty momentum of historical embeddedness brings us to face our groundlessness. A critical relation to historicalness proper opens the doorway to learning to mediate our desire for first causes (grounds) and final states (God).

Although humans neither create nor fully control history, they also do not simply suffer history passively. The desire to understand may not be a defect, but Heidegger indicts the indifferent and complacent acceptance of the search for grounds as compulsive because at a preconscious level we choose to remain habituated and weighted down by the cumulative momentum of 2300 years of history. Influenced by Nietzsche, Heidegger describes the compulsion of western *ratio* as a deliberate posture, an "insurrection" and willful "assault" against Being by humans (QCT, 100/H, 236) rooted in a *"horror vacui"* and "flight" from groundlessness (N4, 31, 155/N11, 65, 210). Not only can we hear echoes of castration anxiety (i.e., the male imaginary) in Heidegger's appeal to Nietzsche but we see that to be destined never simply befalls us. Humans always adopt a posture before, and are not simply neutrally placed within, the ontological sensibilities of a historical *topos*. In the age of representation, western *ratio* pursues certain possible venues of analysis by refusing to critique the supposition that everything has a ground and that reason itself can supply this ground.[13] Though gender-neutral, this analysis portrays a deliberately assumed passivity before the metaphorical associations wrapped around western ideals of rational impartiality, associations attributed to the feminine or absencing side of historical existence. Heidegger's analysis tacitly exposes an erotic economy of desire, a passive aggression toward the uncontrollable features of existence, a compulsion-addiction that grounds the search for impartiality in suppression of sensuous particulars. The significance of this analysis is that mediating our historical-ontological sensibilities comprises a specific and irreducible activity necessary to adopting a critical relation to rational reconstructions of normative ideals.

Modern Representation as Sheer Fantasizing

In "The Age of The World Picture" (1938), Heidegger argues that the central ramification of the modern drive for certainty is that humans begin to lose the capacity to distinguish between reality and fantasy. Modernity ushers in the eclipse of reason's own shadow, namely, fantasia. Accordingly, reason reproduces itself as sheer fantasy, as the dangerous illusion that reason is the ground and master of all that exists. My reading claims that Heidegger's distinction between fantasia (reason's productive ground) and fantasizing (a form of fetishization) anticipates Irigaray's model of critical mythologizing. Without explicitly focusing on the specular optics of modernity, as do Irigaray and Foucault, Heidegger defines modernity as the age in which three interrelated phenomena occur: (a) reality becomes reduced to a mirror image of human being; (b) reason mimetically re-presents reality as a picture or world view; and (c) reason forecloses real historical possibilities for change when it reduces reality to its mirror image. Although Heidegger's concept of fantasy differs in fundamental ways from that of Irigaray, we can interpret his critique of representation as a practical curtailment of masculine utopianism (which fetishizes *archē* and telos) and a tacit recovery of a productive model of fantasy as central to historical development.

For Heidegger, representational thinking depicts what is unique to modern rationality. Representation images reality as an objectifiable totality which, because objectifiable, guarantees Cartesian certainty or, as Heidegger cautions, the dangerous illusion of

security. Modernity, he says, liberates humanity through the introduction of "subjectivism and individualism. But it remains just as
certain that no age before this one has produced a comparable
objectivism" (QCT, 128/H, 81). Three things are central to modern
reason, according to Heidegger. First, there is a "necessary interplay between subjectivism and objectivism," a "reciprocal thinking
of one by the other" (128/81). Though addressed in gender-neutral
terms, this interplay denotes something akin to a specular matrix.
To Heidegger's mind, humanity becomes "subject" in modernity in
a preeminent sense:

> [W]hen man becomes the primary and only real *subiectum*, that
> means . . . Man becomes the relational center of that which is as
> such. But this is possible only when the comprehension of what is
> as a whole changes. In what does this change manifest itself?
> (128/81)

Heidegger answers,

> Where the world becomes picture, what is, in its entirety, is jux-
> taposed as that for which man is prepared and which, correspond-
> ingly, he therefore intends to bring before himself and have before
> himself, and consequently intends in a decisive sense to set in
> place before himself. (129/82)

Behind the epistemological turn to subjectivism lie "events more
profound," namely the reduction of the world to a one-dimensional
mirror made in the image of human being (128/81). While incapable of identifying a dominant conceptual scheme as narrowly
depicting masculine biases, Heidegger does hold that anthropocentrism leads to a truncated grasp of the world and all beings
in it. The reign of the logic of identity culminates, for Heidegger, in
the modern inability to remain in touch with the autodisclosive
character of interaction.

Heidegger resists any model of critical reflexivity built upon
the concept of world views, the second feature identified by
Heidegger as central to modern reason. Instead of advancing an
interactive model whereby individuals attain heightened critical
consciousness by bridging world views, the notion of world view,
Heidegger believes, perpetuates rather than challenges the representational economy of meaning which binds subjectivism to an
objectivism run rampant. Circumscribed by the epistemic subject

and its objectifiable totality, that economy remains incorrigibly caught in the vicious assumption that there exists an identitarian symmetry between reason and Being. The concept of world views merely proliferates the logic of identity with the pernicious effect that individuals become increasingly alienated from one another, enclosed every more deeply in the isolated and disencumbered space of their private world views. For Heidegger, imaging the world as so many pictures deprives humans of the poetic basis for engaging in nonobjectifying relationships because we no longer treat other subjects as autodisclosive, as different. By nourishing an incipient indifference toward the autodisclosive nature of things, modern reason encourages the belief that my view is objective and boxes me into an enhanced reification of all things as objectifiable. Ultimately even humans fall under the haunting aegis of instrumental reason. Loss of the capacity for nondominating forms of recognition to others (difference, particularities) ensues.

To continue my critical use of Heidegger against Heidegger, I find his treatment of the ethos of modernity compelling but I resist his one-sided methodology. Heidegger seriously undervalues interactive possibilities for bridging horizons as a crucial ingredient in attaining an awareness of the limitations of struggles to achieve and reconstruct paradigms of objectivity and normativity. Yet we can reinterpret his point to suggest that one element of critique must be a basic questioning of our fundamental ontological and epistemic sensibilities and this critique leads us to explore the metaphorical fantasies underpinning our paradigms of reason. From a Heideggerian standpoint, the attempt to decenter modern impartiality through bridging world views must remain partial and incomplete because it leaves the view of reason as grounded in self-reflexivity intact. Only by acknowledging that reflective capacities are historically embedded, Heidegger suggests, can we develop a critical relation to the unquestioned ethos and poetic sensibilities grounding self-reflection. This analysis shifts from an examination of human reflection as fallible to exploring how finite historical conditions suffuse all rational projects with fantasies and desires that are themselves fallible. If recognition of the impossibility of achieving a symmetrical and transparent relation between reason and reality is crucial to critique, then Heidegger nonetheless misses the converse point, that decentering the epistemic subject of modernity remains abstract and indeterminate when not filled out through interaction with other critically engaged actors in a shared, public world.

The third feature of modern reason is that it posits the subject at the center of reality and thus makes history appear as the agonal struggle of competing world views and, more centrally, as a conquerable process:

> What is decisive is that man himself expressly takes up this position as one constituted by himself, that he intentionally maintains it as that taken up by himself, and that he makes it secure as the solid footing for a possible development of humanity. . . . There begins the way of being which mans the realm of human capability as a domain given over to measuring and executing, for the purpose of gaining mastery over that which is as a whole. (QCT, 132/H, 84).

The assumption that human being can image, produce, control, will, master, and govern reality closes down the historical process, according to Heidegger. This alleged attainment of perfect symmetry between reality and human reason is the hallmark of folly and ushers in a total eclipse of the autodisclosive nature of phenomena.

In Irigaray's psychoanalytic terms, the ascension of rationality to its zenith witnesses the total eclipse of a critical relation to the male imaginary; the more divested of a poetic basis reason becomes, the less aware it remains of its fetishized foundation achieved through the exclusion of Woman. In Heideggerian terms, what becomes historically explicit (namely, that in metaphysics reason posits itself as ground), lapses into occlusion; the nearest thing to us remains farthest from critique. No longer able to see its shadow, western rationality becomes the very harbinger of destruction, Heidegger forewarns. In the name of the progressive development of humanity, reason sets off full speed ahead on a collision course with its own nihilistic imaginary hidden in the desire to master history. That is, by arrogating to itself the power to determine being as objectifiable, reason's creative reproduction of the world becomes an impotent form of imagining the future; it reduces possibility to a projection of our current ways of thinking. Historical progress folds back on itself, doomed to reproduce the will to mastery which engenders only domination. The idea that humans develop their humanity from the standpoint of objectification Heidegger finds comical, for this idea evinces the fact that we are fast losing touch with a sense of mortality; we forget that we cannot get behind and master history any more than we can conquer the imaginary or collective unconscious.

The relation between Heideggerian thought and Cornell's interpretation of Irigaray appears more clearly at this juncture. This one-dimensional mirroring of reality in the image of human reason produces a sterile and uncreative form of thought. No metaphoric transference can take place in a mimetic repetition of history that proves reductionist, circular, and vicious. And no genuine *utopian* movement toward a new form of interaction, a new *poiēsis*, can emerge from conditions wherein we reify ourselves as masters over history (QCT, 27/VA, 31). Representational thinking heralds at best a limited grasp of the creative impulse and the role of fantasy in metaphorically mediating the fact that reality defies neat categorization. For the modern episteme, creativity is genius, a specific endowment of intellect, an active faculty of imagination. But this conception of creativity depicts an ethos that no longer acknowledges the source of creativity—the ontological excess, the auto-disclosive character of all human and nonhuman beings—which the human mind does not create. For Heidegger, losing touch with our creative relation to real possibility (this excess) transmutes fantasia into a dangerous, truncated form of sheer fantasizing peculiar to instrumental rationality.

In his important "Appendix 8" to "The Age of the World-Picture," Heidegger differentiates between two kinds of fantasy which he equates with the classical view of reality as unconcealment (auto-disclosive) and modern representation:

> In unconcealment *fantasia* comes to pass: the coming-into-appearance, as a particular something, of that which presences—for man, who himself presences toward what appears. Man as representing subject, however, *"fantasizes,"* i.e., he moves in *imaginatio*, in that his representing imagines, pictures forth, whatever is, as the objective, into the world as picture. (QCT, 147/H, 98)

Although he questionably presents Greek thought as pristine and modern representation as sullied, his distinction between *fantasia* and *fantasizing* informs his critique of modern representation. Heidegger argues that the Sophist assertion that "Man is the measure of all things" is not a species of modern subjectivism (143/95). The debate between Plato and Protagoras over the relation of reason to reality (Being), transpires beyond the modern dichotomy between subject and object, according to Heidegger. Presupposing the autodisclosive unconcealment of all things as the necessary condition of thinking, Protagoras questioned how human being could preserve this horizon of disclosure in apprehension. For the Greeks, Heidegger claims, there was not a detached, isolated I that transcendentally imposes its measure on reality. "[M]an can never be *subiectum*" for the Greeks because Being is presencing and truth is unconcealment; whereas for the moderns Being can never be unconcealment because human being is *subiectum* and truth is representation (147/98). The former thinking employs fantasia in order to maintain awareness of differences in sensible particularities and to suspend the impulse to achieve conceptual mastery over the world, while modern representation collapses reality into the mind's (fantasizing) images.

One thing missing in modern representation, from both a Heideggerian and Irigarayan standpoint, is a definitive sense of its accompanying fantasy. Professing to be purely cognitive, conceptual, and nonmetaphoric, modern reason cannot deal with the imaginary basis of rationality; it sharply divides mythos from *logos*. Earlier I pointed out, in my discussion of Irigaray's critique of Lacan, that the attempt to find a pristine moment of the real separated from the imaginary fetishizes Woman (or some excluded Other). Reason then suffers the return of its repressed in the form of anxiety about grounds, either as castration fear in Irigaray, or as ontological *angst* about groundlessness in Heidegger, and finally as nihilism in both (matricide in Irigaray and destruction of the earth and humanity in Heidegger). Heidegger's analysis lends credence to Irigaray's argument that we can only bring about change by dealing with the imaginary basis of production, artistic and social. Instead of marching to the tune of a rationality that sobers up from myth and metaphor, we need to *critically* mediate the metaphoric basis of conceptualization, to critically mediate the sensible proper or the autokinetic nature of reality. Otherwise we end up with no distance on our myths and the nihilistic vengeance of the return of the repressed.

The Heideggerian distinction between fantasia and fantasizing allows us to comprehend his notion of *Gelassenheit* as releasement from the pernicious effects of a specific kind of imagination, fantasizing. What Heidegger calls fantasizing Irigaray more aptly calls fetishizing. Fetishizing refers to a naive foreclosure and repression of fantasy by severing a symbolic system of meaning (in which representational thinking transpires) from its imaginary basis, thereby generating a wild and uncritical (masculine) utopianism in which the repressed rises up as the dreamy, romanticized telos of the (gendered) subject of history. Despite the lack of an explicit declaration of his relation to the metaphorical and even a definitively positive evaluation and critical conception of fantasy proper, Heidegger subdues his earlier fetishizing tendencies through a critical recovery of fantasia. Implicit, though not intended, in this act is a (partial) abatement of the male imaginary. Because all forms of thinking, instrumental and noninstrumental, are forms of *poiēsis* for Heidegger, we can interpret his return to the mytho-poetic as a *critical mediation* of the underlying basis of conceptualization (akin to Irigaray's metaphorical mediation of the sensible) rather than a mythical longing for untainted immediacy. My interpretation plays down the essentializing strain in Heidegger's metanarrative that "[w]estern history has been under the spell of the 'metaphysics of presence'" and emphasizes instead that his mythic rendition of western history moves beyond strategic essentialism; it enacts a critical mediation of the autokinetic (sensible) dimension of reality as such.[14] Heidegger's work cultivates a kind of *poiēsis* (fantasia) which creatively brings into view the auto-disclosive character of all beings.

The Link between Fantasizing and Nihilism

The Heideggerian narrative asserts that western history underwent a reversal from Plato to Nietzsche, a reversal from presupposing the autodisclosive character of reality as the foundation of knowledge to positing human reason as the measure of the real. This story depicts western humanity as progressively dissociating rationality as productive *technē* from its poetic basis, thereby increasingly narrowing the operation of thinking from a creative way of opening up historical possibilities to an instrumental form of rationality. The Greeks, Heidegger notes, understood *technē* as a form of *poiēsis*. *Technē* is not just a skill or technique of fabrication; rather it "belongs to bringing-forth, to *poiēsis*; it is something poetic" (QCT, 13/VA, 16). Thinking, like art, is *poiēsis* and denotes human engagement in the creative process of bringing something forth into appearance.[15] Hence, thinking assists a thing in its creative self-disclosure. What is "decisive" about *technē* "does not lie at all in making and manipulating nor in the using of means, but rather in the aforementioned revealing," in *alētheia* (13/16). Heidegger attributes the source of fantasia not to the intentionality of the imagining mind, but to the dynamic self-showing of a thing from out of itself. *Technē*, understood as technique, manipulation, and fabrication, is a derivative and truncated form of participation in the process of disclosure. Instrumental reason, we can infer, becomes dangerous once severed from an engagement with the ontological fact that things cannot truly be reduced to human conceptualization.

In his 1939 lecture course on Nietzsche, "The Will to Power as Knowledge," Heidegger treats the willful compulsion to bring reality under rational control as both a perversion and extension of Greek thought. The Greek understanding of phenomena as self-showing, he argues, undercuts the distinction between the real and the copy, between concept and image. Presencing names the way that a thing shows itself in its outward appearance (*eidos*) as imagelike: "What is imagelike does not consist in what is fabricated, like a copied imitation. The Greek sense of 'image'—if we may use this word at all—is a 'coming to the fore,' *phantasia*, understood as 'coming to presence'" (N3, 29/NI, 505–6). The western understanding of image undergoes a full reversal within the span of western history. Whereas for Heraclitus, knowledge consists in guarding "the 'view' that something proffers," for modernity image denotes the "representational object" projected by the human mind (29/505). This reversal enacts a shift from *fantasia as preservation* to *fantasizing as imposition of form*, from receptive letting be to conceptual domination. Heidegger claims that the history of metaphysics, by failing to critically mediate the poietic basis of thought in *alētheia* (unconcealment), issues in a debasement of *technē*. Metaphysics severs the productive character of thinking from its primordial creative source and rationality deteriorates into an instrumental desire to surmount reality.

Despite high praise for Greek thought, Heidegger argues that although the Greeks "dwelt" in unconcealment, they failed to "think" it (EGT, 77/VA, 220). Platonism marks the beginning of metaphysics, for Heidegger, while Plato himself proves a transitional figure. Plato's thought is preanthropocentric, prehumanistic, and prevaluational. Nevertheless, by inaugurating the desire to surmount beings toward a transcendent cause, Plato prepares the anthropocentric turn and the hierarchizing features of metaphysics (N3, 58–59/NI, 540–41). Since, like all Greek thinkers, Plato presupposes the autodisclosive nature of phenomena, Heidegger claims that Plato's philosophical problematic centered on how not to misperceive the self-showing appearance of entities. Regarding this self-showing in its outward appearance (*eidos*), Plato attempts to name that which enables all visibleness. The *idea* allows the emergence of a thing from out of concealment or hiddenness to come into view (PD, 262/W, 131). Against the theory that Plato erects a two-world doctrine, Heidegger argues that for Plato presencing (*idea*) is never separate from sensuous form (*eidos*); appearance is not different from reality. "Only what appears can in the first place show an aspect and form" and "[o]nly a thinking which has beforehand thought Being in the sense of presencing into unconcealment (*alētheia*) can think the presencing of what is as idea" (EGT, 56/H, 341).[16]

Yet even without reducing reality to a product of the representing mind and thus to the sterile *mimēsis* of sheer fantasy, Plato unwittingly readies the two-world doctrine. On the one hand, Platonic education teaches steadfastness at wresting presencing from hiddenness "so that one's gaze is made fast to the firm limits of the things standing fast in their outward appearance" (PD, 259/W, 128). By calling *idea* the *agathon* (good), Plato did not think in terms of rank, hierarchy, or moral value because *agathon* did not mean the "*summum bonum*" (N4, 168/NII, 221). Plato's good was not a moral concept, Heidegger argues, but rather designated the "suitable." The *idea* yields knowledge by "mak[ing] a being *fit* to *be* a being," to appear as what it is (169/222). On the other hand, Plato's focus on the permanent visibility of phenomena brings the genuine condition of knowledge, namely, unconcealment (*alētheia*), under the yoke of the *idea* (what reason can perceive). This yoking covers over the fact that unconcealment occurs independently of human reason and that knowledge relies upon the self-showing character of phenomena. Tacitly instituting the highest *idea*, the *agathon*, as the a priori ground of seeing (knowledge), Plato obscures the self-revelatory character of entities and transmutes truth into correct perception (*orthotes*) (PD, 265/W, 136).

This Platonic gesture unleashes the metaphysical ideal of rationality as "correctness of representing through assertion" (266/138). Knowledge of sensible things, *ta physika*, subsequently is made possible by that which surpasses sensuous form—the Being that is *meta ta physika* (N4, 164/NII, 216). "[G]lazing up to the 'ideas'" in order to know the permanent *eidos* within changing appearances, the philosophical quest for knowledge surmounts sensuous form in order to win a foothold in that which enables presencing (the *idea*) (PD, 268/W, 141). Aiming at the education of the *animal rationale*, philosophy becomes humanism, the steadying of the soul by gazing on that which is permanent and not susceptible to change (269/142). Ripe for the two-world doctrine, philosophy becomes theology, the search for the highest *idea* (268/ 141; cf. N3, 58/NI, 541).

Having instituted an ideal of rationality as the mind's ability to grasp the *idea* (Plato) or to categorize beings (Aristotle), classical thought paves the way for representing reality as a static and ultimately objectifiable totality. Once "[t]he totality of beings is the single object of a singular will to conquer," little impedes postulating reason as the very ground of reality (EGT, 37/VA, 343). Despite the slow 2300-year incubation, it was a small conceptual step from classical metaphysics to Leibniz's dictum, *nihil est sine ratione* and ultimately to Nietzsche's will to power (QCT, 142/H, 93).

> Now the essence of the *idea* changes from visibility and presence to representedness for and through the one who is representing.... Being—Idea—becomes a condition over which the one representing the subject, has disposal and must have disposal if objects are going to be able to stand over against him. (N4, 174/ NII, 230)

The reversal, whereby western *ratio* erects itself as the condition of knowledge, marks an occlusion of the dynamic autodisclosive nature of unconcealment. Unconcealment means that all things emerge into a particular constellation of presencing only because some other possible configuration recedes. Associating knowledge with visibility, the optics of modern rationality occludes the epistemic subject's dependence upon the dynamic process of unconcealment, *alētheia*. For Heidegger, Kant "takes the decisive step" in this reversal. When characterizing the activity of the transcendental subject as generating the conditions of objective reality, Kant makes representing the very essence of reality. Being, the totality of what is, can be known because it is representable (174/230).

But it is Nietzsche who exposes the two fundamental features of western metaphysics: first, he tracks the genealogy of modern *ratio* back to the Greek understanding of reason as a desire to surmount sensuous matter; second, he identifies the link between this desire and erecting hierarchal systems of value. Heidegger interprets Nietzsche as showing that Kant's categories are not static but rather dynamic ways of schematizing reality by projecting fixed horizons of possibility. Nietzsche shows that all "taking-something-for-true" (schematization) is a positing of value (evaluation) wherein thought reckons its own conditions of possibility (176/24). Values hold no absolute meaning but instead serve as the conditions of self-enhancement (50/88). All life, not simply human life, accomplishes itself as the self-productive activity (*technē*) of positing the conditions of its self- surpassing, i.e., a horizon which it then moves beyond. "Forming horizons belongs to the inner essence of living beings themselves," the means by which the overwhelming refulgence of life (becoming) creates order out of chaos as a temporary condition of self-enhancement (N3, 86/NI, 573).

Nietzsche, taking his cue from Kant, defines intellection as this praxis of schematizing becoming. Rational schematization is none other than a practical exigency of life, not merely a structure of *ratio*, but the fundamental comportment by which human being inheres in life (86–89/573–77, cf. 68/551). So extending his analysis of representational thought beyond Descartes's ego and Kant's transcendental subject, Nietzsche brings the modern metaphysics of will (Schopenhauer, Hegel, et al.) to completion. He gathers the will to surmount back into its classical roots in *technē* understood as *poiēsis*. Because the projection of a horizon of meaning arises out of a groundlessness (becoming), representation does not interpret a preexistent objective reality. It is poetizing command (will), the free self-legislation of life over itself (N3, 97, 119/NI, 611).

For Nietzsche, Heidegger claims, nihilism arises because metaphysics posits values that uproot life from its inherence in the creative force of will to power. Naively submitting to absolute ideals, Greek metaphysics emasculates western humanity, depriving it of rootedness in creativity (N4, 44/NII, 81). If the Heidegger of the thirties felt seduced by Nietzsche, then the later Heidegger identifies will to power with the culmination of the nihilistic attitude inaugurated with the two-world doctrine of Platonism.[17] Though impressed by the Nietzschean view of thought as creative bringing-forth (*technē*), Heidegger believes that Nietzsche arrogates the power to create to human being. He accuses Nietzsche, along with the Greeks, of neglecting to critically transform the poetic economy of desire that gave birth to metaphysics. What Nietzsche overlooks in harkening back to Greece is the implicit, albeit unthought, possibility of an alternative kind of *poiēsis*.

Heidegger indicts the Nietzschean rendition of the impetus to surmount as nihilistic on two counts. First, it is self-camouflaging: "[M]etaphysics' utmost entanglement in the inauthenticity of nihilism comes to language in the desire to overcome (*Überwinden-wollen*)." In other words, "under the guise of an overcoming of nihilism, [this entanglement] transposes nihilism into the effectuality of its deracinated nonessence" (N4, 231/NII, 375). Second, it reproduces the ethos of mastery as insurrection against the unrepresentable nature of phenomena:

> To *want* to overcome nihilism—which is not to be thought in its essence—and to *overcome* it would mean that man of himself advance against Being in itself in its default. But who or what could be powerful enough to attack Being itself, no matter from what perspective or with what intent, to bring it under the sway of man? An overcoming of being itself can never be accomplished—the very attempt would revert to a desire to unhinge the essence of man. (N4, 223/NII, 366)

For Heidegger, two dangerous outcomes prevail. The first is loss of memory. Without recollecting the poetic excess in our historical being, western humanity poses as "lord of the earth" (QCT, 27/VA, 31) and marches toward the total "Europeanization of the earth and of man" (OWL, 15/US, 103). Instead of a critical mediation of history, this pose reduces historical possibility to a perpetuation of our current form of life. Second, modern representation deteriorates into an ethos of instrumentalism. Reality appears not only as objectifiable but as objects to be stockpiled and used at human whim and disposal. The desire to surmount unfurls the impotence and sterility of instrumental reason (modern *technē*) and its deluded imagination and fantasizing (QCT, 15/VA, 19).

The key danger inherent in the technological attitude, Heidegger warns in semiapocalyptic tones, is that the delusion of mastery can become our reality. Once we lose touch with the self-disclosive nature of beings, we transform human relations into instrumental ones. We can win a Pyrrhic victory through the assertion of rational mastery:

> It is not primarily that in advancing against Being itself thinking falls into what is logically impossible, but that with such an attack on Being it rises to renounce Being itself, and pursues the surrender of man's essential possibility. That pursuit, despite its absurdity and logical impossibility, could be fatefully (*Geschicklich*) realized (*sich verwirklichen*). (N4, 224/NII, 366)

Rather than depict thinking as quietist, the fantasy that we master history can unhinge our essence. In "The Question Concerning Technology," Heidegger characterizes this unhinging as a peculiar "delusion" in which "it seems as though man everywhere and always encounters only himself" when in actuality "*precisely nowhere does*

man today any longer encounter himself, i.e., his essence" (QCT, 27/
VA, 31). Once caught in the instrumental view of ourselves as
masters of reality, we ironically lose the capacity to experience the
autodisclosive nature of self and others. The instrumental or calculative standpoint brings human being "to the very brink of a pre-
cipitous fall; that is, he comes to the point where he himself will
have to be taken as standing-reserve," i.e., as a disposable object
for use (27/31).

The Heideggerian thesis, that all things are autodisclosive,
carries ethical implications. This thesis sketches a connection, however mediated, between recognizing the asymmetrical relation of
reason to reality and the ethical capacity to sustain nonobjectifying
relations to one another. More important, from Heidegger's standpoint, is that without a poetic form of life which lets the irreducible
sensuous particularities of all things be, we lose any sense of urgency about the importance of cultivating meditative or
nonobjectifying forms of thinking. If we let the capacity to muse
atrophy, we fail to hold open the unerasable future dream of genuine humanity.[18] Heidegger clearly lacks the conceptual framework
for discussing a transformation in *poiēsis* as a form of metaphoric
transference. His notion of *poiēsis* refers to an ontological transformation in the way we dwell among things as opposed to altering
our relation to symbolic practices. Yet by claiming that *logos* is
mythos (WT, 10/WD, 7; EGT, 39–40/VA, 325) and that thinking is
fantasia, Heidegger foreshadows Irigaray's position that there is no
reality outside of fantasy, even as she differentiates between psychosis and sanity.

Heidegger demarcates delusion (fantasizing rooted in the abstract, speculative mind) from the fantasia that concretely prepares a critical mediation of ontological sensibilities (Heidegger) or
the social imaginary (Irigaray). Heidegger's recollective thinking
(*Andenken*) and Irigaray's critical mythologizing instantiate situated forms of transmitting ideas aimed at dissolving mere repetition of the same old identitarian logic which postulates a symmetry
between reality (the symbolic) and human being (the male imaginary). Their methods mimetically recollect what is lost, forgotten,
taken for granted as the poetic basis of social transformation. In
this fashion they rethink Being (Heidegger) and the symbolic
(Irigaray) in a nonrepressive and nonreductive fashion. From the
respective standpoints of Irigaray and Heidegger, origin (autokine-
sis or the imaginary) can no longer be presented as a fixed substratum or first cause; nor can goals be projected as static utopias or

regulative ideals good for all times. Each offers a critical stance toward origins by admitting the need to mediate foundational sensibilities. Heidegger's critical mimetic recovery of origins retains an important utopian impulse because he finds it necessary, as does Irigaray, to countermand the dangerous fantasizing impulse of western representation through fostering a transformed fantasia which modifies our poetic sensibilities. While his work does not specifically address the issue of metaphoric transference, Heidegger's transformative mediation of the poietic basis of western thinking enacts metaphoric transference.

5.3 *Gelassenheit:* Heidegger's Reluctant Utopia

One thing Heidegger and Irigaray show us is that the way out of the anthropocentric and specular optics of western metaphysics must be indirect. Whereas Irigaray holds that substituting one symbolic economy of meaning for another does not effectuate metaphoric transference, Heidegger finds that replacing one representation of reality with another leaves the will to dominate intact. Because western rationality has solidified into what Heidegger calls "transcendental-horizonal re-presenting," we confront a vicious circularity (DT, 63/G, 36). Modern re-presentation fetishizes Being as 'reality', i.e., as an objectifiable totality. Reality thus appears circularly as the visible purview of the epistemic subject. As Nietzsche shows, representation posits entities as objects simultaneously with projecting the transcendental horizon against which entities can be interpreted as objects standing before the subject (63/36). Any direct attempt to project a different world view (conceptual horizon) cannot free us of the seduction that we exercise willful mastery over reality. All attempts to turn around and directly re-present what lies behind our backs, specifically, the self-showing of things, only re-produce Being as the subject's visible, transcendental horizon. Re-presentation always comes too late to experience phenomena as unrepresentable; it constitutes a frontal assault upon Being.[19]

Heidegger's sustained effort to think beyond the one-dimensionality of representation, like Irigaray's dissolution of the specular matrix of western metaphysics, has two moments, one practical and one formal. These two moments correspond to the substantive task of transforming the ethos of western tradition and to the recognition that this new *poiēsis* must symbolize its own limits, thereby instituting a formal delimitation of every horizon of

meaning implicit in rational projects. Here I will restrict my discussion to (1) the Heideggerian practice of "weaning ourselves from
will" (60/32) as it bears on intersubjective relations; and (2)
Heidegger's metaphor of the fourfold as a formal effort to shift from
a univocal grasp of normative systems of meaning to a plurivocal
or reiterative ideal.

(1) Getting beyond the Will to Conceptual Mastery. How can we
get beyond transcendental-horizonal consciousness when thinking
simply is representational? Heidegger answers that thinking is
broader than representation. In his 1944–45 essay *"Zur Erörterung
der Gelassenheit,"* Heidegger demonstrates that humans can experience Being as the excess beyond any transcendental-horizonal
standpoint, even though they cannot represent that experience.
One way to discuss this experience, without waxing mystical and
overly obscure as Heidegger often does, is to define it as divesting
myself of the belief that I own and project the images by which I
grasp the world. To experience the autokinetic character of entities
is to realize that things and others evoke images. Heidegger's talk
of meditative thinking as a kind of nonwilling, *Nicht-Wollen*, can be
understood as a precursor to the poststructuralist claim that the
intentionality of the speaker does not create meaning (59/30). Although Heidegger focuses on thinking and not linguistic theory, his
point is that we experience the fact that reality is never reducible
to any given horizon of interpretation only on condition of relinquishing the habit of assuming intentional mastery over meaning.

When Heidegger defines representation (*Vorstellen*) as willing
(*Wollen*), he characterizes intentionality broadly to indicate both
the idea that consciousness is consciousness of something and its
underlying economy of desire. In representation, Heidegger argues,
we perceive a totality of things against a conceptual horizon. The
horizon appears as the transcendent orientation of consciousness
and thus as the condition which makes possible the appearance of
things as a totality. But, Heidegger argues, "[w]hat is evident of the
horizon, then, is but the side facing us of an openness which sur-
rounds us" (64/37). Not only does representation restrict the scope
of thought to the projection of consciousness, it identifies the subject of reason with a truncated desire, that is, the will to surmount
what it is (entities as a whole) toward the totality of what is (the
horizon which brings everything into the scope of human reason).
Heidegger maintains two fundamental suppositions: (i) that humans have an implicit prethematic, prevolitional awareness that

things defy containment in representation and (ii) that we can only experience this prethematic engagement by "weaning ourselves from will" (60/32).

Heidegger's counsel against willing provides a directive to mimetically recover and actively sustain an explicit relation to the implicit prethematic awareness we have of the autodisclosure of others and all things. We do not recover this awareness by struggling willfully with personal motives in a psychological-spiritual way or by appropriating it, but rather indirectly by delimiting the projective horizonal standpoint proper. This delimitation occurs through cultivating recognition that there is a gap between my (lack of explicit) awareness of the autokinetic nature of things and the presumption that consciousness manufactures the life of ideation. Representational thinking in effect habitually leaps to the assumption that we manufacture the interpretive horizon of inquiry. This leap transpires so rapidly, Heidegger implies, that it constitutes the subject of reason through a particular fantasy. In the activity of representation we attach the dangerous illusion of mastery to the practice of transcendental-horizonal thinking. Though inclined to agree with Heidegger's critics that he mistakenly posits representational and nonrepresentational thinking as mutually exclusive activities, there are two Heideggers. The moderate Heidegger allows room for interpreting his critique not as a call to end representation (which is impossible) but instead to transform the economy of desire supporting modern *ratio.* This means that we take critical distance on representation by fostering an alternative poetic economy which enables us to sustain a relation to ourselves and to others through receptivity rather than mastery.[20]

To live beyond the transcendental-horizonal standpoint is not to occupy two different locales, but rather to wake up from the will to mastery though still engaged in representational thinking (DT, 61/G, 32f.). In his 1955 "Memorial Address" to Conradin Kreutzer, Heidegger describes meditative thinking as this counterpoise to calculative mastery. Calculative thinking, which Heidegger finds predominant in the technological era, refers to an aggravated form of representation that not only objectifies but reduces beings to things at the disposal of the epistemic subject. Arguing that technology and technical devices are not the problem, but rather a communal calculative disposition, Heidegger proposes that we must cultivate *Gelassenheit* (letting be) as a new *poiēsis* able to wake up from the will to master:

> We let technical devices enter our daily life, and at the same time
> leave them outside, that is, let them alone, as things which are
> nothing absolute but remain dependent upon something higher. I
> would call this comportment toward technology which expresses
> "yes" and at the same time "no," by an old word, *releasement
> toward things (Gelassenheit zu den dingen).* (54/23)

Releasement toward the unrepresentable excess in things recovers
"openness to the mystery" that things are not simply at human
disposal (55/23). Releasement divests us of a dangerous attachment to the historically situated habit of adopting an instrumental
view of the world.

Weaning ourselves of will fosters a practice that decenters our
relation to western rationality. As a subject of representation, I am
neither ultimately objectifiable nor subjectifiable; my possibilities
can no more be contained in a single re-presentation of my self-
showing than can any other thing. For Heidegger, to let transcendental representation be is fundamental to suspending habitual
identification with the ethos of mastery. Regaining awareness of
the ontological excess beyond any horizon of meaning divests me of
reducing my own subjectivity to the activity whereby consciousness
represents reality as an objectifiable totality.[21] Heidegger wants us
to learn to critically inhabit and maintain the gap between the
necessity of representation and the unnecessary habit of arrogating to ourselves control over thought, language, history, and reality.
We can do the former (represent) while divesting ourselves of the
latter. As conscious and rational beings, we cannot but actively
represent the world to ourselves, yet what we are is irreducible to
this activity. We overcome truncating ourselves through identification with thetic intentionality by engaging forms of thinking that
retrieve a sense of playful, poetic engagement with the defiant
refusal to be things contained in an idea. Heidegger transfigures
the libidinal desire underlying metaphysics by fostering receptivity
to reality as autodisclosive, as process and not substance.

This practical relinquishment of will (understood as attachment to attaining rational mastery over reality) opens up a new
poetic basis for envisioning nonhomogeneous and noncoercive *forms
of intersubjectivity.* Though never distinctly fleshed out in ethical
terms, my interpretation presses Heidegger's work into relevance
for ethics. I propose that cultivating the ability to reside on the
border of one's cultural and historical identity, though not sufficient,
supplies a necessary precondition of nondominating relations to

others, both human and nonhuman.[22] Even as rational reconstruction may be necessary to develop moral theory, Heidegger's work decenters the subject of reason by resisting the unidirectional, one-dimensional, and narcissistic tendency by which the modern episteme reduces the world to its mirror reflection. Despite his clear penchant for meditating on nonhuman others, we can extend his concept of letting be, as a dispositional counterpoise to the drive for conceptual mastery, to ethical relations among human beings.

Since language is the medium of all disclosure and conceptualization, the Heideggerian notion of letting be translates into the proposal that humans develop noninstrumental relations to others *indirectly* via critical mediation of language. Here language circumscribes a transcendental, interpretive horizon of meaning. Retaining awareness of what Irigaray and Kristeva call the metaphorical excess beyond any conceptual horizon enables us *not* to absolutize our standpoint. Heidegger's 1953–54 essay, "A Dialogue on Language between a Japanese and an Inquirer," demonstrates that critical distance on the finite historical-linguistic horizon within which we think comprises an ethical prerequisite for achieving nonviolent communication. Violence and coercion can occur without any deliberate attempt on my part to be cruel and malicious. The inability to maintain explicit awareness that I have been appropriated into a pregiven cultural horizon at a prevolitional level forces others into a violent and distorted self-disclosure. The person must either translate herself into my categories, thereby doing violence to herself, or appear irrational because she cannot speak without challenging my cultural standpoint.

Rather than focus directly on the subject matter, Heidegger devotes three-fourths of the dialogue with his Japanese interlocutor to questioning the words and concepts employed in their conversation (OWL, 4–5/US, 88–90). Neither information nor correct representation of a theory enables Heidegger to understand Japanese aesthetics. The dialogue shows that carefully exploring language, concepts, and images opens the speakers up to an experience of reality. Matters are even more one-sided because Heidegger has minimal knowledge of Japanese philosophy and no language capacity, while his interlocutor knows western tradition and speaks German. Unless Heidegger strives to take distance on western aesthetical categories and the German language, his interlocutor will be forced to translate a complete understanding of the totality of what is into western categories. Now, let me be careful. Heidegger tends to speak about the Oriental Dasein from an Occidental stand-point.[23] He abstracts from personal biases in conversation and this not only privileges a masculine and extremely cognitive view of intimacy but allows him to overlook aspects of Eurocentrism. Despite the potential for a rich notion of intimacy inherent in his theory of nonwilling, Heidegger revels in an abstract, arguably masculine joy felt through intellectual exchange and not interpersonal disclosure. This abstraction allows cultural biases to remain unchallenged in Heidegger's dialogue. For example, Heidegger exhibits no concern to understand the social location of his Japanese interlocutor as one who may suffer prejudice while in Germany. Personal awareness of his own potential ethnocentrism appears irrelevant to achieving distance on a western-centric view of aesthetics. Worse, Heidegger at times paternalistically dictates the integrity of the cultural Dasein of the Japanese, by showing his Japanese interlocutor how western aesthetic categories violate the integrity of Japanese tradition.

I do not wish to ignore the virtue underscored by Heidegger's keen sense that western concepts provide a fundamental outlet for cultural imperialism. Nevertheless, a certain stoic abstraction continues to haunt later Heidegger. This abstraction prevents him from exploring both his personal and his methodological biases, and from extending his insight to the ethical sphere of interpersonal relations. Heidegger's key interest, to advance his own theory of language, envelops and clouds the ethically salient features of the dialogue. His focus on Japanese views of aesthetics circles the discussion back to a confirmation of his own theory. Heidegger's goal, to decenter anthropocentrism, remains incomplete without these more concrete dimensions of interaction. A Eurocentric bias even prevails in the title which locates Heidegger as the "Inquirer" (nothing could be more superior to Heidegger's mind), while the Japanese is merely the "Japanese," presumably the Other (1/84).

Even given these limitations, Heidegger's work substantiates the need to base ethical relations on a postmetaphysical or decentered transcendental-horizonal thinking. I take this to mean that language itself must be questioned. We can apply his insight internally to western culture, since humans appropriate tradition in a variety of ways. The experience of conceptual coercion potentially occurs, not only across the so-called Occidental-Oriental axis, but concretely in any relationship. Envision a person who considers herself a spiritualist but who does not find any orthodox religious practice a suitable expression of her spirituality. During an interview for a job at a religious-affiliated college, she stands before a tribunal of elders who judge her intellectual maturity against the self-evident validity of their hermeneutical horizon. They presume that any adequate expression of religiosity must manifest as conversion to their basic assumptions and to a specific linear journey of maturation. The interviewee carries the burden of translating her self-understanding into a foreign discourse and into inappropriate categories which distort her life.

In this example distortion occurs in the simple attempt to make herself intelligible to the tribunal. To resist employing their conceptual categories would be to tacitly polemicize with them, since they do not regard their ethical task as requiring that they question their hermeneutical horizon. If the woman explains that she is unmarried but has a rich, deeply committed relation to her lover, does that translate inappropriately into sin or intellectual immaturity? If she claims she is married, in order to convey her true commitment, she not only appears duplicitous but feels guilty both because the situation makes her aware that she is not married by their standards and because it ascribes responsibility to her for sincere communication. Under conditions where both parties do not accept the limits of language, discourse, and conceptualization, undistorted and nonviolent disclosure becomes impossible. Until the terms of discourse proper can be called into question, only a distorted self-showing can occur. Because justified by a logic of identity, the elders' conception of ethics reduces similarity (nonidentity) to sameness. Without an ability to experience nonidentity and asymmetrical reciprocity, they have no capacity to bridge horizons, translate, and compare the interviewee's spiritual autobiography with their own. They have no conception of dialogue which questions the premises for dialogue. The logic of identity leads to the position that humans have no ethical responsibility to create conditions of dialogue (and ultimately social conditions) for nondistorting disclosure and communication of those features of identity and social location recalcitrant to complete translation.

Key to this example is that no single person consciously desires to harm the interviewee. No person acts from deliberate malice. And yet extreme coercion can occur. Passivity before the task of cultivating critical distance on systems of representation guarantees ethical failure when humans must interact across vast differences in social location. Though abstractly conceived, the Heideggerian conception of releasement or nonwilling implicitly recognizes the need to become accountable for those forms of conceptual violence that cannot be theorized under traditional conceptions of evil as willful maliciousness (DT, 62/G, 35). The advent of modernity brings recognition that no single historical, cultural, or linguistic horizon necessarily encapsulates the totality of what is. By extension, every person and thing cannot be contained in a concept; all horizons are up for debate. An important element in achieving respect, recognition, and proximity must be attentiveness to language and discursive practices. Respect requires more than admitting that many moral viewpoints exist; it calls us to actively attend to nonidentity.

(2) *The Vision of the Fourfold as Formal Delimitation of Universalism.* Irigaray holds that the universal regulative ideals proposed by the canonical figures in western tradition harbor utopian fantasies of humanity's rational transparency; moreover, these fantasies tacitly follow an identitarian logic that metaphorically associates humanity with male morphology. Just as Irigaray thinks that we must decenter the logic of identity at two levels, so too Heidegger breaks with modern humanism both by fostering an alternative *poiēsis* and by refiguring the formal status of transcendental ideals as non-univocal. Both Irigaray and Heidegger reject the premise that humans become rationally sober when thought achieves a symmetrical mirroring of reality, i.e., when the real is the rational and the rational is the real. Their shared ontological assumption that reality is kinetic, not static, leads to the antithetical conclusion: we become increasingly broad-minded and sober by realizing that there is no perfect transparency between rational reconstruction of reality and phenomena. Rather than a prescript for epistemological skepticism, this recognition ultimately calls for a model of enlarged reasoning based upon dialogue and interaction, a model neither Irigaray nor Heidegger furnishes. What they do offer, however, are formal models for delimiting utopian ideals. They offset the recognition that humans need universal images of humanity by severing every identitarian association between a perspective (man) and an idealized humanity. These formal models are antinormative, in that they deny a single universal image of humanity for all times, yet they offer a way to work toward greater humanity by finding a way beyond the violence of the present.[24]

Though Irigaray clearly connects the logic of identity to social group formation, Heidegger more generally claims that the logic of identity stems from an overdetermined subject-centeredness of late modernity. For Heidegger, our inability to grapple with nonidentity characterizes and is an effect of our basic failure to contend with the fact that we cannot master our own historical process. Late modernity has a specific historical configuration which Heidegger names *das Gestell* (the Enframing). Enframing means that historically the West's basic orientation is to treat things calculatively as "standing reserve," i.e., as objects whose energy and potential can be extracted, stored like stock, readied for consumption at human whim (QCT, 17, 19/VA, 21, 23). The age of Enframing marks the culmination of the western metaphysical search for rational transparency, according to Heidegger, because it locates us before the possibility of reducing ourselves to standing-reserve. The search for rational transparency yields a one-dimensional world in which we no longer find our humanity; moreover, this one-dimensionality spreads through the Europeanization of the world.

We can readily contest Heidegger's quasi-apocalyptic descriptions of western history for ignoring both that calculative treatments of humans were prevalent in other historical periods and that modernity offers a more complex legacy than a simple Enframing of relations as one-dimensional. But I am advancing a reading of Heidegger's philosophy of history as a form of critical mythologizing. Interpreted in this way, his descriptions function in part as strategic interventions which aim, not to accurately depict the past or present, but rather to awaken us to the netherside of the present. Moreover, like Irigaray, I argue that his philosophy of history does not stop with strategic intervention but invokes a positive utopian vision, a way to decenter the present and open up an alternative future. Opening this futural possibility has two moments, one relative to the present and one universally applicable to all futures. By imagining the excessive quality of sensible reality, Heidegger counteracts the ethos which treats things as available for human disposal, but he also formally shatters the desire for a univocal horizon of meaning. If Enframing identifies the desire to have reality image human rationality, then he proposes the fourfold, *das Geviert*, as a multifaceted or reiterative universal that formally symbolizes the asymmetrical and heterogenous nature of reality. Letting metaphysics be proceeds through this formal delimitation of universalism.

Heidegger's poetic talk of the "mirror-play" between the four regions—earth, sky, mortals, and gods—may sound like a yearning for a romantic return to a premodern, neopagan, mythical, and innocent immediacy. But such romantic readings do not suffice. The fourfold arguably functions as a heuristic device for developing the possibility of a critical relation to utopian projects as such (PLT, 179/VA, 172). The fourfold cannot refer to a hidden but pristine reality underlying contemporary life which only the privileged few, the acolytes, poets, and mystics experience. David Kolb aptly calls this kind of misreading "romantic," since "[t]here can be for Heidegger no historically constant basic revelation of things that is then covered over." There is no lost Eden-like origin that we must get back. Much like Cornell's reading of Irigaray, Kolb argues that the fourfold describes a combination of a future world (with a transformed *poiēsis*) and "the 'worlding' of *any* world" (the formal structure of our own temporality).[25]

The fourfold thus denotes the temporal possibility that humans can attain a decentered relation to their own historicalness. It invokes an unerasable utopian moment wherein we cultivate an alternative ethos through this decentering and finally develop a future without metaphysics, i.e., without the historical compulsion to arrive at perfect transparency. Although it retains usage of the metaphor of the mirror, Heidegger's analysis breaks up the univocal trope which posits reality as the mirror image of humanity. Furthermore, it rejects the singularly cognitive focus rooted in the specular optics of metaphysics. Heidegger intends the mirror-play to deliver us back to a rich, holistic attunement to the embeddedness of our identities as constantly held out toward nonidentity with reality and toward the open-ended structure of the future. The fourfold constitutes Heidegger's formal description of the postmetaphysical era. It portrays the possibility that humans could develop a form of life that would not neglect our preconceptual awareness of nonidentity. Historically we need not reduce meaning to static presence, to a univocal horizon, to a one-dimensional mirror reflecting the epistemic subject of modernity.[26]

Through delineating the structure of historical embeddedness as a multifaceted confluence of transcendental horizons of meaning, Heidegger reworks Nietzsche's insight into the perspectival nature of life but on a non-egocentric and asymmetrical basis. The multifaceted structure of Being (the totality of what is) is not synonymous with the concept of world views or a Nietzschean model of rationality as the subject's projective schematization of life under a variety of useful interpretive horizons. Each such horizon absolutizes the subject as source of meaning and yields a totalizing objectification of the world. For Heidegger, it is performatively contradictory to act as though I accept the validity of alternative world views when in fact I take my projected horizon as absolute.

This disingenuous gesture toward difference cannot transform one's subject-centered standpoint. By contrast, Heidegger's argument proposes that demystifying divinities proves the central condition for the possibility of a genuine decentering of the subject of reason. We transgress universals by discovering that reality cannot be contained in a single, univocal interpretive horizon.

Each of Heidegger's four regions (earth, sky, mortals, divinities) provides a horizon of interpretation for poetically bringing-forth into disclosure one face of human existence as a whole and not simply as perceived from a particular standpoint or social location. For example, we can represent existence in terms of the holy or in terms of shared mortality. Each region encompasses a backdrop horizon against which individuals and social groups debate their manifold perspectives. These spheres of meaning, Heidegger indicates, are irreducible and incommensurable because each reveals the world as a whole in a specific and unique way. To assume that a single horizon delivers me to a transparent grasp of reality precludes the recognition of ontological asymmetry between reason and Being. This foreclosure is related to but not the same as the problem of rigid adherence to a particular world view or social standpoint.

Heidegger's analysis adumbrates the view that realizing an asymmetrical relation between representation and reality forms a precondition of becoming receptive to the limits of my situated perspective; it makes possible delimiting debates over competing standpoints. The conditions of dialogue proper, the metaphorical associations of a closed system of meaning, must enter into debate. If we apply this analysis of the fourfold to moral theory, then the formal delimitation of spheres of meaning implies that there could be equally justifiable, yet incommensurable, moral universals and there could be numerous historical pathways for developing utopian visions of humanism genuinely worth inhabiting. Most of all, the delimitation of universalism claims that we cannot approach a new humanism without recognizing that incommensurability does not necessitate relativism or incoherence. To the contrary, we need models of historical progress that can contend with asymmetrical development without assuming assimilation as ideal; and we need a model of moral respect that heeds the ontological irreducibility of human beings to one another.

When we achieve a critical relationship to our own historical and ontological finitude, Heidegger tells us, we touch the source of all conceptualization, that is to say, the inexhaustibility of our possibilities for developing new forms of meaning. Against Heidegger's methodological one-sidedness, I believe that we must extend Heidegger's premise that entities are autokinetic to intersubjective relations. It follows that humans are interdependent upon one another for growth in awareness of the limitations of their standpoints and of systems of meaning as such. Ontologically speaking, every person enables me to know myself differently. In Heideggerian terms, learning to revel in the mysterious, multifaceted, and heterogeneous character of reality makes me capable of sustaining ethical possibilities for love and friendship across sensuous particular differences. But, as a corrective to Heidegger, the ontological irreducibility of people's identities never appears outside of the influences of social location in economic, material, racial, ethnic, and class terms. Becoming decentered in ways that foster ethical relations would entail addressing these factors as well. Still, Heidegger's vision contributes to the displacement of the modern subject as objectifying others as absolutely different and its replacement with the notion that humans can communicate overlapping regions of interpretive experience without reducing differences to the same.

The Heideggerian concept of the mystery of Being, i.e., the self-revealing but simultaneously self-veiling nature of phenomena, can now be shed of associations with a terrifying dark void or romanticized feminine abyss which ambiguously causes elation and castration anxiety. The mystery simply names the inexhaustible, disclosive possibilities of all beings. According to Heidegger, human beings could not wonder or seek knowledge if they had no preconscious, ontological proximity to the self-showing process of others. This proximity depicts a relation to the nonidentity among things, a space in which comparative similarities and differences can be discerned but without subsuming them under hierarchies of classification. In substantive terms, the fourfold portrays a vision of nonhierarchical interaction between different kinds of beings (nature, gods, mortals, heavens). Differences truly obtain only once we relinquish metaphysical systems of hierarchy.

Again, pressing the Heideggerian notion of proximity into the service of ethics means that, when we take ourselves narrowly to be simple subjects of representation, we prevent ourselves from attaining an explicit collective and poetic sensibility of that intimacy which is already implicitly built into our ontological proximity to one another. The fourfold depicts a mirror-play that is not specular. It suggests that recovering an explicit capacity for playful engagement that does not reduce others to specular imaging, engenders nondominating relationships. To gain awareness of the asymmetry between thought and reality avails me of the possibility of entering into proximity with others, human and nonhuman. To enter proximity means to take pleasure in the ontological phenomenon whereby simple contact with another person reveals my identity in ways that I do not experience myself. My presuppositions, the limitations of my narrative about myself, my unconscious desires, and the basic ways I schematize and conceptualize reality suddenly appear in their dramatically finite contours. This illumination of the outer boundaries of my active formation of horizons of meaning is effectuated at an ontological level. Whatever other disagreements in viewpoint two people share and use to challenge one another, Heidegger points to this play as a spontaneous, nondeliberate effect of ontological asymmetry, i.e., of the fact that another person quite simply is not me and does not inhabit the world from precisely the same location as do I. Another person need not directly criticize, challenge, impose her perspective on or objectify me in order for me to become aware of the asymmetry between our conceptual horizons. The self-disclosure of the alter simply reveals my own difference, my personal limits as well as my strengths.

The critical import of Heidegger's philosophy consists in demonstrating that the ontological condition of possibility for ethics stems from the proximity that humans implicitly have yet must explicitly foster with other beings. Proximity denotes the ontological space of the play where, neither symmetrical nor commensurable, everything in the world reveals differences between itself and me in nonhierarchical ways. I enter this space on condition that I renounce any calculative attempt to grasp the alter. Though never without presuppositions, distance on the inclination to universalize prepares an attitude of readiness to experience the finite contours of my standpoint as mirrored to me by the simple existence of others. Though a lyrical image, Heidegger does not depict nearness and proximity as facile immediacy. Not only must I be available to experiencing my limits, but I must learn that intimacy occurs through an indirect letting be and not a direct grasping of the other.

Finally, Heidegger's model of *Gelassenheit* or releasement into the fourfold tacitly acknowledges the interdependence of humans for developing critical awareness of their perspective(s) and, beyond that, an enlarged understanding of other perspectives. While I cannot let another mirror my limits to me unless not threatened by difference, I also need others (both human and nonhuman) to occasion my growth precisely because I am ontologically finite and not simply psychologically resistant (though possibly that). The space of proximity is not undifferentiated, it is not mere closeness. Proximity ultimately calls for mediation and a form of life that could support it. The very space of the fourfold only exists as space on condition that we dismantle the reign of instrumental forms of reason and the material forms of life which support their reign.

5.4 Irigaray and Heidegger: A Concluding Glance

Heidegger and Irigaray offer images of proximity and intimacy that reject the felt need to reduce difference to identity; they contemplate the interval between collapsing others into subsets of my standpoint and objectifying others as completely inaccessible to my understanding. Stephen White finds Heidegger's *Gelassenheit* (releasement into proximity) more applicable to ethics than Derrida's *différance*. Heidegger, like Irigaray, shares an interventionist side with Derridean deconstruction, but White argues that Heidegger additionally offers new ways to live face-to-face without denying difference or positing differences in oppositional terms:

> This interventionist side of *Gelassenheit* would seem to be appro-
> priately realized in the sorts of deconstructive and genealogical
> strategies recommended by contemporary postmodernists like
> Derrida and Foucault. Here, there is a refusal to be a face-to-face
> participant in the discourse of modernity. The point is not to im-
> prove our modern conversations but rather to introduce disso-
> nance into them by means of an impertinent stance, a slapping of
> faces as it were. In this way, we begin to release ourselves and
> others from the hold of the modern political "world."

Against what he perceives as Derrida's allergic reaction to face-to-face encounters (as "reek[ing] of the worst sorts of concepts associated with metaphysical, logocentric modes of thought"), White claims that the Heideggerian interest in "nearness" develops a greater sense of respect for otherness than Derridean *différance*. White remarks that the mood of *Gelassenheit* "is a current of attraction, fascination, and delight, balanced by a current of reticence, sobriety, respect, or mourning."[27]

Like White, I find Heidegger's *poiēsis* of receptivity fruitful for rethinking ethics. The basic intuition motivating Cornell's reading of Irigaray similarly highlights the need to move beyond a deconstructive valorization of slippage of meaning to a modest utopian effort to engender a new social eros, a new poetic way of belonging together. For White, Heidegger's ethical-aesthetics compensates for "the momentum of impertinence" characteristic of deconstructive practices; when overdetermined, he argues, interventionist methods cause "the moral dimension" to suffer and "postmodern thinking opens itself to the charge of mere aestheticism." In White's words,

> [A]n *over*emphasis on disruption and impertinence creates for postmodern thinking a momentum that threatens to enervate the sense of responsibility to otherness, subtly substituting for it an implicit celebration of the impertinent subject who shows his or her virtuosity in deconstructing whatever unity may come along.

Instead of emphasizing "a slapping of faces . . . an impertinence before the unity, and simple presence that faces traditionally claim to embody," we need to reimagine face-to-face interaction in postmetaphysical terms.[28]

Irigaray and later Heidegger share the view that a nonoppositional, nonhierarchical belonging together cannot be achieved by focusing on difference instead of identity. In Krzysztof Ziarek's words, if "difference is always threatened with a possible return to sameness it is then continuously preoccupied with the forestalling of closure."[29] Heidegger envisions *Gelassenheit* as an ethical mood, an openness to nonviolent forms of recognition. His work teaches us to find joy in the ability to coexist in a heterogeneous sphere of mutual presencing without needing to impose substitutability or symmetry on the participants; his later thinking suspends the urge to control the self-withdrawal of people and phenomena, as if we would be swallowed up by the womblike abyss underlying finite existence. Irigaray teaches us to dispel masculine anxiety over impotence and the fear that closeness produces suffocation, destroys plurality, difference, or my sense of identity. Instead of a choice between difference or identity, Heidegger proposes a unifying form of belonging together that roots unity in heterogeneity. Instead of a vertiginous fall before the abyss, the temptation to reject all totalities as totalitarian, all forms of identity as oppressive, Heidegger and Irigaray resist lapsing into a viciously circular and permanent praxis aimed at sustained critique of all identity. Rejection of unity threatens to fall back into nihilism, whereas acceptance that not all forms of identity promote oppressive totalities opens the utopian doorway to cultivating a genuine heterogeneity. And in this fashion, we overcome nihilism.

Heidegger's specific effort to map out a general vision of an alternative mode of existence, I have claimed, comprises an *unerasable utopian moment*. Clearly he does not fashion a static regulative ideal for all times. His substantive vision of communalism is an ideal for our times, a corrective to the social anomie inherent in metaphysics and its deterioration into instrumental reasoning. Future generations will have to determine the substantive ideal that will correct whatever dilemma they face. The status of Heidegger's particular theorization of the excess as the fourfold is both structural and substantive. In its structural moment, it symbolizes the nonidentitarian aspect of existence. Though the content of every utopian vision must change with the generations, the notion of the fourfold implicitly decenters metaphysics, representation, calculation; it provides a formal delimitation of all utopian ideals by showing that no universal can anticipate all temporal and ontological possibilities. Despite the mystifying side of Heidegger's work, we can interpret the fourfold as engendering a critical ethos and not a romantic desire for immediacy. Symbolically, positing an asymmetry between reason and reality builds a critical moment into any universalizable ideal; the ideal itself must keep open that age's possibility for not absolutizing its specific historical-linguistic-cultural eros. This moment will prepare social change within an age and continue to root human desire in attentiveness to mutual care.

PART III

From Reiterative to Interactive Universalism

Concrete Aporias of Recognition

CHAPTER SIX

Heidegger's Apolitical Nostalgia for Immediacy

> Heidegger's thought discourages planned revolutions. Anything
> we might plan and carry out will be within the space of uni-
> versal imposition [*das Gestell*]. We will not found a new realm.
> No revolution based on human action can change the space
> within which we move.
>
> David Kolb, *The Critique of Pure Modernity*

Prevalent dismay toward postmodern antihumanism, expressed by liberal as well as Marxist critics, centers around a
basic worry that antihumanism leads to a thoroughgoing
antinormativism unable to sustain the very emancipatory interests it proclaims. As one precursor to postmodern antihumanism,
the contradictory tension in Heidegger's work between its proto-
and antinormative dimensions deserves attention. An exploration
of this tension could assume varied forms. I restrict my focus to
Heidegger's recollective textual intervention into the historical
transmission of ideas as the vehicle by which he strives to transform the ethos of technological modernity. By enhancing the
protonormative side of Heidegger, I have given a sympathetic
reading of his argument for a nonmastering poetic sensibility,
envisioning this "moral-aesthetic" ethos as a partial basis for an
ethics that can supplement, as Stephen White argues, "responsibility to act" with "responsibility to otherness."[1] Without implying
that this ethos provides a developed moral theory or a concrete
model of community, I have pressed Heideggerian insights into
the service of modeling a postconventional community on mediated relations to the symbolic sources of identity; that model,
while incomplete, postulates the need to repair distortions of disclosure across social and cultural horizons of meaning in order to
sustain egalitarian interaction.

Nonetheless, it is not news that Heidegger's recollective practice of recuperating benumbed sensibilities enjoys a marked disinterest in the relation of linguistic conventions to political context.
Poststructuralists make a clear advance over Heidegger in this
sphere. What interests me, however, is a more basic issue, namely,
that Heidegger's textual practice overlooks the valuative biases
that inform his ideal-typical reconstruction of history. Rather than
reject the therapeutic value and protonormative implications of
Heidegger's strategic renditions of the history of ideas, I want to
argue that the substantive ways he fleshes out his vision yield
partial and perverse outcomes when left ungrounded in an interactive and communicative model of ethics. Though in disagreement
with the particulars of a Habermasian model of discourse ethics, I
hold that filling out an Irigarayan-Heideggerian protonormative
ideal of a self-mediating community based upon identity-in-
difference would have to become materialized in a politics of needs
that must be redeemed by submitting claims to public dialogue.
Toward that end, I constrain my comments to this more limited
claim. Even were we to link interventionist textual practices to
political context, we must theorize the need for interaction as the
ethical means to attaining a critical relation to the valuative biases
of any such practice.

Heidegger's philosophy can be interpreted as an elaborate
performative displacement of modernity from the standpoint of not
being able to abstract completely from one's cultural and historical
topos. Previously I depicted Heidegger's efforts to transgress
scientific rationality—which to his mind instills a form of living
that extends beyond projecting everything in a one-dimensional
mirror image of the intentional subject to rendering everything
available to manipulation—as recovering a postmetaphysical form
of perspectivalism.[2] By postmetaphysical, I mean an epistemologi-
cal-ontological mode of thinking-dwelling that delimits the unitary
metaphysical ideal of finding one context-transcendent standard of
truth by which to hierarchize manifold particulars of existence.
The ethical intuition informing this *modus operandi* resides in the
premise that there is a correlation between the capacity *not* to
absolutize one's standpoint and achieving humanistic ideals. Yet
without grounding this protoethical intuition in a communication
paradigm, Heidegger conflates the premise that there is no transcendent standpoint with antinormativism. Here antinormativism
means not a delimitation of universalism but the strong position
that we should displace universalizing theory as if a new poetics

could deliver up an organically self-sustaining, heterogeneous set of communities in dialogue.

My argument is that, instead of keeping open the productive tension between a moral-aesthetic and its potential contribution to a reworked universalism, Heidegger collapses that tension into a contradiction minimally on two planes, ontological and temporal. His works manifest a nostalgia for immediacy operating as an intrinsic contradiction within his model of a mediated poetics. This nostalgia issues in an abstract and premature negation of false universalism because it repudiates the need to contend with people's diverse social needs. Similarly, on a temporal plane, Heidegger abstractly negates a speculative interest in the future by collapsing the possibility for social change into the immediate and singular task of fostering noninstrumental forms of reasoning in the here and now. The historical project of bringing the metaphysics of presence to closure thus tacitly prescribes here and now as a potential meta-utopia; that is, as the unique phase in history in which conditions are ripe for determining how to end the nihilistic and destructive orientation of western humanity. Given that Heidegger never questions the structural and material preparedness for such a change, his work ushers in a pronounced disinterest in contemporary forms of material suffering. The nonessentialist thesis, that there is no causative logic engendering historical process as intrinsically progressive, degenerates in Heidegger's thought into a categorical denial of any basis on which to plan revolutions. This preemptory foreclosure siphons off the potential emancipatory interest a neo-Heideggerian perspectivalism could hold for the victims of past history.[3]

Contrary to some readings, I do not attribute the problems of quietism, apoliticism, and abstraction from material conditions plaguing Heideggerian thought to the sheer fact that his theory of history appears to be monocausal. Taken as an interventionist with ethical intent, Heidegger need not be read as automatically adhering to a facile logocentrism. His narrative construction of western history solidifies into a monocausal explanation of what ails the contemporary West when he treats his work as a stand-in for dialogical interaction among humans, for normative theory of every kind, and for developing heterogenous models of civil society. With that move, the ethical purpose of his work balloons into a set of self-validating prescripts and a blind refusal to acknowledge the normative force of his theoretical assertions. For this reason, I locate Heidegger's reductive treatment of now as the time to decide

for meta-utopia in a conflict between his maieutic effort to effectuate a holistic transformation of western ethos and the unwarranted,
absolutist conclusions he prematurely draws from his limited ideal-
typical depictions of technological modernity. He reifies his depiction into a grand narrative through distinctly forswearing the need
for further articulation of the causes of our social anomie; then the
ethical import of his call for a new poetics slips into broad prescrip-
tions that lack nuanced theoretical and practical grounding in relation to prevailing social and political conditions. This argument
rescues the protonormative vision of a new poetics by theorizing
the need for these elements to become materialized, and potentially modified, in a concrete practice for legitimating norms. And
it provides a backdrop for a similar analysis of Irigaray that I carry
out in the next chapter.

6.1 The Turn to Situated Criticism

One finds in postmodern literature varied and multiple forms
of a turn to situated criticism. By this turn I mean the view that
social criticism, if it is to avoid the pitfall of serving the interests
of one group over those of another, must give up philosophy as a
metanarrative of legitimation. Along with the view that subjectivity is a discursive construct, situated criticism is a form of nominalism. It designates the rejection of grand narratives in favor of local
narratives or the idea that there are no context-transcendent criteria for legitimation. In her lucid articulation of the shared assumptions of various postmodern theorists and theories—ranging
from Foucault, Derrida, Deleuze and Guattari, Lyotard, Barthes,
Rorty, and Cavell to semiotics, deconstruction, genealogy, and psychoanalysis—Jane Flax identifies a common therapeutic intent of
such critiques of grand narrative:

> Despite their many differences, these discourses are all
> "deconstructive"; they seek to distance us from and make us skep-
> tical about the ideas concerning truth, knowledge, power, history,
> self, and language that are often taken for granted within and
> serve as legitimations for contemporary Western culture.[4]

This therapeutic interest leads these theorists to emphasize description as opposed to the traditional reconstructive or prescriptive function of philosophy. Contemporary views that philosophy

provides no solutions but rather transforms how we think descend, most recently, from Heidegger's distinction between meditative thinking and philosophy as a species of problem solving.

Flax's study well portrays the maieutic and ethical intent of various deconstructive strategies. By arresting the totalizing logic exercised by Enlightenment philosophies, these *strategic devices* decenter the privilege accorded to the white, male, middle-class sector of western society, open the space to reclaim lost voices in history, and encourage humility before the situated character of all knowledge. Yet thinkers both sympathetic and antipathetic to these strategies acknowledge that postmodernist critiques of the grand narrative of the Enlightenment "construct their own metanarratives of the 'death' of the Enlightenment or 'the metaphysics of presence'." Later Flax continues,

> [P]ostmodernists construct stories about the Enlightenment in which the disparate views of a variety of thinkers, including Descartes, Kant, and Hegel, are integrated into (and reduced to) one "master narrative." This master narrative then serves as an adversary against which postmodernist rhetoric can be deployed.[5]

That master narrative, distilled from various modern positions, revolves around three death blows that postmodern thinkers strive to deliver. Flax calls these blows the death of man, the death of history, and the death of metaphysics. The death of man rejects Enlightenment conceptions of subjectivity as coherent and stable and all essentialist theories of human nature, proposing instead that subjectivity is a fiction of language. The death of history issues a death warrant to all teleological conceptions of history in which events unfold for a reason and in a linear and uniform march toward the rational perfection of human existence. The final thesis, indebted to Heidegger, claims that western philosophy has been captured in "the spell of the 'metaphysics of presence' at least since Plato." It repudiates the philosophical desire to master reality as dangerous and invalidates the view that only "philosophy can provide an objective, reliable, and universalizable 'foundation' for knowledge and for judging all truth claims."[6]

While not unfounded as criticisms of Enlightenment *ratio*, certain conceptual tensions suffuse the turn to situated criticism as justified by this grand narrative. My interest, however, does not revolve around hollow claims that this performative contradiction nullifies subversive textual strategies. Instead, I want to situate Heidegger's reading of western history against two conceptual tensions. Benhabib clarifies that what is at stake in the death-of-metaphysics thesis is whether antifoundationalism leads to antinormativism. If philosophy, understood as epistemology, can no longer claim to be the metadiscourse that yields "criteria of validity presupposed by all other discourses," then what conclusion does this warrant? Does the contextual character of knowledge, Benhabib asks, announce the swan song of philosophy (as Heidegger claims), induct philosophy into a sociological version of situated criticism (as Rorty and Lyotard suggest), or call for a reconstructed model for normative theory by deriving criteria for legitimating viewpoints on more fallibilist grounds (as in discourse ethics)? Considering the first two options, Benhabib rightly asserts that "the 'local narratives,' 'les petits récits,' which constituted our everyday social practices or language games" may not "themselves be reflexive and self-critical enough to pass judgments on themselves."[7]

Similarly, Fraser, Nicholson, and Benhabib all question the implications of the death of history. Understood as denoting the process of constructing "master Narratives" that mirror the subject's rationality to itself, history promotes an idealizing desire to master the real: "At the end to his story/time," Flax explains, "Man's reason or labor will be made fully Real, and thus nothing will be alien to or estranged from him. He will be the Sovereign Subject forever."[8] Skepticism toward history as grand narrative recognizes a distinct connection between the desire to master reality and the historical ways that some groups surreptitiously advanced themselves as representing the interests of all humanity. Inspired by Lyotard, Fraser and Nicholson define metadiscourses as large-scale, monocausal narratives which construct totalizing depictions of history as following a single logic. For Lyotard, such grand narratives function as modernist strategies of legitimation; they inherently erect one local perspective as the most superior standard of evaluation. As Fraser and Nicholson elucidate,

> The metadiscourse narrates a story about the whole of human history which purports to guarantee that the pragmatic of the modern sciences and of modern political processes—the norms and rules which govern these practices, determining what counts as a warranted move within them—are themselves legitimate. The story guarantees that some sciences and some politics have the *right* pragmatics and, so, are the *right* practices.[9]

Like Fraser and Nicholson, Benhabib shares with Lyotard a
call to end essentialist and monocausal forms of grand narrative,
but resists his strong, nominalist, and "prima facie rejection of
any historical narrative that concerns itself with the long durée
and that focusses on macro- rather than on micro-social practices." In light of the totalitarian movements of the twentieth
century, Benhabib points out, a weak version of the death of history issues an important indictment of the "hegemonic claims of
any group or organization to 'represent' the forces of history, to be
moving with such forces, or to be acting in their name." But a
strong rejection of macrosocial analysis, she warns, would undercut an "epistemological interest in history." In answer to the question, can pure local narrative substantiate a moral imperative to
struggle for the emancipation of the victims of history, Benhabib
gives a resounding no. And she worries that postmodern historiography abstracts from the lives of actual victims: "[F]or Michel
Foucault there is no history of the victims of history but only a
history of the construction of victimization" and "the monotonous
succession of infinite 'power/knowledge' complexes that materially
constitute selves."[10]

I too hold that, when connected with a thoroughgoing
antinormativism, strong versions of the death of history threaten
to wipe out any dream of progress. Incorporating lost voices of
history into cultural and institutional practices that alleviate the
material conditions of suffering hinges on both the need to evaluate
local circumstance in relation to macrosocial processes and on the
normative task of generating procedures for evaluating competing
narratives. But I also think that examination of the symbolic construction of victimization is not irrelevant to this task. Thus, instead of identifying Heidegger's work with a monocausal narrative
that ushers in the swan song of philosophy as normative theory, I
find it more productive to examine the tensions and contradictions
in his work. I will argue that as a strategist with ethical intent,
Heidegger recognizes difficulties with a monocausal view of history.
His historical praxis reifies into a monolithic and flat picture of
history because he fails to theorize his own recognition that every
textual reconstruction of history is ideal-typical. Further, without
theorizing a communicative model for adjudicating competing claims
of various social groups, Heidegger, by default and without grounds,
elevates the valuative biases built into his story as universal and
self-validating. Left only with the prospect of turning in the here
and now to a new poiesis, this premature enactment of harmony

occludes differences in social power and abolishes the need for ideology critique in setting social and political priorities.

6.2 Heideggerian Eschatology as Performative Subversion

Critical modernists and poststructuralists hold that Heidegger's work evinces remnants of logocentrism to the extent that it relies upon a monocausal view of western history. On this view, the narrative of history as metaphysics of presence continues to rely upon the assumption that a hidden essence guides western humanity to a more rational existence and to provide the standard for judging our *topos* in history, i.e., our possibilities for transgression and critical distance on our world. Without denying that Heidegger consistently poses as the metatheorist of the twentieth century, offering his univocal story of history as inaugurating the sole practice able to save the West from its technological form, I reject any clean division between Heidegger the grand narrator and postmodern nominalist efforts to steer clear of teleology, eschatology, and essentializing views of history. I affirm Benhabib's insight that "much of the postmodernist critique of western metaphysics itself proceeds under the spell of a meta-narrative," namely Heidegger's story about the metaphysics of presence. Still, I resist this clean division not in order to issue a blanket indictment of poststructuralist theorizing as hopelessly caught in monocausal treatments of history. The Heideggerian legacy is more complex. Entanglement in a monocausal view of history arises in Heidegger's work, neither through belief in a deep core of history nor its renunciation (and one finds both strains in his work), but rather because he loses sight of the fact that his story is just one story, one reconstructive evaluation of history. Or he refuses to draw out the theoretical and practical consequences of his mimetic techniques. Imploding Heidegger's unified view of history in favor of multiple renditions does not automatically alleviate interventionist strategies of an uncritical relation to, and the need to theorize ways to compensate for, the biases invoked in any one description of reality.[11]

A political subtext runs through the Heideggerian corpus. Heidegger understands his critique of objectifying rationality, which he takes to be a keystone of modernity, to contribute to overcoming global domination of the world by the West. Though much of his later work rings apolitical, he speaks at crucial moments about the need for the West to relinquish its "unconditioned self-assertion" over the world (BW, 221/W, 17). His thought implies that the spread of western grammar and languages throughout the world promotes an unacknowledged co-optation of other cultures. His "Dialogue on Language" characterizes this co-optation as depriving humanity of basic resources for halting the drive toward an increasingly one-dimensional world. In offering glimpses of the global ramifications of technological rationality, Heidegger descries the increasing "Europeanization of the earth and of man" (WL, 15/US, 103). As a forerunner to the postmodern turn to local narrative, Heidegger's call to rein in the global reach of western culture begins from a strong view of thinking as historically and culturally situated.

Yet basic ambiguities pervade Heidegger's texts. His penchant for attributing deep meaning and archaic origins to key phenomena, texts, or words, rings of essentialism. But these could also be historicist claims, rather than an appeal to an essentializing view of history. A deliberately radical reading acknowledges other comments in the Heideggerian corpus which indicate his awareness that his theory does not delineate the sole, true depiction of a core essence of western history. As early as his 1928 lecture course, *The Metaphysical Foundations of Logic*, Heidegger confronts his need to formulate the purpose of his ontological project within a large scale narrative about western history; ontology cannot be abstracted from historical situation and context. When confronted with this problem, he finds himself enjoined to classify the status of such an appropriation of history as a necessary illusion:

> Not only do we need analysis in general but we must produce the illusion, as it were, that the given task at hand is the one and only necessary task. Only the person who understands this art of existing, only the person who, in the course of action, can treat what is in each case seized upon as wholly singular, who at the same time nonetheless realizes the finitude of this activity, only such a one understands finite existence and can hope to accomplish something in it. (FL, 158/GA 26, 201)

These words explain the function of his philosophical ontology in ontic or everyday life. Sharply distinguishing the objective of his work from the traditional "advice-giving" function of philosophy, he establishes his performative intent. A genuine "repetition" of ancient philosophy must effectuate a "transformation" of western humanity as opposed to the mere "externalized transmission" of traditional problems depleted of their transformational value

(155/197).

The hermeneutical problem of the historical transmission of ideas does not necessarily hinge upon the discernment of a core essence to reality grasped with increased clarity and perfection through the teleological march of history. As historical, humans appropriate tradition one way or another. Heidegger clarifies:

> But, as decidedly as we must find our way back to the elemental force of central problems conceived in their universality and radicality, so would it be fatefully misguided were we to absolutize these very problems and so negate them in their essential function. We humans have a tendency, not just today and just on occasion, by which we either mistake what is philosophically central for what is interesting or easily accessible, or we absolutize a central point immediately, blindly, and once we grasp it, we fixate on a single potential stage of the originating problematic and make it the eternal task, instead of summoning and preparing the possibility of new originations. To do the latter, one need not foresee these originations. One needs to work continually at factical possibilities because of Dasein's finitude. (FL, 155–56/GA 26, 197–98)

Philosophy, in other words, achieves relevance to the human condition when it creates new possibilities of concrete, finite existence. Yet these comments carry a warning. Against his proclivity to assign deep meaning to archaic words, Heidegger cautions that humans generally take for granted traditional legacies, receive the lessons of history in fairly set ways, and thus pose contemporary problems in limited and limiting conceptual patterns. Here the elemental force of tradition rests upon no deep *logos*, but ultimately on the structures of time and language; on the fact that being historical and linguistic means that human existence always has a resevoir of excess possibilities out of which to generate novel forms of life. Most significant, for my purposes, is Heidegger's hypothesis that an inevitable performative contradiction arises when effectuating a radical transformation of existential possibilities within historical process; for any attempt to change one's mode of dwelling must "produce the illusion" that there is only one way to recover the "elemental force" of tradition, it must seize upon "what is" as if a "wholly singular" event (158/201). Projecting a holistic view of past tradition, as if tradition were a monolithic, singular, and hermeneutically monistic field of meaning, is a forceful means for "a breaking open of new horizons" (156/198). But it also has limitations.

There are two sides to Heidegger, the essentializing and the nonessentializing, as John Caputo often demonstrates.[12] In order to reconcile Heidegger's performative treatment of history as univocal with his claim that we should not absolutize any set of problems, we must read Heidegger as a strategist, not in the singularly deconstructive sense, but with a purpose to rejuvenate imagination and new ontological sensibilities. A certain nominalist impulse underlies his comments in that Heidegger posits no noumenal essence to historical reality. Emphasizing this nonessentializing side of later Heidegger leads to the reading I advance of his work as a critical mimetic practice. So read, the Heideggerian corpus relates a large-scale story about western history not in order to discern its essence or telos, but rather as a performative device for opening up a breach with an instrumental ethos and for redirecting the ontological and humanistic desire to be into alternative historical possibilities. Since Heidegger finds a direct link between instrumental reason and false universalism, his ethical ideal of decentering western thought as one of many standpoints marks a return to a more localized perspective that refrains from conceptual domination in order to open up the space within which dialogue can occur fruitfully across cultural differences. Heidegger believes the impetus to prevent the world from becoming a full scale, homogenizing extension of the West must minimally come from the West. His proposal is that the West can arrive at a critical relationship to its *topos* via a kind of historical-immanent criticism or the step-back that transgresses the epoch from within by reorganizing ethical sensibilities.

The nonessentializing side of Heidegger, which resists a conception of tradition as a monistic fabric of meaning (cf. PR, 92/SG, 156), brings us to a basic tension in his eschatological treatment of western history. Heidegger's apocalyptic story of the West's decline proclaims that the contemporary age has a special fated location in history, the chronological time-point where metaphysics exhausts itself as nihilistic and presents a historical possibility hitherto unknown to western humanity. But Heidegger also comments as well that there is no privileged window enabling one to judge our contemporary situation as more opportune than past epochs: "Not only do we lack any criterion which would permit us to evaluate the perfection of an epoch of metaphysics as compared with any other epoch. The right to this kind of evaluation does not exist" (OTB, 56/ZSD, 62). Such patently equivocal comments both treat large-scale historiography as ideal-typical narrative reconstructions undertaken from a specific temporal standpoint (now) and yet deny the status of every reconstruction, including Heidegger's own, as an absolutely objective assessment of history. Heidegger disclaims the need to assess the standards by which humans judge the incommensurable impact of history on diverse social groups. Instead, he closes each epoch into an isolated whole that can measure the critical import of its synchronic excess only against that whole, i.e., only in terms of its efficacy as a mechanism for decentering precisely one univocal depiction of the adversary named modernity. He steals the emancipatory interest in the future from the performative redirecting of human desire in noninstrumental ways by severing the synchronic possibilities for generating meaningful forms of life from a diachronic interest in past and future.

Any nonfatalistic reading of Heidegger, as I am pressing, ultimately implodes Heidegger's eschatological theory of time. More accurately, it minimally differentiates between (a) the context of Heideggerian eschatology as part of one rendition of history and (b) eschatology as an adequate analysis of the temporal structures of historical existence. It questions Heidegger's justifying of his story by appeal to what can only be formal structures (time and language) but not entities issuing forth our fate; and it challenges the incompleteness of an eschatological theory of temporality to the extent that such a model divorces synchronic temporal possibilities from the socially dependent bases of human action in the diachronic unfolding of history and the historically contingent nature of meaning. Still, my purpose is not to rewrite a theory of temporality but only to indicate that the maieutic intent of Heidegger's narrative of western history lapses into an unwarranted reification of tradition as a composite whole and an obfuscation of its own status as an ideal-type reconstruction that harbors social and political implications. The wholesale rejection of the enemy breeds two untenable splits. These include splitting the role of meditative thinking from a speculative interest in the future and divorcing the synchronic excess of meaning from diachronic linguistic usage. Before examining these two splits as inconsistent with Heidegger's own moral-aesthetic goal of decentering western cultural imperialism, I want to specify the features of a thoroughgoing nonfatalistic view of his eschatological story.

A nonfatalistic reading treats his narrative not as a positivistic declaration that the age of technological Enframing (*Gestell*) is the last epoch in history, and thus not as accurate historiography, but instead as a maieutic effort to effectuate an end to specific elements of collective ethos looming large in the present age. This interpretation more strictly adheres to the fact that reconstructions of history are undertaken not only from our current historical location, but finally from varied and differentiated social standpoints with respect to concrete meanings that historical and cultural legacies hold. And it proposes that Heidegger's reification of history into an eschatology runs contrary to the nonessentialist side of his work. Caputo gives a lucid description of Heideggerian eschatology:

> In eschatology the beginning overtakes the end and puts an end to the end; in teleology, the end fulfills the beginning and puts an end to the beginning. In eschatology the beginning outstrips the end so that the end is driven beyond itself. The most extreme end is consequently the point of transition to a new beginning. . . .
> The *legein* in eschato-logy, the gathering together [of beginnings and ends], thus supplies a logic of reversal, a movement in which the beginning spins itself out into oblivion, and then turns itself around into a new beginning.[13]

To rigorously adhere to his maieutic intent, Heidegger must give up grandiose claims to special insight into history, to supply the end that outstrips metaphysics, to inaugurate the new life *in toto*. His narrative so read posits neither a beginning nor end of history, but instead engages in a textual reading of history in terms of a limited and necessarily partial assessment of key elements orienting the age, namely, certain patterns of thinking and living that bolster, perpetuate, even numb people to the dangers of the instrumental and technological orientation of the contemporary West. Projecting the *Kehre* (the prospect of undertaking a reversal wherein we counteract this one-dimensional pull) reveals the fact that every historical circumstance has possibilities for resistance and that this age has resources for countering western nihilism and cultural imperialism.

The parameters of a nonfatalistic reading of Heideggerian eschatology include these. (1) Heidegger's immanent reading of western history (though reductionistic and monolithic) presupposes that there are manifold ways in which to read and rewrite history, none of which delineates all possibilities or desirable goals. These require further evaluation. Yet some stories shed more light on the dangers of our times because they reveal our situation from the standpoint of what has been forgotten. Heidegger's story reveals one price we pay for our current form of life, a profound lack of urgency about instrumental reason. (2) A subversive reading of western history is necessarily pessimistic because, like utopian novels, it glimpses the netherside of our world and fleshes out what our world would become if we were to incrementally expand these trends to their most exaggerated proportions. (3) As depicting one potential fault with the teleological assumption that history moves ever onward in predominantly progressive directions, this dystopian narrative must be circular. It must entertain the possibility that a linear construction of time ideologically suppresses negative consequences of history. Again it images these negative dimensions as backlash effects of what is repressed. But one must be cautious not to interpret this technique as supplying an accurate depiction of the empirical past rather than a way of opening up the specter of what belief in our own rational control over history may or may not mean for us in the present; this dystopian projection, in Heideggerian terms, represents not the empirical past but the 'has-been' (repressed assumptions) uncritically validating our contemporary form of life. (4) Finally, this deliberately pessimistic rendition of the netherside of history aims to jar us from complacency into urgency about technological *ratio*. Such a textual practice treats 'now' from the standpoint that a quantitative extension of the prevailing suppositions of the age do not suffice to undergo historical process well. Taking critical distance on our historical sensibilities requires an investigation into the fact that genuine social change cannot proceed without a transformation in social eros.

Heidegger's apocalyptic and pessimistic reading of western metaphysics as a circle closing in upon itself can be interpreted as critically tracking a possible trajectory of the netherside of instrumental rationality in its contemporary form. By projecting the destructive impulses of calculative reason to an outermost point—total devastation of the earth, the Europeanization of man, a one-dimensional world, manipulation of others in the name of progress toward accepting different world views—his story brings forward alternative ways to be. Admittedly Heidegger at times employs overly evocative and seductive rhetorical tactics. But my point is that, understood as a technique closer to literary forms of utopian thought, the projected end of history is neither predestined nor a developed solution. It strikingly demonstrates the need for qualitative and not mere quantitative change and that this change must permeate to the fleshy ontological and epistemic sensibilities driving the human desire to further its own humanity. Heidegger's transformative-intervention harbors no real concern with whether human beings will, in some material-historical sense, actually bring about an apocalypse. The point is to show us that in this age, now, we partially live out an apocalyptic desire to the extent that the West continues to organize its identity around global domination and the struggle for perfect mastery of the world. We already participate in the destruction of ourselves and the earth. Contrary to *Being and Time*, later Heidegger diagnoses this dysfunction as a historically and culturally learned anxiety about lack of grounds, not finally an ontological or temporal necessity. Put in moral language, we have a responsibility *not* to have to live out every course of action in order to see what damage will be done. It lies within human capacity to ascertain reasons not simply to let history manifest as a quantitative extension of the present.

6.3 Romantic Valorization of Now

Even when read in strict performative and nonfatalistic terms, however, later Heidegger's eschatology digresses into a premature and abstract negation of modernity when left without a corrective to its built-in limits. One central limit of performative strategies is their reliance upon univocal descriptions. As literary meditations— embodying a sustained pedagogical effort aimed at weaning the reader of an instrumental habit of objectifying language and history which thereby tacitly positions him/herself as master of reality—Heidegger's descriptions of modern rationality tender extremely effective challenges. His meditative excurses seem inexhaustible in their ability to confront the reader with a sense of atrophied pleasure in both noninstrumental thinking and nonstoic- and even noncompetitive-based ways of realizing one's autonomous capacities, talents, and skills.

Examples are not difficult to find. Heidegger's peculiar use of language—in such turns of phrase as "language is the house of Being" (BW, 213/W, 164), "*language* remains the master [*Herrin*] of man" (PLT, 146/VA, 140), and "language speaks" and bespeaks us (PLT, 192/US, 14)—works Socratically to raise awareness that grammar structures perception and that in habitual and unacknowledged ways we posit ourselves as subjects in control of meaning in and through representational or denotative speech. These descriptions deliver the reader to a rich sense that ontological and epistemic senses are historically conditioned. Modern man, he says, "becomes the relational center of that which is as such" (QCT, 128/H, 81). With modern representation, "[t]he world picture does not change from an earlier medieval into a modern one, but rather the fact that the world becomes picture at all is what distinguishes the essence of the modern age" (130/83). Heidegger skillfully makes historical circumstance come alive and reveals historical situated-ness as an active ethos and not mere passive insertion in time, thus reminding westerners that they have not always understood themselves as grounded in a transcendental, formative conscious-ness or as self-legislating, autonomous individuals.

Effective as these techniques are, they target modernity as a hermeneutic whole rather than a heterogenous set of meanings and they treat speculative rationality as a uniformly pernicious kind of objectification. Heidegger's treatment of modernity falsely depicts a world fundamentally the same for all westerners and all people; it flattens out history. This flattening constricts the pros-pect of retrieving those facets of modernity that proffer solutions to instrumental usages of reason and, worse, covers over the fact that it simply isolates a particular feature of modernity as the basic enemy of the age. Here I examine two untenable splits that render Heidegger's maieutic practice contradictory with respect to its ethi-cal intent. I suggest that, taken by itself as the total picture of modernity, Heidegger's description encourages romanticizing now as if it were a meta-utopia. Meta-utopia denotes a set of social and material conditions in which humans could embody Heidegger's vision of noninstrumental and nonhierarchical community, thereby harmoniously reconciling needs and multiple visions of the good life. But propping up a uniform view of calculative thinking and proposing it as the sole enemy of contemporary humanity does not furnish liberatory tools proportionate to the very goal of righting cultural imperialism espoused by Heidegger.

The Instrumental/Meditative Split

In the "Memorial Address" Heidegger treats meditative think-ing as a corrective to a one-sided, calculative standpoint (DT, 53–57/G, 22–26). Yet his undifferentiated categorization of modern reason (including conceptual paradigms, world views, and symbolic practices) as objectifying activities, though not false, fails to distin-guish between crass instrumentalism and forms of representation that need not lose touch with poetic sensibilities. This failure grounds the performative activity of taking distance on representational thought in a practical a priori that posits representation and meditative thinking as *mutually exclusive*. An unfortunate tension prevails in Heidegger's practical transgression of modernity as an era we cannot escape and his basing the noncalculative ethos on surpassing strategic forms of struggle; or between his acceptance that the technological apparatus is not the problem and his failure to account for how a noncalculative culture could effectively utilize technology to alleviate suffering and impoverishment. Learning how to think differently may well entail an existential suspension of ordinary habits as part of an initial schooling in coming to perceive naive adherence to socially ingrained patterns of thought. At first, relinquishing the calculative perspective might entail holistically giving up certain ways of willing, projecting, fantasizing. But this meditative schooling, though perhaps felt in the initial stages of edification as precluding objectification of all kinds, yields a partial understanding. It reflects a unidirectional existential experience of the paradoxes built into breaking old habits and mistakenly infers that the paradox is irresolvable. Transformed habits can dialectically inform other activities such that calculating, representing, imagining, and planning revolutions need not assume purely instrumental and manipulative forms.

Expanded to encompass a transformation of collective ethos, Heidegger's anti-Enlightenment mentality slurs the boundary between correcting the totalizing urges of speculative reason and displacing reconstructive philosophy altogether. He nicely counterpoises the social anomie of modernity with the prospect of a rejuvenated lifeworld. And though he admits that overcoming social anomie does not remove us from the technological era, he at best inconsistently follows the parallel tack with respect to philosophy. Often he treats as infeasible the possibility that the step-back from calculative thought might not obliterate the validity of and need for problem solving. Once meditative living is cast as a total response to modernity, the critique of philosophy as foundationalism inevitably collapses into a pernicious antinormativism. By pernicious I mean not simply a discourse that stops short of formulating criteria by which to evaluate forms of suffering, but one that obfuscates its own set of values and presents the task of repairing human suffering as antipathetic to reconstructive theory and oppositional thought.

Even though the postmodern tenet that all evaluations inherently suppress nonidentity and normalize people may be correct, it does not follow that every evaluation equally disempowers the oppressed. To displace normative theory proper amounts for Heidegger to resisting rational speculation and planning the future. His focus on an organic change in poiesis as necessary to engendering a future that is no mere extension of the present notwithstanding, his position is quietistic in that it shoots down the positive uses of critique and speculation along with destructive forms of objectification. Equating objectification with reification, Heidegger's philosophy deprives theory of resources to assess current forms of immiseration on the basis of social and ideological practices. It tends, to the contrary, to single out technology as the basic adversary. Although a significant reminder of the links between objectifying others and cultural imperialism, this textual practice nonetheless ignores those ways that an exclusive focus on technological *ratio* as the enemy can also obscure concern for the material suffering of many.[14] His limited maieutic practice reifies into a monocausal view of the culmination of modernity when it replaces social analysis with a preparatory thinking and treats the task of fostering an alterative ethos as a stand-in for a complex political strategy. Though a noninstrumental ethos could conceivably contribute to a world in which manifold visions of the good subsisted harmoniously, it does not by itself offer a rich enough curative for the ailments of modernity nor should we assume that it provides a self-validating and self-sustaining form of life that can afford to do away with normative theory, critique, and liberation struggle.

The Synchronic/Diachronic Split

Similar problems suffuse Heidegger's view of language. The thesis that language houses our historical *topos* does not intend to postulate language as a meta-entity, but simply as the multifaceted legacy of human interpretations and the possibilities left unharnessed in that legacy. Still, Heidegger's performative interventions into the transmission of words erect a false dichotomy between language as world-disclosive and the diachronic history of linguistic usages. In his practice, Heidegger equates any concession that his work gives only one reading of history with perpetuating the appearance that the author or speaker has full intentional mastery, transcends language, picks and chooses how to symbolize the world. Given his objective to break the standpoint of intentional mastery, he refuses to discuss his own investigation of key words of tradition as a form of re-metaphorizing our world. This refusal forces him to separate the experience of being linguistic from critical social analysis of and morally informed decisions about the actual names, labels, and nominative usages of words we decide to transmit.[15]

Since the "metaphorical exists only within metaphysics," Heidegger differentiates his own performative rejuvenation of language from both the literal and the metaphorical (PR, 48/SG, 89).[16] The claim, that to pick and choose new concepts cannot neutralize metaphysical rationality and its dualistic literal/metaphorical scheme, establishes another unwarranted dichotomy: representation and the critical rejuvenation of new meaning become posited as *mutually exclusive activities*. Here Heidegger obliterates the dialectical relation between the experience of language as a synchronic reservoir of possible meanings and the diachronic history of word usage. In his zeal to countermand metaphysics, Heidegger exaggerates the nature of the breach with current metaphoric usages, thereby founding his own derivation of new metaphors for rethinking human identity on an uncritical and parochial intuitionism (cf. EGT, 77/VA, 220). If Heidegger is right that thinking relies upon the creative, originary, inexhaustible excess of meaning inherent in being linguistic, then his refusal to analyze the metaphorical character of his work in its empirical effects leads to a partial and incomplete practice with deleterious results. Instead of limiting meditative thought to a participatory as opposed to mastering role in the linguistic institution of a world, Heidegger relegates power over discursive practices to language proper. His unidirectional recovery of excess meaning plays down responsibility for language usage, inevitably transmutes language into a metaentity, and severs attentiveness to language as a medium of disclosure from its protoethical import. The task of mediating language, as a fundamental part of disclosive processes, loses its connections to critical reflection on the social implications of what language discloses and to face-to-face relations.

A clear example is Heidegger's penchant for using feminine imagery in recovering the "fundamental words" of western tradition, like the Greek *alētheia* figured as goddess (P 1/Pa 1). There is an inconsistency between the noninstrumental poiesis he advocates based upon nonhatred of the traditionally feminized aspects of life and his complete lack of attention to the social function of feminine metaphors. Heidegger never questions the nonessential character of equating reality (unconcealment) with figurative representations of the feminine. Even though the retrieval of a nonobjectifying thinking arises out of transforming our relation to language (PLT, 146/VA, 140), Heidegger leaves in place the traditional metaphoric association that equates the receptive and nongraspable character of reality with the feminine. That no intuitive or nonpolitical reason explains why the veil of reality must be like woman is utterly inconsequential to Heideggerian thought. We can surmise that *how* we speak the feminine (from out of the originary event of language) need not demand an alteration of *what* we name as feminine (that we deliberately choose to represent our world to ourselves by deciding what is worth transmitting from past tradition).

Dissociating the synchronic event of linguistic excess from the diachronic history of language usage not only results in mystification but catapults the ethical significance of his work into hopeless inconsistencies. How can we learn not to objectify others without examining the empirically specific ways that concepts and images contribute to oppression? Can I understand another's self-disclosure when I abstract language from ideology critique and the institutionalized practices that circumscribe the meaning of her life? Though *alētheia, logos, nous,* substance, subjectivity, will to power, and technology are key words in the western tradition, there is no reason to divorce the elemental power of language from everyday usage and empirical ramifications. Though he assesses the ways that key words become key words by eclipsing other terms, Heidegger overlooks the latent biases of his conceptual genealogies because he adopts a pronounced indifference to the fact that his narrative cuts only one slice into western history. Fixated on the silenced meanings of key words like *alētheia,* he never questions that the feminine itself might be a key term or whether the typically male profession of the shepherd can image a nonhierarchical poiesis.

Justification for retaining certain word usages—nigger, bitch, spick—cannot rest on the view that a set of ontological and epistemic possibilities are called forth by them. Wouldn't precisely a verbal understanding of naming as productive of a world call into question such terms as social constructs? The very activity of naming, because a social practice, must attend to the historiographical career and ideological function of words. Such attention would bring us into an additional moment of critical relation to language left unpracticed and untheorized by Heidegger. His dichotomous distinction between the activity of adhering to the verbal excess in language and attending to the function of metaphorical associations in concrete situations undermines his protoethical ideal of a new poetic foundation for community. That ethical potential of his theory needs to become grounded in a critical mediation of diachronic history, material and social analysis, and an intersubjective paradigm of communication. Without this grounding, the praxis of letting be deteriorates into a pauperized engagement with language. As Calvin Schrag eloquently remarks, "[a] metahistorical approach seems destined to conceal the concrete solicitations of meaning within the mundane lifeworld of historical action, and, to this extent, remains impoverished." To dwell poetically dwindles into a rarified process that, to borrow Werner Marx's words, "lets meanings arrive."[17] But this praxis stands with implacable complacency before the connotations it invokes relative to preexisting symbolic frameworks and social practice. And so Heidegger's historical rejuvenation of meaning squanders its relevance for engaging in face-to-face ethical relations across social location without reducing the other to an image of oneself.

Now as Utopia

I have consistently portrayed Heidegger's thought as proto-utopian and protonormative for two reasons. First, although the substance of his vision of a poiesis based upon letting be offers a response for our age, it redirects ontological desire toward possible social change as opposed to the perpetuation of the present. Second, as a structural analysis of temporality, Heidegger's poetic model reveals the worlding of any world as thus having implications beyond the present. On the one hand, the image of the fourfold mirror play specifically operates as a corrective to the "technological-scientific-industrial character as the sole criterion of man's world sojourn" (OTB, 60/ZSD, 66). It depicts, David Kolb tells us, not "a deeper world but a different way of experiencing the preconceptual and prepropositional inhabitation of our world."[18] As relative to this age, it does not give us a substantive vision that proclaims its staying power for all times. On the other hand, as delineating the structural possibility for taking distance on historical location in general, it reveals the ontological and temporal conditions that structure human existence. Those structures both enable distancing from one's historically embedded identity and indicate that linguistic beings do not have transparent access to the meaning horizons of one another's lives. This model tacitly holds up a normative ideal to resist the myth of the given and to forswear the idolatry of wanting to become a self-transparent humanity. Though this position should commit Heidegger only to weak versions of the death of history and the death of metaphysics, he reductively conflates the limited proto-utopian orientation of his work with a complex assessment of historical needs; and he assumes that rejecting normative theorizing is necessary by appeal to historical location rather than submitting normative claims to public debate. Heidegger's total and uniform rejection of modernity winds up relying upon a deeper world theory to tacitly validate quietism, as Kolb sharply analyses, even though he resists the idea of a deeper world. Because all strategic action would allegedly perpetuate the instrumental logic of this epoch, Heidegger transmutes the need to transgress instrumental *ratio* into a historical dictate, a special epoch in which all productive forms of normative debate and political action have been exhausted. Kolb assesses Heidegger's stance:

> Heidegger believes that the traditional advice-giving function of philosophy is finished. Philosophy has run out of metaphysical grounds on which to base advice, and the new thinking with the peculiar kind of transcendental move he propounds does not reach any measure.[19]

In effect, only the thinking that hears the voice of historicity and places no lien on the empirical past or present can slowly build a noninstrumental doorway to a future world.

The most basic confusion in Heidegger's texts centers around his comments on the nature and role of nonrepresentational thinking. In 1952 he categorically declares that thinking "does not produce usable practical wisdom" and it "does not endow us directly with the power to act" (WT, 159/WD, 161). But it is not clear what relation (meditative) thinking has to moral and political theory. At times thinking appears to perform a propaedeutic function, at others it displaces normative theory. When Heidegger talks in 1964 about the "task of thinking" at the "end of philosophy," he says:

> But above all, the thinking in question remains slight because its task is only of a preparatory, not a founding character. It is content with awakening a readiness in man for a possibility whose contour remains obscure, whose coming remains uncertain. (OTB, 60/ZSD, 66–67)

Yet he also posits thinking as having a chronological time: "The task of thinking would then be the surrender of previous thinking to the determination of the matter of thinking" (73/80). Minimally, he performatively enacts this surrender as a false either/or: either a new ethos or the same old problem solving. Thus, his vision crystallizes into an injunction against normative theory and speculation; it bypasses the question whether traditions can remain sufficiently self-critical to prevent hegemonic formations during this preparatory period; and it inaugurates ending philosophical history as *the* singular task, *the* only alternative to traditional philosophizing available to westerners. By setting the poetic task against problem solving, he projects utopia as organically built without reliance upon norms.

Two undesirable consequences spin off from Heidegger's abstract negation of representation and historiography. First, freedom becomes narrowly construed as releasement through meditative thinking. Obviously Heidegger does not intend a species of stoicism because he considers thinking an activity that modifies our sensibilities and perceptions and informs interaction. Yet he denies us freedom to deliberately govern historical and social change. Residues of stoicism haunt the idea that we find releasement by retreating holistically into poiesis, as if that were possible. Second, because releasement proves quietistic with respect to immiseration, it necessarily indulges a romantic view of the present. 'Now' becomes the valorized end of history in which all the resources to live noninstrumentally already await our patient discovery. Consistent with his refusal to come to terms with his early involvement in National Socialism, Heidegger simply prescinds from political action, everyday life, and real-world concerns. Living in the fourfold comes to incarnate a nostalgic longing for home in the here and now, a premature yearning to stop the struggle of actors in history, and a romantic want of rest.

But who can afford such fantasies except those of material privilege? Who needs to retain spirited interest in strategic action and struggle if not those who suffer economic exploitation? This longing for home, for rest, and for a readily available nonoppositional community devalues historiography and with it an emancipatory hope to overcome oppression. Abstracting historicity from historiography and the social sphere, Heidegger need not clarify the relation of preparatory thinking to sociopolitical change. How do we get to a noncompetitive society? What kinds of institutional change would that entail? In counseling us to wait on the gods (Spieg, 91–

116), Heidegger reduces human thought to an irresponsible and morally reprehensible compliance with the known. The constant slippage, between his critical contribution to a critique of instrumental reason in its ideological usages and his antitheoretical pose, lends itself to a conservative, political agenda. Without a corrective, it could readily fuel reactionary longings for an immediate sense of community whether sought in invidious forms of nationalism, religiosity, ethnicity, or class-based elitism.

Caught in this backsliding undertow, Heidegger's mythos dampens interest in a critical ethos; it forgets that even recollective thought is a reconstruction (one among many possible reconstructions) and proffers a precritical and dogmatic acceptance of whatever history brings (as if history delivers only one primordial possibility). We find no criteria for differentiating between a premodern and a postmodern ethos. That we reject hierarchy in today's world is merely the result of fate, just as the aristocracy of the ancient world was determined by their spontaneous experience of Being. The impossibility of mastering historical progress, rather than encouraging progressive cultural change, drains the noninstrumental ethos of letting be of its productive qualities. Transmuting the ground of this new ethos into simple compliance with the singular allottment of an originary possibility granted the age, Heidegger submerges the historicalness of human existence underneath the powerful and unfathomable unfolding of history according to eschatological necessity. For this reason, Kolb warns, "What becomes difficult for Heidegger at this point is to give that awareness of the worlding of the world some effect on our lives without turning it into a second world or a romantic deeper world."[20]

6.4 The Legacy of Antinormativism

I have argued that Heidegger's quietism as well as his fatalism do not result directly from his grand narrative, but rather from failing to theorize the performative status of his thought as protoethical, rather than as self-validating. By this I mean that his philosophy outlines an alternative poetics without working out a rich vision of postconventional community in distinctly material and social terms; and it calls for a normative ideal of decentering false universalism without developing a new ethical paradigm able to contend with the weaknesses of monological and legislative models of moral reasoning. The archaeological focus on finding a special

locus of transgression of modernity eclipses the main point of therapeutic interventions, namely, to reveal that there is never a total
view of history and that no group can claim to be the privileged
agent of change. Hence, something in addition to transgression has
to replace the death of metaphysics. If we can discern nothing else
from our past, then we can at least know that interaction with and
among diverse standpoints is a viable way to resist homogenization
and essentializing and totalizing standpoints. A methodology which
rejects the old as if it captured the complete reality of early modernity cannot afford to forget that it does provide an adequate basis
for determining what is needed to resolve the problems of modern
societies.

All large-scale renditions of historical locus are, as Benhabib
notes, "ideal-types":

> However one wishes to characterize the relevant context to which
> one is appealing for example as "the Anglo-American liberal tra-
> dition of thought," "the tradition of progressive and intervention-
> ist jurisprudence," "the Judeo-Christian tradition," "the culture of
> the West," "the legacy of the Suffragettes," "the tradition of courtly
> love," "Old Testament views of justice," "the political culture of
> democratic welfare states," etc., all these characterizations are
> themselves "ideal types" in some Weberian sense. They are con-
> structed out of the tapestry of meaning and interpretation which
> constitutes the horizon of our social lifeworld.

Since traditions are not "monolithic, univocal and homogeneous
fields of meaning," every reconstruction of the Enlightenment fixes
on some aspects to the exclusion of others. Without an explicit
recognition of this fact, Heidegger's theoretical explorations hide
the valuative priorities they implicitly promote and deny the necessity of exploring their potential impact on various social groups
and submitting these for public legitimation.[21]

Once taken as the whole story, an ideal-type reconstruction
disavows responsibility for legitimating the values implicit in such
context-transcending (i.e., not context-transcendent) claims. Certainly humans offer narratives as a means of showing to others the
meaning of their perspectives; however, some form of interaction
and intersubjective procedure is necessary to elevate any of these
into the principles that will redress the injustices of the past. Like
Benhabib, I think that an interactive model of practical reasoning
and a communicative procedure for generating norms proffer solutions to these problems. Glossing over the priorities implicit in the

quest to end metaphysics promotes an antinormativism that contradicts Heidegger's vision of a heterogeneous mediation of identity-in-difference. A postmetaphysical conception of social and moral theory needs to be materialized in a theory of interaction. A dialogical model of adjudicating moral claims can check the tendencies of one group to assert its local vision as the whole; it could ideally support the epistemological interest of the victims of history without relying upon teleology; and it fulfills the modern requirement of legitimizing one's standpoint through public discourse without appealing to transcendent reason. Without linking his work to a model of interaction, Heidegger transmutes his analysis of the age of technology into a transcendental standpoint.

Thus Heidegger's philosophy poses the serious question whether overcoming metaphysics can be accomplished without turning to an interactive moral theory to replace the old role of philosophy as the discourse of legitimation. Lacking such a paradigm, his protoethical vision of a postconventional model of a poetics based on mediating difference and his critique of the idealizing desire for mastery fall into contradiction. That contradiction, between a nondominating ethos and maintaining the status quo of domination, arises from a premature negation of modernity, one that leads to a partial perspective and perverse outcomes. Heidegger's untimely translation of his poetic vision into a univocal generational task whose time is now displaces social analysis. It severs the ontological basis for an ethics based on respect for nonidentity from an obligation to address others concretely within their social location. And Heidegger's antinormativism performs a total overthrow of modern universalism as based on the desire for mastery, but at the expense of an imperative to struggle for social justice. Most poststructuralist thinkers neither amputate the sources of meaning from social relations nor subscribe to a one-sided replacement of moral obligation based on right action with an ethics based solely on intrinsic responsibility to others. But I have shown that the deeper sources of Heidegger's valorization of now as meta-utopia, with its tacit support of material suffering, are two. These include his faulty unidirectional grounding of meaning in synchronic sources and his narrowing of the pathway to future possibility into a uniform step-back from metaphysics. The former not only sacrifices critical examination of the diachronic career of word usage but also overlooks the valuative biases in its narrative construction of history. The latter, in addition to collapsing the future into now, proves complicitous with the continued immiseration of the poor. Even given her social conception of language and her rejuvenation of a neo-Hegelian speculative interest in the future, Irigaray, in attenuated form, inherits this dual legacy.

CHAPTER SEVEN

Postmodern Meta-Utopia or Solidarity?

Race, Gender, and Reiterative Universalism

Sexual difference is one of the major philosophical issues, if
not the issue, of our age. According to Heidegger, each age has
one issue to think through, and one only. Sexual difference is
probably that issue in our own time which could be our "salvation" if we thought it through.

> Luce Irigaray, *An Ethics of Sexual Difference*

It is arguable that the focus by postmodernists on Western societies, and particular cultural traits of those societies as traits
sine qua non with an already constituted mega-utopia, renders
their views ethnocentric and colonialist.... Another approach,
however, is that the focus on Western societies not only erases
black and oppressed peoples of Western societies, but renders
their existence irrelevant; that the conditions taken to be important (such as authoritarian uses of enlightenment meta-narra-
tives and valorizations of historical subjects) allow postmodernists
to take the verities of a particular cultural strata and array
them as features of the nature of knowledge and reason ... that
the characteristics that postmodernists believe are important as
conduits for liberation from authoritarianism are deleterious for
the liberation of the oppressed within Western societies.

> Leonard Harris, "Postmodernism and Utopia"

The problem of the twentieth century is the problem of the
color-line.
> W. E. B. Du Bois, *The Souls of Black Folk*

In the late 1970s and early 1980s, W. E. B. Du Bois's forthright
challenge, that *the* "problem of the twentieth century is the problem

233

of the color-line," came home to roost within U.S. feminist theory.[1] Women of color challenged white feminists to recognize and to contend with the exclusionary racial bias that their theories and practices often exhibited even where an express commitment to combat racism existed. The importation of French poststructuralist theories, undertaken as one of several responses to this challenge, has been viewed as ambivalently motivated by numerous feminist and race theorists. Kelly Oliver hypothesizes that, for some, this political importation offered U.S. feminists a way to deflect criticism onto the French feminists by contrasting U.S. theories with the obvious "essentialism and elitism" inherent in the works of Irigaray, Cixous, and Kristeva.[2]

It would certainly be remiss to imply that pervasive feminist interest in French theory is symptomatic of white defensiveness. Yet Irigaray's own dictum—that sexual difference is, as one translation puts it, "the burning issue" (SD, 165) of our age—forebodes a monism doomed to conflict with a Du Boisian centering of race as the problem facing U.S. feminist theory. Definitive differences separate Heidegger's puzzling mystifications of destiny from Irigaray's lucid critique of patriarchy. That Irigaray has not explicitly theorized the intersection of race and gender could be chalked up to her particular concern to challenge the limited conception of gender-oppression held by liberal feminists within France. In spite of her own oversight, there are central reasons why many Anglo-feminists do *not* regard her methodology as *a priori* unsuited for redressing the racial exclusion that has most recently faced the second wave of feminism since the early 1980s. Yet given the robust Heideggerian influence on her work, I want to address the potential danger to eclipse race ensconced in her monistic approach to gender as paradigmatic of all forms of oppression and, correlatively, as "our salvation" in the twentieth century.

What makes poststructuralist theories attractive to many U.S. feminists—feminist theorists of various racial, ethnic, national, class, and sexual backgrounds—includes but cannot be reduced to the recognition that multiple epistemic perspectives exist. Poststructuralist theories share with many other schools of thought the view that there are no purely impartial and context-independent criteria for justifying knowledge claims.[3] Like other feminist epistemologies, the poststructuralist commitment to perspectivalism accommodates the fact that women of diverse racial, sexual, and other backgrounds may well have different localized experiences of the very same social and historical reality that issues in gender-based oppression(s). The peculiar attractiveness of poststructurlist theories is not solely epistemological, but rather methodological. Poststructuralist theories promise a powerful *methodological* vehicle for demonstrating how dominant cultural practices erect one group's point of view as normative, thereby exposing the very machinations of false universalizing as these correlate to systemic domination and subordination.

Instead of reconstructing a univocal conception of 'Woman's oppression' or a normative ideal of the 'liberated Woman', much poststructuralist theorizing tends to be interventionist, deconstructive, or strategic. It unmasks the ways that cultural discourses constrain women's possibilities for identity and autonomy. Whatever other theoretical commitments distinguish various poststructuralist positions, interventionist methodologies are commonly considered, firstly, to be eminently suited to unmasking the multiple yet specific (localized) forms of women's oppression while avoiding false universalism. They are understood, secondly, to be motivated by and to encourage ethical humility. That ethical impulse consists in adhering to as well as raising the theorist's critical awareness of the limits of her own perspective. Those engaged in these methodological praxes implicitly strive to encourage a solidarity-based attitude among women of materially and socially different situations by relinquishing the presumed authority that any one situation represents that of all women.

Nevertheless, some poststructuralist theorists are prone to confusing the minimal recognition *that* multiple epistemic authorities exist with having accomplished the *critical task* of addressing the interests of diverse marginalized groups. The thin recognition that I cannot universalize my own perspective yields no automatic critique of my standpoint. The nominalist underpinnings of poststructuralist theories, critics imply, cannot engender a utopian vision based upon a moral and epistemological interest in the self-determination of other oppressed groups. By nominalism I mean two things: first, the critical ontological view that only individuals and not real essences exist; secondly, the epistemological claim that universals exist only as we name them in language and not as substantive essences. Irigaray's work evinces certain nominalist undertones in that she (i) views subjectivity primarily as a discursive construct and (ii) treats social reality as primarily textual or symbolic in a foundational sense. For thinkers like Leonard Harris, these *nominalist underpinnings* embroil poststructuralists in theoretical praxes that ignore differences in social power among oppressed groups. They foster an *epistemological myopia* that comfortably disavows responsibility to local sites of liberation struggle other than one's own. Utopian visions of multicultural pluralism unfold into an invidious perpetuation of our racially segregated world.

Rather than indict Irigaray's nominalist focus on identity as a discursive construct as necessarily reproducing racial and economic privilege, I want to treat this anemic ethical consciousness as rooted in a conceptual confusion between abstract, as opposed to concrete, negation of one's racialized and material social location. Drucilla Cornell's utopian reading of Irigaray offers a serious and promising attempt to adapt French theory to the problem of racial exclusion. Cornell's work strives to correct for the deficiencies of nominalism both by moving beyond intervention to formalizing the need for a utopian practice that accommodates the interests of manifold struggling groups under her concept of reiterative universalism. Moreover, she balances this utopian practice with an ethical theory that rejects stereotypical fantasies of others as exotic and absolutely different (nonhuman). Even so, I will argue that Cornell only partially compensates for the biases of Irigaray's abstract, idealistic tendency to posit gender as foundational to other forms of oppression. In order to complete this corrective to Irigaray, it is necessary to supplement Cornell's model of reiterative universalism with an interactive theory of asymmetrical recognition.

7.1 From Hermeneutical Monism to Pluralism

The maieutic focus of Heidegger's tale of the West's decline flattens out history as a text characterized by hermeneutical monism of meaning. This flattening, in turn, glosses over the social and political priorities reflected in his ideal-typical reconstruction of modernity. The more promising implications of Heideggerian ontology for a vision of heterogeneous community fall vulnerable to collapse under his romantic embrace of now as meta-utopia. He illicitly moves from a therapeutic praxis of critical mythologizing to prescribing a general remedy for what ails modern society; he abstractly negates modernity because he fails to assess the multiple meanings of modernity for various groups and to achieve a critical and differentiated grasp of the political interests implicit in his position. Due to his staunch antimodernism and antinormativism, Heidegger never develops an ethical theory of recognition which could replace transcendental philosophy as the discourse of legitimation. By giving the impression that a single cause of social anomie exists, his work presents a single task confronting our age. Concealed within his persistent and uncritical appeal to destiny (his reconstruction of history) as justification for his utopian vision is the specter of the metaphysics he so heartily strove to rise above. A core *logos* permeates history as a destinal bestowal.

A distinguishing feature of poststructuralist theories of language is the rejection of a Heideggerian holistic view of history in favor of the view that multiple local narratives exist within a tradition. Derrida, for example, implodes Heidegger's conception of language as an *Urstiftung* or unitary origin and bestowal of meaning. John Caputo observes,

> Even to think the "history of metaphysics" as a "destiny of Being" (*Seinsgeschick*), to enclose it thus within the unified and undivided essence of "metaphysics," is to remain within the project of metaphysics and to arrest the play, to tame the flux. It is to organize it into a history and to center that history on a destiny— when all there is (*il y a*) is the plurality and plurivocity of dispatches flying in every different direction.[4]

Poststructuralist theories of language share with Heidegger an insistence that meaning inheres in language and not authorial intentions; but they explicitly treat meaning as rooted in social practices and highlight that there are multiple ways to interpret history. No single reading of history can claim to discover the noumenal message that decodes our present and bestows our second rebirth. So correcting Heidegger's twin mistakes, namely, rooting historiography in the unfolding of a deeper synchronic historical principle and divorcing diachronic historical change from social conditions, it is arguable that poststructuralist theories retain a definitive interest in reworking Enlightenment ideals of humanism, autonomy, and pluralism.[5]

There can be no doubt why poststructuralist theories are attractive to many theorists who find themselves on the wrong side of the normalizing gaze of the white, male, bourgeois subject of the Enlightenment. Jane Flax identifies the death of history as a fundamental objective common to all postmodern and poststructuralist thought. History, understood as the master narrative of man's "Being" unfolding in time toward its pregiven rational goal, is questioned as a fiction.[6] Imploding the view that historical progress mirrors a rational core undermines the claim of single groups to represent the rational force of history. There is no epistemologically impartial standpoint from which to measure pragmatic discourses, to evaluate the telos of history, and to claim to act unequivocally in the name of preordained progress. The nominalist recognition of plural sites of meaning comprises a postmodernist strategy aimed both at decentering the male, bourgeois subject of western Enlightenment reason and at breaking up homogenizing tendencies within groups struggling for their self-determination. Respect for difference, we presume, must entail curbing one's own interest in representing the totality of human reality.[7]

The productive promise that U.S. feminists have found in poststructuralist philosophies has been, to put it simply, twofold. First, by treating personal identity as a discursive social construct and not a pregiven essence, poststructuralist theories have often advanced feminist efforts to uproot fixed assumptions about the alleged nature of Woman. Secondly, the nominalist view that only local narratives—or context-specific justificatory standards—exist enables feminists to break away from the demand for coherence. Not only does this view avoid the essentialism inherent in theoretical efforts to pinpoint a universal conception of patriarchy that "subjugates all women everywhere,"[8] but it uproots the correlative assumption that women need to adopt a single strategy for liberation. Without reducing Irigaray to a simple Heideggerian still committed to an essentialist theory of women's historical oppression, I wish nonetheless to question seriously whether her utopian practice of imagining a feminine-universal inherently cultivates a critical awareness of its own social position. When posed in terms of race, this question means, does her concept of the feminine-universal, even grasped as reiteratively capable of being fleshed out in multiple forms (Cornell), actually serve to further segregate women's various identities? In what way would imaging multiple manifestations of the feminine-universal (in terms of racial and economic difference) avow or disavow the ethical imperative to examine whether the theoretical and practical priorities of one women's group prove detrimental to the situation of other women (or oppressed groups)?

bell hooks's work poses this question. She relies upon postmodernist theorizing to counteract essentialist conceptions of racial oppression. In her essay "Postmodern Blackness," she states:

> Employing a critique of essentialism allows African-Americans to acknowledge the way in which class mobility has altered collec-

tive black experience so that racism does not necessarily have the same impact on our lives. Such a critique allows us to affirm multiple black identities, varied black experience. It also challenges imperialist paradigms of black identity which represent blackness one-dimensionally in ways that reinforce and sustain white supremacy.

Here hooks elicits the aid of postmodernist theory to "rearticulate the basis for collective bonding" or black solidarity that neither presupposes an ideal of the "authentic" black identity nor leads one to internalize white hegemonic conceptions of "black authenticity." By dismantling univocal conceptions of race-based oppression, hooks works both to counter false demands placed on black women to privilege racial exclusion over gender concerns within black struggles and to pave the way toward coalitions among feminists that do not rely upon a unitary conception of women's experience.[9]

Even so, it would be premature to *infer* that any given poststructuralist strategy for exposing hegemonic conceptions of identity—understood as the keystone underpinning a politics of difference and an ethics devoted to recognition of Otherness—necessarily proves inclusive of the sociopolitical interests of the racially oppressed. In the same essay, hooks qualifies her laudatory comments with the sobering claim that many postmodern theorists use the critique of identity in ways detrimental to the racially oppressed: "Without adequate knowledge of and contact with the non-white 'Other', white theorists may move in discursive theoretical directions that are threatening and potentially disruptive of that critical practice which would support radical liberation struggle." Moreover, "[g]iven a pervasive politic of white supremacy which seeks to prevent the formation of radical black subjectivity, we cannot cavalierly dismiss a concern with identity politics."[10] hooks's concerns are pointed and instructive. They imply that antiessentialist critiques of identity and grand narrative must not deteriorate in neo-Heideggerian fashion into a romantic, allegedly principled, yet utterly abstract embrace of cultural difference by failing to theorize the need to defer to the experience of oppressed groups. Especially when posed in abstraction from those who experience material conditions of racial and economic exploitation, she cautions, an embrace of heterogeneity obfuscates the social concerns of blacks. Worse, as a stand-in for interaction across racial borders, it impedes blacks from acquiring critical voice and asserting themselves into the text of history.

Black scholarly debates over the potential usefulness as well as terrible dangers of postmodernist theories for advancing the needs of the racially oppressed reinforce hooks's concerns. Jon Michael Spencer attacks postmodernism as a "conspiracy to explode racial identity." Patricia Hill Collins echoes hooks's positive view of postmodern theory as useful for dismantling "Blackness as a master status," whereas Molefi Kete Asante, like Spencer, sees a "conservative agenda to construct a postmodernist web of a multiplicity of identities in order to befuddle the real issue," namely "giving agency to African people which might mean African solidarity and African self-determination." These debates raise a central concern. Instead of expanding "discursive theoretical" strategies to become more inclusive, white theorists, including feminists, can unwittingly use the recognition that multiple voices exist to disavow ethical and social responsibility to "incorporate the voices of displaced, marginalized, exploited, and oppressed black people."[11]

This type of failure to grapple systematically (in theory and praxis) with one's own racialized and material location as a theorist belies an epistemological myopia. That is, it falsely assumes that discursive accounts of difference or group specificity have a built-in protection mechanism against white solipsism. The nominalist view that only local narratives exist has no automatic protection mechanism which keeps the theorist from falsely universalizing or improperly assessing the biases rooted in her own context-specific standpoint. That myopia does not, however, inhere in poststructuralist methodologies per se. But neither does the methodological recognition *that* multiple epistemic authorities exist suffice to accomplish the *critical task* of addressing the interests of diverse marginalized groups, whether in utopian, moral, or political theory. To the contrary, even when African-American and Anglo-American feminists critique the same thing—such as the grand narratives of European Enlightenment—they often bring different concerns with them. And these differences matter because they refract conflicting societal positions of power relative to one another and not simply to a common enemy.

This fact accounts for the ambivalence exhibited by many African-American, Third World, and postcolonial theorists toward poststructuralism. Even as poststructuralist theories conjure new hope for overcoming racial, economic, and other forms of apartheid, the postmodern world simultaneously portends the relegation of the disenfranchised to their preestablished places in well-anchored and aged systems of apartheid. With the break-up of the former

Soviet Union, the postmodern world has been enveloped by a social climate of retrenchment to local forms of life that often do not adhere to a broad moral obligation and humanistic vision that transcends local interests. Some labeled Yugoslavia the first postmodern war; others, Viet Nam. And Frantz Fanon's reminder is no less applicable today, that the colonial world incorrigibly remains "a world divided into compartments."[12]

I want to argue that feminist theory cannot afford to embrace the heterogeneity of women's fragmented struggles of resistance as if a perfectly level vista stretches across these diverse and disjointed struggles. Since women are implicated in preexisting hierarchies of material and political power locally and globally, theorists must develop some conceptual basis for solidarity, granting that theory cannot stand in for the actual work of establishing these relations. My objective is not to dictate a single, authentic feminist methodology; however, I think outer parameters exist beyond which a variety of feminist methodologies cannot tread without becoming an impediment, not simply to building alliances and solidarity, but to meeting the diverse needs of women. In keeping with my focus, I address similar challenges to poststructuralist theory directed at theorizing utopia.

7.2 Postmodernism as Meta-Utopia?

Without denouncing all versions of postmodernism as neo-Heideggerian acquiescence before the end of history and the inefficacy of oppositional resistance to modernity, I will argue that feminist utopianism can at least avert complicity with racial and class privilege by avoiding two problems. In his critique of Baudrillard's depictions of the postmodern urban center, Leonard Harris identifies these two challenging problems: (i) treating now as a meta-utopia and (ii) uncritically valorizing the fragmented self of postmodernity. These two theoretical positions, he claims, suffer from the problem of the self-referentiality or the continued hegemony of the western, white, materially secure subject. Sharing with postmodern theorists an interest in overcoming Enlightenment authoritarianism, Harris nonetheless argues that treating now as meta-utopia represents the interests of a specific social sector while masking the immiseration of the racially poor. Moreover, projecting fragmented subjectivity as ideal serves to renounce the moral competencies needed for disdaining immiseration and exercising oppositional resistance.[13]

If Baudrillard does not repeat Heidegger's romantic abandonment of political interests, Harris's analysis suggests that his treatment of the urban West as utopia is no less pernicious. Because
postmodernists share with pragmatists an effort to naturalize epistemology, Harris claims that,

> [w]hat is unique about the postmodern project, in relation to notions
> of utopia, is the view that the world has come to the end of his-
> tory. There are two components of the view that the end of history
> has arrived which are of particular importance to my argument:
> (a) The belief that the idea of inevitable progress, development
> towards utopia, or something close to these has been discredited,
> and (b) the belief that models of the world in which the nature of
> the subject is realized (models which once masked ideological he-
> gemony) are now delegitimated. Now, in effect, is the postmodern
> meta-utopia.[14]

Far from claiming that his critique exhausts the wide range of
postmodern and poststructuralist positions, Harris focuses on specific postmodern descriptions of the urban West. Nonetheless, if we
are to take seriously Cornell's ideal of reiterative universalism,
then we must address whether Harris's criticisms are applicable by
extension. He argues that depictions found in Baudrillard's *America*,
Deleuze and Guattari's *Anti-Oedipus*, and Raban's *Soft City* treat
the contemporary western urban center as representing a meta-
utopian framework. Following Nozick, Harris defines meta-utopia
as "an environment or framework in which different utopian visions are permitted." Unpacking this concept, he shows that an
appeal to meta-utopia implies that we have entered a historical
period in which the social climate "permits or makes it possible for
individuals or groups to pursue their vision of utopia" and, moreover, does "not allow any one vision to force its way of life on
anyone else."[15]

Harris's argument is that such descriptions of the contemporary West are normatively loaded and "indefensible" because they
render "invisible the immiserated."[16] I read this critique in neo-
Hegelian terms: Even if postmodern criticisms of the false universalizing tendencies of Enlightenment reason and traditional
utopianism are correct, does it follow that we have arrived at a
juncture in history when various groups have equal resources to
pursue "differentiated visions of the good or community grounded
on the heterogeneity of identity"? Whether pragmatists or
poststructuralists, we can agree that there are no "universal rules

of rationality" which convey objective truth or "iron laws of nature" that govern historical evolution. But, Harris charges, "it does not follow that the inferences drawn from [these] views support cogent descriptions" of the contemporary, urban West.[17] Rather than denounce the ideal of postmetaphysical rationality or an alternative conception of pluralism than we find in liberal humanism, Harris focuses his critique on the normative assumptions embedded in the way we describe the present historical juncture.

This criticism turns the notion of critical fantasizing back on its head: Harris encourages us to ask what fantasy is deployed in those descriptions? To Harris's view, a certain postmodern pluralism commingles with the pernicious fantasy that utopia is present at hand. And he asks whose interests are currently served by that fantasy? Harris's answer is that this fantasy only tangibly exists for those who already have the material and psychological resources to consume a morsel of diversity, albeit a superficial consumption. Baudrillard's view of the urban West implies that we can universalize the pursuit of plural goods as reflecting the interests of all without additional mediation, i.e., without consulting plural descriptions of our historical juncture. Targeting the *particular* textual evaluation of social conditions built into valorization of the present as a meta-utopia enables Harris to reveal that a pernicious fantasy suffuses that vision. That fantasy stems from a faulty moral premise which perpetuates existing conditions of immiseration and economic depravity and the process by which these conditions take root in racial and ethnic segregation.

For example, Harris notes that Baudrillard's descriptions systematically fail to mention the misery and economic poverty of those urban inhabitants who do not have the means to roam freely through the spaces of postmodern architecture or ethnically diverse boroughs. Break dancers, he argues, do not have the luxury of enjoying the space of the postmodern building that ideally allows one to travel, in imagination, through the multiple ethnic and historical time periods reflected in its architecture. The dancers, by virtue of their situation of economic immiseration, lack access to the "diffractured time" represented by this space. Nor can they experience the imaginary community of diversity as a positive feature of the postmodern city because they lack both economic resources (credit cards) and the social acceptance requisite to travel through "each racialized neighborhood." By contrast, middle class (mainly white) subjects can travel, Harris says,

> with a sort of schizophrenic taste for food, freely moving from one
> ethnic neighborhood to another, sampling cuisine as we go, imag-
> ining membership in each, paying with our credit card in each
> restaurant, ordering food the same way in each restaurant, using
> the same language in each, and yet imagining that we have fun-
> damentally travelled to different lands of cuisine in some sense
> other than having simply tasted different foods. We have touched
> different cultures.[18]

Such images of our contemporary western world, Harris charges,
both presuppose a racialized world (marketing consumption of the
exotic) and "normalize segregation":

> If postmodern concepts provide an appropriate way of describing
> the West, then it is not at all clear why the fundamentally para-
> sitic relationship of race is excluded from accounts: the world of
> race and race relations, I believe, festers in an unholy alliance
> with the world depicted by postmodernists.

Rather than take such a description of the postmodern world as
the "basis for cultural pluralism," Harris issues a moral imperative
to think of it as an "anathema against" true diversity.[19]

Harris drives his critique home by claiming that Baudrillard's
vision is hegemonic in that it represents the interests and possibilities of a particular cultural group:

> The postmodern vision of now is an elliptical hegemonic vision. By
> this, I mean that the concept of the subject in the postmodernist
> project under consideration [Baudrillard and Lyotard] is self-ref-
> erential, i.e., elliptical—we must presuppose a composite sense of
> self-identity in order to make sense of a fragmented self which
> can experience fragmentation; and the referent is hegemonic in
> the sense that the human subject is grounded on a valorized model
> of Western decentered and materially secure whites with access to
> the resources associated with modernity.[20]

This self-referentiality has two moments. First, the reductive
postmodern preference for examining social oppression in terms of
symbolic practices, images, fantasies, and metaphors isolates a "narrow spectrum of social reality" and takes it to "represent the very
character of social life." Baudrillard's description of the urban West
does not presuppose a belief in racial inferiority; rather, Harris
argues, his exclusive and preferential focus on images "renders the

immiserated irrelevant and blacks, in particular, as ornaments without agencies or resistance." Baudrillard recuperates "well-worn stereotypes" by the elliptical way that his descriptions refuse to connect image to the real experiences of the impoverished and instead elevate his "tourist report[ing]" to the "accurate presentation" of reality. The very act of relegating the experience of immiseration to the "tangential" prevents any genuine "transcription" of the symbolic meaning of race in its substantive impact on the lives of people.[21]

Second, Harris continues, the utopian ideal of "a social identity capable of ready transportation" is also hegemonic. Harris's critique indicates more than the ineffectualness of this ideal to dismantle a world that valorizes specific competencies while socializing whites and the wealthy to possess these traits. It additionally points to how this ideal perpetuates the keystone to the hegemony of that world, specifically, the "benign blindness" to racial exploitation constitutive of white consciousness. For Harris, the valorization of a radically ephemeral identity is disingenuous and egregious. The prototypical postmodern subjects "can remake their identities without foundational commitments." But those who can realistically pursue the cosmopolitan pleasures of multiethnic forms of the good life already possess, not simply a composite sense of agency, but an agency based upon basic material resources and racial security. Certainly all mentally sane subjects, including the disenfranchised, rely upon a composite memory of being social actors capable of exercising choice and preference. But, Harris notes, the postmodern ideal of fluidity further presupposes a subject not laboring under the "dehumanizing negation of their being as humans," a subject with a sense of inclusion in "the moral community of humans," a subject able to exercise choice with success over time. Finally, Baudrillard's urban subject lacks moral indignation about social wrongs.[22]

We could readily counter that not all poststructuralist theories valorize now as meta-utopia. To the contrary, many focus (following Adorno and Horkheimer) on the fetishization of image as an indicator of fundamentally dangerous features of advanced industrialized societies. In apocalyptic tones, they characterize now as a misshapen dystopia: the hegemony of capitalism has become "utterly triumphant" and "capitalism has shown itself remarkably indifferent to both the destruction or retention of fundamental (religious, metaphysical, or even ideological) truths and the beliefs dependent upon them."[23] But Harris's critique cannot be so readily dismissed because we can extend it beyond the substance of Baudrillard's *America* into formal theoretical concerns. His analysis poignantly demonstrates that nominalism—both the turn to local narrative and the view of identity as a discursive construct—does not automatically avoid false universalism. To the contrary, the postmodern turn to local narrative often justifies a metanarrative that singles out the experiences of western racially and economically privileged groups and elevates them as key to unlocking the global hegemony of the West. The very convergence of theory on symbolic practices thus ironically deadens an emancipatory interest in generating social conditions for the historical self-determination of the racially exploited.

Harris's critique rests upon the claim that postmodern theories normalize "ghoulish separateness" through the *simultaneous totalization of social reality as symbolic and as fragmented*. This critique isolates the conceptual profile of invidious forms of nominalism. Fragmenting reality into self-contained sites of meaning obscures the precondition of hedonistic, cosmopolitan revelry, namely, the abhorrent pluralism of our racially segregated world and the exclusion of the underclass from partaking of this hedonism. At issue is not a facile equation of this exclusive focus on discursive sources of oppression with white solipsism. Reifying a symbolic practice into a hermeneutically monistic whole engenders only an abstract negation of one's local standpoint. Local meanings thus appear as composite, homogenous units of embodiment of that symbolic reality rather than competing ways of constructing ideal-typical presentations of western history.[24] This produces a perverse dialectic in which the racially privileged wear glasses that reflect themselves even as they embrace difference. This embrace elliptically reproduces the morally objectionable diffidence peculiar to antiblack racism manifest as the view that, since whites cannot possibly understand what it means to be black, the black problem must be a problem of blacks. Though as white I cannot directly experience being socially located as black, I nevertheless can understand a great deal about black social location and I certainly have direct experience of processes of racialization from the side of being white.

At times, Harris's commentary indicates that the very focus on symbolic sources of oppression is uniformly indicative of material privilege whereas economic concerns are natively prioritized by the impoverished. On the one hand, I agree that postmodern discourse problematically occludes the language of impoverishment and disenfranchisement when it opts for the equalizing language of marginalization. On the other hand, it does not follow that the basic enemy of material depravity is primarily economic and only secondarily symbolic, even though the lives of the impoverished may be consumed by the cycle of poverty, by the struggle for survival and against despair, with distracting their children from the allure of drugs, and with compensating for the long-term effects of the aesthetic depravity of the Bronx and of living in fear. These uniform associations notwithstanding, I do not think Harris's commentary intends to rehash old lines of debate between idealist versus materialist, existentialist versus Marxist, or most recently poststructuralist versus Marxist approaches to ideology critique.[25] There is a difference between reifying reality as symbolic or reifying symbolic practices into univocal wholes, on the one side, and addressing the symbolic sources of oppression, on the other. Instead of a strong rejection of all poststructuralism, I find it more fruitful to take Harris's analysis as a challenge to forms of nominalism which lead to invidious cultural pluralism. Invidious means that they sanction color-blindness in whites and, as a necessary consequence, normalize segregation.

Nominalist strategies of decentering Enlightenment universalism through a proliferation of local narratives can, indeed, ignore the question of whose interests will come out on top, given that local groups begin with unequal resources. Instead, "[e]ach differentiated subject or community of subjects is understood to pursue incremental transformation of capitalism within its own site of experience."[26] Harris's analysis begs for a theory of coalition. And it begs for a model of flexible identity which differentiates productive aspects of composite identity (coherence) from authoritarian (nonfluid) traits. Rather than reject all coherence, a productive model of flexible identity isolates basic competencies necessary for sanity and agency while displacing those features of the western ideal of coherence associated with the stoic emotional life—psychic rigidity, anal retentiveness, sexual repression, homophobia, racialized phobia, fear of flesh, mucous, and so forth. These have historically supported a logic of sacrifice linked to the episteme of impartial reason which is challenged by race and feminist theorists alike.

I want to address a common thread underlying calls for models of coalition and for a moral psychology that serves oppositional resistance. These appeals add up to a single moral imperative and theoretical question: If the turn to local narrative does not suffice to cultivate critical awareness of our social locations as theorists, then what must we theorize in order to decenter the influence of

social location on the praxis of theorizing? If a central manifestation of abstract negation of one's social location is lack of moral
interest in sites of struggle other than one's own, then what practice must theory encourage as requisite to cultivating such a moral
competency? Arguably an interactive paradigm comprises a crucial
ingredient in generating critical distance on my own social position
as a theorist and an agent. To the extent that nominalism relies
upon a notion of self-contained local cultures that can coexist with
basic anathemas of our age—such as forms of class oppression
rooted in racial differentiation—it romanticizes present social conditions. Textual practices which emphasize marginalized voices
remain abstract and empty without interaction. Ultimately my
position calls for an ethical paradigm of asymmetrical reciprocity.

7.3 Irigaray's Approach to the Masculine Symbolic

Irigaray definitively connects Heideggerian ontology to symbolic and social practices. And she clearly recognizes that transforming the symbolic basis for social eros must be filled out through
intersubjective relations. Yet a neo-Heideggerian one-sidedness
continues to pervade Irigaray's work at two levels. These define
two kinds of monism that I will call paradigmatic-foundationalist
and descriptive-hermeneutical. Deborah King defines *monism* as
the claim that social relations can be distilled down to *one* dimension that underpins all other forms of oppression. King's definition
highlights the paradigmatic-foundationalist brand of monism, while
the existential-hermeneutical brand of monism refers to treating
contingent social locations as homogeneous rather than heterogeneous sites of meaning. In the works of Heidegger and Irigaray
these two forms of monism are interconnected. Just as Heidegger's
maieutic effort to cultivate a new ethos abstractly negates a univocal and homogeneous conception of modernity in ways that flatten
out the variegated needs of the victims never included in the ben-
eficial dimensions of western modernity, so too Irigaray's efforts to
release women's libido from patriarchal symbolism through writing
threaten to ignore "the material base of social relationships" and to
"flatten out differences of race, class, and history, limiting the
multifaceted variety of women's experience."[27] Whereas Heidegger's
abstract negation of modernity relies upon a reductive synchronic
reconstruction of modernity divorced from its diachronic basis in
history and society, Irigaray in a more attenuated form similarly

reduces the patriarchal symbolic to certain synchronic and trans-historical features.

The history of second-wave feminism unfolded through competing monistic claims about the foundational and common cause of women's diverse experiences of oppression. Was that cause legal or cultural, gender or economic based, rooted in ideal or material relations? Were the ideal and the material united under a third category or semiautonomous in their functions? The interlocking features of race and gender, mixed race, and hybrid social locations brought into question such monistic searches for the singular conceptual bedrock sustaining the complex edifice of women's oppression. Because Irigaray's peculiar combination of radical feminist precepts and nominalist linguistic commitments do not save her from the monistic tendency to treat race and economic relations as secondary effects of gendered cultural values, we must question the value of her work for advancing U.S. feminist concerns. At a foundational level, her work is reductionistic is two ways. First, she masks the empirical-historicist claim that gender is *the* unique problem of the twentieth century and as such utterly paradigmatic for transforming all other social relations. This claim is in turn grounded in a second premise, namely, an idealist reduction of social reality to symbolic relations. Irigaray thereby puts forward the symbolic order as the foundational keystone for unlocking women's alienation. A nominalist approach to reality as linguistic, materialist critics challenge, reflects class and race privilege; moreover, this reductive foundationalism leads as a necessary consequence to hermeneutical reductionism. By presupposing commonality, this approach homogenizes descriptions of women's experiences.

Though deeply sympathetic to the demand that feminist theory connect symbolic practices to material need and reveal rather than efface racial and class circumstance, I think these materialist critiques confuse two levels of analysis. In attacking poststructuralist theories *in toto,* they falsely equate focusing on language with foundationalism and hermeneutical reductionism. By assuming that a basic commitment to the premise that reality is linguistic *necessitates* monism of meaning at both a foundational and descriptive level, they overlook that maieutic interventions into the symbolic sources of a group's oppression need not lead to a reductive treatment of reality as symbolic. I think that both kinds of monism are interrelated in Irigaray's work; nonetheless, I want to argue that methodological occlusions of race do not arise as a necessary consequence of treating symbolic practices as relatively autonomous from, though connected to, material institutions. One approach is to advance a counterreductive standpoint theory which tacitly equates focus on symbol and imagery with race and class privilege. My approach considers it more instructive to explore theoretical correctives to the reductive tendencies of these interventionist strategies. There is no need to disparage the productive investigations by poststructuralists of the rapid commodification of symbols, ranging from Anita Hill to Rodney King, in the service of neoliberal capitalism.

Like Heidegger, there are two sides to Irigaray's work, the overly idealist tendency to treat symbolic systems as transhistorical and the maieutic attempt to sublate and redirect energy requisite to dream, hope, and finally undertake the hard theoretical and practical labor necessary to diagnose societal ills, propose resolutions, and actually work toward them. Irigaray's idealism does lead her to conflate these two sides of her work. She questionably assumes that her maieutic interventions yield enough information to represent women's needs and to undertake the reconstructive work of moral, social, and political theory requisite to articulate those needs. Her work abstractly leaps from a limited textual practice aimed largely at consciousness raising and rejuvenation of an autonomous social desire to a material specification of needs. It rests upon a flawed premise that an abstract textual practice suffices to establish ethical humility among women who occupy axes of power relative to one another.

I want to argue that, in Irigaray's case, the occlusion of material differences among women, and its correlative truncated political consciousness, stems primarily from the premise that the patriarchal symbolic has a stable, fixed structure. I assume that descriptive reductionism (homogenizing women's situations into hermeneutical wholes) is potentially connected to, but also potentially independent of, either materialist or idealist foundationalist assumptions (that the material produces the ideological or vice versa). Irigaray, in other words, conflates two ways of comprehending the signifier Woman. These are (i) treating Woman or the feminine-universal as a heuristic device for fleshing out concrete, material genealogies of actual women's histories of victimization; and (ii) defining the symbolic structure governing western culture's myths and fantasies as organized around an association of maleness with having the phallus (i.e., the universal subject of reason who has control over meaning) and being the phallus (the excluded, unmediated, erotically satisfied relation to the lost feminine/mother). The former lends itself to a pluralist methodology based upon the premise that there is no singular foundational cause of women's oppression but instead manifold, intersecting features of social reality. After reviewing Irigaray's foundationalism, I will critically examine whether Cornell's notion of reiterative universalism successfully reconciles Irigaray's maieutic project with material genealogies and corrects Irigaray's effacement of race and class.

Irigaray's Paradigmatic-Foundationalist Monism

Though the woman problem avails us of an integral thread that unravels the warp of the social fabric in its manifestly complex aspects, it is not the paradigmatic thread. Minimally, the race problem equally binds the weave of fantasy, culture, and organization of material production constitutive of civil and institutional relations in U.S. and western societies. Like many race theories, Lewis Gordon's *Bad Faith* makes plausible cases for the following views: that antiblack racism suffuses the social fabric; that the empirical referent for the most abject and lowly in this world is blackness and not femininity; and that sex, which denotes the real limit of reason, equally lends itself to linkage with race as with gender. In Gordon's terms, the antiblack world posits the ultimate locus of phallic control as whiteness and not masculinity. In both theory and practice, Irigaray commits herself to the view that gender is the primary key to transforming western societies. As an empirical-historicist claim, we could readily dismiss it as unwarranted. Yet her methodology prioritizes this empiricist-historical claim about gender. This priority effaces the plural and competing forms of the logic of identity which equate not only maleness but also whiteness and manifold other signifiers with the universal subject or the position of mastery over language. Like other French theorists, Irigaray never tires of associating the feminine with the dark continent while exhibiting a disturbingly dull, if not completely benumbed, attitude to the racial connotations of these metaphors.

In Stephen Pluhacek's and Heidi Bostic's spring 1996 interview with Irigaray, it is clear that Irigaray follows Heidegger's critique that simple multiplication of world views does not break with the transcendental logic of identity. She argues that mere proliferation of the universal subject of meaning yields multiples of one, and thus cannot dismantle the logic of identity which equates a social group with the universal subject of reason. Against critics, Irigaray recognizes the problem of hermeneutical monism of meaning, stating that

> to deconstruct reference to unity, to the absolute, to the ideal, to the transcendent, etc., without bringing about a reorganization of the energy invested in such values risks the disintegration of the subject to the benefit of the savage reign of death drives or of the coming to power of an even more totalitarian authority.[28]

This reorganization of energy calls for a new set of cultural values that would defy the logic of identity, thereby surmounting the binary logic of metaphysics. In other words, we must relinquish the unmediated, naturalized relations between the sexes without yearning for a final sublation of one under the other. Fostering a new cultural form of bonding based upon mediating gender identity would counteract the current practice of relegating gender relations "to need . . . to instinct . . . to natural fecundity." Instead it would form nonhierarchical civil relations in general. It is easy to extend her limited intervention into gender to a demand relevant to other social groups. The demand not to naturalize relations issues an appeal to create social conditions that would enable all associated with nature to become subjects dialectically mediating themselves as "for-self" and not just "in-self."[29]

But what Irigaray gives in one hand she takes away with the other. Rather than argue the weak claim that gender avails insight into, without proving an exhaustive analysis of, the logic of identity, she categorically states that gender supplies the dialectic that restores "all singularity." She illicitly moves from a limited maieutic focus, in which she analyzes some particular symbolic sources of women's oppression, to postulating gender as the Archimedean fulcrum of social change. This move makes two simulataneous conflations, one hermeneutical, the other foundational. First, she conflates the idea of examining how western philosophy invokes ideal-typical depictions of Woman's nature with analyzing the manifold symbolic and material sources of women's diverse forms of oppression. Second, she conflates the correct assumption that gender suffuses all civil relations with the false assumption that gender denotes the unique facet of global reality able to open the window to the social contract in all its pernicious effects. Glossing the interviewers' suggestion that class privilege could render an analysis of the two sexes less than adequate to change social reality, Irigaray states that gender categorically is the trait that "belongs universally to all humans." This premise sanctions a methodological and practical subordination of "differences between cultures" to "hierarchical treatments of the relations between the genders."[30]

Given the history of U.S. feminism and U.S. race relations, it is imperative to set aside as a now-obvious falsity her assumption that gender suffices to ground multiculturalism. This supposition yields a myopic episteme that impedes achieving an ethically decentered relation to one's standpoint as a socially embedded theorist. Irigaray's claim that rethinking the man-woman relation, symbolically and historically, establishes a unique fulcrum for humanistic social evolution makes her excursus into symbolic myths questionable in numerous regards that extend beyond ignoring racialized social location. We could ask, for example, What kind of imaginary is deployed in the obvious lesbian imagery of the two lips when Irigaray elliptically centers the man-woman relation in ways that might work against the political cause of gay and lesbian movements? Questions of this kind highlight the epistemic difficulty of undertaking textual practices (such as utopian fantasizing) in ways that foster a sufficiently critical grasp of the practitioner's material location and of the fantasies resultant from this social location. The more central question is, Must her explorations of the two lips, interpreted as a methodological strategy for rethinking intersubjective relations that are not atomistic, reinforce heterosexism or antiblack racism?

The graver difficulty is whether Irigaray's methodological privileging of gender stems not simply from a false empirical-historicist claim but from her poststructuralist brand of idealism. Reverberating in Harris's critique of Baudrillard, Hartsock's resistance to Foucault, or Stabile's challenge to Haraway's technophilia is a common indictment of postmodern nominalism as decontextualizing symbolic systems and a mutual appeal to correct the antimaterialist facets of poststructuralist theorizing. For many, Irigaray's nominalist view, that identity-formation is *primarily* a linguistic construct, entangles her work in an a priori idealist reification of reality as symbolic. That reification, in turn, treats nondiscursive causes of oppression as secondary effects of language. The very methodological privileging of language, critics charge, evinces racial, western, modernist biases and threatens to reinstate the ghettoization of nonwhite and/or poor women to their predefined social groupings. As Stabile queries, "[t]o what extent is the emphasis on imagination, creativity, and literacy a class-based claim that can only disable and disarm a politicized feminism?"[31]

Nancy Fraser traces this problem in Irigaray's work to her structuralist inheritance. Saussure treats language systems, Fraser notes, as "synchronic rather than diachronic," and this leads him to posit language as a "static and atemporal," "monolithic," and fixed symbolic system. Many poststructuralist feminists in the U.S. are quick to point out that Lacan, not Irigaray, locks people into their preexisting social locations. Lacan, they argue, fails to move beyond Saussurean structuralism because he simultaneously theorizes sexual identity as discursively constructed (the result of social practices) and yet maintains "that the symbolic order must necessarily be phallocentric since the attainment of subjectivity requires submission to 'the Father's Law'."[32] Part of Irigaray's project aims to decenter what she sees as this double-bind in Lacan by reconnecting symbolic practices to the effects they exert on actual women's lives. A main intention of poststructuralist feminist revisionings of Lacan is to reject the paradigm of a fixed psychosymbolic order. That fixity necessarily positions men and women in a power-differential relative to the phallus by forcing language and sexuality under preexisting forms of representation. By elevating so-called feminine libido out of the sphere of the natural into that of the social, Irigaray challenges Lacan's ahistorical and fixed conception of the patriarchal symbolic. Hers is a strategy for displacing the libidinal organization of western societies around the phallus, i.e., around a single universal subject. Irigaray, in other words, rejects the necessity of castration, sacrifice, antagonism.

Even so, I partly agree with Fraser that the Saussurean model of language, "presupposed in Lacan," is in fact only "abstractly negated but not entirely superseded in deconstruction and in related forms of French women's writings." Dorothy Leland well exemplifies this point. While admitting that Irigaray's work discloses key aspects of the ideological control exerted in western cultures over women's sexuality, Leland nonetheless argues that Irigaray falls prey to three interrelated mistakes. First, she abstractly "views [women's] alienation as a feature of sociality *per se*"; second, this abstract view treats alienation as caused by a masculine symbolic system that operates beneath "the vast and variegated texts of social, political and economic life"; third, having severed the foundational cause of alienation from material conditions, Irigaray cannot supply an adequate political psychology. Analyzing alienation as "a free-floating ideological and psychological structure" does not enable women to "recognize the grounding of internalized oppression in culturally and historically specific institutions and practices" and intersubjective relations.[33]

These analyses rightly indicate that, in spite of her criticisms of Lacan, Irigaray takes over two unwarranted Lacanian tenets. The first is the foundationalist reduction of social relations to their symbolic dimensions which supplies her justification for the empirical-historicist claim that gender is the window to the future. The second is the view that men enjoy greater psychological benefits from the masculine symbolic than women, independently of class and race. Lacanian psychoanalysis erroneously derives these claims from the view that sex is different from all other aspects of identity. Sexual difference, as Joan Copjec clarifies, "is a real and not symbolic difference."[34] This claim neither advances a species of biological essentialism nor extends Freud's dictum that anatomy is destiny. Sex is neither purely nondiscursive nor purely a discursive construct, but rather denotes the limit point where meaning breaks down, a physical reality that resists total sublation into symbolic mediation. Broadly construed, sex offers a concrete referent for indicating the tension between identity and nonidentity, i.e., the fact that all sensible reality defies subsumption both under foundationalist myths of a naturalistic given and the totalizing urge of all conceptualization to subsume nonidentity under sameness.

Lacanians, like Copjec, defend the view that, while racial, ethnic, and class differences stem directly from symbolic meaning and other social relations, sexual difference does not. Though this makes sex pivotal to human development, it leads Copjec to misconstrue gender as more basic than other things in identity development. We cannot confuse sex as a limit marker (that opens us to our own nonidentity with ourselves) with supposing that developmental processes revolve around gender in ways that are more basic than racial and other social influences. This view of Oedipalization is unwarranted. If sex denotes the biological reminder of nonidentity, then other features of human existence can also designate the ontological gateway to nonbeing. Gender, race, class, and other matrices are coextensive features of symbolic reality that refer to the tension between being and nonbeing, having and not having. Elizabeth Abel demonstrates that all these sociosymbolic axes of power simultaneously inform identity-formation; and all permeate the very structuring, channeling, sublating, and manipulating of sexual energy or erotic desire.[35] I think it is empirically false to hold that gender socialization (and its connections, proximate or remote, to sexual orientation) predates a child's affective and cognitive recognition of race (for example) as a symbolic and material issue. To the contrary, white parents often hold this view arguably because their children experience no obvious aporia during ontogenesis which precludes reconciling their sense of inclusion in the human race with their racial markings.

In a forceful effort to decode the symbolic sources of antiblack racism, Lewis Gordon's work disproves the Lacanian view that Oedipalization, understood as structured around gender, exhausts sexual identity development. If for Lacan, castration identifies a linguistic transaction inaugurated through entrance into a patriarchal system of meaning, then Gordon shows that castration equally pertains to miscegenation. We live in a world thoroughly ensconced in antiblack values. For Gordon, the socio-erotica of lynching cannot be explicated on a model that associates linguistic castration solely with gender. Like sex, blackness denotes the "ontological limit of human reality," that is, nonbeing. Rather than abstractly assume that the phallus is masculinity, Gordon proposes that symbolic systems reflect specific values of this world. Instead of using a Lacanian model to justify the methodological focus on gender as paradigmatic, Gordon argues that, empirically speaking, blackness functions in this world as the global referent for the abject, lowly, and despicable. Yet he concurs that gender and race, among other things, equally suffuse symbolic and material reality and thus impose themselves on identity-formation with radically pernicious effects on our respective erotic lives and on human agency.[36]

Gordon's work challenges the two fundamental tenets of Lacanian psychoanalysis: (i) that the phallus is masculinity; and (ii) that black men qua maleness enjoy greater psychic power than white women in this hetero-patriarchal and antiblack world. There are, then, manifold aspects of human reality relegated to the allegedly unmediated nature that subsists outside the rationally decipherable features of reality. Black flesh, like female erotica, is one such signifier. Rather than a facile equation of femininity with darkness, Gordon's analyses suggest that fleshing out specific differences in the symbolic codification of otherness matters when fostering ethical self-transformation. Whereas 'blackness' conjures raw, cannibalistic, and exotic desire, the 'feminine' discussed by Irigaray portrays an enveloping, womblike space, an "[u]nmitigated yearning for the intrauterine nest" (Irigaray, E, 127). It is plausible that these symbolic associations indicate different kinds and possibly degrees of social resilience to critical metaphorical mediation.

To the degree that Irigaray's work is prone to an abstract negation of the Lacanian conception of the symbolic order, it perpetuates the blanket assumption that gender is most basic to identity-formation; and it promotes a truncated ethical sensibility unable to acknowledge the possible race (or class) biases pervading her work. Yet despite my agreement that Irigaray's foundationalism leads to this strong critique, I nonetheless hold that there are two sides to Irigaray. Though clearly based on the recognition of death drives and inherited assumptions about ontogenesis, Irigaray's analyses of symbolic practices, unlike Kristeva's, are not directly reliant upon a Lacanian theory of identity-formation.[37] Instead of the strong critique, that poststructuralist nominalism necessarily reflects race and class biases, only a weak thesis is justifiable. Not all poststructuralist methodologies share Irigaray's foundationalist monism. In addition, there is no reason not to set her maieutic goals free from her faulty foundationalist view that the pivotal axis of identity-formation via language acquisition is gender and none other.

Materialist critics are right to caution that poststructuralism tends to reduce social reality to symbolic practices, thus rendering material features of oppression unimportant. Yet these two problems are not necessarily related. Correlations between racialized class location and prioritizing economic over symbolic concerns may well stem from social embeddedness. But these correlations cannot be postulated as absolute at a theoretical level or we end up with a reductive standpoint theory that equally threatens to relegate groups uniformly to their preexisting social positions. A sophisticated pantextualism, based upon the insight that humans have no linguistically unmediated access to reality, does not necessitate denying the analytic distinction between discursive and nondiscursive features of reality in a narrow sense. Explorations of the masculine imaginary need not be understood as exhaustive of either social reality or symbolic practices. Given that I share the materialist view that identity-formation is mediated by both nondiscursive and discursive social practices, I agree that symbolic systems, though semiautonomous, are bidirectionally as opposed to unidirectionally related to material conditions. But though theory should not abstract discursive practices completely from actual victims, social agents, and existing social practices, it must also acknowledge that discursive practices can take on a life their own, a life greater than the collective will and the institutions that ground it, a life that could conceivably adapt to alternative forms of economic production.

For this reason, I reject the reductive materialist charge that the very focus on symbolic practices necessarily reflects racial power and material privilege. We can interpret Irigaray's neo-Heideggerian view to mean that transforming our cultural forms of metaphorically coding the body does not have to collapse all praxis into symbolizing, distill all features of reality down to discursive aspects, or assume that such metaphorical mediations suffice to delineate guidelines for social change without exploring their links to material conditions. Such as unmediated displacement of constructing a materialist basis for social action in favor of a limited textual praxis would collapse now into a meta-utopian fantasy that diminishes moral culpability for one's race and class location. Instead of this false utopianism, Cornell's theory of *reiterative universalism* presses a more critical, Derridean side of Irigaray that partly corrects the latter's inclination to abstractly reify reality as symbolic. First, Cornell argues for a pluralist as opposed to monist methodology. She assumes that women's circumstances are diverse not homogeneous. Second, Cornell repairs Irigaray's synchronic approach to symbolic associations of Woman with man's Other, arguing that these associations must be fleshed out in terms of empirical genealogies of women in their diverse historical and social locations. After examining Cornell's compelling theory, I will argue that Irigaray's descriptive monism flattens women's experiences. While reiterative universalism partially compensates for this tendency, it needs to become grounded in human interaction.

7.4 Reiterative Universalism Revisited

Since one of the explicit objectives of postmodern feminist theorizing has been to bring the theorist to an awareness of the biases and relative power inherent in her social position, Cornell's insightful appropriation of Irigaray merits attention. Like others, Cornell does not regard Irigaray's methodology as intrinsically tied to any specific set of material conditions, whatever complex matrix of racial, economic, and other factors those conditions might exhibit. The most salient feature of Cornell's reading is her effort to reconcile the nominalist theory that Woman is a linguistic fiction with undertaking multiple genealogies of women. This view attributes the abstraction in Irigaray's texts largely to the tradition that Irigaray critiques and not to Irigaray's own position. Much of the U.S. reception of Irigaray's work emphasizes that her primary aim is not to lay out a full-fledged political theory but instead to intervene in the psychosexual imaginary of western culture as transmitted in key texts of that tradition. Given that the modest objective of these interventions is to cultivate the psychic resistance necessary to overcome the disabling effects of gender-based domination, Cornell's utopian interpretation presses to attach this newly won eros to the work of engendering existential conditions for a world free of racial tensions (see Irigaray, TS, 166).

On this view Irigaray clearly does not equate women—their specific and diverse identities—with how Woman is represented within western tradition. Rather, she demonstrates that the symbolism inherent in the western philosophical corpus, from Plato to Hegel, denies women any symbolic association by which to identify as specifically female *and* as subject. The phallocratic symbolic system curtails women's ability to image themselves as self-determining and inhibits experimentation with their autonomous self-expression. If the phallocentric organization of symbolic practices projects Woman or the feminine as what lies outside impartial reason, then Woman functions as a social imaginary that grounds a masculinely codified universal subjectivity and defies symbolization. Given that for Irigaray, individuated imagination is bound to the symbolic resources of a society's norms, actual women are denied a self-derived fantasy of their autonomy when forced to play the role of being the fantasized object of the male imaginary, the *archē* and telos of man's unfulfilled desire (Irigaray, TS, 77, 94–95).[38] Irigaray's writings focus on recovering a female imaginary, i.e., a way for women to symbolize their own desires as universal.

Accordingly, Cornell interprets Irigaray's work as a form of critical utopian fantasizing or mythologizing, aimed at counteracting the "depletion of the feminine imaginary in the name of the masculine symbolic." In *Beyond Accommodation*, Cornell defines the feminist utopian project of rewriting the feminine as consistent with material analyses of women's victimization:

> The mimetic writing of feminine specificity, including the reworking of myth, can then be combined with the articulation of the determinate situation of women within our legal and political context, and with the genealogical exposure of how we are formed as objects within the masculine symbolic. *The mistake is to think that we cannot engage in all three aspects of the project, and worse, that one excludes the other.*

Cornell's reading is instructive in at least two ways. First, Cornell carefully argues that Irigaray's strategy of imaginative universalizing does not reinstate a single normative model for what female sexual identity has been or should look like. "This use of the feminine as imaginative universal does not, and should not, pretend to simply tell the 'truth' of Woman as she was, or is," Cornell says. "This is why our mythology is self-consciously an artificial mythology." According to Cornell, Irigaray is not wedded to a transhistorical view of women's oppression, since she does not describe the way women "are" or have been. Nor does Irigaray erect a static ideal of who women ought to become.[39]

Hence, the primary function of critical fantasizing is to detach women's imaginative and erotic energy from the claws of patriarchal symbolism in order to free up resources for social analysis and to rejuvenate hope. This energy can be freed, Cornell argues, by effectuating metaphoric slippage in our preestablished interpretive frameworks: "What matters is that the retelling of the feminine as imaginative universal gives body to the 'elsewhere' which makes this one appear as 'fallen,' and gives us the hope and the dream that we may one day be beyond it."[40] Critical mythologizing thus examines traditional mythic representations of Woman. Even as these preexisting myths about Woman constrain women's self-reflection and action, they prove susceptible to more than one interpretation. Critical appropriations of preexisting mythologies about Woman provide a medium through which to release the utopian desire needed to guide women's liberation struggles toward personal and social transformation, that is, toward a truly novel future.

Secondly, this utopian reading leads Cornell to claim that Irigaray's work can be adapted to opening up racial, national, and ethnic differences among women in a way that fosters mutual understanding. Because Woman as such does not exist but rather women are only as they exist within the manifold texts that determine their situations, Cornell argues that there can be no inherent contradiction between analyzing *the* masculine symbolic structure of western tradition and fleshing out the specificity of women's various historical circumstances. Cornell's argument is that symbolic constructions of Woman do not exist a priori as free-floating universals, but only a posteriori in their localized manifestations. Again, this theoretical position relies upon the nominalist intuition that no substantive or real universals exist for which we find only particular instantiations in material reality. Rather, the universal-particular dichotomy gives way to exploring women's specificities or how, in fact, tradition has imposed linguistic and symbolic group-ings onto people in ways that ground and support material condi-tions of oppression.[41]

So recognizing that Woman is only an allegory or myth, Cornell rejects the charge that postmodern methodologies privilege white women's experiences and thereby force women of color into the additive problem of tagging race or ethnicity onto white woman's account of femaleness. Rather, concrete critical mythologies treat women's different forms of oppression holistically. Cornell claims that imaginative universalism is "reiterative universalism" because the universal, in this case Woman, "is only as it is told, in its difference." Using Toni Morrison's *Beloved* as an example, Cornell states:

> Far from homogenizing the situation of Woman, the allegory of
> *Beloved* relies on myth to dramatize the very difference of the
> Afro-American mother's situation. In this sense, the "universals"
> expressed in myth are not and cannot be just the mere repetition
> of the same. Indeed, the "universal," the symbol of the "killing
> mother," cannot be known except as it is in context.[42]

Here Cornell explicitly links the textual practice of mythologizing to the ethical task of fostering a political psychology able to recog-nize both the material and ideological bases of women's actual forms of oppression. Extending Irigaray, Cornell holds that retelling myths can raise social awareness of how racial difference intersects with gender and in such a way that African-American women are not stereotypically depicted as absolutely different from or not human like Euro-American women. Fleshing out specificity does not re-duce black women to a subset of a white woman, where the latter represents humanity on a more universal plane. Susan Babbitt comments, "[Cornell's] point about *Beloved* . . . is that we see what is wrong with a basic social myth—a presumption about how women's experience in general is characterized—when we apply it to the experience of an African-American woman and it fails to make sense."[43]

Similar to Heidegger's decentering of transcendental-horizonal thinking, Cornell casts *Beloved* against the hermeneutical horizon of the Medea myth long held in the West as a universal represen-tation of Womanhood. By transmuting essence into allegory, Cornell fleshes out the concrete material and social specificity of the African-American mother's reality in slavery. This retelling of Medea as *Beloved* reveals that killing one's children under slavery cannot exemplify, as with Medea, the overbearing mother who protects her children from patriarchy, because under slavery the mother cannot even "guarantee [the children] . . . an autonomous life in even the most minimal sense." In this fashion, Babbitt suggests, Cornell shows how *Beloved* encourages a political consciousness and an ethical sensibility of the ways in which Sethe, precisely as human as me, is treated differently: "If we were to think of Sethe in terms of the then dominant conceptual framework, the difference between Sethe and a white woman is that Sethe is *less* than fully human, not just that she is unjustly treated *as* human."[44]

Finally, Cornell argues that *Beloved* not only transforms the significance of the Medea myth but "challenges on a very profound level the idealization of mothering as the basis for a unique feminine 'reality'."[45] Although not explicit, it is plausible that this version of critical mythologizing effectuates a transvaluation of cultural values in ways dependent upon examining their material bases. Cornell implies that a nonhierarchical community based upon differences among humans could emerge only on condition that humans develop the capacity to conceptually mediate the ways that race and gender intertwine in diverse ways without associating one group with the universal subject of humanity. Since these mediations do not preclude material conditions, it is conceivable that this capacity would remain partial and incomplete without developing a moral ability to perceive and disdain economic immiseration. Finally, this ethicopolitical consciousness is attainable only by dismantling our social elevation of motherhood into a romanticized ideal as if that ideal exists independently of women's social conditions. Cornell's analysis of slavery suggests that deromanticizing motherhood as a cultural ideal would require U.S. society to come to grips with how it supports material forms of production that effect inhumane ramifications, both economic and psychological, for women and, I would add, for others as well.

7.5 The Little Distance that Still Fragments?

Cornell's extension of Irigaray's method to incorporate the question of racial, ethnic, and national diversity impressively shows how critical mythologizing can contribute to fostering ethical and political awareness of the differences among women. Cornell uproots Irigaray's view of gender as paradigmatic of all forms of oppression; however, she partly overlooks Irigaray's descriptive-herme-neutical monism. I suggest that Irigaray's dyadic conception of the patriarchal symbolic order, as organized around a simple dyadic masculine-feminine hierarchy, continues to depict the perspective of white, middle-class women as normative or universal. When Cornell finds no difficulty steering between a formal concept of *the masculine symbolic* as a bipolar configuration and examining the manifold social and material differences in women's situations, she fails to clearly distinguish her plural explorations of the influence that symbolic depictions of Woman have on women's lives from Irigaray's illicit premise that a woman's oppression is a priori determined against the phallus defined strictly in terms of maleness rather than mediated by additional symbolic factors, like whiteness.[46] Relying upon Irigaray's restricted view of the symbolic order, in order words, distorts the very sharp advance that Cornell's theory of reiterative universalism makes over Irigaray.

For reasons that I will clarify shortly, I am sympathetic to Cornell's definition of Woman as nonexistent except as fleshed out a posteriori. My critique is weak rather than strong. I suggest not that we abandon reiterative universalism, but only that defining Woman a priori in opposition to the masculine phallus belies the biased standpoint that all women experience their oppression in terms of a simple dyadic masculine-feminine hierarchy. This premise reproduces Irigaray's foundationalist view of gender at a descriptive level that continues to diminish power differentials among women. Here I wish to identify several interrelated aspects of that normative bias inherent in Irigaray's descriptive-hermeneutical monism and show how each threatens to segregate women in their preallocated racial or other groupings. Yet I make this analysis in order to free Cornell's notion of reiterative universalism from being pulled into the undertow of Irigaray's ties to invidious monist tendencies.

First, Irigaray's Lacanian formal approach to the symbolic as masculine is *reductionistic* and for that reason it obscures some of the complexity of women's relations to one another. Irigaray rightly holds that women's various forms of oppression are not substantively the same in content. Yet Irigaray not only recognizes that oppressed women are formally like one another in that they are marginalized as women, she treats this formal equivalence as foundational when she predefines Woman. This approach trivializes in advance key substantive differences in women's kinds of oppression, thereby reducing those differences to only secondary manifestations of a primary, shared condition. The issue is not one of laundry-listing forms of oppression, as if it is possible or desirable to add oppression onto oppression so as to rank these from best to worst forms. Rather, the premise that the feminine plays a special role over other terms, such as black or exploited, as the discursive basis of women's oppression, is not only unwarranted but may reflect the social advantage that Harris, Hartsock, hooks, Fraser, Leland, and others criticize.

Cornell makes a strong contribution to specifying differences in women's unique historical, cultural, economic, and political situations. What concerns me is that Irigaray's a priori view of Woman as structured around a primary enemy, the masculine symbolic, undercuts Cornell's argument that Woman is simply an empty signifier until fleshed out in terms of women's a posteriori circumstances. Unlike Cornell, Irigaray's view of the symbolic tacitly harbors substantive claims about women's actual situations or minimally centers attention on gendered features of women's oppression as if these override other aspects of women's circumstance. Thus, she fragments traditions or sub-traditions into *discrete* manifestations of a univocal, dyadic symbolic structure. Women's specificities then become identified not simply as unique in some regards, but rather are isolated as pristine wholes, untainted and untouched by one another at the most basic level.

For Irigaray, these specificities are not examined as overlapping, interrelated, yet often *competing* and *incommensurable* analyses of complex, multifaceted symbolic imagery (racial, gendered, and so on) and shared global economic conditions. Such a nonmaterialist approach to patriarchal symbolic practices readily allows the white postmodern theorist—in specifying her experience of the feminine—to ignore fundamental conflicts of interest between her theoretical and practical endeavors and those of women of color. Presumably since women are the same in that they are marginalized under the masculine symbolic, they need not worry that differences in their respective material and philosophical positions may impede the advancement of some other women. But, since a given woman's experience of gender oppression does not necessarily sensitize her to racial or class oppression, a methodology that a priori displaces attention away from differences in power among women and toward a common enemy better serves those with material security and racial privilege than those lacking these.

Secondly, these comments imply that Irigaray's dyadic approach to symbolic structures poses problems for achieving the goal of cultivating a new poiesis. For designating the masculine phallus as the keystone in the symbolic sources of women's oppression cordons off in advance any examination of those specific conflicts among women—conflicts in perspective, in economic and political relations to one another, in symbolic position, and in strategies for social change—that permeate all the way down to the core attitudes and to the basis for the respective positions they hold. Again, Cornell's retelling of Medea through *Beloved* admirably succeeds in revealing important differences in relative power between white women who are viewed as human and those who are not so regarded. Her critical mythologizing fosters some level of empathy for and understanding of some differences among women. Nevertheless, Cornell's success in bringing the reader to see the relative freedom that white women have enjoyed historically over enslaved, is attributable to two things: (i) her twin critical premises that ultimately only women exist and that Woman has substantive meaning only as it has been predefined and reified by tradition; and (ii) her own ethical concern to apply Irigaray's textual practice in ways sensitive to the complex issues or race, nation, and gender.

My point is twofold. First, Woman as predefined by tradition does not solely revolve around the masculinely codified subject position (having the phallus) but instead appears mediated by multiple candidates for this position, whiteness among them. Second, without a corrective that frees the signifier Woman from this dyadic presupposition, fleshing out differences between women does not necessitate such sensitive applications as we find in Cornell. Indeed, fleshing out the feminine-masculine dyad in its local manifestations does not require the theorist to completely traverse the distance between abstractly seeing that there are differences in relative power between Euro- and African-American women (or between Medea and Beloved) and concretely facing the fact that one's own racialized and socioeconomic power as white partakes of the exploitation of others. By methodologically shying away from the sticky area wherein conflicts in perspective and circumstance may prove incommensurable, Irigaray's view of the signifier Woman avoids having to provide a textual practice of reiterative universalism requisite to support solidarity and alliances among women. Her model could conceivably stop short with a politics of heterogeneous anarchism, wherein local groups win their psychic resistance through discrete efforts to project a critical utopian vision of liberation independent of other struggles but without reconciling the potential cross-purposes of their utopian visions.[47]

In principle, Cornell demonstrates that critical mythologizing could be applied to exploring these intersections of various women's lives. My argument, however, is that Irigaray's assumption that the symbolic sources of women's oppression can be reduced to an Oedipal triangulation structured around the male codified phallus impedes this possibility and so must be challenged. Thus, even when fleshing out important material differences in how women are specifically placed as Other to the norm of masculine subjectivity, the very activity of specifying what is unique to an oppressed group qua that group isolates and preserves a space of distancing among groups. It is arguable that, in actuality, Euro-American women and African-American women, again taking only two examples, do ultimately live in one another's texts and mythic traditions because they share complex and overlapping histories. But, given the pervasiveness of white solipsism, this reality does not necessitate that we find one another in our critical mythologizing especially if the retelling of myths focuses on what is unique to a group's existence. At what point, then, will such discrete projects of critical fantasizing lead women to cultivate that social consciousness needed to assume responsibility for whether or not their respective situations and practices undercut the struggles of others? In disclosing this world as fallen, when do our respective myths add up to a viable picture of larger relations of domination and subordination that implicate some women in relative degrees of power over other women?

The psychosexual fantasies which fuel the oppression of women in the U.S. emerge out of a variety of institutionalized practices, including antiblack racialized social norms and a capitalist political economy. While I agree with Irigaray and Cornell that tapping into the psychosexual fantasies of U.S. culture is key to unlocking sexist ideologies, nothing in Irigaray's view of the feminine-masculine dyad as this key encourages white feminist theorists to grapple with their racial locus and to overcome the fears, habits, advantages, and fantasies bound up with that locus. To the contrary, analyzing gender oppression strictly in terms of a bipolar hierarchy tends to abstract from an examination of the racial and class dynamics of one's own—not just the Father's—cultural fantasies.

Because Irigaray's bipolar conception of the symbolic order centers on masculine-feminine signifiers, it tends to eclipse other kinds of symbolic and not only material power relations. Hence, it cannot uncover the erotic fantasies that circulated, e.g., in nineteenth-century U.S. society around the complex knot embedded in

relations among the white slaveholder, his wife, the black female
slave, and the black male slave. And my question is, if white women
and black women are left to retell the myths of their allegedly
composite traditions of gender oppression and even if women can
learn from retelling these differences, then who will work on this
complex knot?[48] Materializing dyadic configurations of masculine-
feminine symbolism does not suffice to bring white women and
black women in the U.S. to confront the distrust that suffuses their
relationships to one another. Those relations are mediated not simply by competition for the phallus—a masculine symbol of power—
but rather by a larger set of societal configurations. This larger
circumstance constitutes a multidimensional set of symbolizations.[49]
Acknowledging race as a symbolic as well as material factor in
women's struggle for liberation challenges the conception at the
base of Irigaray's work that power is purely masculine or phallic.
Moreover, as a modest strategy for psychic resistance, Irigaray's
bipolar analysis of the symbolic order seems unable to encourage a
socially therapeutic investigation into the legacy of Jim Crow. Can
we conceive the 'fantastic' process whereby a woman recovers her
autonomy as achievable from within a discrete analysis of her
specific situation? How will an autonomy so achieved be complete
or make the transition to solidarity if not grasped as fundamentally tied to the larger global relations that form the matrix delineating the oppression of others?

Thirdly and finally, Irigaray's dyadic conception of the masculine symbolic tends to burden women of color with the task of
factoring race and socioeconomic status into analyses of their specific
forms of gender oppression, while absolving white women of this
task. Hermeneutical monism not only ghettoizes women but in this
very ghettoization perpetuates racialized hierarchies within feminist theory. Even if, however, we reject Irigaray's monism, an abstract textual practice could fall prey to this problem because we
enact such textual interventions within preexisting relations of racial
hierarchy. Irigaray's hermeneutical monism readily slips into allo-
cating a larger share of responsibility for analyzing and fighting
racism to women of color. Unlike Cornell, Irigaray's own appeals to
mythic presentations of the feminine never touch on the racial and
class features of white women's location in the seemingly racially
pure masculine-feminine dyad. Why do her analyses of white
women's gender-based disadvantage not indicate the social, political, and economic power that often accompany being located as
white? We cannot leave the prospect of linking race and gender to

the good faith of the theorist who applies this method, but must instead theorize the need for reiterative universalism to be connected to interaction.

7.6 Toward a Dialectic of Utopia and Interaction

I have argued that Irigaray's dyadic conception of the phallocratic or masculine symbolic system abstracts discursive practices from the preexisting racialized economic system as well as other nondiscursive sources of women's oppression. Her approach to symbolic systems of meaning treats sexism first as rooted in mythologies centered on race- and class-pure gender roles and only secondarily sees these gender roles as housed in other symbolic and nonsymbolic relations. Accordingly, this approach encourages the illusion that materially secure, racially privileged women experience sexism in a pure form independently of the very socioeconomic and racialized features of our society they enjoy. Playing down the complex discursive and material factors influencing identity-formation and treating mythical traditions as hermeneutically monistic leads to disturbing effects. At the very least, it feeds into the traditional impulse of U.S. antiblack racism criticized by Du Bois; that is, it makes the "black problem" a problem of blacks.[50]

These are strong criticisms that echo the voices of many critics of poststructuralist nominalism. Nonetheless, I want to pave a middle way between materialist and idealist views of symbolic practices. On one side, I agree with Fraser that we should embrace a "model that treats languages as sets of multiple and historically specific institutionalized social practices" in lieu of the abstract Lacanian model.[51] But I agree only insofar as 'institution' is broadly construed to include cultural values and does not denote a narrow reduction of symbolism to a simple, one-to-one effect of economic institutions. On another side, Cornell rightly defends the need to rejuvenate a critical utopian practice clearly neglected by Fraser's more pragmatic explorations of symbolic imagery. This underlies the force of Cornell's concerted effort to divest the abstract signifier Woman of substantive meaning in itself and to reconcile its usage with the kinds of pragmatic explorations of the impact of symbolic imagery on actual women's lives. Because pragmatic examinations of group circumstance critically expose axes of domination, they stop short of redirecting erotic energy to the possibility of a postconventional *Sittlichkeit*. By contrast, transforming identitarian associations of humanity with maleness, whiteness, and other attributes, makes a necessary contribution to this goal, while it nonetheless remains insufficient to provide guidelines concerning the material conditions needed to support such a future communalism. I propose that, instead of abandoning multiple mediations of the sensible-transcendental, we can correct for the lack of concrete guidelines for applying reiterative utopianism. Since reiterative universalism does not automatically prevent epistemic myopia, we must supplement it by calling for interaction as a way to fill out the political consciousness necessary to engage in utopian thinking.

In this light, I wish to conclude with two programmatic statements. First, any U.S. feminist methodology committed to contending with psychosexual cultural fantasies needs to offer a more complex, non-bipolar hermeneutical analysis of the symbolic sources of women's oppression than Irigaray's Lacanian-influenced framework allows. Such an alternative model can be found in Cherríe Moraga's analysis of the mythology of Malinche in Mexican history. Moraga analyzes one specific discursive source, also a mythology, contributing to homophobic oppression of lesbians in Mexican and Chicano communities. Her analysis demonstrates that Mexican conceptions of women's alleged inferiority are deeply intertwined with ethnic concerns to resist Anglo-imperialism. Moraga shows how the concern to resist cultural genocide has reinforced heterosexist conceptions of family unity. Although centered on a culturally specific myth, Moraga's materially concrete isolation of the distinctive features of the Chicana's struggle opens up, rather than obscures, the contours of women's diverse and complicated social locations relative to one another in a shared world history of colonizer and colonized. And it reveals the complexities involved in differently motivated liberation struggles within a local context.[52]

For example, she argues that resistance to Anglo-imperialism has led mistakenly to fear of giving up patriarchal power within the family, since the family, historically speaking, has provided Mexican and other Latino communities a key source of empowerment against cultural hegemony. As empirically and historically concrete, Moraga's analysis of the Malinche myth harbors no a priori assumptions that the feminine or la Raza must form *the* centralized symbolic axis around which the Chicana is oppressed. Precisely by avoiding such monistic assumptions, Moraga's focus on the uniqueness of Mexican heritage can reveal the multiple axes of power and powerlessness embedded in complex relations of culture, economics, gender, and race both within a nation and across lines of national interest. For this reason, her analysis has general applicability beyond its obvious concern to reveal the difficulties that the Chicana lesbian faces. It calls other women to accountability for whatever investment in these networks of domination and subordination they may have.[53]

If Moraga's analysis exemplifies Fraser's pragmatic model of symbolic analysis, then it also does not specify a utopian vision of a community based upon an ethical capacity to symbolically mediate identity-in-difference. Though Cornell wants to undertake such genealogical analyses, she additionally exposes the specific need to target the ways that all ultimate categories of classification—such as space and time—inevitably carry metaphorical associations. A crucial moment in breaking the logic of identity exceeds the pragmatic goal of fostering ethical relations across difference. Cornell (following Irigaray) argues that one necessary, though not sufficient, condition of sustaining such relations is fostering the capacity to think of metaphysical concepts and divine principles in multiple ways, i.e., codified via the imagery of female morphology or black morphology and so on. The way to break a univocal association between God and (white) man cannot be attained by pragmatically divesting conceptualization of morphological (read: metaphorical) associations with bodies, nature, the elements, space, time, and the like. Rather, we need to cultivate a critical relationship to those associations by multiplying them. This method, similar to policies of bilingualism, has both a pragmatic and a symbolic goal. Bilingual education would not only enable U.S. citizens to become a more pluralistic society, it would symbolically decenter a dominant Anglo-cultural ideal even though we learn only two and not five languages.[54] Similarly, the pragmatic-historical goal, implied in the task of invoking multiple sensible-transcendentals, is to cultivate a new form of life. Symbolically, the very ideal of such plurivocal invocations of the sensible-transcendental decenters every possible metaphysical packaging of a universal, including the notion that there is a feminine-universal proper.

This brings us to the impasse of feminist utopian thinking. Rather than a reactionary feminist utopianism which uncritically celebrates women's essence, history, or culture as the basis for a conflict-free, noninstrumental, peaceful future world, Cornell's reiterative universalism elevates the metaphorical values equated with the feminine, not to the celebratory practical goal of instituting a feminized future community, but as a critical mechanism for weaning human beings of the totalizing urge in the logic of identity, an urge to reduce similarity to sameness. The 'critical moment' divests the concept of femininity of any inherent, nonhistorical value, while the 'universal moment' decenters the view that only women have feminine attributes. Cornell's sublation and alteration of these more romantic feminist utopian visions does not yield a full analysis of the material and other social causes of women's oppression. But it is not incommensurate with such analyses.

Critics of Irigaray argue that all notions of the feminine-universal reinstate the already rampant and pernicious values attributed to femininity. Thinkers like Judith Butler, for example, advocate enhancing pluralism through an antiessentialist dispersal of boundaries and through provoking dissonance with all categories of identity. Her Foucauldian program to proliferate local sites of power bodes an undeniably attractive normative vision of a future world wherein humans embody all thinkable combinations of sexed-gendered-cultural identities. More importantly, the very language of thinking identities in terms of categories of sex and gender (we could add race and ethnicity) would become obsolete. Instead, "the history of gender may well reveal the gradual release of gender from its binary restrictions."[55] At one level, I share the ideal of a future beyond sex, gender, and race as we know them. But this kind of Foucauldian program, though consistent with Fraser's pragmatic model of discursive practices, sidesteps the meta-utopian problem of collapsing the future into the present. It yields a warmed-over postmodern liberalism consistent with market individualism in its current form and equally susceptible to strategic problems of founding liberation on heterogenous anarchism instead of coalition.

Carol Stabile argues that reactionary feminist utopianism seeks to define the future through a profound nostalgia for a mythic, matriarchal past, while postmodern pluralism invokes a hyperreal aesthetic itch for a future of an "endless play of difference" altogether disconnected from the archaic past.[56] Each, she says, effaces the material and ideological conditions of the present and fails to offer any viable means to work toward an alternative future. Materialist feminists, like Fraser and Stabile, insist that we can correct the problem of collapsing the future into an imaginary meta-utopian now by connecting analyses of symbolic practices to the material institutions which sustain them. Though I agree that material analyses correct tendencies to elliptically imagine now as utopian, this corrective remains insufficient to theorize the critical symbolic basis for a communal sense of bonding based upon identity-in-difference. Cornell's reiterative universalism strives to occupy a middle position between nostalgia for the past and an imaginary futuristic pluralism that coexists with segregation and colonial fragmentation. But reiterative universalism can hold this middle position only on two conditions. One condition entails abandoning the assumption that the signifier Woman or the feminine-universal revolves univocally around masculinity or the phallus. Another condition requires compensating for the abstraction of reiterative universalism through a paradigm of communicative interaction.

There is no perfect way to imagine an association between the feminine and humanity which avoids a particular conceptual problem, namely, that the very term 'feminine' seems to posit gender as the transcendental signified in patriarchal symbolic practices. Concretely there are only 'feminine/white/able-bodied . . . universals' and 'black/educated/female . . . universals' and so forth into the infinity of the singular universals embodied by every individual. Thus, I disagree with Irigaray that the utopian moment stems solely from the repressed feminine in language. This position confuses the premise that a utopian moment is built into language with the additional claim that the western symbolic system has a fixed formal structure that is organized around a feminine-masculine dyad. Cornell loosens the former claim from the latter. Although I agree with Cornell that language systems harbor the possibility of creating new meanings, I also emphasize that both time and language grant human beings their utopian possibility of creating novel forms of life. Even though every attempt to analyze the particular symbolic sources of one kind of oppression is limited, I still find plausible Cornell's argument that socially oppressed groups need to imagine themselves as humanity. And I find her position plausible for two basic reasons, one conceptual and the other historical. Conceptually, we can restate the need for critical utopian thinking in terms of the activity of conceptualization. To the extent that all representation inevitably invokes totalities, the question is not how to stop thinking in totalities but rather how to develop a critical relation to this phenomenon. Humans are incorrigibly metaphysical in that they tend to overuniversalize even ideal-typical reconstructions of reality. Pragmatic sobriety is not enough to remain critical. Since conceptualization relies upon metaphorical associations and concept is never without image, a critical relation to conceptualization must entail learning to critically mediate, rather than abandon, the imagistic. Historically, the way to the future is paradoxical. We cannot bypass learning to redress phobias about

fleshy particulars. Whether this means we will eventually stop thinking in terms of fleshy differences or not is premature to predict.

A delimited textual practice of imagining forms of the feminine-universal need not contradict material genealogies of women's
situations, then, if our first corrective places the notion of feminine-
universal under erasure. This means that we grasp it as a heuristic
device, formal and empty in itself; and, further, that we reject an
a priori formal definition of the feminine as organized around the
normativity of masculinity, but instead assume that it is an open-
ended signifier necessarily mediated by multiple signifiers, like
whiteness, bourgeois, First World, masculine. With these
qualifications, the practice of utopian thinking becomes consistent
with fleshing out women's actual situations, as it no longer rests
upon the monistic and additive assumption that gender functions
as the linchpin in their oppression. Even given this first corrective,
an additional one is needed. We must assume that such textual
practices alone—both because by definition abstracted from real
relations and because enacted within preexisting social relations—
do not necessarily suffice to bring a theorist to critical awareness
of her own symbolic and material power. Undertaking the practice
of imaginative universalism, in ways that equally reveal a white
woman's whiteness and a black woman's blackness, must be dialectically based upon nontextual kinds of interaction. Just as pragmatic analyses of social location prove incomplete without the
utopian moment, so does reiterative universalism remain abstract
and partial without grounding in material conditions and an interactive praxis of communication.[57]

This brings me to my second programmatic conclusion. If theoretical interventions into symbolic practices are to reflect ethical
humility, then they cannot begin with the assumption that as women
we already have a common empathy for our respective plights.
Preexisting relations of power among women challenge precisely
the assumption that women can rely upon even the minimalist
view that being oppressed as women suffices to bind women together in a collective liberation struggle. María Lugones and Vicky
Spelman reminded feminist theorists some time ago that not all
women "talk the same language" and that women of various ethnic
backgrounds are "ill at ease" in one another's worlds, theories, and
languages.[58] Given that discussions of the Other can perpetuate paternalistic motives, feminist theorizing cannot unlearn these motives purely through textual exposures, whether or not those practices
reveal, as do Cornell and Moraga, intersections of race and gender.

Only by doing more than specifying women's diverse positions can western feminist theory move critical utopian projects beyond the epistemological problem of overuniversalizing a given individual, group, or cultural perspective. Not only must theory confront the fantasies embedded in relations of power among women, but it can do so only by positing interaction as a necessary condition of its possibility. Nor can theory avoid false universalism by advocating heterogeneous anarchism as a political strategy in which each group works incrementally and discretely toward its own vision of liberation without assessing the ramifications, especially negative, that vision and struggle might yield for others. Although developing the imaginative basis for such a theory of social liberation extends beyond my objective, one of the noticeable and frightening deficiencies of Irigaray's work is its failure to articulate a category of interaction as a necessary condition for cultivating critical utopian thinking, for conceptualizing this world as fallen, and for fostering social agency in terms of coalitional alliances if not a deeper solidarity among the oppressed.

Arguably an interactionist paradigm proves necessary even for advancing a theoretical strategy restricted to Irigaray's goal to foster, via critical fantasizing, a new postconventional poiesis based upon a collective capacity to mediate identity-in-difference. Dialogue with one another is an effective vehicle for giving up presumed authority, if not a necessary means by which to develop a critical relation to my circumstance. If the objective of reiterative or imaginative universalism is, in part, to unlearn the habits and attitudes that divide women and delimit their individual and collective agency, then how can women from different walks of life attain this objective without actually engaging with one another? Unlearning racial myopia requires the cultivation of enlarged thinking; that is, the ability to grasp any social event or phenomenon in terms of its multiple dimensions and its disjunctive and conflicting impact on various groups or individuals. More complex hermeneutical analyses of gender dynamics of the type undertaken by both Moraga and Cornell clearly contribute to this goal; however, enlarged thinking requires that we come into contact with, gather information about, and, most importantly, allow ourselves to meet and be challenged directly by those whose circumstances differ from our own in key regards.

Not long ago, I heard a feminist state in public that she does not want to know the people behind the margins of a text, but prefers to read the text first and then determine whether or not she wants to get to know the person. In a complex world such as ours, abstract examinations of symbolic systems, which pit Woman against the masculine codified phallus, allow the theorist to selectively edit what texts she reads and what voices she finds in the texts, and even blatantly to ignore those whose voices have been systematically denied epistemic authority. If prejudice is a "stabilized deception of perception" that selectively edits out differences threatening to one's own identity, then the epistemological concern to develop a reflective relation to my standpoint as a practitioner of textual analysis may be achievable only via social interaction.[59] Theoretical contributions that encourage overcoming fragmentation and divisiveness await a richer utopian vision and a thicker intersubjective theory of women's social agency than we can directly lift from Irigaray's work.

Those possibilities for autonomy must be understood as not only social but global because we live in a world of structural and institutional interdependence, a world in which at this particular historical juncture the powerful benefit from fragmentation among the less powerful and the powerless. Social agency, then, should not be understood solely as local power over one's regional or group-specific concerns. Rather these local freedoms must be understood and analyzed as decisively curtailed when other members of society or sectors of the globe are denied participation in the decisions and policies that affect their daily lives. To the extent that women's possibilities are determined by preexisting global relations of material and social conditions, recovering local autonomy hinges upon combatting global structures that produce the multiple, yet interrelated, exploitative mechanisms that sustain diverse forms of oppression in the first place. Heeding Cornell, Lugones, and Spelman, we could undertake the difficult labor of a critical mythologizing that would trace the complexity of this, our fallen world, thereby opening up the horizon for a truly different future. Multiple mediations of concrete-universals do not by themselves yield a complete foundation for social change. They must eventually join with programmatic steps toward material change.

CHAPTER EIGHT: EPILOGUE

Asymmetrical Reciprocity

From Imaginative Universalism to Ethical Concretion

Postmodernism inherits a certain romanticism from modernity. As John McGowan succinctly puts it, the romantic effort to "recreate the ethical totality of society through a revitalized mythology conveyed to the people in poetry and the other arts" finds its latest proponent in postmodernist thinking. Modern romanticism had two tributaries, one spiritualist and one realist. The former "favor[ed] changes in consciousness" as the basis for achieving ethical totality and the latter employed "more directly political and worldly methods of change." Even some sympathetic to postmodern ideas question which tributary it navigates. Cornel West, for example, asks "Is it not ironic that the recent American preoccupation with French recuperation of the textually playful and politically transgressive side of high modernism should lead us back to our own racially heterogeneous postmodernism?"[1] In partial response to this query, I have argued that we do not need to throw the baby of a critical ontology rooted in the autokinetic nature of things out with the bathwater of regressive political ideology (Heidegger); and that we do not need to prematurely reject the call for a critical mediation of morphology along with white solipsism (Irigaray). But, in order for a reenchantment of the lifeworld not to wane lyrical in ways that fuel chronic mythological stereotypes or a meta-utopian effacement of the economically impoverished, it must be connected to a material politics of needs and to a communicative paradigm of ethics based upon asymmetrical reciprocity.

Irigaray and Heidegger develop models of social attunement based, respectively, upon amorous exchange and proximity. Rather than call their respective poetics fully developed models of postconventional *Sittlichkeit* or community, I suggest that they supply the critical ontological and temporal bases for developing new forms of community based upon a critical relation to myth, a heterogeneous public sphere, and an ethics of asymmetrical reciprocity. Irigaray, more distinctly than Heidegger, grounds the possibility for nonantagonistic forms of social attunement in the mediation of origins and ends. In Heidegger's language, she lets divinities be. Drucilla Cornell rightly brings forward this critical side of Irigaray, while I have shown it to be of Heideggerian vintage. Letting divinities be means that we attain to sobriety about existence by mediating, not eliminating, transcendentals and sensibles, symbolic representation and imaginary processes. The importance of Cornell's interpretation is that it introduces the possibility that a reenchantment of our drastically disenchanted lifeworld is not inherently contradictory to critique.

West's remarks rightly indicate that utopian and aesthetic strategies for a reenchantment of the lifeworld do not automatically prove conducive to analyzing, let alone providing means for resolving, material conflicts. Nor, as I have shown, does the turn to local narrative (situated criticism) necessitate ethical humility (i.e., that a theorist or local group achieve sufficiently critical distance on her/their form of life). It follows that an unqualified turn to local narrative does not necessarily suffice to adjudicate competing claims to normative rightness or to reconcile conflicting, heterogenous strategies for political change. Even so, I suggest that a critical poetics (which calls for an ongoing mediation of sensible givens and teleological goals) can be articulated in ways not irreconcilable to analyzing its rootedness in the material dimensions of society or to critique understood as rational reconstruction of norms. My argument is that we must correct Heidegger's methodological tendency to abstract the synchronic dimensions of history from the diachronic transmission of ideas and his displacement of social and material relations as secondary effects of ontology. Similarly, we must reject Irigaray's proclivity to ground social reality in a fixed, synchronic conception of language and her clear relegation of material forms of exchange to the status of secondary effects of symbolic reality.

Precisely these undialectical assumptions, which sever ideation from vested interests in material oppression, undermine the critical importance of the twin Heideggerian ontological insights that phenomena are autodisclosive and that historical existence is oriented to temporal excess. Instead of supporting historical process, Heidegger's philosophy collapses into a species of political quietism and the contradictions inherent in proclaiming now a meta-utopia. And these one-sided moves bog Irigaray's neo-Hegelian utopianism down in textual abstraction. As a consequence, her work falls prey to this aporia, that it undermines recognition of the racially immiserated in the name of cultivating a critical relation to the mythic foundations of society and promoting nonantagonistic forms of recognition. Yet by abandoning Irigaray's ties to structuralism and her monistic assumptions, we can salvage the ideal of a poetic rejuvenation of the utopian dream of social change by preventing it from harboring inherent contradictions and turning it toward analyzing material aspects of existence. And we can then reconcile a moral-aesthetic focus on obligation to the concrete other with the need to overcome a facile embrace of diversity that elliptically recenters white, materially secure identities, prepared for ready transport to other worlds (Harris).

In lieu of Heidegger's and Irigaray's unidirectional methodological privileging of language over material conditions, I have argued for, not simply a dialectical model of agency, but a dialectical method on multiple levels. This means that the poetic basis for social attunement must be regarded as dialectically informed by material aspects of life. And it suggests that a textual practice of awakening atrophied sensibilities cannot stand in for actual interaction with other human beings. A theory interested in fostering ethical humility (critical distance on its own stance) must fill out the *textual and monological* activity of reiterative universalism in dialectical tandem with an *interactive and dialogical model* of ethics. Like Benhabib, Young, Fraser, and others, I advocate a communicative model for generating postconventional moral theory and arriving at political judgments. Though I embrace the need for imaginative, utopian thinking, I hold that distortions of all hypothetical forms of reasoning (e.g., solipsism, stereotyping) must be countered through interaction.

In this work I did not directly address the material sources of suffering but instead focused on the threat of self-referentiality circling around Heidegger and Irigaray. I continue my limited emphasis by centering my concluding comments on the need to supplement the utopian search for a new poiesis with an ethics of asymmetrical reciprocity. I move toward that supplement in a series of four gestures. My first gesture suggests that grounding symbolic practices in Heideggerian ontology compensates for overly abstract forms of nominalism which treat identities as purely fluid and linguistic. I assume that vast hierarchies in material relations distort agency and social desire in perverse ways and, correlatively, that a condition for realizing a poetics of playful recognition would entail transforming current material relations. Oppression, in other words, cannot be alleviated solely at the level of imaginative universalism. But I suggest that a critical ontology provides a basis for critiquing processes of fetishization and thus forms a bridge to material concretion. My second gesture shows that a textual practice that avoids self-referentiality must be grounded in interaction. My third gesture addresses Harris's concern that postmodern subjects lack the moral competencies to hate immiseration. I believe that a specific political self-awareness, a kind of enlarged mentality, is necessary to understand people's diverse social situations. I suggest that Kristeva's subject in process can hate immiseration, but only if the subject develops enlarged mentality. My fourth and final gesture claims that reiterative universalism does not by itself provide a complex political strategy for change. It remains incomplete, monological, and partial when not pinned down in an ethics of asymmetrical reciprocity.

From Postmodern Nominalism to Nondistorting Presencing

The strength of critical utopianism consists in demonstrating that a fundamental relation exists between theodicy and the capacity to exercise agency. To symbolically equate God with whiteness and maleness (to take two examples) structures the social desire for humanism in specific and obscene ways. By unearthing Irigaray's debt to Heidegger's ontology, I have argued that the relation between identity (desire) and ideal systems of representation (humanity) is not reducible to a free-floating symbolic phenomenon. Instead, decoding these metaphorical associations uncovers the existential fact that human sensibilities solidify into particular shapes through historical and material processes. Their central differences notwithstanding, Luce Irigaray and Lewis Gordon share the view that there is a definitive relation between images of the divine and how humans experience odyssey. So long as the divine figures around an identity logic, which equates humanity with masculinity and whiteness, then the collective ideal of humanism devolves into manifold perversities that distort the erotic desires and motivations underlying ethical and social interaction.

Where, Gordon argues, the project of human existence envisages the ideal humanity as fullness of presence to itself; and where humanity (Presence, Light) is postulated as identical to whiteness, striving to be white becomes synonymous with the human project. And, since God (self-transparent, apodictic self-justification) symbolizes this impossible man, God is the white man. Against Hegel's master-slave dialectic, the collective project of becoming humanity

"carries the infamous assimilation aporia": in attempting to become human, black consciousness is forced to internalize a white
foundational ego, to embody a "misanthropic consciousness toward
the oppressed." These socioerotics force on black consciousness either the constant denial of blackness in the effort to become human
or the constant recognition of being black in a world that hates
blackness. Assimilation presents a double-bind, a "warped desire,"
that cuts short the ability to be oneself (black) as human (white).
Gordon astutely brings forward the stakes involved in the antiblack value system, namely "neither the black man nor the white
man is truly human in an antiblack world." The ultimate desire for
God as white means for black consciousness self-hatred or self-
denial and for white consciousness supreme misanthropy, i.e., the
desire to be God. The consequences of this situation may seem
startling on Gordon's analysis. But I believe he is right: that blacks
are eternally damned and whites have no salvation.[2]

The problem is not only material and institutional—how to
develop a politics of difference that would not require assimilation
to whiteness and that could eliminate black economic impoverishment? It is also ontological or sociogenetic—how to "throw out the
white God without hating the white man?" That whites face a
situation of "moral condemnation" in coming to terms with their
racial locus describes the perversity of the antiblack world and
does not profess an absolute claim. The question is: How can blacks
twist free of the double-bind without revenge and how can whites
struggle for humanity without hating themselves as white? How
could we achieve such a socioerotic transformation of the ontological desire to be?[3] Gordon never sanctions the poststructuralist notion
of a sensible-universal or a utopian projection of reiterative universalism, nor is it clear that he would. Yet he shares with Irigaray
the view that we must develop an alternative ontological and social
eros, one that enables the oppressed to mediate their own identity
as 'for-itself,' and no longer simply the 'in-itself' of a white humanity. A nondistorting self-expression cannot occur as long as symbolic resources preclude a noncontradictory mediation as mixed
race and human, as black and human, as leprous and human, and
so forth.

My suggestion is that if we ground Cornell's idea of reiterative
universalism in Heidegger's ontology, then symbolic practices would
no longer be so idealist (uncoupled from material forces) nor so
fluid (nominalist) that they could support capital fetishism. Cornell's
model works toward two goals. First, with respect to cultural myths

and utopian images of humanity, reiterative universalism offers a vehicle for dismantling the spurious neoconservative premise that nations and communities need a univocal mythic core in order to foster individuals with strong identities and to bind the collectivity together. Conversely, her work also resists the liberal pattern of ignoring people's continued desire for a mythic enchantment of the lifeworld. Instead she shifts that energy toward a genuinely new possibility of sustaining communities based upon identity-in-difference. Second, the ethical intent underlying Cornell's ideal of imaginative universalism ultimately rests on the premise that we cannot become tolerant as a society until we overcome fear of specificity. Gordon expresses a similar concern that we need to deal with one another in the flesh (though he does not specify reiterative universalism as a solution). I ought to be able to recognize myself in the social 'we' without having to prune my flesh and blood away, but also without making another do so by taking my flesh and blood as a value in itself.

Nonetheless, these two goals leave open the question, Where do imaginative projects fit in the world of capital and conservative co-optation of multiculturalism? While extolling multiculturalism as an important ideal for U.S. society, I lament that it is used to befuddle the dynamics of antiblack racism and to mystify U.S. imperialism in a racialized world. The usual momentum of history plows ever onward on the side of conservative and reactionary forces. Perhaps the greatest weapon wielded by neoliberal forces entails convincing the public that neither selfish individuals nor capitalists but rather the organized collective action of social groups is to blame for democratic unfreedom.[4] A key weapon in their arsenal consists of appropriating multicultural images while repudiating multiculturalism's more radical and progressive interests. Whatever duplicitous shapes neoliberalism adopts in its alignment with flexible capital accumulation, one fundamental mask it dons takes the shape of a superficial, disingenuous, and fetishized appropriation of diversity. Corporations are selling a multicultural meta-utopia; and they sell the idea that utopia has arrived. It sits just on our horizon; we simply need a little time to harvest and extend the rewards of capital to everyone. Underneath the overt lies a covert message: U.S. citizens can resolve racial conflicts without structurally altering society and without self-transformation. Once during Prague Spring, Alexander Dubček promised the very real option for socialism with a human face. Now neoliberal forces dangle the hyperreal carrot of capitalism with a smiley face.

I do not deny that a happy coincidence aligns postmodern capital with fluid postmodern identities. But I regard such sociohistorical formations dialectically, both as potentially progressive and as potentially regressive. The poststructualist emphasis on fluidity of identity and proliferating sites of struggle, on the one side, can readily be harnessed to feed capital's organic thriving on fragmentation, on the other. Superficial emphasis on fluidity may be ripe for addiction to the distracting fetish of images in the technological era. But return to a base/superstructure model to solve the chicken-or-egg problem seems unwarranted. Did the aesthetic focus on plurality precede or emerge from capital? Does it represent potential resistance to or merely a reflection of social fragmentation? My answer is both. The aesthetic focus on symbolic practices and fluidity of identity need not support flexible accumulation and the elliptical forms of hegemony that capital incarnates across class and race difference. Any utopian vision, poststructuralist or socialist, is somewhat vulnerable to abuse by capital fetishization.[5]

Thus the delimited utopianism I have been defending needs to resist a premature valorization of the cosmopolitan attitude as meta-utopia. In a disingenuous form, meta-utopia exists all around me whether or not I live in the urban center. It is posted on the wall of my elevator in D.C. as a campaign for HIV/AIDS. Manifold restaurants advertise multiethnic dining; a picture of racially diverse customers entices you to dine for a good cause; a portion of profits will be donated to feeding HIV/AIDS victims who are no longer able to cook for themselves and require hospice services. I like the advertisement and support the cause. Since I have to participate in capitalism, I prefer to have some proceeds go to causes I plead. But none of this resolves the contradictions of capitalist domination. The very stock which supports ecological causes may also be another profit-tactic of the companies that create ecological destruction. The advertisement sells harmonious race/gay/straight relations while ignoring the fact that in D.C. much of the white, gay as well as straight, community is racist and politically conservative.

Abstract selling of harmony coincides with de facto perpetuation of antiblack racism and impoverishment. The desire packaged in the ad is a fetish. It represents an exotic world that can deliver me to ecstasy now and at no moral cost, if indeed I am racially and economically privileged (as I am). I need not change my lifestyle nor undertake the laboriously slow work of transforming my desire. In packaging a racialized imaginary, the image sanctions exoticism and reconciles it with the mundane. The everyday world of

U.S. society figures as already consistent with genuine resolution of racial conflict, yet race feeds the erotic force of titillation in the image. Blackness images the border where my identity breaks down, where I am cast into displacing my love for myself onto love of the object but without responsibility to change who I am, my lifestyle, my politics, let alone my desire. Fetishism is this displacement without ontological and epistemic transformation. In exotic ecstasy, I am cast outside myself while remaining myself. Also horribly individuated, the imaginary transgression promotes the view that desire is individual, not social, thereby displacing my identity from the concrete into sheer fantasia. Utopia can be mine on condition that I participate in the long-standing illusion that I can overcome my racism without giving something up. Racism has always been consistent with being 'nice' and 'white'. What I, as white, take to be rational and real continues to take precedence in this symbolic ad, namely, my desire to end racism without trial and tribulation, without giving up power, without divesting myself precisely of the want of being recognized as one of the better whites who is for racial change. In a word, without human interaction.

Against this horizon, I suggest that reiterative universalism is susceptible to collapsing now into meta-utopia only when it does not (a) connect symbolic practices to material conditions and (b) theorize a model of recognition based on interaction, though I primarily address the latter. By relaxing her nominalist underpinnings and intensifying her debt to Heidegger's ontology, I rescue Irigaray's work from abstraction. For this grounding supplies a criterion for distinguishing the fetish from forms of fantasy that free human relations from distortion. Though Cornell works within an idealist paradigm, her Irigaray-based utopianism need not support fetishization or co-optation of multiculturalism. A critical ontology, in other words, supports an ideal of social eros that allows for concrete forms of nondistorting self-expression. It demonstrates that symbolic practices grounded in a totalizing urge fetishize set visible markers designated ambiguously as signs of inferiority and as sites for discovering one's own exoticness. Against this dissociation of these visible markers from the whole person by patriarchal culture, racial symbolism, capitalism, and numerous other forces, Irigaray and Cornell strive to cultivate the poetic capacity to reground image in real disclosure of persons.

Reiterative universalism thus measures possibilities for social transformation by the need to create conditions—cultural, symbolic, and material—that will enable the nondistorted presencing of all individuals and groups. Those conditions must allow forms of self-expression not caught in the double-bind of believing in one's humanity while being presented as not human. A necessary though insufficient condition for realizing such a world is developing a critical relation to fantasy and myth. By rejecting a symbolic/figurative, concept/image dichotomy, Irigaray and Cornell return the role of poetic imagery to its concrete function of enabling people to mediate their fleshy particulars. This call for a social eros embodied through difference is not inconsistent with the need to transform economic relations, though a transformation of social eros would be partial when not informed by an examination of those material practices that contribute to current forms of social desire. Thus their analyses of social desire at ontological and symbolic levels make a central contribution to moral and political theory. They articulate the insight that a transformed social eros, while partially based upon economic and other social factors, is an irreducible problem of human existence rooted in the existential fact that humans symbolize their world to themselves. Even as capitalism thrives on fetishizing images as entertainment, the appeal of images has an ontological basis which exceeds material conditions. Cultivating a heterogeneous society issues an ethical appeal to create material and nonmaterial conditions for the nondistorted self-expression of individuals.

From Textual Abstraction to Ethical Concretion

In *The Philosophy of the Limit*, Cornell links her theory of reiterative universalism to a fuller conception of ethical recognition. Her ethical theory can be read as the foundation for the textual practice enacted through her interpretation of *Beloved*; there she shows how critical mythology, based on memory and yearning, leads the reader into a bridging of horizons with the world of Sethe. That bridging of horizons fosters an ethical understanding of Sethe as both human like the Euro-American woman yet different. Part of that empathy brings one, Cornell argues, to question the norms of motherhood that force women to raise children under the impossible material and ideological conditions of slavery. Cornell proposes a model of ethics based upon phenomenological symmetry and ethical asymmetry: ethical sensibilities maintain the balanced attunement that neither relegates the other to absolute alterity nor ignores her difference. Though the ontological irreducibility of people's social locations supports a model of ethical reciprocity based upon asymmetry, I still hold that a textual practice does not suffice to yield that recognition.[6]

Phenomenological symmetry demands recognition of the other as human, as an I. Yet recognition must be balanced by ethical asymmetry or the ability to acknowledge the other's nonidentity. Relying on Derrida, Cornell rejects Levinas's a priori ethical deference before the face of the Other because this type of "phenomenological asymmetry" reifies the Other: "Derrida explicitly reminds us of the Hegelian lesson that the hypostatization of difference— alterity is absolute—reinstates absolute identity." An ideal of nonviolent relations must resist romanticizing the Other. Ethical asymmetry, she argues, "would degenerate into the worst sort of violence" unless based upon phenomenological symmetry. Though not sanguine about her terminological usage of symmetry and asymmetry, I agree with Cornell that ethical recognition based upon asymmetry cannot treat the Other as exotic. Rather than fall into grave difficulties over whether a phenomenological description of people in their social circumstances could yield symmetry, I prefer to focus holistically on developing models of asymmetrical recognition which are not Levinasian. My earlier critique of Kristeva rejected her ethic of love for necessitating a phase of idealized collapse into a concrete person. The antithetical correlate to interpersonal collapse would be, as Cynthia Willett argues of Levinas, another supplicating ephiphany evoked by the "fraternal stranger" who is so transcendent that "the Other is, *precisely in her concrete difference, i.e., her embodied specificity*, effaced." Neither gesture—idealized collapse or exoticized submission—achieves an ethical stance of respect. I agree with Cornell and Willett that such models only fuel stereotypical images of others.[7]

But I also concur with Willett in holding that what is morally objectionable about idolatry and supplication is that these activities eclipse actual face-to-face encounters. In idolatry I worship hypothetical, generally stereotypical fantasies about the other rather than learn to understand the other as she represents herself. Cornell also talks of face-to-face relations. Still, every time she exemplifies her ethical paradigm she restricts the cultivation of ethical recognition to textual practices and never fully extends it to face-to-face interaction with others. This leads her to leave reiterative universalism as a nondialogical practice wherein communities simply remember to be self-critical. Filling out what she means by ethical asymmetry, Cornell ties its significance to deconstruction in terms of two things: a critical utopian vision of community and ethical humility.[8]

Although humans must dream an "ideal of community as the hope for a nonviolent ethical relationship to the other," Cornell insists, no community can identify itself as the ideal embodiment of heterogeneity, no matter how ethical.[9] Such identification would collapse into a naive communalism, a nostalgia for home, and hegemonic identity. To ward off these collisions, Cornell defers the unerasable utopian moment as a negative ideal of communicative freedom; that is, a critical ideal of community constantly reminds that no human form of life, no positive law, can afford to regard itself as the perfect manifestation of nonviolent recognition. I accept the ideal of a postconventional theory of *Sittlichkeit* (community) based upon resisting the desire for immediacy and a homogeneous vision of the good. Nonetheless, staking the maintenance of this community solely on its self-sustaining critical ability to resist hegemonic totalities from within evades the deeper issue. After the hard lessons of the twentieth century, we cannot let a poetics or communalism perform all this labor. Indeed we should strive to undertake the hard labor of transforming the emotional, erotic, and existential undercurrent of racial and (hetero)sexist biases running beneath a surface commitment to social equality. Yet Cornell's idea of imaginative universalism needs to be complemented by a concrete paradigm of social interaction.[10]

So let me turn to my more limited purpose by addressing the second issue of ethical humility. I propose that a textual practice does not suffice to develop a critical relation to my social location. Or, since it depends upon who undertakes this textual practice, theory should not assume that deconstructive strategies suffice to foster a highly evolved critical consciousness. The question I ask is this: What must we theorize in order to show what it means to become individuals capable of an ethical relation to symbolic imagery and to discursive presentations of those whose lives I know only a little? In *Beyond Accommodation*, Cornell explicitly claims that imaginary or reiterative universalism is ethical:

> Ethical feminism "envisions" not only a world in which the viewpoint of the feminine is appreciated; ethical feminism also "sees" a world "peopled" by individuals, "sexed" differently, a world beyond castration. Through our "visions" we affirm the "should be" of a different way of being human.[11]

And in *The Philosophy of the Limit*, she identities the very practice of deconstruction as keeping alive this possibility of ethical relations.

Through the "constant displacement of representational systems that attempt to capture the Other," Derridean deconstruction
"embodies the promise" of "fidelity to otherness" in two ways.
"[G]ender hierarchy is unethical," Cornell maintains, because rooted
in a symbolic "denial of women's phenomenological symmetry."
Levinas, in other words, erroneously bases ethics on an "unknown
other" perfectly consistent with a romanticized projection of Woman.
Though this analysis seems to imply the need for human interaction with a known other, Cornell continues to treat ethics as a
purely textual matter. She assumes that a deconstructive practice
of reading lets the other speak because it envisages an Irigarayan
ideal of love. Irigaray's model of lovers yields a normative vision of
phenomenological symmetry/ethical asymmetry, since lovers embrace one another but without encompassing the other "in a pregiven
unity." The ethical moment in Cornell's Derridean-Irigarayan
deconstructive work consists in contributing to the realization that
all humans are phenomenologically symmetrical, i.e., human. And
it fosters this realization by intervening in popular and canonical
discourses that deny women's symmetry.[12]

I acknowledge this contribution as important. And I believe
humans could become capable of truly critical forms of life. But it
would also be dangerous to trust that the ethico-ontological sensibilities embedded in a form of life would guarantee that it never
become one-dimensional. Any theory of ethical community needs to
be supplemented by a dialogical model of interactive universalism,
i.e., a communicative praxis that affords the representation of diverse standpoints as an institutional basis for decision making and
as a prerequisite to this community's sustenance. Moreover, once
ethical recognition and communicative freedom are restricted to
interventionist practices, then ethics becomes divorced from actual
individuals, human interaction, the existing institutions that perpetuate oppression, and the people who sustain these practices. No
longer moored in the complexities of social location, this model of
ethical recognition violates that upon which it is premised, namely,
the supposition that another's experience is irreducible to my own.
It follows that I attain a more optimal understanding of another's
experience, and in turn new insight into my own social location,
through face-to-face interaction.

Because I take seriously the poststructuralist idea that analyzing the texts of tradition can be instruments of change, I
question the ability of textual practice alone to encourage a well-
tuned comprehension of and obligation to those whose plight

differs markedly from my own. Only a fuller model of ethical recognition based upon dialogue can bridge the gap between textual practice and ethical interaction. Though contributing to fostering that ethical awareness in basic and significant ways, reiterative universalism remains abstract and monological without grounding in direct face-to-face encounters. What should replace a Levinasian a priori romanticization of responsibility to the Other cannot be a substitute romanticization of heterogeneous and local communities of identity-in-difference able to keep hegemony at bay simply by negating their own perspectives.[13] Individuals capable of nonfetishized relations to cultural imagery; individuals able not to misinterpret literature written by marginalized people; individuals not suffering from the elliptical hegemony of reproducing the world in their own class, race, gender image need more than a preliminary awareness that their social location delimits their perceptions. They need a highly developed political consciousness and an extremely differentiated openness to continued moral growth.

Toward a Dialectical Mediation of the Plural Subject and Social Fragmentation

I recognize any number of criteria as conditions for the social agent capable of moral responsibility to and solidarity with others. These include, minimally, the ability to evaluate ideological features of institutions and social customs, a capacity to face my own false consciousness, and, as Leonard Harris argues, an ability to disdain immiseration. Harris forcefully maintains two basic criticisms of postmodernist valorizations of noncoherent and fluid identities. First, he contends that "a social identity capable of ready transportation requires . . . an already constituted sense of cognitive location." Second, he charges the "transient, ephemeral or fragmented" postmodern identity of being incongruous with the specific traits necessary to disdain immiseration, traits like "self-esteem, sacrifice, diligence and dedication to a liberation project."[14] A full-blown nominalist view of identity as linguistic performance would yield a model of subjectivity so radically fluid and unstable that it could hardly be distinguished from the schizophrenic. While questionable that most postmodern positions actually adhere to such a strong brand of nominalism, two things are clear. Some theorists do disingenuously fail to recognize that they presuppose a composite self. Mostly, however, those of us engaged in postmodern theorizing have not spent time developing differentiated models of identity which clarify these matters. Here I make a partial contribution.

For Harris, the postmodern concept of the plural self is disingenuous; it presupposes, but without acknowledgment, a racially and materially secure agent who enjoys a strong sense of composite identity. By composite identity he means having "intact memories," a "coherent range of experiences over time," awareness of having "an identity which changes, as all identities do, but within a range of similar meanings as distinct from actual schizophrenic personalities." By not theorizing those competencies necessary to exercise autonomy "postmodernists make the possibility of composite senses of self-identity seem either tangential to a future world or already given." Harris's point is well taken. The ability to map change and to exercise choice, the self-esteem necessary to image oneself as capable of completing goals, and, as Harris says, the belief that you merit inclusion in the human race are necessary to normal levels of social functioning.[15]

Moreover, theories that embrace fragmented identities, while excluding discussion of core competencies, ignore the basic psychic conditions necessary for evaluating misery as morally wrong and acting against it. Making a list similar to that of Harris, Seyla Benhabib declares that "self-reflexivity, the capacity for acting on principles, rational accountability for one's actions and the ability to project a life-plan into the future" are the traits required for the ability to make moral judgments, undertake moral action, and commit to liberation struggle. These are the traits needed if one is to achieve that "consistency of reasoning" necessary to "hold, over time, disdain for unnecessary misery." Harris illuminates:

> If, as I argue, the postmodern concept of the subject lacks a viable sense of composite self-identity, not only is it difficult to see how persons enthralled in postmodern culture could be agents of resistance, but how could they have the attitudes associated with the desire to resist? How could they feel morally indignant about personally felt infringements and wrongs, let alone social wrongs?[16]

We need only look to adolescence to find examples of a spontaneous capacity for moral outrage coupled with a thoroughly sustained inability to evaluate the causes of social oppression and thus to assess one's own participation in those systemic forms of domination. Episodic outrage can dissipate as rapidly as it emerged in a given identity. Thus I agree with Harris that cultivating an identity capable of moral sensibility and social resistance requires consistency in thought and action. Yet I add that attributes of flexibility, lack of moral rigidity, awareness of one's finitude, and openness to the complexities of life are equally central to developing moral competencies.

Did fluid identities precede or emerge from capital? Do they offer potential resistance to or embody a naive acceptance of social fragmentation? My answer is again it could be both. The notion of plural identity need not yield an elliptical valorization of a morally obscene cosmopolitan attitude or a phantasmatic desire to be so ephemeral that I can avoid social responsibility to combat anti-black racism. Postmodern theory does need to develop models of identity that differentiate specific kinds of psychic flexibility from simply being ephemeral; and it needs to learn not to posit attributes such as flexibility as antithetical to other prerequisites of ethical action; rather, it should encourage the ability to close the gap between a false self-image and one's actions as they take on meaning within social and material contexts. Nonetheless, an uncritical valorization of a unified subject of history, incapable of learning the virtues of patience and magnanimity that stem in part from understanding one's own nonidentity, also overlooks central moral competencies. We do not need to go to Kristeva's former Bulgaria in order to identify the Marxian activist subject whom she calls paranoic. We can simply look to Marxist groups in the U.S. to find a long history of male authority, a dogmatic resistance to postmodern ideas, and a staunch inability to recognize their own masculinism rivaling the blindness of the very liberal conceptions of rationality they disdain.

Kristeva's *sujet en procès*, I argued, provides such a paradigm that balances psychic flexibility with consistency in action. Though she does work out a developed theory of virtue, her ethical subject is not so very fluid and ephemeral that it lacks an ability to disdain immiseration. On the contrary, she balances the capacity for cogent self-expression with the ability to take pleasure in the creative process of one's continued self-transformation. She harmonizes the need for identification with shared meanings (belonging to the human race) and the critical desire to challenge these meanings in nonparanoic ways. Finally, she resists stoic and authoritarian personalities without embracing all forms of fluidity as ends in themselves. Her work shows that decreasing narcissism, solipsism, and the preference for isolation—all of which are psychologically tied to fantastic forms of fetishizing others—must proceed by way of intensifying one's affective investment in human and social interaction. According to Kristeva, we increase our ability to be concerned with immiseration when we become less rigid and more flexible. Her work offers means for distinguishing the desire for episodic transgressions, perhaps epitomized in the ephemeral self, from the genuine psychological preconditions of ethical capacity.

In addition, however, we should differentiate psychological-ethical flexibility from those social conditions that consistently threaten to disintegrate one's sense of stability, to deprive one of feeling pleasure in performance, or to fragment one to the point of incapacitation. Many non-postmodern feminists, like Gloria Anzaldúa or Norma Alarcón, also recognize a plural self. And they praise specific virtues learned from occupying multiple social locations. Here the plurality of subjectivity operates at a sociopolitical as well as psychological-existential level. María Lugones, for example, demonstrates that "world-traveling" has moral implications. World-traveling entails bridging conceptual and social horizons. It refers to the ability to cultivate an enlarged understanding by coming to see another person as she appears three-dimensionally in her own world. World-traveling, she explains, is not intimacy: "Intimacy is constituted in part by a very deep knowledge of the other self and 'world' traveling is only part of having this knowledge." But without world-traveling, she says, "the other is only dimly present to one."[17]

Rather than perceiving another person one-dimensionally against my world horizon, I must work hard to see her as an agent in a world not dependent upon my self-understanding. Though we share a broader social environment, I cannot begin to understand another person when I reductively assess her actions against my own perceptions of and reactions to that shared set of societal conditions, i.e., when I measure her solely in terms of what I do or do not want to become. Only upon recognizing that was Lugones able to see, for example, that her mother was "not exhausted by the mainstream Argentinian patriarchal construction of her." By implication, we recognize that another "shines as a creative being" when we see that she exists in some measure as for-herself and that at least some other people regard her as such.[18]

If Lugones's notion of world-traveling fills out a concrete practice of not reducing the other to my self-image, then it also does not valorize social conditions of fragmentation. Valuing fluidity as openness to nonidentity (Kristeva) and the competency of world-traveling (Lugones) should not be confused with an uncritical valorization of the social conditions under which one learned those competencies. Much literature by women of color exemplifies the pain of excommunication, the ongoing limitations of being denied a social world able to allow a holistic manifestation of who they are. Anzaldúa, for example, discusses being able to be Chicana but not lesbian in Chicano circles, while being able to be lesbian but not Chicana in largely Anglo-lesbian communities.[19] A differentiated model of the plural yet ethical self would need to pinpoint when social conditions undermine the achievement of a psychological sense of competent self-expression; when material conditions promote untenable forms of fragmentation; and when the otherwise illuminating discovery that there are plural aspects of myself feed ethical irresponsibility. In order that the discovery of these plural aspects encourage self-growth and expansion, we need to identify questionable modes of valuing plurality in oneself.

Most of all, a psychological model of flexible identity remains undeveloped without a political notion of enlarged mentality. Kristeva's notion of the subject in process provides a psychological paradigm consistent with a flexible yet ethical self. But the Kristevan ideal of becoming a stranger to myself (developing psychological flexibility) offers only a starting point for ethics. It does not get one to a well-developed political consciousness able to assess the differential impact of a social practice in its negative ramifications for those whose situations differ markedly from my own. Lugones's model better approximates an effort to gain that kind of enlarged thinking even though it is not dialogical. Enlarged political awareness is a precondition, not simply an extension, of ethical capacity. Kristeva's psychoanalytic model of coming to terms with the stranger in oneself makes an important contribution to ethics. A nonphobic relation to my own groundlessness forms a psychological precondition, she argues, of not relegating others to abjection. A crucial stage in psychic and moral development entails gaining the ability to suspend projecting stereotypes and fears onto others, no longer to experience uncontrollable visceral reactions to those socially marked as different from me, and to stop reacting to people as threats to my personal identity.

Though important, I suggest that this capacity does not present a developed model of the social consciousness able to disdain the immiseration of others. While central to analyzing phenomena like homogeneous group identity, authoritarian personalities, and spurious nominalist forms of balkanization in Central-East Europe, Kristeva's psychoanalytic theory does not yield a thick model of political consciousness. The willingness to contend with my own strangeness and my own violence, though utterly necessary, do not supply sufficient conditions to awaken to a sense of moral respect

for others. One fundamental aspect of the oppositional consciousness requisite to liberation struggle, brought out by Harris's work,
is the capacity—at the end of European metaphysics, history, and
philosophy—to resist the gravity of this era, to reject a bland leveling down to equivalence of all life forms, and to oppose treating
now as a vibrant ethnic salad bar delectable only for the materially
secure. For this a political understanding is needed.[20]

I hold it to be an existential truth that becoming sensitized
to one's own experience of a form of marginalization does not
automatically translate into a critical capacity concerning other
aspects of that oppression or other forms of oppression. An individual initially becomes sensitized only in partial ways to gender
oppression given that sexual orientation, economic privilege, race,
ethnicity, national identity, age, and other factors play important
roles in our experiences of gender oppression. The order in which
any person becomes cognizant of diverse forms of oppression cannot be generalized as if the stages of developing social consciousness necessarily come in a certain order. Developing an increasingly
differentiated social consciousness occurs in a variety of ways
relative to the person's identity and social location. Awakening to
a preliminary ethical sense of those experiences of oppression
closest to mine does not deliver me to a sufficiently differentiated
political understanding to sustain a real (not simply imaginative)
moral obligation to those with social needs distinct from mine in
definitive regards. Definitive means all those forms of oppression
for which nothing in my personal journey directly provides an
understanding.

Coming to know the stranger in myself is thus only a psychic
point of departure for attaining an enlarged mentality that aims at
moral recognition and solidarity. As central, that psychic capacity
awakens ethical sensibilities grounded in internal obligation as
opposed to external laws and makes me able *not* to disdain difference. But recognizing that my visceral desire to annihilate another
has nothing to do with that person is not yet a positive understanding of another. A good deal more begins after this point. Ethical
theory must move beyond the psychoanalytic model if it is to conceive a specifically ethical and political consciousness that will feel
morally obligated to struggle consistently and with duration against
precisely those forms of immiseration not of immediate concern in
my world but from which I benefit everyday. More often than not,
acquiring this ability requires interaction with others.

Asymmetrical Reciprocity

In *Situating the Self*, Seyla Benhabib proposes a postmetaphysical model of interactive universalism. In lieu of the three illusions of modernity—the illusion "of a self-transparent and self-grounding reason, the illusion of a disembedded and disembodied subject, and the illusion of having found an Archimedean standpoint, situated beyond historical and cultural contingency"—she advocates (following Habermas) a paradigm shift. That shift moves from a disencumbered, monological, and legislative conception of the rational subject able to generate universally valid norms to a contextualized, situated, dialogical model of rationality. The moral point of view, in other words, does not presuppose a free-floating set of truths. Rather truths must receive validation through public forms of discourse; moral objectivity becomes refigured "as a contingent achievement of an interactive form of rationality rather than as the timeless standpoint of a legislative reason."[21]

While Irigaray and Cornell work to form the mythic basis for a postconventional *Sittlichkeit* by displacing the substitutionalist logic that spuriously reifies symbolic practices around a single group morphology, Benhabib develops normative theory that replaces *substitutionalist* with "*interactive* universalism." As Benhabib explains,

> Universalistic moral theories in the Western tradition from Hobbes to Rawls are substitutionalist, in the sense that the universalism they defend is defined surreptitiously by identifying the experiences of a specific group of subjects as the paradigmatic case of the human as such.

Just as substituting a patriarchal with a matriarchal symbolic would elevate a new group to symbolic superiority, so an alternative monological model of universalism will not redress the ways that theory unintentionally reinstates solipsism. Benhabib defends interactive universalism—a dialogical praxis governed by procedures for generating universals, validating claims, and adjudicating conflicts of interest—on the grounds that only a dialogical model "acknowledges the plurality of modes of human being" and "takes difference as its starting point," even as it need not sanction all differences as morally salient or all views as morally valid.[22]

Benhabib's argument is that universalizability is *epistemically incoherent* when directed to an abstract rather than concrete other and when undertaken hypothetically (monologically) rather than through actual dialogue with concrete others. I find this argument from epistemic incoherence perspicuous and persuasive, but hold that the ontological grounds for making this claim are inconsistent with her retention of an ideal of reversibility of perspectives. Directed specifically to Rawls and Kohlberg, Benhabib claims that their model of reciprocity presupposes a "definitional identity" that "recapitulates a basic problem with the Kantian conception of the self, namely, that noumenal selves cannot be *individuated.*" Understood as the imaginative ability to take the viewpoint of others, reciprocity, when directed hypothetically behind a veil of ignorance to others, simply erases differences and empirical features of context potentially salient in moral decision making. Once individuals are treated solely as generalized, i.e., in terms of abstract rational agency, a loss of plurality of perspectives ensues. If identity and agency are a priori divested of all concrete determinants and treated as morally irrelevant, this model lapses into epistemic incoherence. As a consequence, Benhabib notes, hypothetical reciprocity "leads to *incomplete reversibility.*"[23]

Benhabib's corrective to Habermasian discourse ethics offers a sensitive account of the fact that "[n]either the concreteness nor the otherness of the 'concrete other' can be known in the absence of the *voice* of the other."[24] Yet the argument from epistemic incoherence loses much of its force when Benhabib pins the ideal of a dialogical rather than hypothetical communicative ethics on the attainment of a yet more perfect reversibility. Like others, I think the ideal of reversibility presupposes its attainability on the idea that we can approach it through verisimilitude. This ideal roots expanded understanding in striving to occupy all positions. But by encouraging those erotic sentiments associated with seeing myself mirrored as humanity's collective transparency to itself, an ideal of reversibility contradicts Benhabib's basic point, namely, that any ethics based upon fusion with another (cognitive or affective) loses the criteria necessary to distinguish self from alter.

Laurie Shrage carries this line of critique further, arguing that Benhabib's insistence on the "unproblematic nature of 'reversibility of perspectives' seems to belie a positivist conception of knowledge of the other which is inconsistent with her post-Enlightenment aims." Shrage argues that Benhabib stops short of providing tools for coping with the incommensurability of interpretive horizons of the participants in communication because she assumes the relative commensurability of conceptual horizons. Further, "if one assumes the commensurability of conceptual frameworks, the task of reversing perspectives becomes an unchallenging and trivial enterprise."[25]

Though I read her as allowing for incommensurability, Benhabib nonetheless diminishes its significance by delimiting her critique of Rawls and Habermas to a "procedural one." Shrage is right to suggest that Benhabib's "ideal interlocutors have or can easily acquire the practical knowledge of others they need to engage in practical reasoning." Or, minimally, her approach still opens the door to the problem of elliptical self-referentiality. In substantiating her critique, Shrage shows that Benhabib's attitudes toward polygamy tend to present its defenders as conventional, not as postconventional, moralists.[26] My proposal is that Benhabib's delimitation of her analysis to a procedural corrective misses the stronger ontological and temporal implications of her analysis. The ideal of reversibility closes off the very ontological and temporal basis for the claim that appeal to noumenal selves leads to misplaced abstraction of the very distinction between self and alter that is needed to engage in practical reasoning.

Benhabib's argument for a dialogical practice rests on the claim that autonomy becomes hopelessly abstract and depleted of its moral and political significance when stripped of its embeddedness in referential systems of meaning. The rationality implicit in the concerns of the moral agent proves unintelligible outside its connection to choosing real historical possibilities. Rawls inherits a Kantian problem. Benhabib explicates, "the Kantian concept of the autonomous self, as a being freely choosing his or her own ends in life . . . slips into a metaphysics according to which it is meaningful to define a self independently of *all* the ends it may choose and all and any conceptions of the good it may hold."[27] These claims imply that epistemic partiality does not necessarily or solely stem from psychological resistance based upon learned prejudices that influence perceptions and attitude; nor must it arise purely from ignorance (though these often contribute to cognitive and affective distortions). A crucial reason why epistemic partiality can never be posited as a final state achieved by the self-legislating subject through monological reasoning is that we never transparently grasp another's social location and personal history. The epistemic limitations of all knowers must be countered, even for the postconventional identity, through continued interaction with others because ontology and temporality make a reversibility of perspectives impossible.

In this book, I have attempted to recuperate Heidegger's basic ontological dictum that all things are autodisclosive. This insight

informs Marcuse's view that all nondistorting conceptualization
reveals the way in which a thing is identical to the universal but
also different from the universal. Nonideological speculation resists
the totalizing urge of the logic of identity. Similarly, I appeal to the
poststructuralist view that all conceptualization evokes image. This
position indicates that the incommensurability of conceptual horizons minimally arises from the fact that communication is never
purely conceptual but also always metaphorical. Benhabib proclaims
the need for interactive universalism precisely to compensate for
the distortions of metaphor and fantasia as these sully hypothetical forms of reasoning. But she never addresses how to contend
with the persistence of mythic imagery as it may severely distort
actual dialogical processes, thereby undermining an ideal communicative ethics. Irigaray and Heidegger better address the fact that,
as Stephen White declares, language is not merely "an 'action-
coordinating' medium" but also a "'world-disclosing' medium."[28] The
possibility of nondistorting communication must mediate the incommensurable symbolic and conceptual frameworks as well as the
diverse social worlds inhabited by the participants.

My view finds confirmation in Young's innovative development
of these points through Irigaray. Against Benhabib, Young argues
that rooting moral respect in reversibility of perspectives both "obscures the difference" of another and is incoherent because an
ontological impossibility; "it is ontologically impossible for people in
one social location to adopt the perspective of those in the social
positions with which they are related in social structures and interaction." To the contrary, because every social location is "constituted by its internal relations to other standpoints," human relations
are "*asymmetrical* and *irreversible*." When elaborating the ontological basis for this asymmetry, Young appeals to Irigaray's notion of
the interval and applies it to communication. The interval, as a
necessary condition of communication, sustains distance between
two subjects and thus allows them to approach one another. For
Young, "[t]his ethical relation is structured not by a willingness to
reverse positions with others, but by respectful distancing from
and approach toward them." The interval must be maintained in
communication in order to avoid reducing similarity to sameness.
Similarity and difference can thus emerge without projecting my
desires onto the other, without indifferently reducing the other to
myself, and without exoticizing difference as absolutely Other.[29]

Young shows that asymmetry presupposes temporal nonconti-
nuity as well as positional nonidentity. Heidegger's work provides

the background for this social ontology. That language is a world-disclosing medium implies that perfect "copresence of subjects in communication" is impossible. Humans can, in others words, achieve a sense of perfect transparency to one another only via illusion, deception, and flights of fancy. Because personal history is complex, involving "experiences, assumptions, meanings, symbolic associations," humans can communicate aspects of their historical identity. But, as inexhaustible, the process of communicating one's nonidentity must be unfinished, since the other can never live my life and vice versa. In addition, because social positions "cannot be plucked from their contextualized relations and substituted for one another," relations are inherently asymmetrical. And all positions "are multiply structured in relation to many other positions."[30]

A sound basis for communication then rests upon understanding that there will always be a remainder. Cultivating critical awareness of that remainder means that I cannot represent the other; that while I can understand another person I will never occupy her location or history as she does; that I must work hard to arrive at an understanding. Maintaining awareness of the interval differentiating self from alter is a precondition of recognizing that other humans are 'for-themselves'. Communication cannot be reached so long as I think that I project the conceptual ground of discourse for the other (as, for example, in forms of white paternalism toward blacks) or that any two horizons of existence could be fused (as in forms of meta-utopian fantasia that obfuscate relations of power between two individuals). In a world marred by antiblack racism and misogyny, the capacity to mediate the metaphorical dimensions of communication and the incommensurability of horizons proves central to transforming the social eros governing those very interactions.

With this in mind, I return briefly to Gordon's argument that the Hegelian ideal of recognition cannot be fulfilled so long as God, or humanity's self-transparency, is connected to whiteness and to light. The white superior cannot come down to humility and the black inferior cannot rise up to status of humanity under these conditions. The humanitarian goal to become self-present (light) carries in its train the need to wipe out blackness, in oneself and in the world. This fact supports forms of socioerotica between black and white that necessarily delimit possibilities for ethical interaction or I-Thou relations. In terms of political struggle, this means that whites, like me, have to abandon the need to be representatives of humanity (God, light, purity) and the gatekeepers to all that is humane. Racial justice is not primarily for whites, Gordon attests. Centered around what motivates the desire for recognition, Gordon poses the poignant question whether ethical relations and solidarity are possible where generosity reflects white power and thus funds the illusion that, in struggling for racial justice, whites sacrifice. Correlatively, how can blacks struggle for liberation without adopting a posture of indifference toward whites? How can black consciousness be self-determining or act 'for-itself' while caring what whites think and do? Caught in this *web* of distorted ethical possibilities, a genuine transformation of social eros would require manifold changes in the material and social structures of society. Still, a communication model that theorizes the necessity for placing a taboo on the idolatry of imaging humanity in univocal terms—and thus requires that we liberate the concept of humanity from its ties to any one set of symbolic and morphological associations—opens the space to transform some important dimensions of that social eros.[31]

As a corrective to textual abstraction, I contend along with Benhabib and Young that only an enlarged mentality can sustain such projects without elliptical hegemony. My contention is that a form of interactive universalism theorizes the concrete basis to foster enlarged thinking. I define enlarged thinking in distinctly social and political terms as a specific ability to ascertain a social phenomenon in its complexity and multiple dimensions. Enlarged mentality further entails the ability to recognize and understand the disjunctive and incommensurable ramifications of a given social policy, event, or state of affairs on various social groups. And I suggest that developing an evolved ethical consciousness relies upon an enlarged political awareness. Premature universalizing of one's own standpoint follows, not simply from fear of nonidentity, but from an additional failure to strive for such an increased understanding. That failure could have multiple existential sources, including lack of desire to give up power and benefits.[32]

Irigaray's textual practices decenter univocal conceptions of humanity and open space for a nonreductive copresencing to one another. Yet as a method for enabling theorists to develop a critical relation to their identities, I have shown that her work remains prone to self-referential difficulties when not grounded in an interactive paradigm of communication and when supported by monistic assumptions. Similarly, Benhabib resists hypothetical imagination. And she cautions that, whereas a Rawlsian model of reversibility leads to cognitive partiality based upon indifference to concrete particular selves, feminist proponents of an ethics of care rooted in "sentiments of empathy and benevolence" can just as readily project others as fantasized mirror images of themselves.[33] Like Benhabib and Cornell, I hold that reciprocity would neither graft the other to myself nor stoically retreat into indifference. Yet Benhabib's model of reversibility also does not free us of the threat of cultural solipsism. She presupposes but does not theorize the logic of ontological irreducibility.

My version of a neo-Heideggerian social ontology and an Irigarayan model for mediating the metaphorical excess of meaning demonstrates that a model of asymmetrical reciprocity, not reversibility, maintains the space requisite to work toward enlarged thinking. A model of asymmetrical reciprocity better suits Benhabib's ideal of eliminating both cognitive and affective forms of fusing the other to myself. It moves Kristeva's subject in process out of the psychological sphere of acquiring familiarity with my own strange plurality and into the public domain. In that definitive social space, overlapping histories and social positions meet but with remainder. And, as communicative, asymmetrical reciprocity pins Irigaray's abstract reflections down in concrete social and material relations. Both Benhabib and Young agree that enlarged thinking extends beyond while encouraging empathy. Yet in associating enlarged thinking with understanding and judgment, we must take care not to ignore its affective dimensions. Stoic indifference to black suffering is part of white supremacy. Stoical restraints on one's emotional and motivational life not only limit one's basic perceptions of others but also stand in the way of enlarged thinking and moral and political decision making.

Notes

Introduction

1. Oliver notes ambiguities in labeling Kristeva, Irigaray, and Cixous the "holy Trinity," in *Reading Kristeva*, 163–68. Moi notes the Heideggerian influence on Lacan, in *Sexual / Textual Politics*, 98. On Cixous's debt to Heidegger, see Conley, *Hélène Cixous*, 102–12, 118–19, 151–52. On the Heideggerian origins of deconstruction, see Bernasconi, "The Transformation of Language" and "Seeing Double."

2. Bigwood defines Heidegger's notion of Being as "the constellation of art, science, politics, and religion within which an historical people dwells" (EaM, 3; cf. Heidegger, BW, 168/H, 31). In addition to Graybeal, Bigwood, Kristeva, and Irigaray, I mention only the most sustained analyses of Heidegger in feminist literature. Hodge provides an excellent comparison of Heidegger and Irigaray in her "Irigaray Reading Heidegger"; cf. her general work on *Heidegger and Ethics*. Bartky, *Femininity*, chap. 6, makes positive use of Heidegger's notion of attunement; see also her critique of later Heidegger, "Originative Thinking." Chanter, *Ethics of Eros*, chap. 4, addresses the influence of Heidegger on Irigaray. For a more sustained comparison of Heidegger and Irigaray, see Mortensen's *The Feminine and Nihilism* and "Woman's (Un)Truth and Le Féminin." Armour's "Questions of Proximity" looks to Heideggerian thought in order to justify a particular interpretation of Irigaray's relation to Derrida. Holland's "Heidegger and Derrida Redux," "Derrida and Feminism," and *The Madwoman's Reason* isolate similarities and differences in Heidegger and Derrida. Chapter 7 of Iris Young's *Intersecting Voices* both criticizes and makes use of the Heideggerian concept of dwelling in order to develop a critical feminist approach to the idea of home. Although a less sustained analysis, Adell's *Double-Consciousness / Double-Bind* treats Heidegger in this definitive comparison of European deconstructive techniques and the black literary tradition. And McAfee, "Abject Strangers," turns to Heideggerian ontology, as I will, to compensate for contradictions in Kristeva's grounding of her subject in process in Freudian biological theory. See also Brown, *Fear, Truth, Writing*.

3. Derrida, *Spurs*, 83; cf. 109–21, as well as "Geschlecht: Sexual Difference" and "Geschlect II." See Caputo, "'Supposing Truth to Be a Woman . . .'," 15–21; Parens, "Derrida, 'Woman', and Politics," 291–301. On the "feminine" as allegory, see Cornell, *Beyond Accommodation*, 35, 79–88. For Heidegger's brief defense of the gender neutrality of Dasein, see W, 54 and his discussion in FL, 136/GA 26, 171; for his disturbing tendency to essentialize the two genders, see his commentary on Trakl, OWL, 170–75, 184, 195/US, 50–55, 65, 78.

4. Butler, "Variations"; cf. *Gender Trouble*. Hekman, "Reconstituting the Subject."

5. Wolin, *Politics*, 38, 29 (in order).

6. Wolin, *Culture Criticism*. See Fraser's assessment of Foucault, *Unruly Practices*, 21.

7. Alcoff, "Cultural Feminism," 306, 308, 309 (in order). Fraser, "False Antitheses," 172.

8. Weir's work, *Sacrificial Logics*, demonstrates that not only existential philosophies and phenomenology but also psychoanalytic feminist theory, of both the object-relations and poststructuralist persuasions, uncritically adopt Kojève's definition of freedom as negation of what is. Weir persuasively argues that this view prevents feminists from theorizing "nondominating relationships between identity and difference" (3). Willett's equally groundbreaking *Maternal Ethics* shows how this Kojèvean legacy bogs down the desire for recognition in antagonistic forms of struggle and in cathartic forms of transgression that have historically supported systematic forms of oppression of women and nonwhite peoples. In lieu of freedom as negation, she develops a model of recognition based upon the sincere, ecstatic capacity to derive social pleasure from interaction across difference.

9. Hartmann, "The Unhappy Marriage."

10. Outlaw, "Africana Philosophy"; Gordon, *Existence in Black*, 2–3.

11. Representative parallels to Irigaray's critiques of Hegel include Fanon, *Black Skin*; and Gordon, *Bad Faith*. The themes of the double-bind, anonymity, voicelessness, and diminished agency are too pervasive in Africana philosophy and feminist literature to summarize.

12. Butler's "Variations" presents an alternative utopian view to Cornell's vision in "Feminism, Negativity, Subjectivity."

13. Harris, "Postmodernism and Utopia."

14. Young, "Asymmetrical Reciprocity."

Chapter 1. Heidegger and Kristeva

1. Oliver clarifies that the term, *le symbolique*, has two senses for Kristeva, *l'ordre symbolique* and *la dimension symbolique*. The former refers to the totality of signifying processes and is synonymous with the social order; while the latter identifies a specific aspect of signification. "To enter the Symbolic order is to take up a position, which is possible only through the symbolic function. Yet not all signification involves taking up a position; or, at least, there is more to taking up a position" (*Reading Kristeva*, 39, cf. 10). On the historical and political background of Kristeva's conception of "the social as a signifying space," see Hennessy, *Materialist Feminism*, 46–48; and Moi, *Sexual / Textual Politics*, chaps. 5 and 8.

2. According to Kristeva, the semiotic, like Freud's unconscious, is a "theoretical supposition" which is nonetheless real (RP, 69). Although in RP she maintains the chronological anteriorness of the semiotic, Kristeva later maintains the anteriorness of the symbolic in order to avoid positing biological processes outside of language. See Graybeal, LF, 13–15; and Oliver, *Reading Kristeva*, 105–6. On Kristeva's view of the *chora* as receptacle, borrowed from Plato's *Timaeus*, see Grosz, *Lacan*, 150–54; and Oliver, *Reading Kristeva*, 35.

3. See Oliver, *Reading Kristeva*, 41–46.

4. Weedon *(Feminist Practice,* 51) is discussing Lacan's notion of misrecognition. On differences between Kristeva and Lacan, see Silverman, *The Subject*, 122, passim; Oliver, *Reading Kristeva*, esp. chaps. 1 and 3; Moi, *Sexual / Textual Politics*, 161; Grosz, 154–60.

5. Kristeva regards catharsis as a constructive dimension of literary production because, through catharsis, humans reenact the religiously ritualized defense against murderous impulses that founds society. Kristeva's praise for the therapeutic effects of catharsis can be linked to her tendency to valorize mere release from social regulation of *jouissance*. Nonetheless, she explicitly locates the value of subversive literature in its ability to undermine the absoluteness of the symbolic and to promote a critical relation to the social order (RP, 75–78). Still, her later distinction between the cathartic effects of literature and the knowledge effect of analysis suggests that challenging the absoluteness of the symbolic does not, in itself, provide a criterion by which to differentiate the manifold conclusions (reactionary and otherwise) one can draw from this detheologizing moment (TL, 276; BL, 19–20). See Willett's critique in *Maternal Ethics*, 20–21; also Suleiman, "Pornography." Oliver *(Reading Kristeva*, 101ff., 117) gives a more sympathetic view.

6. As early as 1919, Heidegger conceives of philosophy as a "deconstructive return" *(abbauendes Rückgang)* to the prephilosophical experience covered over by dominant interpretations. This view offers a parallel

to Kristeva's conception of phenomenology. On the genesis of the *Destruktion* as critique of Husserl, see Makkreel, "The Genesis"; van Buren, "The Young Heidegger and Phenomenology"; Kisiel, "Genesis." For early intimations of a theory of signification in Heidegger's dissertation on Duns Scotus, see Caputo, "'Grammatica Speculativa'."

7. Sheehan, "On Movement and Destruction," 536, 538.

8. Sheehan, "On Movement and Destruction," 536. On *Ent-lebnis*, see Van Buren, "Hermeneutics of Facticity."

9. Like numerous commentators, Graybeal (LF, 97–98) argues that Heidegger's claim to the ethical neutrality of falling is counteracted by the valuative language he uses. See Kellner, "Authenticity"; Martinez, "An 'Authentic' Problem," 14–15; Ciaffa, "Toward an Understanding," 51ff.

10. Key portions of this section are taken from my more detailed, comparative analysis of Kierkegaard and Heidegger, "Heidegger's Reading."

11. See Schrag's *Existence and Freedom* for a definitive comparison of Kierkegaard and Heidegger. It is difficult to reconcile Heidegger's theoretical terminology with the standardized usage of the term "existential" to refer to philosophies of existence. Against other translations, I follow Schrag's use of the English existential (rather than existentiell) to denote Heidegger's *existenziell* or "existence in its concrete determinations" (17). I will use the adjective *existenzial* to depict the self's prethematic engagement in the world; and I will translate the noun, *Existenzialien*, as existentialia to designate the structures underlying concrete ways of existing (18).

12. Caputo, "Hermeneutics as Recovery," 355–56.

13. Graybeal (LF, 127) grants that intimations of an ethical ideal are weak in Heidegger and challenges Kristeva's (RP, 129) staunch criticism that Heidegger's use of fable is a "regressive mythological travesty." I agree that Kristeva's critique is simplistic, but I examine what provokes the view that Heidegger undercuts social agency and progress.

14. Kisiel, in his "Genesis," 33, maintains that the Kierkegaardian language in *Being and Time* reflects, not an existential interest, but Heidegger's ec-static conception of Dasein. Admittedly *Being and Time* is not simply existential philosophy, but the work as a whole gives credence to Caputo's interpretation and has spawned an extensive body of existentialist interpretations. My argument is not that the intent to synthesize existential and phenomenological insights constitutes a misreading but rather that Heidegger's model of critical thought proves a deficient attempt to achieve that synthesis. I want to show that, precisely for the existential reader, his theory of authenticity is deceptively radical; thus his textual practice fuels reactionary ideological associations while parading itself as progressive. Also see van Buren's important work which shows how the Kantian transcen-

dentalism of 1927 breaks with the concreteness of Heidegger's earlier personalist view of factical life: "The Young Heidegger" and "The Young Heidegger and Phenomenology."

15. See Kierkegaard, *Postscript*, 348ff.; *Sickness*, 13; *Either/Or*, 1: 1, 26, 42, 289.

16. Kierkegaard, *Repetition*, 229, 307, 315.

17. Kierkegaard, *Anxiety*, 28, 31; *Postscript*, 74f., 242, 246; *Two Ages*, 91, 99.

18. Kierkegaard, *Point of View*, 60, 118, 112.

19. Kierkegaard, *Two Ages*, 63.

20. Ibid., 86, 90–91.

21. Kierkegaard, *Point of View*, 94–99, 115. For a comparison of Kierkegaard and Kristeva, see Lorraine, "Amatory Cures." On the compatibility of inwardness and ideology critique, see Westphal, *Kierkegaard's Critique*, esp. chap. 7; Marsh, "Kierkegaard and Critical Theory"; and Matuštík, *Postnational Identity*.

22. See Schrag, *Existence and Freedom*, 17–19 and n. 11 above.

23. Although Scharff ("Habermas," 192) rightly interprets Heidegger's discussion of empathy as a critique of Husserl, I read such claims as dealing a double blow to Husserl and existential philosophy (Kierkegaard). That double blow stems from a conflation of the formal critique of Husserlian epistemology with a rejection of the psychological or existential notion of edification. Heidegger replaces interior examination with a more pragmatic, less fussy view of the subject as holistically embedded in a context of meaning. If, for Heidegger, the ontological analysis of care markedly undercuts and renders defunct self-examination, then Heidegger's refusal to credit Kierkegaard as a key source for his own work becomes more intelligible, though not on that account justified.

24. Sandra Bartky's "Shame and Gender" (in *Femininity*, 83–98) exemplifies such a method. Working with Heidegger's notion of mood as attunement, she employs a dialectical analysis of the relation between one's social condition as female in a patriarchal society and the defining moods that characterize one's basic comportment toward others and one's options in the world.

25. Berthold-Bond, "A Kierkegaardian Critique," 124, 127. Numerous commentators have proposed various strategies for resolving the contradiction inherent in Heidegger's treatment of authenticity as concretely engaged in everyday existence, on the one hand, and his equating everdayness with inauthenticity, on the other. See Zimmerman's "On Discriminating Everydayness"; Ciaffa, "Toward an Understanding"; and Martinez, "An 'Authen-

tic' Problem." I follow Berthold-Bond in locating the problem with authenticity in its abstractness. Zimmerman especially vindicates Heidegger from the critique that he denigrates everyday life by showing that everdayness is a horizon of meaning rather than an inauthentic way of existing. But my analysis suggests that Heidegger's abstract approach denigrates ordinary discourses to the extent that it collapses ethical distinctions between kinds of discourse, e.g., envious gossip and empathy.

26. Berthold-Bond, "A Kierkegaardian Critique," 129, quoting Hegel's *Phenomenology*, 120.

27. For an explication of Stoic fatalism as "invit[ing] action" in, not withdrawal from, the world, see Bréhier, *The Hellenistic and Roman Age*, esp. 61–65. My concern to develop a moral psychology that addresses the relation between affect, perception, and judgment does not rest upon a facile claim that Heidegger needs a care ethics. See, e.g., Anzaldúa, "Bridge"; Benhabib, "Generalized"; Collins, "The Social Construction"; Gordon's critique of Appiah, *Bad Faith*, chaps. 12 and 13; Jaggar, "Love and Knowledge"; Meyers, *Subjection*; Walker, "Moral Understandings"; Young, "Impartiality."

28. Kierkegaard, *Postscript*, 314, 323ff.; *Two Ages*, 92.

29. See Harries, "Heidegger as Political Thinker," 647, for an analysis of Heidegger's voluntarism.

30. For serious critiques of Heidegger's pseudoconcrete and asocial theory of authenticity, see Stern (Anders), "On the Pseudo-Concreteness"; B. W. Ballard, "Marxist Challenges to Heidegger"; Kosík, *Dialectics*, 121, passim; and Lukács, *Die Zerstörung*, 139. While some points in Scharff's rebuttal to Habermas's critique of Heidegger's SZ=BT are valid, Habermas ("Work and Weltanschauung," 439) is correct that SZ=BT suffers from "methodological solipsism."

31. Similarly, Kierkegaard slurred the boundary between his method of literary transference (indirect communication) and his paternalistic tactic of "freeing" Regina (his beloved). Kierkegaard later repents this Socratism. For diverse assessments of Kierkegaard's relation to the feminine and to feminism, see Brown, "God, Anxiety"; Berry, "Kierkegaard and Feminism"; and Howe, "Kierkegaard."

32. Kierkegaard, *Either / Or*, 2: 291ff.

Chapter 2. Heidegger, Irigaray, and the Masculine Ethos of National Socialism

1. Tugendhat, *Der Wahrheitsbegriff*, 360–61.

2. Positions on the relation of Heidegger's theory to his politics span two poles. Whereas staunch apologists for Heidegger have sought, as

Sheehan has shown, to critique the man in order to save the theory, radical critics have found uniform coherence between *Being and Time* (SZ=BT) and his authoritarian politics. For the former group, Heidegger's political engagement marked an anomaly that violated the 1927 effort to existentialize a Kantian conception of autonomy; for the latter, it signaled a contiguous extension of early Heidegger's latently authoritarian evocative method that came as no surprise. While not an unadulterated continuum, there is also no pure lack of relation between 1927 and the period from 1929 to 1935. Certainly Heidegger's embrace of Nietzsche and German chauvinism in the thirties marks a development in his work, but his love of soldiers, his generational sensibilities, his collectivist view of Dasein, and the practical orientation of his philosophy all antedate and lay the foundation for this evolution. Wolin and Schürmann represent nuanced positions: each admits that no logical necessity connects SZ=BT to the *Führerprinzip*; each accepts that mediated links exist between 1927 and 1932; but finally they disagree about the possibility of salvaging aspects of the Heideggerian corpus in support of democratic political philosophy. On the three historical waves of debate, see especially Zimmerman, *Confrontation*, 279, n. 19; also Sheehan, "A Normal Nazi"; Rockmore, *Heidegger*, chap. 8; Wolin, *Politics*, "Preface" and chap. 1.

3. Zimmerman dates Heidegger's view that "his generation was destined to make a radical new beginning" to 1919 (*Heidegger's Confrontation*, 16–19). Van Buren also dates the influence of Spengler on Heidegger's critique of modern rationality as rooted in a technological ethos of mastery, calculation, rule-oriented behavior to 1919, *The Young Heidegger*, 321.

4. Wolin, *Labyrinths*, 1–12, passim. I do not intend to undermine the inestimable value of Wolin's sustained efforts to demythologize the cult of Heidegger and even the cultlike dimensions of deconstruction. To the extent that these cults may exist in the U.S., they arguably pertain preeminently to white malestream thought. My point is that his critique fails to differentiate antihumanist strategies that retain an interest in reworking normative theory and those that do not, and so tends to denigrate both. With the exception of Arendt, Wolin focuses his critique on malestream thinkers, like Bataille and Derrida, without addressing feminist theoretical works that strive to assimilate transgressive strategies into newly reworked humanist visions. Young, *Justice*, and Meyers, *Subjection*, offer two representative works.

5. Jünger's thought exercises a decisive influence on Heidegger's own theory of *Seinsgeschichte* (History of Being).

6. Wolin, *Politics*, 32, 36; on the crisis mentality, see 22–27.

7. Wolin, *Politics*, 21; see his pointed comment:

For a philosophy of existence whose central concept is that of authenticity, and for which the supersession of an academic philosophy divorced from life becomes a *point d'honneur*, a translation of the categorical framework into the terms of concrete life itself becomes an *existential imperative*. Only via such a process of categorical transposition—from the plane of ontological analysis to the domain of life-praxis itself—can the true *existential ramifications* of the philosophical doctrine first become manifest. (67)

8. Excellent accounts of the diverse movements that set the stage for the rise of NS can be found in Herf, *Reactionary Modernism*, chap. 2; and Zimmerman, *Heidegger's Confrontation*, chap. 1. Herf differentiates reactionary modernists, like Jünger, from other conservative revolutionaries. Reactionary modernists realized that technology was essential to national power and claimed that "Germany could be *both* technologically advanced *and* true to its soul" (3). Their ideas considerably prepared popular reception of Nazi ideology. See also Wolin, *Politics*, 22–27. For Kristeva's critique of Heidegger, see RP, 129.

9. Wolin, *Politics*, 28, 29–30.

10. On decisionism, see Wolin, *Politics*, 29, 35–39, 63 and *Terms of Cultural Criticism*, 88–89; cf. Habermas, "Discourse Ethics."

11. Wolin, *Politics*, 31. On the relation of fascism to aesthetics, see Benjamin, "Theorien"; Bohrer, *Ästhetik*; Hillach, "Aesthetics of Politics"; Herf, *Reactionary Modernism*, 12, 31, 47; Stollman, "Fascist Politics"; Wolin, *Labyrinths*, 103–22; Zimmerman, "Ontological Aestheticism," esp. 60.

12. Wolin, *Politics*, 31, 63, 65; for the full discussion of fatalism, see 53–66. The task of circumventing Nietzschean individualism by rooting the fate of individuals in the collective nation was deliberately promoted by Nazis in order to mobilize popular interest in Nietzsche for party purposes. Aschheim's illuminating work, *The Nietzsche Legacy*, addresses this transmutation; see chap. 8, esp. 236–39, 249; cf. 158. Cf. Harries, "Heidegger as Political Thinker," 649–50.

13. Wolin, *Politics*, 57.

14. See Schneeberger, *Nachlese*, for the German, speeches nos. 44, 69, and 132.

15. That Heidegger holds no ideal of impartial reason does not prevent him from seeking a pristine insight into the disclosure of Being. The entire 1935 lecture course, *An Introduction to Metaphysics*, works within a dichotomous logic that pits commonplace thought against the pure vision of Being where the latter is untainted by social forces or personal psychology.

16. Schürmann, "Political Thinking," 216 (quoting from Harries, "Heidegger as Political Thinker," 669; and Schneeberger, *Nachlese*, 47–48, 63–64, 135–36); see also his *Heidegger On Being and Acting*, 12–21.

17. Schürmann all too readily dismisses the more serious critiques of Heidegger's philosophy. Yet, when commenting on the criticisms of NS advanced by Heidegger's Nietzsche lectures, he pointedly states that "articulating a coherent political thinking is quite different from courageously aiming occasional criticisms" ("Political Thinking," 194).

18. Schürmann discusses Heidegger's names for various epochal modes of Being in "Political Thinking," 196–200, and "Questioning," 359–61. These names include "Physis, Logos, Hen, Idea, Energeia, Substantiality, Objectivity, Subjectivity, the Will, the Will to Power, the Will to Will" (Heidegger, IuD 66/134).

19. Schürmann, "Political Thinking," 197; "Ontological Difference," 107.

20. Schürmann, "Political Thinking," 200, 213, and 214 (citations in order); see also his "Ontological Difference"; for his most elaborate account of these ideas, see *Heidegger on Being and Acting*. Birmingham offers an Arendtian interpretation that reaches a similar conclusion, namely, that Heidegger's political philosophy preserves a heterogeneous public space and secures freedom against a sovereign will; see her "Logos," 44–46, 52 and "Time," 42–43.

21. See, for example, Irigaray, SP, 47f., 304, 320, passim. In *Luce Irigaray*, Whitford clarifies the complexity of Irigaray's notion of the imaginary (51–57) and her idealized, rather than literal, notion of morphology (58–59). The notion of the imaginary stems from Lacan and Freud who held that any mental representation of reality is partially filtered through bodily drives and unconscious fantasies. See Lacan, *Écrits,* 1–7, passim; Freud, "The Ego and the Id," 1–66, and "The Unconscious," 14, 159–215; and Irigaray's critique, TS, 34–67.

22. Moi, *Sexual/Textual Politics*, 132; see also her fine explication of how *Speculum* is organized around a "speculum-like structure" (130); cf. Irigaray, TS, 68–85.

23. For these metaphors, see Nietzsche, *Will to Power*, aphorisms 141, 204, 861, 951.

24. Cf. Nietzsche, *Zarathustra*, 17, 76–77, 123.

25. Bigwood explains,

What we find happening with Nietzsche's metaphysics is that the ontological movements of concealment (movements like receiving, sheltering, holding, and reclining) are suppressed. *Phusis* is pushed to create beyond its limits, to overcome, expose, resist and compel, for its character is now nothing else but Will to Power. (EaM, 88)

26. On Heidegger's admiration for militarism, see Kisiel, "Heidegger's Apology," 38–40; Zimmerman, "Philosophy and Politics," 12; Caputo, "Heidegger's *Kampf*," 61–62, 72–77; Franzen, "Sehnsucht," 78–92.

27. Wolin, *Politics*, 4.

28. Herf, *Reactionary Modernism*, 23–24; see also his discussion of Hannah Arendt's work on the reactionary tradition, 24.

29. Theweleit, *Male Fantasies*, 1: 30, 33–34, 37, 41 (cited in order).

30. In *Money, Sex, and Power*, Hartsock demonstrates how the erotic dimension of masculine social bonding is founded on matricide, i.e., a mythic fetishization and symbolic expulsion of Woman from society. She argues additionally that the emergent community of men is fragile and truncated (chap 8).

31. Theweleit, *Male Fantasies*, 1: 229; Zimmerman, "Ontological Aestheticism," 78.

32. Theweleit, *Male Fantasies*, 1: 230, 239; Dwinger, *Auf halbem Wege*, 509. Cf. Heidegger, SA, 31–33/SB, 11–13.

33. Theweleit, *Male Fantasies*, 1: 240–42.

34. For citations, see Herf, *Reactionary Modernism*, 15, 16.

35. Ibid., 73.

36. Jünger, *Copse 125*, ix.

37. Jünger, *Kampf*, 57. Jünger totally effaces women from reality by anthropomorphizing war as a father figure that tests strength of soul and smelts a new blood, a "race of trench soldiers" who are hardy and brave: "Men of this strong and courageous blood in which the superfluous vitality of a nation is shown . . . are more warmly and strongly alive to [life's] joys than any others" (*Kampf*, 13; *Copse 125*, x, 2). See Herf's commentary, 73–75; Benjamin holds that Jünger suffers from a "boyish rapture" that leads to a cult of war, in "Theories," 121, passim.

38. Zimmerman, "Ontological Aestheticism," 78 (brackets are Zimmerman's, quoting from Theweleit, *Male Fantasies*, 1: 229–30); and 59.

39. Citations taken from Jünger, "Technology as the Mobilization," 271, 287, 276, 280–81, 289, 288, which is a translation of portions of *Der Arbeiter*.

40. Herf, *Reactionary Modernism*, 33. Heidegger's works do not exhibit the rampant anti-Semitism of other ideologists. It is notable, however, that the "new nationalism" advocated after the Great War by Spengler, Schmitt, and the Jünger brothers did not rely on biological theories. Though clearly anti-Semitic, these thinkers "believed that German superiority lay in historical traditions and ideas rather than biology" (35). See also Benjamin, "Theories."

41. I use the term 'man' deliberately. It is consistent with Heidegger's focus in the 1930s on manhood and there is no evidence that Heidegger as-

sumes that women could be great creators. Van Buren identifies numerous gender ambiguities in Heidegger's choice of language to depict human being, see "Stories," 222–23.

42. I rely upon Fried's discussion and translation of Heidegger's EHD, 61 ("Heidegger's *Polemos*," 181); cf. GA 47, 149–50, from which Fried also quotes.

43. Jünger, "Technology as the Mobilization," 272.

44. I follow Fried, "Heidegger's *Polemos*," 164, in which his longer version makes apparent that Heidegger confuses the imagery of harmony with that of conflict.

45. Sophocles's poem curiously supplies Heidegger with poetic imagery very similar to that employed by the Freikorpsmen. Heidegger interprets: "Man embarks on the groundless deep, forsaking the solid land." He undertakes a "violent excursion upon the overpowering sea" and a "never-resting incursion" that "disturbs tranquility and growth, the nurturing and maturing of the goddess [earth] who lives without effort" (IM, 154/EM, 118). He also glorifies Oedipus "as the embodiment of Greek being-there" while thoroughly effacing Antigone (107/81).

46. Zimmerman, "Ontological Aestheticism," 75.

47. Fried, "Heidegger's *Polemos*," 180.

48. Ibid., 167.

49. Ibid., 173 (Fried's translation).

50. I follow Matuštík's argument in *Postnational Identity*, 120–24, and *Specters of Liberation*, chap. 2, that the charge of decisionism against Kierkegaard is a category mistake. See my "Heidegger's Reading," 56–59.

51. Habermas, "Historical Consciousness," 262. Others find strong complementarity between Kierkegaardian inwardness and Marxian critiques of ideology. Marsh suggests that Kierkegaardian inwardness "can strengthen and enhance communicative praxis" especially against the ideological operations of the culture industry ("Kierkegaard," 206). In *Kierkegaard's Critique,* Westphal locates Kierkegaard's ideology critique in the *Postscript*, 115–25; cf. 33–42. Matuštík turns to Kierkegaard's theory of indirect communication in order to correct homogenizing tendencies in Habermas's model of communicative action, *Postnational Identity*, part 2.

52. This is Derrida's reading in "Geschlecht: Sexual Difference." Marcuse's Heideggerian-influenced Marxism in *One-Dimensional Man* and Schrag's *Communicative Praxis* develop such possibilities.

53. Schürmann, "Political Thinking," 221; see 201–15 on the five proposals (i–v).

54. Ibid., 202, 205, 207, 210.

55. Schürmann, "Political Thinking," 209, 210–11. While diametrically opposed to my view, Birmingham's work makes a significant advance over Schürmann in that she interprets the achievement of authenticity as necessarily rooted in intersubjective communication. See her "Logos" and "Time."

56. Wolin, _Politics_, 14.

57. Dauenhauer, "Does Anarchy," 371–73.

Chapter 3. Agency, Affect, and the Postmodern Subject

1. Butler, _Gender Trouble_, 142. Though in agreement that "critical capacities are culturally constructed," still other feminists challenge that poststructuralist talk about resignification depletes the normative concept of autonomy of its critical, oppositional force by failing to differentiate between critical and naive transmutations of meaning. See Fraser, "False Antitheses," 172; and Alcoff, "Cultural Feminism," 309.

2. Cf. Bartky's similar claim, "Sympathy and Solidarity," 178.

3. Weir, _Sacrificial Logics_, 145–46, passim.

4. Kristeva rightly acknowledges that the desire to communicate, while clearly developed through language acquisition, must derive energy from a source which exceeds the effects of socialization. Correlatively, this desire must orient humans, in a kind of _parousia_, toward inexhaustible possibilities for critique of existing social practices, thus funding the want of making new meaning together. Still, I criticize Kristeva's effort to provide a linguistic account of the prosocial character of human motivation because she locates the extralinguistic source of the impulse to self-expression in a Freudian drive theory.

5. Willett, _Maternal Ethics_, 103. Her critique of Hegel is highly relevant. Hegel's assumption "that human beings are in part animals driven by asocial desires," Willett claims, leads him to delineate a stoic and cathartic model of freedom. The self emerges as free through a will which "must be a bold indifference to life and death" and which issues in a "radical break from nature." Thus, Hegel rejects "the body and its desires, women, and African men" (all those who are associated with the lower appetites) from personhood (105). By contrast, French existential philosophy took its cue from Kojève's reading of Hegel and thus regarded human as opposed to animal desire as the motivational core of the self. Willett clarifies that Kojève's use of the French '_désir_' is "closer to the '_eros_' of Plato's _Symposium_ than the German '_Begierde_' [used by Hegel] or the English 'desire' with their more animalistic or naturalistic connotations" (58, brackets mine, cf. 109).

6. Butler, *Gender Trouble*, 143.

7. Hekman, "Reconstituting the Subject," 46 and 50; Butler, *Gender Trouble*, 8. I address their works more fully in my "Toward a Dialectical Concept of Autonomy."

8. Butler, *Gender Trouble*, 145; Hekman, "Reconstituting the Subject," 53–54.

9. Hekman, "Reconstituting the Subject," 59. In *Feminist Practice*, Weedon nicely fills out this antihumanist model in Foucauldian terms. Personal identities are plural and incoherent, she claims, because we comprise the "site" of competing, even contradictory discursive practices. Yet we are also the subjects of discourse: "[A]s we move out of familiar circles, through education or politics, for example, we may be exposed to alternative ways of constituting the meaning of our experience which seem to address our interests more directly" (33). By highlighting that creative competencies are linguistically grounded, poststructuralists introduce an important corrective into earlier existential accounts of situated subjectivity. But creative iteration is a form of mediation when it is not simply naive.

10. Butler ("Gender Trouble," 333–39) rightly argues that the trope of inner space is sheer fantasy (here relying upon the psychoanalytic work of Roy Schafer). But, in her effort to eliminate the bathwater of a normative ideal of coherence for sex-gender-sexuality development, she throws out the baby of all forms of coherence. Thus she jettisons activities like learning to bring imagination and action together which, when stabilized, yield a competency.

11. Weir, *Sacrificial Logics*, 146, 3 (quoted in order). See Fraser, "False Antitheses," 172–73. This chapter represents a modification of my earlier critique, "Toward a Dialectical Concept of Autonomy," of Kristeva as remaining caught in a stoic Freudian paradigm.

12. Weir, *Sacrificial Logics*, 19, 20, 21; for her comments on Hegel, 22–23. Cf. Hegel, *Phenomenology*, 19–28.

13. Weir, *Sacrificial Logics*, 161, 151 (quoted in order). Weir shows that, for Kristeva, thetic identity is the constant reenactment of the shift from making sounds to making meaning. This practice involves an investment in an ability to symbolize which is not simply defensive but also takes pleasure "in the capacity to signify" (159, 167). Oliver also emphasizes Kristeva's insistence that separation from dependency on the (m)other cannot be purely defensive, but must be motivated by pleasure as well; see her *Reading Kristeva*, 33–36, 44–47. If symbolic capacity were purely a substitute for lost pleasure (immediacy), then thetic identity would be permanently neurotic. Because it would be the very dichotomous position of an impossible desire for mastery which avoids dissolution, it would be motivated by complete attachment to secure control over meaning.

14. Later I will argue that, by grounding the genesis of this intentionality at the stage of pre-Oedipal identification, Kristeva consistently reduces complex existential motivations back into a biologically determined evolution of libidinal processes; this reduction corrodes the qualitatively new agency she ascribes to existential capacities.

15. A Kristevan account of this irreducible element of desire must also be ontologically original, I later argue, rather than a secondary pre-Oedipal attainment. It must be present in the rudimentary awareness of the infant as exceeding libidinal pleasures and familial processes of identification and manifest as staking out a psychosocial space for creative self-expression in resistance to external influences.

16. See Young's account of aversive racism, in *Justice*, 141–48.

17. While Kristeva often talks of self-transformation as a reactivation of drives, her analysis implies, by contrast, that simple reactivation of asocial drives does not satisfy. Rather, only through harnessing that energy in a transformative direction does the subject become a critical actional, rather than reactionary, being. Kristeva casts the revolutionary subject as reactional in that it seeks to transform itself from the outside.

18. I am sympathetic to critics who charge Kristeva with heterosexist biases. We could question whether the premise that autoeroticism is an original state tacitly posits a correlation between fetishistic pleasures and immature development. I am pressing an existential interpretation in which stoic narcissism and nonstoic identity are the operative words, rather than fetishism or other alternative pleasures. The point is not to ignore the relation between proliferating sexual identities/pleasures and social change, but instead not to assume that the political pursuit of a wide range of sexual identities automatically theorizes what will enable a person to have critical distance on her socialized idenity. If we abandon Kristeva's drive theory, then we can allow that developing critical identity may be not only consistent with, but best served by fostering a society with a wide range of sexual identities. For different readings of Kristeva's views on feminine sexuality, see articles by E. Ziarek, "Kristeva and Levinas"; Wiseman, "Renaissance Paintings"; Weir, "Identification"; and Butler, "The Body Politics," in Oliver, *Ethics, Politics, and Difference*. See also Butler, *Gender Trouble*, 86–88; Weir, *Sacrificial Logics*, 173–83; Oliver, *Reading Kristeva*, 140–41.

19. Crownfield, "The Sublimation of Narcissism," 59. In spite of Kristeva's proclivity to use the term narcissism to refer to both the triadic and dyadic moments, Crownfield suggests we use "narcissan" to refer to primary identification while reserving "narcissism" proper for collapsing the triadic structure of identification (64, n.1).

20. Identification is neither pure incorporation (which reduces being to having and thus devours and assimilates the preobjectal other) nor pure

rejection (which entails libidinally cathecting the partial object as an total object, an absolute alterity; this cathexis would be associated with the necessity of repressing affective bonds to the mother in order to become a subject). See Kristeva, TL, 25–26.

21. Freud names the metaphorical object of desire the imaginary Father (Kristeva, TL, 26).

22. Whereas Weir (*Sacrificial Logics*, 181) and Oliver (*Reading Kristeva*, 84) argue that the loving Other need not be a father figure but only a third, Lorraine ("Amatory Cures," 105) claims that the Great Other must be a father. What is crucial for Kristeva, Lorraine notes, is that the stern and repressive law of symbolic meaning become fused with a loving father; this loving dimension of the paternal law allows individuals to take semiotic pleasure in outlaw desires, to communicate nonidentity, and to accept their fallibility and peculiarities. Cf. Kristeva, BS, 23–24.

23. See Oliver, *Reading Kristeva*, 119.

24. Or she can do so only on the grounds that such qualitative leaps are characteristic of the natural evolution of all matter, including the libidinal energy which supports psychic development. But this leads to another problem: that intentionality is depleted of its meaning as grounded in freedom. Rather than truly transform the asocial character of autoeroticism, humans sublate the immediacy of autoerotic pleasure into the demand that another person cohabit my immediate life of desire and need.

25. "Thanatos is pure while Eros has, since the beginning, been permeated with Thanatos" (Kristeva, TL, 31).

26. Primary identification rests upon the energy-consuming activity of repressing the innate cannibalistic orientation of oral drives and the autoerotic pleasures of expulsion characteristic of anal processes. Through this fusion of one's existential desire to be with the desire to be loved, Thanatos can be brought to serve psychological maturation. But the possibility for psychological maturation occurs only when my desire to express my nonidentity outweighs my indulgence in psychotic or fetishistic pleasures, i.e., if and only if there is a primary idealized identification with a Great Other at the very foundation of the ego. Thus the very desire for the real is synonymous with compensation for the death drive.

27. Kristeva discusses borderline psychological cases, including morbid forms of identification with the mother, as failures to make the complete transition away from autoeroticism. On borderline cases and women's melancholy, see Oliver, *Reading Kristeva*, 84–85; Weir, *Sacrificial Logics*, 178–83.

28. This constraint of cannibalistic desire makes impossible a clean distinction between metaphor and metonymy. Given that this deferral toward the metaphorical Other sublates death drives, why would the ability to de-

vour words necessarily provide a prosocial ground for intersubjective relations? Language and communication could be a new medium of competition, a vehicle for overwhelming others, for verbal duels, for asserting an alleged superiority. Kristeva illicitly cleanses the idealized orientation toward metaphoricity of any misogynistic or antagonistic associations by postulating metaphoricity as essentially prosocial while charging metonymic fantasy life, or failures to break with autoerotic pleasures, as the culprit in psychologically immature relations.

29. I do not wish to deny the reality of transference love or even that humans generally must undergo a process of psychological maturation in order to become capable of love.

30. See Willett's critiques of Kristeva and Levinas, *Maternal Ethics*, chaps. 1 and 4.

31. Kristeva's theory implies that perhaps one day, from a phylogenetic standpoint, we could eradicate the death drive and evolve possibilities for alternative forms of socialization. But the Kristevan notion of the death drive appears to delimit such possibilities in the here and now. This assumption leads her to confuse historical conditions with the necessity of hysterical love. For a convincing alternative development theory, see Willett's use of Stern, in *Maternal Ethics*, 4–30 and chap. 2.

32. Lugones, "Playfulness," esp. 276–83. Willett offers a particularly illuminating critique of Lacan's mirror stage, arguing instead that "[t]he mirror holds the attention of the infant not because it provides a static image of wholeness but because it recalls the interactive qualities of intersubjectivity" (*Maternal Ethics*, 68).

33. McAfee's "Abject Strangers" similarly turns to Heidegger to supply a nonambivalent relation to alterity.

34. It lies beyond the scope of this chapter to hammer out the details of synthesizing Heideggerian ontology and Kristeva's biological-based theory of psychosexual development. Suffice it to say that I do not intend a trivial displacement of biological processes, including aggressive impulses. My claim is that a broader social orientation is present in infants. Yet I think this prosocial orientation stands in tension with biochemistry to some extent. The ontological or existential dilemma is that the infant must develop individuality by differentiating itself from intersubjectivity. It is possible that biochemistry, by contrast, may be incorrigibly individuated and thus pull the infant in an antithetical direction, thereby creating felt difficulties in connecting with other humans. To my mind, a genuine account of the relation between ontology and biology would be complex and dialectical. Here I simply want to suggest that we must assume a broader social orientation exists in infancy in order to account for the human capacity to derive pleasure from harmonious social interaction.

35. Heidegger grounds the desire for creative self-expression in a kind of existential rather than psychological ambivalence. Like Kristeva, the early Heidegger sees language as both seducing us into fallenness and as allowing for alternative modes of expression. Yet early Heidegger associates intersubjectivity with naive adherence to discursive practices, thereby leading to a one-sided and abstract negation of existing social norms. This negation reinstates the individual as antagonistic to socialness rather than develops his basic insight that subjectivity is intersubjectivity (*Mitsein*).

36. Rosi Braidotti also conceptualizes the subject as a "dynamic interaction of desire with the will . . . not just libidinal desire, but rather ontological desire, the desire to be" ("On the Female Subject," 182). And Schrag's *The Self After Postmodernity* offers a model which portrays the self as both a speaking and an agentive subject.

37. Heidegger's methodology, both early and late, consistently leads him to discuss attunement in abstract terms. Where Heidegger talks about my attunement to the world in epochal terms, Sandra Bartky (*Femininity*, chap. 6) extends the notion of attunement to a consideration of the ways that U.S. patriarchy encourages males and females to develop asymmetrical senses of their orientation toward creative self-expression. Against both Kristeva and early Heidegger, the fixation with death corresponds to a Homeric ideal recast in capitalism (see Hartsock, *Money, Sex, and Power*, chaps. 8 and 10).

38. Gordon, *Bad Faith*, esp. chap. 15 and part 4.

39. Existential thinkers like Lewis Gordon argue that the enduring value of existential philosophies consists in their demonstration that attitudes toward evidence are not merely passive (*Bad Faith*, part 2). While not sanguine about the Sartrean underpinnings of Gordon's particular existential philosophy, I agree that we cannot account for phenomena like racism and misogyny without retaining a concept of "bad faith" or, in Kierkegaardian language, willed ignorance. But I would qualify such concepts by altering the categorical formulation that humans willfully resist evidence that invalidates their racial prejudice, and replacing it with the modified claim that, at any given point in time, human subjects either strive to become willing or remain unwilling to assume responsibility for the results of their socialization and their ongoing formation of identity.

40. Moreover, there are many cases in which the unwillingness to face something stems not from limitations rooted in deep psychic beliefs but rather much more directly from finitude proper, from felt limits in the present, fears and desires about one's immediate work, or recent changes in social location. Finding oneself in one's first salaried job may indeed alter one's capacities to make decisions which lack of material security allowed. While cognizant of this influence, it functions not simply as an external force but rather as a self-directing psychic fantasy, perhaps manifest as a felt desert for the work I devoted to getting where I am. Humans

do derive momentum from the immediacy of their surroundings. Willingness to identify those effects opens me to the possibility of not absolutizing my social location, not being in denial about my cowardice, not being unaware that I am dangerously close to easy compromise on ethical and political issues.

41. An important, albeit ironic, implication of locating racist attitudes in prereflective choices is that, while not all racist invective reflects a history of pathological hatred of blacks, this does not make individual racist acts less egregious. Gordon offers the example of the white patient, who, just before complete psychological break down, unleashes racial invective at a black worker in order to convince himself that he is not really at bottom (*Bad Faith*, 73). At first glance this example might lead the reader to think that, fortunately, even when s/he makes a racist 'slip up,' at least this is no full reflection of her/his character. But, to the contrary, Gordon's point is precisely that reference to one's 'true character' or 'true self' in such self-interpretations operates as denial of the gravity of the situation. The failure here is no mere 'lapse' in character, not just a being out of sink with the 'real me.' Such claims obscure the *active* character of choice and the foundational character of the action. For in this act I fashion my identity anew, seeking to give myself value through negation of another.

Chapter 4. A Critical Mimetic Recovery of Origins

1. Whereas for Irigaray western metaphysics is patriarchal, Heidegger never makes this connection in any explicit way. Naming nihilism in terms of gender clearly modifies and transforms our experience of what nihilism is in ways that Heidegger's gender-neutral language cannot evoke. Even so, I exploit the region of overlap between them without on that account intending to diminish their differences. Hodge's "Irigaray Reading Heidegger" provides an excellent summary of these similarities and differences.

2. See Caputo on late Heidegger's eschatology, in *Radical Hermeneutics*, 160–86; see also Derrida, *Margins*, 25–27, 124–36; "Of an Apocalyptic Tone," 80–81. For fine discussions of Irigaray as essentialist, see Schor, "This Essentialism," 38–58; Fuss, *Essentially Speaking*, 55–72; Whitford, *Luce Irigaray*, 71–74, 84–89, 94–95.

3. For Cornell, Derridean deconstruction harbors an unerasable utopian structure and Irigaray's work embodies this utopian moment. See Cornell's *Beyond Accommodation*, 107, passim.

4. Cornell, *Beyond Accommodation*, 167. Bigwood (EaM, 38) argues that Heidegger's origin is not a "virginal a priori" or first cause but rather an event, a genesis where things emerge into unconcealment but without ground or reason. Cf. Heidegger, WT, 152/WD, 98; QCT, 6–12/VA, 11–16.

5. Butler, "Variations," 136–39 and "Gender Trouble."

6. Young, *Justice*, 98–99.

7. Cornell, *Beyond Accommodation*, 166.

8. Ibid., 168.

9. Ibid.

10. Ibid., 168–69.

11. Irigaray makes comments which support strategic readings, e.g., "the issue is not one of elaborating a new theory of which woman would be the *subject* or *object*, but of jamming the theoretical machinery itself, sus- pending its pretension to the production of a truth and of a meaning that are excessively univocal" (TS, 78, cf. 76, 90, 150). Whitford offers a helpful treatment of these varied interpretations of the "two lips," in *Luce Irigaray*, 171–72; the quotation from Grosz is found in Whitford; see Gallop, *"Quand nos lèvres,"* 78; Fuss, "'Essentially Speaking'," 66; and Grosz, "Derrida, Irigaray, and Deconstruction."

12. Cornell criticizes Whitford for neglecting the utopian dimension in Irigaray's writing and addresses the threat of conservativism *(Beyond Accommodation*, 77–78). On Lacan's "closed circuit" of metaphoric substitution, see Oliver, *Reading Kristeva*, 171; also see Irigaray, TS, 76f. On the conservativism of re-metaphorization, see Gallop, *"Quand nos lèvres,"* 83.

13. See Whitford's cogent summary of the terminological usages of metaphor and metonymy from Jakobson via Lacan to Irigaray, in *Luce Irigaray*, 178–81.

14. Cornell, *Beyond Accommodation*, 78.

15. Ibid., 36.

16. Ibid., 37.

17. Silverman, *The Subject*, 183, 141 (in order).

18. Whitford, *Luce Irigaray*, 44–45. Cf. Irigaray, Gen, 91–104. Note Silverman's critique of Lacan: "It is preposterous to assume either that woman remains outside of signification, or that her sexuality is less culturally organized or repressed than her male counterpart" *(The Subject*, 189).

19. Irigaray continues, "by remaining absent as 'subject', she lets them keep, even guarantees that they can keep, the position of mastery" (TS, 95).

20. Whitford, *Luce Irigaray*, 50. Irigaray criticizes Heidegger for colonizing the feminine as well. See my chap. 3 on the relation between Heidegger's desire to appropriate female powers and his involvement in National Socialism.

21. Whitford, *Luce Irigaray*, 68.

22. Cornell, *Beyond Accommodation*, 169.

23. Ibid., 87–88.

24. See, for example, McKluskie, "Women's Language," 57–58 and 60; and Burke, "Irigaray," 303.

25. Cornell brings Derrida and Irigaray together in advancing this interpretation, in *Beyond Accommodation*, 87.

26. Feminist utopias do not eliminate struggle. See Whitford, *Luce Irigaray,* 18–19; Kristeva, WT, 202–5; Rose, "Dreaming the Future," esp. 121, 128; Irigaray, TS, 130.

27. For Irigaray, the economy of solids supports closed metaphoric systems that exclude the feminine. On her critique of Heidegger's earth metaphor as well as his notions of appropriation, construction, and building (forms of erection), see OA, 10, 17ff., 35, 71–72, 85; SP, 133; and R, 213–18, with Whitford's comments R, 163. For Kristeva's critique, see RP, 131. Cf. Whitford, *Luce Irigaray,* 150–51, 156–57; Bigwood, EaM, 76–81; and Young who criticizes Heidegger's notion of dwelling as male-biased in her *Intersecting Voices*, chap. 7.

28. I want to note two things. First, Irigaray notwithstanding, Derridean deconstruction can be fruitfully interpreted as providing a utopian moment, as Cornell demonstrates in *Beyond Accommodation*, 79–118. Second, while Heidegger lacks Derrida's concern for gender, his work arguably offers a more substantive ethics of responsibility to others than does Derridean deconstruction, as White claims in "Heidegger," 80–103.

29. In a note on her translation of Heidegger's *"Überwindung der Metaphysik"* ("Overcoming Metaphysics"), Stambaugh argues that, although he employs the "familiar word *Überwindung,*" Heidegger "means it in the sense of the less familiar word *Verwindung"* (EP, 84 n. 1/VA, 67). I agree with Stambaugh and mention that this essay contains notes worked out during the years of the Nietzsche lectures from 1936–46, though not published until 1951. During this time, Heidegger's thought shifts away from the will to overcome toward an ethos of letting be. In his 1944–45 essay, *"Zur Erörterung der Gelassenheit,"* he discusses letting be as "keeping awake" for an experience of unconcealment, as opposed to willing that awakening. He distinguishes *"Erwachen"* (awakening ourselves) from *"Wachbleiben"* (keeping awake) (DT, 61/ G, 32).

30. Cornell, *Beyond Accommodation*, 167.

31. Ibid., 167–68, 179, 168 (in order quoted).

32. Hegel, *Phenomenology*, 375.

33. Cornell, *Beyond Accommodation*, 169; see 179–83 for her critique of strategic essentialism, particularly as represented by Spivak's "In a Word";

and Fuss's "Essentially Speaking." Hodge shows that Irigaray and Heidegger deliberately inhabit "the dynamic dependence and incompatibility between the philosophical ideal of rigorous conceptual structure and human experiences of time, difference, and incompleteness" ("Irigaray Reading Heidegger," 202).

34. Cornell, *Beyond Accommodation*, 181.

35. Fuss shows that false universalism is a species of essentialism (*Essentially Speaking*, 2).

36. While Cornell never develops a concrete identity politics, I am suggesting that her work implicitly addresses the concern that political activism inevitably occurs as identity politics. Phelan's "(Be)Coming Out" makes this point well in her critique of Butler, esp. 778–86.

37. On her use of Walzer's notion of reiterative universalism, see Cornell, *Beyond Accommodation*, 194–96; Cornell rejects the label nominalism for her own Derridean-Irigarayan position, yet she clearly rejects the existence of real universals, 85, 183, 190f.

38. Cornell, *Beyond Accommodation*, 178 (on artificial mythology) and 169 (remaining quotations).

39. On memory as recollective imagination, see Cornell, *Beyond Accommodation*, 178; on the Derridean logic of the double gesture, 170–72; on eliminating hierarchy, see her treatment of Morrison's *Beloved*, 194–96. Young, *Justice*, 97.

40. Ziarek, "Proximities"; see also *Inflected Language*, chaps. 1 and 2.

41. Oliver, *Reading Kristeva*, 172.

Chapter 5. *Gelassenheit:* Heidegger's Reluctant Utopia

1. Schürmann, "Heidegger and Meister Eckhart," 115.

2. Being is not an absolute entity, final ground, or explanatory principle of human existence.

3. Cornell, *Beyond Accommodation*, 107.

4. Whitford, *Luce Irigaray*, 44.

5. Ibid., on the comparison of Bachelard and Sartre, see 55; on Sartre's view of imagination, 54; on the elements, 55.

6. Whitford, *Luce Irigaray,* on the synthesis of phenomenology and psychoanalysis, see 54; on the elements, 56. Though she finds it useful to compare Irigaray to Sartre, Whitford carefully notes that the phenomenological influence derives largely from Merleau-Ponty. Similarly, since

Irigaray never mentions Bachelard, Whitford speculates that Irigaray inherits this influence from French culture.

7. Whitford, *Luce Irigaray,* 56, notes that Irigaray uses Castoriadis's word, magma, to speak about the imaginary as a creative source. See Castoriadis, *L'Institution imaginaire,* 253. See also Weedon's discussion of the relation between Althusser's work and poststructuralism, *Feminist Practice,* 27–32.

8. I borrow the terms 'autodisclosive' and 'autokinetic' from Sheehan and use them interchangeably, see "On Movement and Destruction," 536.

9. While I do not want to ascribe my own position to these thinkers, I nonetheless read Heidegger, Marcuse, Irigaray, and Iris Young as subscribing to this ontological position. Moreover, this notion of the imaginary differentiates Irigaray from less idealistic approaches to social eros and fantasy like Hartsock's in *Money, Sex, and Power,* esp. chap. 8.

10. Whitford, *Luce Irigaray,* 58–59, quoting from Gallop, *"Quand nos lèvres,"* 79.

11. See Whitford's discussion, *Luce Irigaray,* 66–67. Throughout this book, I consistently maintain that the real, because it denotes the possible, is not some kind of Kantian noumena. Rather, we come to know the real in the forms of life we develop, in our collective and intersubjective accomplishments. These accomplishments always produce something qualitatively greater than humans intend and plan.

12. I am arguing that Heidegger's step-back, whereby we attain a critical relation to our own finitude, would remain partial without other more standard types of philosophical critique.

13. In *Der Satz vom Grund* Heidegger describes the compulsion to ground in more ethically neutral language, less clearly related to castration anxiety. While this language could indicate later Heidegger's attempt to distance his thought from his earlier politically charged talk, the moral neutrality of his analysis continues to reflect the recurrent stoic side of his work. In contrast to Heidegger's stoic tendency to depict humans as caught in the erroneous ways of a history not of their making and doing, my interpretation stresses his critique of agency as strategically transformative and not as a relinquishment of ethical responsibility. We seize upon our epochal interpretive horizon—either deliberately or by default, consciously or unconsciously—in order to feel grounded but equally so as to suppress awareness of our primordial groundlessness. To dogmatically take over the legacy of history is to undertake a naive mimetic repetition of our own historicalness; it tacitly posits our form of life as the progressive standard by which to judge history. Succumbing to the weight of the past is not passivity in a neutral sense, but rather aggression toward (flight from) origins. Humans are ethically responsible for the historical process by which they translate

past perspectives into new grounds for the present, even though they are born into a world that they did not make.

14. Flax, *Thinking Fragments*, 34. See Benhabib, *Situating the Self*, 211.

15. See Zimmerman, *Heidegger's Confrontation*, 230.

16. See also Heidegger, N4, 91–95/NII, 135–41.

17. For changes in Heidegger's position, see W. Marx, *Heidegger and the Tradition*, 106–13, 139–43, 155f., 220–24, 227–31. Also see Bigwood, EaM, 96–103.

18. This is the gist of Heidegger's insistent appeal that the nihilistic destruction of humanitarian existence could ensue, even if we do not bring about actual technological annihilation; see his OWL, 15/US, 103; and WT, 30/WD, 11–12.

19. Heidegger's prescription to adopt a nonwillful posture can be seen as an effort to actuate human progress at a juncture in western history wherein the impediment to progress is the belief that we can master nature and reality.

20. My interpretation of Heidegger as offering a nonunivocal concept of the transcendental is indebted to Schürmann's innovative and definitive reading in *Heidegger on Being and Acting*, 223–25, passim. But I ultimately contend, against Schürmann, that theoretical anarchism offers no adequate vision of political and moral relations without developing interactive paradigms for reconstructing universalism.

21. Heidegger discusses the other side of the horizon as "an enchanted region" (DT, 63/G, 38); and states that "Releasement is indeed the release of oneself from transcendental re-presentation and so a relinquishing of the willing of a horizon" (80/57).

22. Heidegger mistakenly thinks that letting be supplies the sufficient condition of nondominating relations or that we learn to let be *sans* interaction with others.

23. Heidegger thinks Dasein in broad strokes as though there is a single, unitary Japanese or German Dasein, thus ignoring that highly individualized appropriations of the eastern and western traditions exist on the basis of ethnicity, nation, class, sexual orientation, and so forth.

24. My interpretation differentiates between (a) the formal delimitation of utopian ideals and (b) antinormativism. I suggest that (a) does not entail (b) rejecting rational reconstructions of moral principles. But it calls for a postmetaphysical ethics built on a communicative, concrete, dialogical reason as opposed to a legislative, abstract, monological search for the moral point of view. While Habermas, Benhabib, Fraser, Young, Jaggar, Lugones, and others disagree about how to reconstruct this paradigm, they

all take a communicative or interactive turn. For a fascinating alternative effort to link Heidegger, through Bloch, to utopian thinking, see Ramsey, *The Long Path to Nearness*.

25. Kolb, *The Critique of Pure Modernity*, 190, 191 (quoted in order). Heidegger's sparse if not entirely cryptic comments on the fourfold, coupled with his numerous though undeveloped accounts of Being as *Ereignis* (the event of appropriation), encourage romantic mystifications of his work. Like Kolb, Sheehan, Caputo, and others, I think we need to demystify Heidegger and abandon laboriously abstract expatiations on concepts like *Gelassenheit*. If the step-back before the synchronic and discontinuous dimension of history *(Ereignis)* does not contribute to acquiring critical distance on our historical perceptions, then Heidegger's work offers little of spiritual value in transforming individuals and western society. Worse, neo-Heideggerian mystification adopts Heidegger's own questionable tendency toward self-aggrandization by planting feathers in the caps of those who dogmatically speak his language. Such a notion of mimesis could hardly deliver one to the inner circle of deep truth. This is not the Heidegger of critical interest.

26. Kolb, *The Critique of Pure Modernity*, 191.

27. White, "Heidegger," 86, 93, 95 (quoted in order). White's noteworthy analysis supports and clarifies my project in three basic ways. First, he criticizes Heidegger's tendency to speak abstractly of everyday face-to-face encounters and to focus instead on encounters with Being as such (83), while he nonetheless harnesses Heidegger for face-to-face ethics. Second, he compensates for Heidegger's antinormativism by reconciling an ethics of responsibility to others with moral legitimation (80–81, 87–89). Third, he recognizes Schürmann's significant interpretation of Heidegger as delimiting universal ideals while arguing against Schürmann that this delimitation cannot yield implications for moral and political theory without additional mediation by other concepts and types of analysis (82–90).

28. White, "Heidegger," 96 (on the moral dimension), 95 (last two quotations). Gordon makes a similar critique of what he calls deconstruction's style-centrism *(Bad Faith*, 169–70).

29. Ziarek, "Proximities."

Chapter 6. Heidegger's Apolitical Nostalgia for Immediacy

1. White, "Heidegger," 81, 79 (in order). White incisively shows that paradigms focusing on a responsibility to act (as in Habermas) grasp "language primarily as an 'action-coordinating' medium" while an ethics of responsibility to otherness understands language "as a 'world-disclosing' medium" (81).

2. Heidegger, to my mind, divides modernity into two distinct phases: an early modern period centering around paradigms of representation and the twentieth-century spread of a nihilistic will to power. See Kolb, *The Critique of Pure Modernity*, 144–50.

3. Kolb, *The Critique of Pure Modernity*, 197–98.

4. Flax, *Thinking Fragments*, 29. In Lyotard's particular brand of postmodernism, we find a clear version of nominalism as local narrative, i.e., as the view that only situated, context-dependent criteria of evaluation exist (*The Postmodern Condition*, 23). See Benhabib's discussion, *Situating the Self*, 225.

5. Flax, *Thinking Fragments*, 12, 30 (in order). In his critical analysis, Harris also explains that these textual devices "are not intended as 'privileged' windows or naked eyes on an objective world" ("Postmodernism and Utopia," 32–33).

6. Flax, *Thinking Fragments*, 34, 30 (in order); on the three deaths, see 32–35.

7. Benhabib, *Situating the Self*, 224, 225. She attributes the strong death blow to normative theory to Heidegger, while taking Rorty as exemplary of a weak decentering of philosophy as a discourse of legitimation. Cf. Rorty, *Philosophy and the Mirror of Nature*, 131f.

8. Flax, *Thinking Fragments*, 33.

9. Fraser and Nicholson, "Social Criticism without Philosophy," 22. See Lyotard, *The Postmodern Condition*.

10. Benhabib, *Situating the Self*, 219–20, 222, 223 (in order). The strong version of the death of history thesis, in Fraser's and Nicholson's words, "throws out the baby of large historical narrative with the bathwater of philosophical metanarrative" ("Social Criticism without Philosophy," 25). Fraser and Nicholson argue, rightly I believe, that we still need large-scale analyses of the "broad-based relations of dominance and subordination along lines like gender, race, and class" that cut across local practices and thus provide some basis for normative judgments that are context-transcending though not context-transcendent (23).

11. Benhabib, *Situating the Self*, 223. My primary concern does not lie in accusing postmodernism of a performative contradiction for relying upon ahistorical, synchronic claims about history (Heidegger), language (Derrida), or patriarchy (Irigaray) while adhering to a form of nominalism. Thinkers like Derrida, Lyotard, and Irigaray at least allow that multiple representations of the same history exist as contrasted with Heidegger's truly more unified view of history. But this does not automatically prevent them from absolutizing their standpoint. In the next chapter, I will explore those ways

in which specific usages of Irigaray, even if they do not completely forget that their story is one of many, nonetheless fail to examine the priorities asserted in that one story.

12. Caputo, "Incarnation and Essentialization," 32–33.

13. Caputo, *Radical Hermeneutics*, 164.

14. Bernstein, *The New Constellation*, 136.

15. Bruns, *Heidegger's Estrangements*, 125; see also Brunzina, "Heidegger on the Metaphor and Philosophy," 184–200.

16. Brunzina clarifies that this refusal comprises Heidegger's active polemic with the customary view that rational knowledge (philosophy) requires the literal-metaphorical distinction. Rationality so defined refers to that activity which pursues "the ideal of a type of meaning and expression that . . . implies the distinction between a direct and proper sense and an oblique and transferred sense"; in other words, "rational account, necessarily opting for the *clear differentiation* of meaning, must necessarily as well see itself as aiming for an articulation in *proper* expression rather than transferred, that is, literal language rather than metaphorical" ("Heidegger on the Metaphor and Philosophy," 194).

17. Schrag makes this comment in response to W. Marx's "The World in Another Beginning," 253. See Marx's fuller comment:

> It is perhaps doubtful whether one can, within the context of the philosophy of the latter-day Heidegger, legitimately speak of "meanings" and of "sense." However, in order to illustrate the difference between Heidegger's early conception of language and his later one, one might say that *Sage*, as the *Sage* of world, Being, and *Ereignen*, lets meanings arrive; this in contrast to word and speech being founded in meanings, as was the case earlier, or as Heidegger put it at the time, "To significations, words accrue." (255)

18. Kolb, *The Critique of Pure Modernity*, 191–92.

19. Ibid., 194.

20. Kolb, *The Critique of Pure Modernity*, 193; see his fuller discussion of Heidegger's attitude toward politics, 193–200. For an even more critical assessment of later Heidegger's work, see Bartky's view that originative thought is vacuous and not fruitful for historical change ("Originative Thinking," 376, passim). For a corrective to Heidegger's tendency to abstract from the material dimensions of life and to collapse utopia into a meta-utopian 'now', see Ramsey, *The Long Path to Nearness*. See also Schrag, *Communicative Praxis* and *The Self After Postmodernity*.

21. Benhabib, *Situating the Self*, 226, 225–26 (in order).

Chapter 7. Postmodern Meta-Utopia or Solidarity?

1. Du Bois, *Souls*, 23.

2. Oliver, *Reading Kristeva*, 168.

3. See Alcoff and Potter, "Introduction."

4. Caputo, *Radical Hermeneutics*, 169–170. See Derrida, "Of an Apocalyptic Tone," 63–97; and *Margins*, 111–36.

5. Following Flax, I interpret postmodern and poststructuralist theories as issuing a threefold death blow to Enlightenment humanism: (i) the death of the coherent subject; (ii) the death of history as an intrinsic order; (iii) the death of the metaphysics of presence and its idealizing desire to master the real (*Thinking Fragments*, 31–35). Yet like Benhabib, I distinguish between weak and strong versions of each death blow (*Situating the Self*, 213–25). The strong nominalist thesis of rejecting all large scale narratives (in the manner of Lyotard) is distinct from the weak thesis which rejects only essentialist and monocausal narratives. I agree with Benhabib, Fraser, and Nicholson that only the weak version is commensurate with an ideal of pluralism that eradicates the problems I address below. Yet theorists from both camps intend to recuperate those voices left out of history. Cf. Fraser and Nicholson, "Social Criticism without Philosophy."

6. Flax, *Thinking Fragments*, 33.

7. Phelan, in "(Be)Coming Out," 784, notes: "Grand theories work by subsuming all struggles under a single rubric, delaying or denying the importance of other categories"; and "Local politics and the theories that sustain them privilege no one axis of oppression but, instead, open space for a multiplicity of claims and struggles."

8. Fuss, *Essentially Speaking*, 2. Her comprehensive definition treats essentialism as referring to any of three positions: (i) the belief in a substantive "female essence"; (ii) univocal and universal notions of womanhood, femininity, or women's oppression; and (iii) totalizing conceptions of symbolic practices. Essentialist conceptions of women's oppression inevitably abstract from the specific historical, social, and material conditions of women.

9. hooks, *Yearning*, 28, 29 (in order).

10. hooks, *Yearning*, 26, cf. 25. Phelan nicely reconciles antiessentialism with identity politics. She replaces the essentialist view of coming out as a "process of discovery" with an antiessentialist view of coming out as self-creation. Where the former regards coming out as overcoming the denial that one's hidden and authentic sexuality is lesbian, the latter reinterprets coming out as the self-creative act of becoming woman-identified and expressing that act in the adoption of a lesbian lifestyle. Acknowledging that

identities have only "provisional subject positions," this provides an open-ended basis for undertaking, rather than undercutting, local identity politics. Her work neither falls prey to essentialism nor prevents coalitional alliances. See her "(Be)Coming Out," 773, 779, passim.

11. Spencer, "Trends of Opposition," 2; Collins, "Setting Our Own Agenda," 53; Asante, "Racing to Leave the Race," 50; hooks, *Yearning*, 25. These debates succinctly unfold in *The Black Scholar* 23, no. 2 (1993) and 23, nos. 3, 4 (1993). hooks has long pleaded the problem of effacement. In *Ain't I a Woman*, she argued that many white theorists use African-American culture to: (i) find innovative directions to move in theory; (ii) undertake self-reflection; or (iii) contribute to discussions of race. But none of these projects recognizes the work of people of color as fertile soil for the production of theory proper. For a summary of the unique contributions of black feminist theory, see Smith 1983, xix–lvi.

12. Fanon, *Wretched*, 37. Kumkum Sangari differentiates two distinct motives underlying "First World" and "Third World" critiques of false universalism. Whereas the "First World's crisis of meaning," Sangari says, stems from "the felt absence of the will or the ability to change things," the "Third World" encounters difficulties realizing its will. For Sangari, the hegemonic ideologies of neocolonialism so distort social reality that the disenfranchised have trouble finding a point of leverage from which to jump-start liberation struggles ("Politics of the Possible," 161). As a Euro-American theorist, Nancy Hartsock holds that French postmodern theories, which "represent the voice of the powerful being forced to come to terms with the voices of the disenfranchised," do not suffice to form alliances ("Theoretical Bases," 257); cf. "Rethinking Modernism," 196.

13. Harris, "Postmodernism and Utopia," 35.

14. Ibid., 33.

15. Ibid., 33 (all quotations).

16. Ibid., 31.

17. Ibid., 42, 31–32, 36.

18. Ibid., 37–38.

19. Ibid., 40.

20. Ibid., 43.

21. Ibid., 35.

22. Harris, "Postmodernism and Utopia," 36, 42, 35, 36 (quoted in order); on moral attributes, see 40–41. Schrag develops a portrait of the self which reconciles the narratival basis of subjectivity with the material embeddedness of existence, *The Self After Postmodernity*.

23. McGowan, *Postmodernism and Its Critics*, 13, 14 (quoted in order). Bill Martin, Jameson, Spivak, and Braidotti advance versions of poststructuralist Marxism that strive to avoid these problems. See also Cutrofello; and Brown, *Fear, Truth, Writing*.

24. Harris, "Postmodernism and Utopia," 38. The point is that such totalizing views of life tacitly assume a metanarrative rooted in my specific group experience and this promotes a view of local narratives as fragments of the whole seen from my standpoint.

25. I retain a dialectical approach because such chicken-and-egg paradoxes are otherwise irresolvable. Does the black criminal become deviant because U.S. society symbolizes black intelligence as dangerous and thus deviant? Or does the black criminal pursue the life of crime because impoverished and the ideology of the ruling class perpetuates this class setup by promoting images of black males as criminal? My answer is both/and. The issue is that racial stereotyping and racial oppression, though intrinsically linked to the ideology of capitalism, nonetheless can operate independently of a capitalist economic organization of society.

26. Harris, "Postmodernism and Utopia," 38. Some postmodern, especially Foucauldian, social theory weds the acceptance of diverse epistemic perspectives to a politics of heterogeneous anarchism. Stabile defines heterogeneous anarchism as the view that politics is necessarily fragmented, that "the only similarity among [struggling] groups is their struggle—from very different positions and in isolation from one another" ("Feminism without Guarantees," 49). A major concern of the debates about postmodernism in *The Black Scholar* 23, nos. 2, 3, and 4 (1993) is that the very focus on a loose, anarchistic proliferation of sites of struggle may reflect the luxury afforded by the axes of power that white, middle class, educated men and women share but blacks do not. Cf. Albrecht and Brewer, "Bridges of Power"; Alperin, "Social Diversity"; Anzaldúa, "Bridge"; Bunch, "Making Common Cause"; Peterson, "Alliances"; Hall, "African-American Women"; Phelan, "(Be)Coming Out"; Reagon, "Coalition Politics"; Smith, "Introduction."

27. King, "Multiple Jeopardy," 51. McKluskie, "Women's Language," 57, 60 (in order cited).

28. Pluhacek and Bostic, "Thinking Life As Relation," 343–44.

29. Ibid., 355, 345 (in order).

30. Ibid., 351, 358 (in order); cf. 343–44.

31. Stabile, *Technological Fix*, 46. By addressing women's difference as fragmented incarnations of a symbolic whole, this reification obscures how every ideal-typical description of the symbolic order arrays some features of reality as definitive.

32. Fraser, "The Uses and Abuses," 182. See Weedon's critique of Lacan, *Feminist Practice*, 71–73, 93, 150; Silverman, *The Subject*, 185–88; also Cornell and Thurschwell, "Feminism, Negativity, and Intersubjectivity," 147. For an alternative model of the narratival foundations of praxis that avoids these problems, see Schrag, *The Self After Postmodernity*.

33. Fraser, "Uses and Abuses" 180. Leland, "Lacanian Psychoanalysis," 120, 121, 121, 114 (in order). Cf. Weedon's argument that Irigaray holds an essentialist theory of female pleasure, *Feminist Practice*, 65.

34. Copjec, "Sex and the Euthanasia of Reason," 21.

35. Abel, "Race, Class, and Psychoanalysis?"

36. Gordon, *Bad Faith*, 1; for his discussion of the thesis that the phallus is white skin, see esp. 124–29, and passim. Although I find Gordon's analysis instructive, I am cautious about hijacking the phallus for analyses of racial exclusion. Rather than multiply incarnations of the phallus, I suggest that we assume neither that the phallus is the sole signifier around which identity-formation takes place nor that gender permeates identity more deeply than does race. Whatever distinguishes race from gender permeates identity more deeply than does race. Whatever distinguishes race from gender in relation to biology, we cannot deny that racialization suffuses erotica all the way down to the unconscious basis of sexual desire. I say this while recognizing that reproductive capacity may remain a fairly permanent source of vulnerability for anatomically distinct humans long after racism and gender-based oppression no longer exist.

37. On Irigaray's attitude toward her class, see Pluhacek and Bostic, "Thinking Life," 358. Whitford clarifies Irigaray's social view of the symbolic order: "[I]t is the symbolic which is sick" (*Luce Irigaray*, 44). The French inclination to equate sex and gender as basic to identity formation could stem from the French language which lacks a definitive adjectival distinction between female and feminine. See Moi, *Sexual/Textual Politics*, 97. Because Kristeva treats ontogenesis as a direct mediation of biology by language, her biologism depicts drives as transhistorical and not as effects of material relations, although partially mediated by language. See Henessey's critique, in *Materialist Feminism*, 49.

38. In both SP and TS Irigaray demonstrates that the western philosophical corpus is organized around a phallocentric libidinal economy. By this she means that western rationality "promulgates" a patriarchal value system that selectively valorizes the imagery of solids over that of liquids, an optics of sight over one of touch, visibility over mucosity, "property, production, order, form, unity and . . . erection" over the "continuous, compressible, dilatable, viscous, conductible, diffusible" (TS, 86, 111).

39. Cornell, *Beyond Accommodation*, 178, 171 (long quotation), 178, 78 (in order). Fuss, *Essentially Speaking*, 55–72 and Whitford, *Luce Irigaray*, 84–97, 177ff. argue persuasively that Irigaray does not seek to replace the

preexisting western phallic symbolic system with a new, static, and dominant matriarchal symbolic system revolving around the vaginal image of women's two lips. But Cornell argues that Whitford neglects the utopian dimension in Irigaray's work and that the only way to prevent a symbolization of the female imaginary from solidifying into a substitutive, but static symbolic is to understand Irigaray's thought as a variety of critical fantasy or critical mythology (77). Bartky (*Femininity*, 33–62) provides a more concrete analysis than Irigaray of the connection between patriarchal symbolism and women's lack of self-determination.

40. Cornell, *Beyond Accommodation*, 186.

41. Cornell, *Beyond Accommodation*, 181. I do not mean to attribute a full-blown nominalism to Cornell as this would distort comprehension of her work. Because she understands gender in contextual terms as a social construct with real effects, Cornell aptly claims that she is not a nominalist. Here I intend only to note how poststructuralist theories take one element of nominalism—that universals exist only *post res*—and utilize this intuition to break the binary logic of thinking particulars as subsumed under universals at the expense of exploring the irreducible specificity of particular things.

42. Cornell, *Beyond Accommodation*, 195 (all quotations).

43. Babbitt, "Identity, Knowledge, and Toni Morrison's *Beloved*," 3.

44. Cornell, *Beyond Accommodation*, 194. Babbitt, "Identity, Knowledge, and Toni Morrison's *Beloved*," 4. I treat Cornell's ethical theory, as filled out in her *Philosophy of the Limit*, in the concluding chapter. But again Cornell rightly realizes the need to connect textual practice to an ethics.

45. Cornell, *Beyond Accommodation*, 195.

46. Ibid., 195.

47. The recent Zapatista movement in Chiapas offers a good example of the way that local liberation and regional autonomy depend upon global resistance to neoliberal economic and political policies.

48. It would be inaccurate to imply that a good many authors have not worked on this topic. I wonder whether reliance upon certain uses of poststructuralism either gives the impression that such works do not already exist or fails to contribute to such work. For comments on sexual relations in the slaveholding system, see e.g., hooks, *Yearning*, 57–64; Davis, *Women, Race, Class*, chaps. 1–4. For a critique of the ethnocentrism latent in earlier white feminist analyses of race-sex dynamics (for example, Beauvoir's *The Second Sex*, Millet's *Sexual Politics*, Firestone's *The Dialectic of Sex*), see Simons, "Racism and Feminism." King's "Multiple Jeopardy," Hurtado's "Relating to Privilege," and Higginbotham's "African-American Women's History" make excellent contributions to isolating key differences in women's forms of oppression.

49. For example, should we materialize the masculine-feminine dyad in discrete white-on-white, black-on-black relationships? Even if we flesh out the white male–black female or white female–black male relationship, this would not deliver us to the white female–black female relationship as it exists in a larger racialized and genderized world. Such relations are not finally bipolar. Spike Lee's *Jungle Fever* suffices to suggest that the social practices that embody the fears, erotic fantasies, and aggression bound up with this multidimensional knot, though perhaps modified in form, have not left the world of U.S. race relations. Or perhaps the definitively racist subtext of *A Time to Kill* better exemplifies this fact.

50. Du Bois, *Souls*, 15.

51. Fraser, "The Uses and Abuses," 177.

52. Moraga, "From a Long Line of Vendidas," 204–5.

53. Ibid., 208–11.

54. Bilingual education could decenter the viewpoint that real Americans speak English, help curtail the imperalist mentality that all the world should speak U.S. English, and conceptually open venues to perceive the world differently. While no single student or educational system could be expected to learn or teach five languages representative of our culturally diverse society, two languages are practically manageable and symbolically indicative of a normative ideal of cultural pluralism.

55. Butler, "Variations," 142.

56. Stabile, *The Technological Fix*, 44; for her extended dicussion, see "Introduction," and chaps. 1 and 5.

57. Babbitt's cogent analysis of Cornell comes to a similar conclusion in "Identity, Knowledge, and Toni Morrison's *Beloved*," 17.

58. Lugones and Spelman, "Have We Got a Theory for You!" 23.

59. Anzaldúa ("Bridge," 226) employs Alexander Mitscherlich's definition of prejudice (see 231 n. 15 for reference); but it is her discussion of prejudice that interests me (216–31).

Chapter 8. Asymmetrical Reciprocity

1. McGowan, *Postmodernism*, 5, 6 (in order). West, *Prophetic Fragments*, 170.

2. Gordon, *Bad Faith*, 151 (misanthropy), 105 (warped desire), 150 (human relations).

3. Ibid., 153, 155 (in order).

4. Vieux, "In the Shadow of Neo-liberal Racism," 25.

5. An innovative effort to reconcile Derridean deconstruction with materialism can be found in Bill Martin's *Matrix and Line*.

6. Cornell, *Beyond Accommodation*, 186–90, 194–96; *The Philosophy of the Limit*, 53–54. I am indebted to Jodi Dean for the insight that Cornell's second book, *The Philosophy of the Limit*, provides the theoretical and ethical foundations for the project of critical utopianism advanced in the first book, *Beyond Accommodation*. See also Dean, "Beyond the Equality/Difference Dilemma," 160–63.

7. Cornell, *The Philosophy of the Limit*, 54. Willett, *Maternal Ethics*, 76, 81 (in order). In her "Asymmetrical Reciprocity" Iris Young mistakenly equates Irigaray's view of alterity with that of Levinas (19).

8. See Cornell, *The Philosophy of the Limit*, 50, 53, 56–61, and chap. 3.

9. Cornell, *Beyond Accommodation*, 56.

10. Cornell turns to philosophy of law to support such possibilities.

11. Cornell, *Beyond Accommodation*, 131.

12. Cornell, *The Philosophy of the Limit*, 80, 81, 86, 87.

13. Unless issuing a moral-imperative to redress material conditions of asymmetry, the ideal of ethical asymmetry remains overly idealist. And poetic sensibility must find its complement in concrete practices for managing conflicts and diversity of needs. Why should Cornell's concept of ethical asymmetry not denote, in addition to cultural nonidentity, material nonequality? My answer is that it can. Pressing the Heideggerian side of Irigaray allows for a more holistic description of ethical asymmetry by discussing the manifold conditions—symbolic, material, and interactive—necessary to achieve moral respect.

14. Harris, "Postmodernism and Utopia," 36, 40.

15. Ibid., 36.

16. Benhabib, "Feminism and Postmodernism" 139. Harris, "Postmodernism and Utopia," 40–41, 41 (in order).

17. Lugones, "Playfulness," 289.

18. Ibid., 290.

19. Anzaldúa, "Bridge," 217–19; also *Borderlands / La Frontera*. Cf. Alarcón, "The Theoretical Subject(s)," 364–65. These works are representative of a much more pervasive phenomenon of the double-bind which many groups suffer.

20. Omi and Winant demonstrate the irreducibility of race to "ethnic-, group-, class-, or nation-based perspectives," in *Racial Formation in the United States*, 52–54, passim. For representative discussions of additive approaches to race and gender, see Spelman, *Inessential Woman*, chap. 5; King,

"Multiple Jeopardy"; Hurtado, "Relating to Privilege": Abel, "Race, Class, and Psychoanalysis?"; Smith, "Introduction"; Davis, *Women, Race, Class*.

21. Benhabib, *Situating the Self*, 4, 6.

22. Ibid., 152–53 (all quotations).

23. Ibid., 161, 162.

24. Ibid., 168.

25. Shrage, *Moral Dilemmas*, 14 (all quotations).

26. Benhabib, *Situating the Self*, 169; on polygamy, see 42–43. Shrage, *Moral Dilemmas*, 14; see her discussion of polygamy on 17.

27. Benhabib, *Situating the Self*, 161.

28. Marcuse, *One-Dimensional Man*, 212. White, "Heidegger," 81.

29. Young, "Asymmetrical Reciprocity," 346, 348, 352 (in order).

30. Ibid., 352–353 (all quotations).

31. See Gordon, *Bad Faith*, 154–55 and 119–20.

32. I follow Benhabib and Young in adopting Arendt's concept of enlarged thought. Young defends Arendt's notion as incongruous with Benhabib's application of it to reversibility. See Benhabib, *Situating the Self*, 53–54, 137–41; Young, "Asymmetrical Reciprocity," 358–361; and Arendt, *The Human Condition*, 52–57.

33. Benhabib, *Situating the Self*, 168.

Abbreviations

Works by Heidegger

English reference will be followed by the German. Where a single text provides the English translation page by page alongside the German original (e.g., LR) only a single reference is given. And where margin numbers in the German align with margin numbers in the English translation one reference will be supplied (e.g., SZ).

BW   *Basic Writings*. Ed. David Farrell Krell. New York: Harper and Row, 1977.

DT   *Discourse on Thinking*. Trans. John M. Anderson and E. Hans Freund. New York: Harper and Row, 1966.

EGT   *Early Greek Thinking*. Trans. David Farrell Krell and Frank A. Capuzzi. New York: Harper and Row, 1975.

EHD   *Erläuterungen zu Hölderlins Dichtung*. Vierte, erweiterte Auflage. Frankfurt am Main: Vittorio Klostermann, 1981.

EM   *Einführung in die Metaphysik*. Tübingen: Max Niemeyer, 1953.

EP   *The End of Philosophy*. Trans. Joan Stambaugh. New York: Harper and Row, 1973.

FC   *The Fundamental Concepts of Metaphysics: World, Finitude, Solitude*. Trans. William McNeill and Nicholas Walker. Bloomington: Indiana University Press, 1995.

FL   *The Metaphysical Foundations of Logic*. Trans. Michael Heim. Bloomington: Indiana University Press, 1984.

G   *Gelassenheit*. Pfullingen: Günther Neske, 1959.

GA 26   *Metaphysische Anfangsgründe der Logik im Ausgang von Leibniz*. Frankfurt am Main: Vittorio Klostermann, 1978.

GA 39   *Hölderlins Hymnen "Germanien" und "Der Rhein."* Frankfurt am Main: Vittorio Klostermann, 1980.

GA 43   _Nietzsche: Der Wille zur Macht als Kunst._ Frankfurt am Main: Vittorio Klostermann, 1985.

GA 47   _Nietzsches Lehre vom Willen zur Macht als Erkenntnis._ Frankfurt am Main: Vittorio Klostermann, 1989.

GA 56/57   _Zur Bestimmung der Philosophie._ Frankfurt am Main: Vittorio Klostermann, 1987.

GA 65   _Beiträge zur Philosophie (Vom Ereignis)._ Frankfurt am Main: Vittorio Klostermann, 1989.

H   _Holzwege._ Frankfurt am Main: Vittorio Klostermann, 1977.

ID   _Identity and Difference._ Trans. Joan Stambaugh. New York: Harper and Row, 1969. Since this edition contains the English translation and the German original, pagination will cite the English/German. [_Identität und Differenz._ Vierte, unveränderte Auflage. Pfullingen: Günther Neske, 1957.]

IM   _An Introduction to Metaphysics._ Trans. Ralph Manheim. New Haven: Yale University Press, 1959.

LR   "Letter to the Rector of Freiburg University, November 4, 1945." In _The Heidegger Controversy,_ ed. Richard Wolin, 61–66.

N1–2   _Nietzsche: The Will to Power as Art_ (N1) and _The Eternal Recurrence of the Same_ (N2). Vols. 1 and 2. Trans. David Farrell Krell. New York: Harper and Row, 1991.

N3–4   _Nietzsche: The Will to Power as Knowledge and as Metaphysics_ (N3) and _Nihilism_ (N4). Vols. 3 and 4. Ed. David Farrell Krell. New York: Harper and Row, 1991.

NI, NII   _Nietzsche._ Two volumes. Pfullingen: Günther Neske, 1961.

OTB   _On Time and Being._ Trans. Joan Stambaugh. New York: Harper and Row, 1972.

OWL   _On the Way to Language._ Trans. Peter D. Hertz. New York: Harper and Row, 1971.

P   _Parmenides._ Trans. André Schuwer and Richard Rojcewicz. Bloomington: Indiana University Press, 1992.

Pa   _Parmenides,_ GA 54. Frankfurt am Main: Vittorio Klostermann, 1982.

PD   "Plato's Doctrine of Truth." Trans. John Barlow. In _Philosophy in the Twentieth Century,_ vol. 3, ed. William Barrett and Henry D. Aiken, 251–70. New York: Random House, 1962.

PLT   _Poetry, Language, and Thought._ Trans. Albert Hofstadter. New York: Harper and Row, 1971.

PR   *The Principle of Reason.* Trans. Reginald Lilly. Bloomington: Indiana University Press, 1991.

PT   "Political Texts, 1933–1934." In Wolin, *The Heidegger Controversy*, 40–60.

QCT   *The Question Concerning Technology and Other Essays.* Trans. William Lovitt. New York: Harper and Row, 1977.

Rich   "Letter to Richardson." In William J. Richardson, S. J., *Heidegger: Through Phenomenology to Thought.* The Hague: Martinus Nijhoff, 1963.

SA   "The Self-Assertion of the German University." In *The Heidegger Controversy*, ed. Richard Wolin, 29–39.

SB   *Die Selbstbehauptung der deutschen Universität / Das Rektorat, 1933 / 34: Tatsachen und Gedanken.* Frankfurt am Main: Vittorio Klostermann, 1983.

SG   *Der Satz vom Grund.* Pfullingen: Günther Neske, 1957.

Spieg   "Only a God Can Save Us." *Der Spiegel's* interview with Martin Heidegger (1966). In *The Heidegger Controversy*, ed. Richard Wolin, 91–116. Originally pubished as "Nur ein Gott kann uns noch retten," in *Der Spiegel*, 31 May 1976.

SZ=BT   *Being and Time.* Trans. John Macquarrie and Edward Robinson. New York: Harper and Row, 1962. *Sein und Zeit.* Frankfurt am Main: Vittorio Klostermann, 1977.

US   *Unterwegs zur Sprache.* Frankfurt am Main: Vittorio Klostermann, 1985.

VA   *Vorträge und Aufsätze.* Sechte Auflage. Pfullingen: Günther Neske, 1954.

W   *Wegmarken.* Frankfurt am Main: Vittorio Klostermann, 1976.

WD   *Was heisst Denken?* Tübingen: Max Niemeyer, 1954.

WT   *What is Called Thinking?* Trans. J. Glenn Gray. New York: Harper and Row, 1968.

ZSD   *Zur Sache des Denkens.* Tübingen: Max Niemeyer, 1969.

Works by Julia Kristeva

BL   *In the Beginning Was Love: Psychoanalysis and Faith.* Trans. Arthur Goldhammer. New York: Columbia University Press, 1987.

BS   *Black Sun*. Trans. Leon S. Roudiez. New York: Columbia University Press, 1989.

DL   *Desire in Language: A Semiotic Approach to Literature and Art.* Ed. Leon S. Roudiez. Trans. Thomas Gora, Alice Jardine, and Leon S. Roudiez. New York: Columbia University Press, 1980.

Osc   "Oscillation between Power and Denial." In *New French Feminisms,* ed. Elaine Marks and Isabelle de Courtivron, 165–67.

PH   *Powers of Horror: An Essay on Abjection*. Trans. Leon S. Roudiez. New York: Columbia University Press, 1982.

Psy   "Psychoanalysis and the Polis." Trans. Margaret Waller. *Critical Inquiry* 9, no. 1 (September 1982): 77–92.

RP   *Revolution in Poetic Language*. Trans. Margaret Waller. New York: Columbia University Press, 1984.

Str   *Strangers to Ourselves*. Trans. Leon S. Roudiez. New York: Columbia University Press, 1991.

TL   *Tales of Love*. Trans. Leon S. Roudiez. New York: Columbia University Press, 1987.

W   "Woman Can Never Be Defined." In *New French Feminisms,* ed. Elaine Marks and Isabelle de Courtivron, 137–41.

WT   "Women's Time." In *The Kristeva Reader,* ed. Toril Moi, 187–213.

Works by Luce Irigaray

AM   *Amante marine. De Friedrich Nietzche*. Paris: Éditions de Minuit, 1980.

E   *An Ethics of Sexual Difference*. Trans. Carolyn Burke and Gillian C. Gill. Ithaca, N.Y.: Cornell University Press, 1993.

Diff   "Sexual Difference." In *French Feminist Thought,* ed. Toril Moi, 118–30.

Dis   "The Power of Discourse and the Subordination of the Feminine." In *The Irigaray Reader,* ed. Margaret Whitford, 118–32.

Gen   *Sexes and Genealogies*. Trans. Gillian C. Gill. New York: Columbia University Press, 1993.

ML   *Marine Lover of Friedrich Nietzsche*. Trans. Gillian C. Gill. New York: Columbia University Press, 1991.

OA	*L'Oubli de l'air chez Martin Heidegger*. Paris: Éditions de Minuit, 1983.
Par	*Sexes et parentés*. Paris: Éditions de Minuit, 1987.
R	"He Risks Who Risks Life Itself." In *The Irigaray Reader,* ed. Margaret Whitford, 213–18.
SD	"Sexual Difference." In *The Irigaray Reader,* ed. Margaret Whitford, 165–77.
SP	*Speculum of the Other Woman*. Trans. Gillian C. Gill. Ithaca, N.Y.: Cornell University Press, 1985.
TS	*This Sex which Is Not One*. Trans. Catherine Porter with Carolyn Burke. Ithaca, N.Y.: Cornell University Press, 1985.

Other Abbreviations

EaM	Bigwood, Carol. *Earth Muse: Feminism, Nature, and Art*. Philadelphia: Temple University Press, 1993.
LF	Graybeal, Jean. *Language and "The Feminine" in Nietzsche and Heidegger*. Bloomington: Indiana University Press, 1990.
NS	National Socialism

Bibliography

Abel, Elizabeth. "Race, Class, and Psychoanalysis? Opening Questions." In *Conflicts in Feminism,* ed. Marianne Hirsch and Evelyn Fox Keller, 184–204. New York: Routledge, 1990.

Adell, Sandra. *Double-Consciousness / Double-Bind: Theoretical Issues in Twentieth-Century Black Literature.* Urbana and Chicago: University of Illinois Press, 1994.

Alarcón, Norma. "The Theoretical Subject(s) of *This Bridge Called My Back* and Anglo-American Feminism." In *Making Face, Making Soul / Hacienda caras,* ed. Gloria Anzaldúa, 364–65.

Albrecht, Lisa and Rose M. Brewer. "Bridges of Power: Women's Multicultural Alliances." In *Bridges of Power,* ed. Lisa Albrecht and Rose M. Brewer, 2–22.

Albrecht, Lisa and Rose M. Brewer, eds. *Bridges of Power: Women's Multicultural Alliances.* Philadelphia: New Society Publishers, 1990.

Alcoff, Linda. "Cultural Feminism versus Poststructuralism: The Identity Crises in Feminist Theory." In *Feminist Theory in Practice and Process,* ed. Micheline R. Malson et al., 295–326. Chicago: University of Chicago Press, 1989. Originally published in *Signs: Journal of Women in Culture and Society* 13, no. 3 (spring 1988).

Alcoff, Linda and Elizabeth Potter. "Introduction: When Feminisms Intersect Epistemology." In *Feminist Epistemologies*, ed. Linda Alcoff and Elizabeth Potter, 1–14.

Alcoff, Linda and Elizabeth Potter, eds. *Feminist Epistemologies.* New York: Routledge, 1993.

Alperin, Davida. "Social Diversity and the Necessity of Alliances: A Developing Perspective." In *Bridges of Power,* ed. Lisa Albrecht and Rose M. Brewer, 23–33.

Anzaldúa, Gloria. *Borderlands / La Frontera: The New Mestiza.* San Francisco: Spinsters/Aunt Lute, 1987.

————. "Bridge, Drawbridge, Sandbar or Island: Lesbians-of-Color *Haci-enda Alianzas.*" In *Bridges of Power,* ed. Lisa Albrecht and Rose M. Brewer, 216–31.

Anzaldúa, Gloria, ed. *Making Face, Making Soul / Haciendo caras: Creative and Critical Perspectives by Feminists-of-Color.* San Francisco: Spinsters/Aunt Lute, 1990.

Arendt, Hannah. *The Human Condition.* Chicago: University of Chicago Press, 1958.

Armour, Ellen. "Questions of Proximity: 'Woman's Place' in Derrida and Irigaray." *Hypatia: A Journal of Feminist Philosophy* 12, no. 1 (winter 1997): 63–78.

Asante, Molefi Kete. "Racing to Leave the Race: Black Postmodernists Off-Track." *The Black Scholar: The Multicultural Debate* 23, nos. 3, 4 (1993): 50–51.

Aschheim, Steven E. *The Nietzsche Legacy in Germany 1890–1990.* Berkeley: University of California Press, 1994.

Babbitt, Susan E. "Identity, Knowledge, and Toni Morrison's *Beloved*: Questions about Understanding Racism." *Hypatia: A Journal of Feminist Philosophy* 9, no. 3 (summer 1994): 1–18.

Balibar, Etienne and Immanuel Wallerstein. *Race, Nation, Class: Ambiguous Identities.* Trans. Chris Turner. New York and London: Verso, 1991.

Ballard, B. W. "Marxist Challenges to Heidegger on Alienation and Authenticity." *Man and World* 23 (1990): 121–41.

Bartky, Sandra Lee. *Femininity and Domination: Studies in the Phenomenology of Oppression.* New York: Routledge, 1990.

————. "Originative Thinking in the Later Philosophy of Heidegger." *Philosophy and Phenomenological Research* 30 (1970): 368–81.

————. "Sympathy and Solidarity: On a Tightrope with Scheler." In *Feminists Rethink the Self,* ed. Diane Tietjens Meyers, 177–96.

Beauvoir, Simone de. *The Second Sex.* Trans. E. M. Parshley. New York: Vintage, 1973.

Benhabib, Seyla. "Feminism and Postmodernism: An Uneasy Alliance." *Praxis International* 11, no. 2 (July 1991): 137–49.

————. "The Generalized and the Concrete Other: The Kohlberg-Gilligan Controversy and Feminist Theory." In *Feminism as Critique,* ed. Seyla Benhabib and Drucilla Cornell, 77–95.

———. *Situating the Self: Gender, Community, and Postmodernism in Contemporary Ethics.* New York: Routledge, 1992.

Benhabib, Seyla and Drucilla Cornell. "Beyond the Politics of Gender." Introduction. In *Feminism as Critique,* ed. Seyla Benhabib and Drucilla Cornell, 1–15.

Benhabib, Seyla and Drucilla Cornell, eds. *Feminism as Critique.* Minneapolis: University of Minnesota Press, 1987.

Benjamin, Walter. "Theorien des deutschen Faschismus." In *Gesammelte Schriften,* vol. 3, ed. Hella Tiedemann-Bartels, 238–50. Frankfurt am Main: Suhrkamp Verlag, 1972.

———. "Theories of German Fascism: On the Collection of Essays *War and Warrior,* edited by Ernst Jünger." *New German Critique* 17 (spring 1979): 120–28.

Bernasconi, Robert. *The Question of Language in Heidegger's History of Being.* Atlantic Highlands, N.J.: Humanities Press International, 1985.

———. "Seeing Double: *Destruktion* and Deconstruction." In *Dialogue and Deconstruction,* ed. Diane Michelfelder and Richard E. Palmer, 233–50.

———. "The Transformation of Language at Another Beginning." *Research in Phenomenology* 13 (1983): 1–23.

Bernstein, Richard J. *The New Constellation: The Ethical-Political Horizons of Modernity/Postmodernity.* Cambridge: Massachusetts Institute of Technology Press, 1992.

Berthold-Bond, Daniel. "A Kierkegaardian Critique of Heidegger's Concept of Authenticity." *Man and World* 24 (1991): 119–42.

Berry, Wanda Warren. "Kierkegaard and Feminism: Apologetic, Repetition, and Dialogue." In *Kierkegaard in Post/Modernity,* ed. Martin J. Matuštík and Merold Westphal, 110–24.

Birmingham, Peg. "Ever Respectfully Mine: Heidegger on Agency and Responsibility." In *Ethics and Danger: Essays on Heidegger and Continental Thought,* ed. Arleen B. Dallery and Charles E. Scott with P. Holley Roberts, 109–23. Albany: State University of New York Press, 1992.

———. "*Logos* and the Place of the Other," *Research in Phenomenology* 20 (1990): 34–53.

———. "The Time of the Political." *Graduate Faculty Philosophy Journal* 14, no. 1; 15, no. 2 (1991): 25–42.

Bock, Gisela and Susan James, eds. *Beyond Equality and Difference: Citizenship, Feminist Politics, and Female Subjectivity*. London and New York: Routledge, 1992.

Bohrer, Karl Heinz. *Ästhetik des Schreckens: Die pessimistische Romantik und Ernst Jüngers Frühwerk*. Munich: Hanser, 1978.

Bordo, Susan. "Feminism, Postmodernism, and Gender-Scepticism." In *Feminism/Postmodernism*, ed. Linda Nicholson, 133–56.

Braidotti, Rosi. "On the Female Feminist Subject, Or: From 'She-Self' to 'She-Other'." In *Beyond Equality and Difference*, ed. Gisela Bock and Susan James, 176–92.

Bréhier, Émile. *The Hellenistic and Roman Age*. Trans. Wade Baskin. Chicago: University of Chicago Press, 1965.

Brown, Alison Leigh. *Fear, Truth, Writing: From Paper Village to Electronic Community*. Albany: State University of New York Press, 1995.

———. "God, Anxiety, and Female Divinity." In *Kierkegaard in Post/Modernity*, ed. Martin J. Matuštík and Merold Westphal, 66–75.

Bruns, Gerald. *Heidegger's Estrangements: Language, Truth, and Poetry in the Later Writings*. New Haven: Yale University Press, 1989.

Brunzina, Ronald. "Heidegger on the Metaphor and Philosophy." In *Heidegger and Modern Philosophy*, ed. Michael Murray, 184–200. New Haven: Yale University Press, 1978.

Bunch, Charlotte. "Making Common Cause: Diversity and Coalitions." In *Bridges of Power*, ed. Lisa Albrecht and Rose M. Brewer, 49–60.

Burke, Carolyn. "Irigaray through the Looking Glass." *Feminist Studies* 7, no. 2 (summer 1981): 288–306. Reprinted in *Engaging With Irigaray*, ed. Carolyn Burke, Naomi Schor, and Margaret Whitford, 37–56.

Burke, Carolyn, Naomi Schor, and Margaret Whitford, eds. *Engaging With Irigaray: Feminist Philosophy and Modern European Thought*. New York: Columbia University Press, 1994.

Butler, Judith. "The Body Politics of Julia Kristeva." In *Ethics, Politics, and Difference*, ed. Kelly Oliver, 164–78.

———. "Contingent Foundations: Feminism and the Question of 'Postmodernism'." *Praxis International* 11, no. 2 (July 1991): 155–65.

———. *Gender Trouble: Feminism and the Subversion of Identity*. New York: Routledge, 1990.

———. "Gender Trouble, Feminist Theory, and Psychoanalytic Discourse." In *Feminism/Postmodernism*, ed. Linda Nicholson, 324–40.

———. "Variations on Sex and Gender: Beauvoir, Wittig and Foucault." In *Feminism As Critique*, ed. Seyla Benhabib and Drucilla Cornell, 128–42.

Caputo, John D. "Demythologizing Heidegger: *Alētheia* and the History of Being." *Review of Metaphysics* 41 (March 1988): 519–46.

———. "Heidegger's *Kampf*: The Difficulty of Life." *Graduate Faculty Philosophy Journal* 14, no. 2; 15, no. 1 (1991): 61–83.

———. "Heidegger's Scandal: Thinking and the Essence of the Victim." In *The Heidegger Case*, ed. Tom Rockmore and Joseph Margolis, 265–81.

———. "Hermeneutics as Recovery of Man." *Man and World* 15 (1982): 343–67.

———. "Incarnation and Essentialization: A Reading of Heidegger." *Philosophy Today* 35, no. 1 (spring 1991): 32–42.

———. "Phenomenology, Mysticism, and the '*Grammatica Speculativa*': A Study of Heidegger's '*Habilitationsschrift*'." *Journal of the British Society for Phenomenology* 5, no. 2 (May 1974): 101–17.

———. *Radical Hermeneutics: Repetition, Deconstruction, and the Hermeneutic Project*. Bloomington: Indiana University Press, 1987.

———. "'Supposing Truth to Be a Woman . . .': Heidegger, Nietzsche, Derrida." *Tulane Studies in Philosophy* 32 (1984): 15–21.

———. "Thinking, Poetry, and Pain." *Southern Journal of Philosophy* 28, supplement: "Heidegger and Praxis" (1989): 155–81.

Castoriadis, Cornelius. *L'Institution imaginaire de la société*. Paris: Seuil, 1975. [*The Imaginary Institution of Society*. Trans. Kathleen McLaughlin. Cambridge: Polity Press, 1987.]

Chanter, Tina. *Ethics of Eros: Irigaray's Rewriting of the Philosophers*. New York: Routledge, 1990.

Chodorow, Nancy. *The Reproduction of Mothering*. Berkeley: University of California Press, 1978.

Ciaffa, Jay A. "Toward an Understanding of Heidegger's Conception of the Inter-relation between Authentic and Inauthentic Existence." *Journal of the British Society for Phenomenology* 18, no. 1 (January 1987): 49–59.

Cixous, Hélène and Catherine Clément. *The Newly Born Woman*. Trans. Betsy Wing. Minneapolis: University of Minneapolis Press, 1986.

Cohn, Carol. "'Clean Bombs' and Clean Language." In *Women, Militarism, and War*, ed. Jean Bethke Elshtain and Sheila Tobias, 33–55. Savage, Mass.: Rowman and Littlefield Publishers, Inc., 1990.

Collins, Patricia Hill. "Setting Our Own Agenda." *The Black Scholar: The Multicultural Debate* 23, nos. 3, 4 (1993): 52–55.

———. "The Social Construction of Black Feminist Thought." *Signs: Journal of Women in Culture and Society* 14, no. 4 (1989): 745–73.

Conley, Verena Andermatt. *Hélène Cixous: Writing the Feminine.* Lincoln: University of Nebraska Press, 1984.

Connell, George B. and C. Stephen Evans. Introduction. In *Foundations of Kierkegaard's Vision of Community*, ed. George B. Connell and C. Stephen Evans, vii–xxii. Atlantic Highlands, N.J.: Humanities Press, 1992.

Copjec, Joan. "Sex and the Euthanasia of Reason." In *Supposing the Subject*, ed. Joan Copjec, 16–44. New York and London: Verso Press, 1994.

Cornell, Drucilla. *Beyond Accommodation: Ethical Feminism, Deconstruction, and the Law.* New York: Routledge, 1991.

———. *The Philosophy of the Limit.* New York: Routledge, 1992.

———. *Transformations: Recollective Imagination and Sexual Difference.* New York: Routledge, 1993.

Cornell, Drucilla and Adam Thurschwell. "Feminism, Negativity, Intersubjectivity." In *Feminism as Critique*, ed. Seyla Benhabib and Drucilla Cornell, 143–62.

Crownfield, David R. "The Sublimation of Narcissism in Christian Love and Faith." In *Body / Text in Julia Kristeva: Religion, Women, and Psychoanalysis*, ed. David R. Crownfield, 7–64. Albany: State University of New York Press, 1992.

Cutrofello, Andrew. *Discipline and Critique: Kant, Poststructuralism, and the Problem of Resistance.* Albany: State University of New York Press, 1994.

Dallmayr, Fred. *Between Freiburg and Frankfurt.* Amherst: University of Massachusetts Press, 1991.

Dauenhauer, Bernard P. "Does Anarchy Make Political Sense? A Response to Schürmann." *Human Studies* 1 (1978): 369–75.

Davis, Angela Y. *Women, Race, and Class.* New York: Random House, 1983.

Dean, Jodi. "Beyond the Equality/Difference Dilemma." *Philosophy and Social Criticism* 20, no. 1, issue 1 (1994): 155–70.

Deely, John N. *The Tradition via Heidegger.* The Hague: Martinus Nijhoff, 1971.

Derrida, Jacques. "*Geschlecht:* Sexual Difference, Ontological Difference." *Research in Phenomenology* 13 (1983): 65–83.

———. *"Geschlecht* II: Heidegger's Hand." In *Deconstruction and Philosophy: The Texts of Jacques Derrida*, ed. John Sallis, 161–96. Chicago: University of Chicago Press, 1987.

———. *Margins of Philosophy*. Trans. Alan Bass. Chicago: University of Chicago Press, 1982.

———. "Of an Apocalyptic Tone Recently Adopted in Philosophy." Trans. John P. Leavey. *Semeia* 23 (1982): 63–97.

———. *Of Grammatology*. Trans. Gayatri Chakravorty Spivak. Baltimore: The Johns Hopkins University Press, 1976.

———. *Of Spirit: Heidegger and the Question*. Trans. Geoffrey Bennington and Rachel Bowlby. Chicago: University of Chicago Press, 1989.

———. *Spurs: Nietzsche's Styles/Éperons: Les styles de Nietzsche*. Trans. Barbara Harlow. Chicago: University of Chicago Press, 1979.

Derrida, Jacques and Christie V. McDonald. "Choreographies." *Diacritics* 12 (summer 1982): 66–76. Reprinted in *The Ear of the Other: Otobiography, Transference, Translation*, ed. Christie V. McDonald, trans. Peggy Kamuf. Lincoln: University of Nebraska Press, 1985.

Dilthey, Wilhelm. *Introduction to the Human Sciences, Selected Works*. Vol. 1. Ed. Rudolf A. Makkreel and Frithof Rodi. Princeton: Princeton University Press, 1989.

Dinnerstein, Dorothy. *The Mermaid and the Minotaur: Sexual Arrangements and Human Malaise*. New York: Harper Books, 1976.

duBois, Page. *Sowing the Body: Psychoanalysis and Ancient Representations of Women*. Chicago: University of Chicago Press, 1988.

Du Bois, W. E. Burghardt. *The Souls of Black Folk*. Greenwich, Conn.: Fawcett Publications, 1968.

Dwinger, Edwin Erich. *Auf halbem Wege*. Jena: 1939.

Fanon, Frantz. *Black Skin, White Masks*. Trans. Charles Lam Markmann. New York: Grove Press, 1967.

———. *The Wretched of the Earth*. Trans. Constance Farrington. New York: Grove Press, 1963.

Farías, Victor. *Heidegger et le nazisme*. Trans. Myriam Benarroch and Jean-Baptist Grasset. Paris: Verdier, 1987.

Ferry, Luc and Alain Renaut. *Heidegger and Modernity*. Trans. Franklin Philip. Chicago: University of Chicago Press, 1990.

Firestone, Shulamith. *The Dialectic of Sex: The Case for Feminist Revolution*. New York: William and Morrow, 1970.

Flax, Jane. *Thinking Fragments: Psychoanalysis, Feminism, and Post-modernism in the Contemporary West*. Berkeley: University of California Press, 1990.

Forst, Rainer. "How (Not) to Speak about Identity: The Concept of the Person in a Theory of Justice." *Philosophy and Social Criticism* 18, nos. 3, 4 (1992): 293–312.

Foucault, Michel. "Why Study Power: The Question of the Subject." In *Michel Foucault: Beyond Structuralism and Hermeneutics*, 2d ed., ed. Hubert L. Dreyfus and Paul Rabinow, 208–26. Chicago: University of Chicago Press, 1983.

Frank, Manfred. "Limits of the Human Control of Language: Dialogue as the Place of Difference between Neostructuralism and Hermeneutics." In *Dialogue and Deconstruction*, ed. Diane P. Michelfelder and Richard E. Palmer, 150–61.

Franzen, Winfried. "Die Sehnsucht nach Härte und Schwere. Über ein zum NS-Engagement disponierendes Motiv in Heideggers Vorlesung 'Die Grundbegriffe der Metaphysik'." In *Heidegger und die praktische Philosophie*, ed. Annemarie Gethmann-Siefert and Otto Pöggeler, 78–92. Frankfurt am Main: Suhrkamp, 1988.

Fraser, Nancy. "False Antitheses: A Response to Seyla Benhabib and Judith Butler." *Praxis International* 11, no. 2 (July 1991): 166–77.

———. "The French Derrideans: Politicizing Deconstruction or Deconstructing the Political?" *New German Critique* 33 (fall 1984): 127–54.

———. *Unruly Practices: Power, Discourse and Gender in Contemporary Social Theory*. Minneapolis: University of Minnesota Press, 1989.

———. "The Uses and Abuses of French Discourse Theories for Feminist Politics." In *Revaluing French Feminism*, ed. Nancy Fraser and Sandra Lee Bartky, 177–94.

Fraser, Nancy and Sandra Lee Bartky, eds. *Revaluing French Feminism: Critical Essays on Difference, Agency, and Culture*. Bloomington: Indiana University Press, 1992.

Fraser, Nancy and Linda Nicholson, "Social Criticism without Philosophy: An Encounter between Feminism and Postmodernism." In *Feminism/Postmodernism*, ed. Linda Nicholson, 19–38.

Freud, Sigmund. *Beyond the Pleasure Principle*. Ed. and trans. James Strachey. New York: W. W. Norton and Co., 1961.

———. "The Ego and the Id." *Standard Edition of the Complete Works of Sigmund Freud*, vol. 19, ed. and trans. James Strachey, 1–66. London: The Hogarth Press, 1951–73.

———. "The Unconscious." *Standard Edition of the Complete Works of Sigmund Freud,* vol. 14, ed. and trans. James Strachey, 159–215. London: The Hogarth Press, 1951–73.

Fried, Gregory. "Heidegger's *Polemos.*" *Journal of Philosophical Research* 16 (1990–91): 159–95.

Fuss, Diana. "'Essentially Speaking': Luce Irigaray's Language of Essence." *Hypatia* 3, no. 3 (winter 1989): 62–80.

———. *Essentially Speaking: Feminism, Nature, Difference.* New York: Routledge, 1989.

Gallop, Jane. "*Quand nos lèvres s'écrivent:* Irigaray's Body Politic." *Romantic Review* 74, no. 1 (January 1983): 77–83.

Garry, Ann and Marilyn Pearsall, eds. *Women, Knowledge, and Reality: Explorations in Feminist Philosophy.* Boston: Unwin Hyman, 1989.

Gethmann, Carl Friedrich. *Verstehen und Auslegung. Das Methodenproblem in der Philosophie Martin Heideggers.* Bonn: Herbert Grundmann, 1974.

Gordon, Lewis R. *Bad Faith and Antiblack Racism.* Atlantic Highlands, N.J.: Humanities Press, 1994.

———. "Black Existential Philosophy." In *Existence in Black,* ed. Lewis R. Gordon, 1–9.

Gordon, Lewis R., ed. *Existence in Black: An Anthology of Black Existential Philosophy.* New York: Routledge, 1997.

Goux, Jean-Joseph. "Luce Irigaray Versus the Utopia of the Neutral Sex." In *Engaging With Irigaray,* ed. Carolyn Burke, Naomi Schor, and Margaret Whitford, 175–90.

Griffiths, Morwenna and Margaret Whitford, eds. *Feminist Perspectives in Philosophy.* Bloomington: Indiana University Press, 1988.

Grimshaw, Jean. "Autonomy and Identity in Feminist Thinking." In *Feminist Perspectives in Philosophy,* ed. Morwenna Griffiths and Margaret Whitford, 90–108.

———. *Philosophy and Feminist Thinking.* Minneapolis: University of Minnesota Press, 1986.

Grosz, Elizabeth. "Derrida, Irigaray and Deconstruction." *Intervention* 20 (1986): 70–81.

———. *Lacan: A Feminist Introduction.* London: Routledge, 1990.

Guignon, Charles B. *Heidegger and the Problem of Knowledge.* Indianapolis: Hackett Publishing Co., 1983.

———. "On Saving Heidegger from Rorty." *Philosophy and Phenomeno-logical Research* 46, no. 3 (March 1986): 401–17.

———. "The Twofold Task: Heidegger's Foundational Historicism in *Being and Time.*" *Tulane Studies in Philosophy* 32 (1984): 53–59.

Habermas, Jürgen. "Discourse Ethics: Notes on a Program of Philosophical Justification." In *Moral Consciousness and Communicative Action*, trans. Christian Lenhardt and Shierry Weber Nicholsen, 43–115. Cambridge: MIT Press, 1990.

———. "Historical Consciousness and Post-traditional Identity: The Federal Republic's Orientation to the West." In *The New Conservativism: Cultural Criticism and the Historians' Debate*, ed. and trans. Shierry Weber Nicholsen, 249–67. Cambridge: MIT Press, 1989.

———. *Postmetaphysical Thinking.* Trans. William Mark Hohengarten. Cambridge: MIT Press, 1992.

———. "Work and Weltanschauung: The Heidegger Controversy from a German Perspective." *Critical Inquiry* 15 (winter 1989): 431–56.

Hall, Nora. "African-American Women Leaders and the Politics of Alliance Work." In *Bridges of Power*, ed. Lisa Albrecht and Rose M. Brewer, 74–94.

Harding, Sandra, ed. *Feminism and Methodology.* Bloomington: Indiana University Press, 1987.

Harries, Karsten. "Heidegger as Political Thinker." *Review of Metaphysics* 29 (June 1976): 642–69.

Harris, Leonard. "Postmodernism and Utopia, an Unholy Alliance." In *Racism, the City, and the State*, ed. Malcolm Cross and Michael Keith, 31–44. London and New York: Routledge, 1993.

Hartmann, Heidi. "The Unhappy Marriage of Marxism and Feminism: Towards A More Progressive Union." In *Women and Revolution: A Discussion of the Unhappy Marriage of Marxism and Feminism*, ed. Lydia Sargent, 1–41. Boston: South End Press, 1981.

Hartsock, Nancy C. M. *Money, Sex, and Power: Toward a Feminist Historical Materialism.* Boston: Northeastern University Press, 1983.

———. "Rethinking Modernism: Minority vs. Majority Theories." *Culture Critique* 7 (fall 1987): 187–206.

———. "Theoretical Bases for Coalition Building: An Assessment of Postmodernism." In *Feminism and Social Change: Bridging Theory and Practice*, ed. Heidi Gottfried, 256–74. Urbana: University of Illinois Press, 1996.

Hegel, G. W. F. *Phenomenology of Spirit.* Trans. A. V. Miller. New York: Oxford University Press, 1977.

Hekman, Susan J. *Gender and Knowledge: Elements of a Postmodern Feminism.* Boston: Northeastern University Press, 1990.

———. "Reconstituting the Subject: Feminism, Modernism, and Postmodernism." *Hypatia: A Journal of Feminist Philosophy* 6, no. 2 (summer 1991): 45–63.

Hennessy, Rosemary. *Materialist Feminism and the Politics of Discourse.* New York: Routledge, 1993.

Herf, Jeffrey. *Reactionary Modernism: Technology, Culture, and Politics in Weimar and the Third Reich.* New York: Cambridge University Press, 1984.

Higginbotham, Evelyn Brooks. "African-American Women's History and the Metalanguage of Race." *Signs: Journal of Culture and Society* 17, no. 2 (1992): 251–74.

Hillach, Ansgar. "The Aesthetics of Politics: Walter Benjamin's 'Theories of German Fascism'." *New German Critique* 17 (spring 1979): 99–119.

Hitler, Adolf. Speech to youth group before Berlin Olympics, 1936. On video at the Holocaust Museum, Washington, D.C.

Hodge, Joanna. *Heidegger and Ethics.* London and New York: Routledge, 1995.

———. "Irigaray Reading Heidegger." In *Engaging With Irigaray,* ed. Carolyn Burke, Naomi Schor, and Margaret Whitford, 91–209.

Holland, Nancy J. "Derrida and Feminism." *APA Newsletters* 91, no. 2 (fall 1992): 40–43.

———. "Heidegger and Derrida Redux: A Close Reading." In *Hermeneutics and Deconstruction,* ed. Hugh J. Silverman and Don Ihde, 219–26. Albany: State University of New York Press, 1985.

———. *The Madwoman's Reason: The Concept of the Appropriate in Ethical Thought.* University Park: Pennsylvania State University Press, 1998.

hooks, bell. *Ain't I a Woman: Black Women and Feminism.* Boston: South End Press, 1981.

———. *Yearning: Race, Gender, and Cultural Politics.* Boston: South End Press, 1990.

hooks, bell and Cornel West. *Breaking Bread: Insurgent Black Intellectual Life.* Boston: South End Press, 1991.

Howe, Leslie A. "Kierkegaard and the Feminine Self." *Hypatia: A Journal of Feminist Philosophy* 9, no. 4 (fall 1994): 131–57.

Hühnerfeld, Paul. *In Sachen Heidegger: Versuch über ein deutsches Genie.* Hamburg: Hoffman und Campe, 1959.

Huntington, Patricia. "Fragmentation, Race, and Gender: Building Solidarity in the Postmodern Era." In *Existence in Black,* ed. Lewis R. Gordon, 185–202.

———. "Heidegger's Reading of Kierkegaard Revisited: From Ontological Abstraction to Ethical Concretion." In *Kierkegaard in Post/Modernity,* ed. Martin J. Matuštík and Merold Westphal, 43–65.

———. "On Castration and Miscegenation: Is the Phallus White Skin?" *Philosophy Today.* Society for Phenomenology and Existential Philosophy Edition (spring/summer 1998): forthcoming.

———. "Toward A Dialectical Concept of Autonomy: Revisting the Feminist Alliance with Poststructuralism," *Philosophy and Social Criticism* 21, no. 1 (1995): 37–55.

———. Review of Richard Wolin's *The Politics of Being: The Political Thought of Martin Heidegger. Auslegung* 18, no. 1 (winter 1992): 72–78.

Hurtado, Aída. "Relating to Privilege: Seduction and Rejection in the Subordination of White Women and Women of Color." *Signs: Journal of Women in Culture and Society* 14, no. 4 (1989): 833–55.

Ijsseling, Samuel. "Heidegger and the Destruction of Ontology." *Man and World* 15 (1982): 3–16.

Jaggar, Alison M. "Love and Knowledge: Emotion in Feminist Epistemology." In *Women, Knowledge, and Reality,* ed. Ann Garry and Marilyn Pearsall, 129–55.

Jung, Mathias. *Der Glaube an Gott und das Denken des Seins—Zum Verhältnis von Philosophie und Theologie bei Martin Heidegger.* Frankfurt am Main: Fachbereich Philosophie, J/W Goethe-Universität, ms.

Jünger, Ernst. *Der Arbeiter: Herrschaft in der Gestalt. Werke.* Vol. 6. Essays II.

———. *Copse 125: A Chronicle from the Trench Warfare of 1918.* New York: Howard Fertig, 1988.

———. *Der Kampf als inneres Erlebnis.* Berlin: 1922.

———. "Technology as the Mobilization of the World through the *Gestalt* of the Worker." In *Philosophy and Technology: Readings in the Philosophical Problems of Technology,* ed. Carl Mitcham and Robert Mackey. New York: Free Press, 1972.

Kellner, Douglas. "Authenticity and Heidegger's Challenge to Ethical Theory." In *Thinking about Being: Aspects of Heidegger's Thought*, ed. Robert Shahan and J. N. Mohanty. Norman: University of Oklahoma Press, 1984.

Kierkegaard, Søren. *The Concept of Anxiety*. Trans. Reidar Thomte and Albert B. Anderson. Princeton University Press, 1980.

―――. *Concluding Unscientific Postscript*. Vols. 1–2. Trans. Howard V. Hong and Edna H. Hong. Princeton: Princeton University Press, 1992.

―――. *Either / Or*. Vols. 1–2. Ed. and trans. Howard V. Hong and Edna H. Hong. Princeton: Princeton University Press, 1987.

―――. *Fear and Trembling* and *Repetition*. Trans. Howard V. Hong and Edna H. Hong. Princeton: Princeton University Press, 1983.

―――. *The Point of View of My Work as an Author*. Trans. Walter Lowrie. London and New York: Oxford University Press, 1939.

―――. *The Sickness unto Death*. Trans. Howard V. Hong and Edna H. Hong. Princeton: Princeton University Press, 1980.

―――. *Two Ages: The Age of Revolution and the Present Age. A Literary Review*. Trans. Howard V. Hong and Edna H. Hong. Princeton: Princeton University Press, 1978.

King, Deborah K. "Multiple Jeopardy, Multiple Consciousness: The Context of a Black Feminist Ideology." *Signs: Journal of Women in Culture and Society* 14, no. 1 (1988): 42–72.

Kisiel, Theodore. "The Genesis of *Being and Time*." *Man and World* 25 (1992): 21–37.

―――. "Heidegger's Apology." In *The Heidegger Case*, ed. Tom Rockmore and Joseph Margolis, 1–51.

Kolb, David. *The Critique of Pure Modernity: Hegel, Heidegger, and After*. Chicago: University of Chicago Press, 1988.

Kosík, Karel. *Dialectics of the Concrete: A Study on Problems of Man and World*. Trans. Karel Kovanda with James Schmidt. Boston: D. Reidel, 1976.

Krell, David Farrell. *Intimations of Mortality: Time, Truth, and Finitude in Heidegger's Thinking of Being*. University Park: Pennsylvania State University Press, 1986.

Kundera, Milan. *The Unbearable Lightness of Being*. Trans. from the Czech by Michael Henry Heim. New York: Harper and Row, 1984.

Lacan, Jacques. *Écrits: A Selection*. Trans. Alan Sheridan. New York: W. W. Norton and Co., 1977.

Lacoue-Labarthe, Phillipe. *Heidegger, Art and Politics: The Fiction of the Political*. Cambridge: Basil Blackwell, 1990.

Lauretis, Teresa de. *Alice Doesn't: Feminism, Semiotics, Cinema*. Bloomington: Indiana University Press, 1984.

Leaman, George. *Heidegger im Kontext: Gesamtüberblick zum NS-Engagement der Universitätsphilosophen*. Berlin: Wolfgang Geisler, 1993.

Leland, Dorothy. "Lacanian Psychoanalysis and French Feminism: Toward an Adequate Political Psychology." In *Revaluing French Feminism*, ed. Nancy Fraser and Sandra Lee Bartky, 113–35.

Lorraine, Tamsin. "Amatory Cures for Material Dis-ease: A Kristevian Reading of *The Sickness unto Death*." In *Kierkegaard in Post/Modernity*, ed. Martin J. Matuštík and Merold Westphal, 98–109.

———. *Gender, Identity, and the Production of Meaning*. Boulder, Colo.: Westview Press, 1990.

Löwith, Karl. *Denker in Dürftiger Zeit*. Frankfurt am Main: S. Fischer, 1953.

———. "The Political Implications of Heidegger's Existentialism." Trans. Richard Wolin. In *The Heidegger Controversy*, ed. Richard Wolin, 167–85.

Lugones, María. "Playfulness, 'World'-Traveling, and Loving Perception." In *Women, Knowledge, and Reality*, ed. Ann Garry and Marilyn Pearsall, 275–90.

Lugones, María C. and Elizabeth V. Spelman. "Have We Got a Theory for You! Feminist Theory, Cultural Imperialism, and the Demand for 'The Woman's Voice'." *Women's Studies International Forum* 6, no. 6 (1983): 573–81.

Lukács, Georg. "Existentialism or Marxism?" In *Existentialism versus Marxism*, ed. George Novack, 134–53.

———. *Die Zerstörung der Vernunft, Werke* 9 (1954). Darmstadt: Luchterhand, 1974.

Lyotard, Jean Francois. *The Postmodern Condition: A Report on Knowledge*. Trans. Geoff Bennington and Brian Massumi. Minneapolis: University of Minnesota Press, 1984.

Magnus, Bernd. *Heidegger's Metahistory of Philosophy: Amor Fati, Being and Truth*. The Hague: Martinus Nijhoff, 1970.

Makkreel, Rudolf A. "The Genesis of Heidegger's Phenomenological Hermeneutics and the Rediscovered 'Aristotle Introduction' of 1922." *Man and World* 23 (1990): 305–20.

Marcuse, Herbert. *One-Dimensional Man: Studies in the Ideology of Advanced Industrial Society.* Boston: Beacon Press, 1964.

——. "Sartre, Historical Materialism and Philosophy." In *Existentialism versus Marxism,* ed. George Novack, 165–72.

Marks, Elaine and Isabelle de Courtivron, eds. *New French Feminisms: An Anthology.* New York: Schocken Books by arrangement with University of Massachusetts Press, 1980.

Marsh, James L. "Kierkegaard and Critical Theory." In *Kierkegaard in Post/Modernity,* ed. Martin J. Matuštík and Merold Westphal, 199–215.

——. *Post-Cartesian Meditations: An Essay in Dialectical Phenomenology.* New York: Fordham University Press, 1988.

Martin, Bill. *Matrix and Line: Derrida and the Possibilities of Postmodern Social Theory.* Albany: State University of New York Press, 1992.

Martinez, Roy. "An 'Authentic' Problem in Heidegger's *Being and Time.*" *Auslegung* 15 (winter 1989): 1–20.

Martinez, Roy, ed. *The Very Idea of Radical Hermeneutics.* Atlantic Highlands, N.J.: Humanities Press, 1997.

Marx, Karl. "The German Ideology." In *Karl Marx Selected Writings,* ed. David McLellan, 159–91. New York: Oxford University Press, 1977.

Marx, Werner. *Heidegger and the Tradition.* Trans. Theodore Kisiel and Murray Greene. Evanston, Ill.: Northwestern University Press, 1971. Originally published in German as *Heidegger und die Tradition.* Stuttgart: W. Kohlhammer, 1961.

——. "The World in Another Beginning: Poetic Dwelling and the Role of the Poet." In *On Heidegger and Language,* ed. Joseph J. Kockelmans, 235–59. Evanston, Ill.: Northwestern University Press, 1972.

Matuštík, Martin J. *Postnational Identity: Critical Theory and Existential Philosophy in Habermas, Kierkegaard, and Havel.* New York and London: Guilford Press, 1993.

——, Martin J. Beck. *Specters of Liberation: Great Refusals in the New World Order.* Albany: State University of New York Press, 1998.

Matuštík, Martin J. and Merold Westphal, eds. *Kierkegaard in Post/Modernity.* Bloomington: Indiana University Press, 1995.

McAfee, Noëlle. "Abject Strangers: Toward an Ethics of Respect." In *Ethics, Politics, and Difference,* ed. Kelly Oliver, 16–34.

McGowan, John. *Postmodernism and Its Critics*. Ithaca, N.Y.: Cornell University Press, 1991.

McKluskie, Kate. "Women's Language and Literature: A Problem in Women's Studies." *Feminist Review* 14 (summer 1983): 52–61.

Mehta, J. L. *Martin Heidegger: The Way and the Vision*. Honolulu: University Press of Hawaii, 1967.

Meyers, Diane Tietjens. *Subjection and Subjectivity: Psychoanalytic Feminism and Moral Philosophy*. New York: Routledge, 1994.

Meyers, Diane Tietjens, ed. *Feminists Rethink the Self*. Boulder, Colo: Westview Press, 1997.

Michelfelder, Diane and Richard E. Palmer, eds. *Dialogue and Deconstruction: The Gadamer-Derrida Encounter*. Albany: State University of New York Press, 1989.

Miller, Nancy K., ed. *The Poetics of Gender*. New York: Columbia University Press, 1986.

Millet, Kate. *Sexual Politics*. Garden City, N.Y.: Doubleday and Company, 1970.

Moi, Toril. *Sexual / Textual Politics: Feminist Literary Theory*. London and New York: Routledge, 1988.

Moi, Toril, ed. *French Feminist Thought: A Reader*. Cambridge: Basil Blackwell, 1987.

———. *The Kristeva Reader*. New York: Columbia University Press, 1986.

Moraga, Cherríe. "From a Long Line of Vendidas: Chicanas and Feminism." In *Feminist Frameworks: Alternative Theoretical Accounts of the Relations between Women and Men*, 3d ed., ed. Alison M. Jaggar and Paula S. Rothenberg. New York: McGraw-Hill, 1993. Excerpted from "A Long Line of Vendidas," In *Loving in the War Years: Lo que nunca pasó por sus labios*. Boston: South End Press, 1983.

Morrison, Toni. *Beloved*. London: Picador, Pan Macmillan Publishers Limited, 1988.

Mortensen, Ellen. *The Feminine and Nihilism: Luce Irigaray with Nietzsche and Heidegger*. Oslo: Scandinavian University Press, 1994.

———. "Woman's (Un)Truth and *le féminin:* Reading Luce Irigaray with Nietzsche and Heidegger." In *Engaging with Irigaray*, ed. Carolyn Burke, Naomi Schor, and Margaret Whitford, 211–28.

Moruzzi, Norma Claire. "National Abjects: Julia Kristeva on the Process of Political Self-Identification." In *Ethics, Politics, and Difference*, ed. Kelly Oliver, 135–49.

Neske, Günther and Emil Kettering. *Martin Heidegger and National Socialism: Questions and Answers.* Trans. Lisa Harries. New York: Paragon House, 1990.

Nicholson, Linda, ed. *Feminism/Postmodernism.* New York and London: Routledge, 1990.

Nietzsche, Friedrich. *Thus Spoke Zarathustra: A Book for All and None.* Trans. Walter Kaufmann. Harmondsworth: Penguin, 1978.

———. *The Will to Power.* Trans. Walter Kaufmann and R. J. Hollingdale. New York: Vintage Books, 1968.

Novack, George, ed. *Existentialism versus Marxism: Conflicting Views of Humanism.* New York: Dell Publishing, 1966.

Oliver, Kelly. "Fractal Politics: How to Use 'The Subject'." *Praxis International* 11, no. 2 (July 1991): 178–94.

———. "Julia Kristeva's Feminist Revolutions." *Hypatia: A Journal of Feminist Philosophy* 8, no. 3 (summer 1993): 94–114.

———. *Reading Kristeva: Unraveling the Double-bind.* Bloomington: Indiana University Press, 1993.

Oliver, Kelly, ed. *Ethics, Politics, and Difference in Julia Kristeva's Writing.* New York: Routledge, 1993.

Omi, Michael and Howard Winant. *Racial Formation in the United States: From the 1960's to the 1980's.* New York: Routledge, 1986.

Ott, Hugo. *Martin Heidegger: Unterwegs zu seiner Biographie.* Frankfurt and New York: Campus Verlag, 1988.

Outlaw, Lucius. "African, African American, Africana Philosophy." *Philosophical Forum* 24, nos. 1–3 (fall–spring 1992–93): 63–93.

Palmer, Richard. *Hermeneutics: Interpretation Theory on Schleiermacher, Dilthey, Heidegger, and Gadamer.* Evanston, Ill.: Northwestern University Press, 1969.

Parens, Erik. "Derrida, 'Woman', and Politics." *Philosophy Today* 33 (winter 1989): 291–301.

Phelan, Shane. "(Be)Coming Out: Lesbian Identity and Politics." *Signs: Journal of Women in Culture and Society* 18, no. 4 (summer 1993): 765–90.

Pheterson, Gail. "Alliances between Women: Overcoming Internalized Oppression and Internalized Domination." In *Bridges of Power,* ed. Lisa Albrecht and Rose M. Brewer, 34–56.

Pluhacek, Stephen and Heidi Bostic. "Thinking Life as Relation: An Interview with Luce Irigaray." *Man and World* 29 (1996): 343–60.

Pöggeler, Otto. *Martin Heidegger's Path of Thinking*. Trans. Daniel Magurshak and Sigmund Barber. Atlantic Highlands, N.J.: Humanities Press International, 1987. Pagination in the margins, which I will use, refers as well to the original text, *Der Denkweg Martin Heideggers*. Pfullingen: Günther Neske, 1963.

Rajan, Tilottama. "Trans-positions of Difference: Kristeva and Post-structuralism." In *Ethics, Politics, and Difference*, ed. Kelly Oliver, 215–37.

Ramsey, Ramsey Eric. *The Long Path to Nearness: A Contribution to a Corporeal Philosophy of Communication and the Groundwork for an Ethics of Relief*. Atlantic Highlands, N.J.: Humanities Press, 1998.

Reagon, Bernice Johnson. "Coalition Politics: Turning the Century." In *Home Girls*, ed. Barbara Smith, 356–68.

Rockmore, Tom. *Heidegger and French Philosophy: Humanism, Antihumanism and Being*. New York: Routledge, 1995.

Rockmore, Tom and Joseph Margolis, eds. *The Heidegger Case: On Philosophy and Politics*. Philadelphia: Temple University Press, 1992.

Rorty, Richard. *Philosophy and the Mirror of Nature*. Princeton: Princeton University Press, 1979.

Rose, Hilary. "Dreaming the Future." *Hypatia: A Journal of Feminist Philosophy* 3, no. 1 (spring 1988): 119–37.

Sangari, Kumkum. "The Politics of the Possible." *Cultural Critique* 7 (fall 1987): 157–86.

Scharff, Robert C. "Habermas on Heidegger's *Being and Time*." *International Philosophical Quarterly* 31, no. 2, issue 122 (June 1991): 189–201.

Schneeberger, Guido. *Nachlese zu Martin Heidegger*. Bern: Guido Schneeberger, 1962. Selections of Schneeberger have been translated into English in *German Existentialism*, trans. Dagobert D. Runes. New York: Philosophical Library, 1965.

Schor, Naomi. "This Essentialism which Is Not One: Coming to Grips with Irigaray." *Differences* 1, no. 2 (1989): 38–58. Reprinted in *Engaging With Irigaray*, ed. Carolyn Burke, Naomi Schor, and Margaret Whitford, 57–78.

Schrag, Calvin O. *Existence and Freedom: Towards an Ontology of Human Finitude*. Evanston, Ill.: Northwestern University Press, 1961.

———. *Communicative Praxis and the Space of Subjectivity*. Bloomington: Indiana University Press, 1989.

———. *The Self After Postmodernity*. New Haven: Yale University Press, 1997.

Schürmann, Reiner. "Heidegger and Meister Eckhart on Releasement." *Research in Phenomenology* 3 (1973): 95–119.

———. *Heidegger on Being and Acting: From Principles to Anarchy.* Bloomington: Indiana University Press, 1990.

———. "The Ontological Difference and Political Philosophy." *Philosophy and Phenomenological Research* 40, no. 1 (September 1979): 99–122.

———. "Political Thinking in Heidegger." *Social Research* 45 (spring 1978): 191–221.

———. "Questioning the Foundation of Practical Philosophy." *Human Studies* 1 (1978): 357–68.

Seigfried, Hans. "Descriptive Phenomenology and Constructivism." *Philosophy and Phenomenological Research* 37, no. 2 (December 1976): 248–61.

Sheehan, Thomas. "A Normal Nazi." *New York Review of Books* 40 nos. 1, 2 (January 14, 1993): 30–35.

———. "On Movement and Destruction." *The Monist* 64, no. 4 (October 1981): 534–42.

Shrage, Laurie. *Moral Dilemmas of Feminism: Prostitution, Adultery, and Abortion.* New York: Routledge, 1994.

Silverman, Kaja. *The Subject of Semiotics.* New York: Oxford University Press, 1983.

Simons, Margaret A. "Racism and Feminism: A Schism in the Sisterhood." *Feminist Studies* 5, no. 2 (1979): 384–401.

Smith, Barbara, Introduction. In *Home Girls,* ed. Barbara Smith, xix–lvi.

———. "Toward a Black Feminist Criticism." In *Feminist Criticism and Social Change: Sex, Class, and Race in Literature and Culture,* eds. Judith Newton and Deborah Rosenfelt. New York: Methuen, Inc., 1985.

Smith, Barbara, ed. *Home Girls: A Black Feminist Anthology.* New York: Kitchen Table: Woman of Color Press, 1983.

Spelman, Elizabeth V. *Inessential Woman: Problems of Exclusion in Feminist Thought.* Boston: Beacon Press, 1988.

Spencer, Jon Michael. "Trends of Opposition to Multiculturalism." *The Black Scholar* 23, no. 2 (1993): 2–5.

Spivak, Gayatri Chakravorty. "In a Word," Interview with Ellen Rooney. *Differences: A Journal of Feminist Cultural Studies* 1, no. 2 (1989): 124–55.

Stabile, Carol A. "Feminism without Guarantees: The Misalliances and Missed Alliances of Postmodernist Social Theory." *Rethinking Marxism* 7, no. 1 (1994): 48–61.

Steiner, George. *Martin Heidegger*. Chicago: University of Chicago Press, 1978.

Stern (Anders), Günther. "On the Pseudo-concreteness of Heidegger's Philosophy." *Philosophy and Phenomenological Research* 8 (December 1947): 337–71.

Stollmann, Rainer. "Fascist Politics as a Total Work of Art: Tendencies of the Aestheticization of Political Life in National Socialism." *New German Critique* 14 (spring 1978): 41–60.

Suleiman, Susan Rubin. "Pornography, Transgression, and the Avante-Garde: Bataille's *Story of Eve*." In *The Poetics of Gender*, ed. Nancy K. Miller, 117–36.

Theweleit, Klaus. *Male Fantasies*. Vol. 1. *Women, Floods, Bodies, History*. Trans. Stephen Conway. Minneapolis: University of Minnesota Press, 1987.

Tugendhat, Ernst. *Der Wahrheitsbegriff bei Husserl und Heidegger*. Berlin: Walter de Gruyter, 1970.

van Buren, John. "Heidegger's *Sache*: A Family Portrait," *Research in Phenomenology* 22 (1992): 161–84.

———. "Hermeneutics of Facticity." In *The Very Idea of Radical Hermeneutics*, ed. Roy Martinez, 166–84.

———. "Stories of Being." In *Transitions in Continental Philosophy*, ed. Arleen B. Dallery and Stephen H. Watson with E. Mayra Bower, 211–25. Albany: State University Press of New York, 1994.

———. "The Young Heidegger and Phenomenology." *Man and World* 23, no. 3 (July 1990): 239–72.

———. "The Young Heidegger: Rumor of a Hidden King (1919–1926)." *Philosophy Today* 33 (summer 1989): 99–108.

———. *The Young Heidegger: Rumor of the Hidden King*. Bloomington: Indiana University Press, 1994.

Vieux, Steve. "In the Shadow of Neo-liberal Racism." *Race and Class* 36, no. 1 (1994): 23–32.

von Hermann, Friedrich-Wilhelm. *Subjekt und Dasein: Interpretationen zu "Sein und Zeit."* Frankfurt am Main: Vittorio Klostermann, 1974.

Walker, Margaret Urban. "Moral Understandings: Alternative 'Epistemology' for a Feminist Ethics." *Hypatia* 4, no. 2 (summer 1989): 15–28.

Wallace, Michele. *Black Macho and the Myth of the Superwoman.* New York: Dial Press, 1979.

Weedon, Chris. *Feminist Practice and Poststructuralist Theory.* Cambridge: Basil Blackwell, 1987.

Weir, Allison. "Identification with the Divided Mother: Kristeva's Ambivalence." In *Ethics, Politics, and Difference,* ed. Kelly Oliver, 79–91.

———. *Sacrificial Logics: Feminist Theory and the Critique of Identity.* New York: Routledge, 1996.

West, Cornel. *Prophetic Fragments.* Trenton: Africa World Press, 1988.

———. *Race Matters.* Boston: Beacon Press, 1993.

Westphal, Merold. *Kierkegaard's Critique of Reason and Society.* Macon, Ga.: Mercer University Press, 1987.

———. "The Ostrich and the Boogeyman: Placing Postmodernism." *Christian Scholar's Review* 20, no. 2 (December 1990): 114–17.

White, Stephen K. "Heidegger and the Difficulties of a Postmodern Ethics and Politics." *Political Theory* 18, no. 1 (February 1990): 80–103.

Whitford, Margaret. "Irigaray, Utopia, and The Death Drive." In *Engaging With Irigaray,* ed. Carolyn Burke, Naomi Schor, and Margaret Whitford, 379–400.

———. *Luce Irigaray: Philosophy in the Feminine.* New York: Routledge, 1991.

———. "Luce Irigaray's Critique of Rationality." In *Feminist Perspectives,* ed. Morwenna Griffiths and Margaret Whitford, 109–30.

Whitford, Margaret, ed. *The Irigaray Reader.* Cambridge: Basil Blackwell, 1991.

Willett, Cynthia. *Maternal Ethics and Other Slave Moralities.* New York: Routledge, 1995.

Wiseman, Mary Bittner. "Renaissance Painting and Psychoanalysis: Julia Kristeva and the Function of the Mother." In *Ethics, Politics, and Difference,* ed. Kelly Oliver, 92–115.

Wolin, Richard. *Labyrinths: Explorations in the Critical History of Ideas.* Amherst: University of Massachusetts Press, 1995.

———. "Left Fascism: George Bataille and the German Ideology." *Constellations: An International Journal of Critical and Democratic Theory* 2, no. 3 (January 1996): 396–428.

———. *The Politics of Being: The Political Thought of Martin Heidegger.* New York: Colombia University Press, 1990.

———. *The Terms of Cultural Criticism: The Frankfurt School, Existentialism, Poststructuralism.* New York: Columbia University Press, 1992.

Wolin, Richard, ed. *The Heidegger Controversy: A Critical Reader.* Cambridge: MIT Press, 1993.

Young, Iris Marion. "Asymmetrical Reciprocity: On Moral Respect, Wonder, and Enlarged Thought." *Constellations: An International Journal of Critical and Democratic Theory* 3, no. 3 (1997): 340–63.

———. *Intersecting Voices: Dilemmas of Gender, Political Philosophy and Policy.* Princeton: Princeton University Press, 1997.

———. "Impartiality and the Civic Public: Some Implications of Feminist Critiques of Moral and Political Theory." In *Feminism As Critique,* ed. Seyla Benhabib and Drucilla Cornell, 56–76.

———. *Justice and the Politics of Difference.* Princeton: Princeton University Press, 1990.

Ziarek, Ewa. "Kristeva and Levinas: Mourning, Ethics, and the Feminine." In *Ethics, Politics, and Difference,* ed. Kelly Oliver, 62–78.

Ziarek, Krzysztof. *Inflected Language: Toward a Hermeneutics of Nearness, Heidegger, Levinas, Stevens, Celan.* Albany: State University of New York Press, 1994.

———. "Proximities: Irigaray and Heidegger on Difference," unpublished paper. Delivered at the IAPL, "Passions, Persons, Powers" Conference, University of California at Berkeley, May 1992. Contact: Department of English, University of Notre Dame.

Zimmerman, Michael. *Eclipse of the Self.* Athens: Ohio University Press, 1981.

———. *Heidegger's Confrontation with Modernity: Technology, Politics, and Art.* Bloomington: Indiana University Press, 1990.

———. "On Discriminating Everydayness, Unownedness, and Falling in *Being and Time.*" *Research in Phenomenology* 5 (1975): 109–27.

———. "Ontological Aestheticism." In *The Heidegger Case,* ed. Tom Rockmore and Joseph Margolis, 52–89.

———. "Philosophy and Politics: The Case of Heidegger." *Philosophy Today* 33 (spring 1989): 3–20.

Index

Abel, Elizabeth, 255
Adell, Sandra, xiv
Adorno, Theodor, 245
affect, 77–116. *See also under*
  Kristeva.
agency, 77–116. *See also* identity;
  subjectivity; *under* Kristeva.
  as creativity, xxiii, 78, 86,
    178
  as (linguistic) competencies, 78,
    83, 106, 113, 241, 245, 247,
    280, 290–292
  dialectical model of, xvi, xvii,
    xxiii, 78–87, 279
  in Heidegger, as heroic, 3–31.
    See also stoic logic.
  in Kristeva, as existential
    striving to be, 78–80, 102.
    See also Kristeva, desire.
  as (performative) resignification,
    xxiii, 78, 81–83, 113. *See also*
    postmodern, subject.
  as social, 274–275
  voluntarist conceptions of, xvi,
    xvii, 77, 83–84, 109, 112. *See*
    also stoic logic.
  willingness vs. willed self-
    regulation, 77, 79, 86, 109–116.
    See also willingness.
Alarcón, Norma, 292
Alcoff, Linda, xix, 81
Althusser, Louis, 164
anarchist/communist threat, 37–38,
  55

antiblack racism, xxii, 110, 112–113,
  251, 256, 266, 280–283, 291,
  299. *See also* Gordon; race.
  black and white consciousness,
    245, 280–281, 300. *See also*
    double-bind.
  motivated deception and socio-
    genic choice, 17, 111, 114
  as willed ignorance, 112, 115
antifoundationalism, 42, 47, 156,
  210. *See also under*
  Heidegger.
antimodernism. *See* premodern;
  under National Socialism.
antinormativism, xv, xviii, xxviii,
  xxix, 42, 68, 82, 147, 194,
  208, 211, 228–231, 325n.24.
  See also under Heidegger;
  Irigaray; postmodern.
Anzaldúa, Gloria, 161, 292, 293
Aristotle, 183
Armour, Ellen, xiv
Asante, Molefi Kete, 240
asymmetrical reciprocity, xvi, 148,
  193, 248, 277, 279, 280, 295–
  301. *See also* communicative
  ethics; Young; *under* Cornell.
  ethical asymmetry, xxxi, 286,
    335n. 13
Auschwitz, 44
authenticity. *See also* stoic logic;
  under Heidegger.
autodisclosure. *See under* Heidegger.
autonomy, xxii, 84, 275, 297

365